HIGHWAYMEN

Dedication
Mum, this one's for you! Unbelievably, it's my twentieth book and what better to give
you — I'm sure there is a family tradition that your side of the family were 'Irish horse
thieves'. And what a family to be part of. All my love.
Sam Willis

Publisher's Note
The highwaymen's 'Lives' in this book were taken from *A General History of the Lives
and Adventures of the Most Famous Highwaymen, Murderers, Street-Robbers, &c. To which
is added, a genuine account of the voyages and plunders of the most notorious pyrates...*,
published in 1734. To aid readability, modern styling has been applied to the use
of italics and initial caps for nouns, but spellings and punctuation have generally
been left as they appeared in the original volume for authenticity.

This edition first published in 2020 by
The British Library
96 Euston Road
London NW1 2DB

Cataloguing in Publication Data
A catalogue record for this publication is available from the British Library

ISBN 978 0 7123 5274 1

Design styling by Blok Graphic, London
Typesetting by IDSUK (DataConnection) Ltd
Printed and bound in the Czech Republic by Finidr

A General History of the Lives, Murders and Adventures of the

Most Notorious

HIGHWAYMEN

Captain Charles Johnson
Introduced by Sam Willis

CONTENTS

P. La Vergne Inv.   M. V.Gucht Sculp

The Golden Farmer &c.

INTRODUCTION

The book you are holding is a box of historical treasures. This edited collection of highwaymen's lives comes from Captain Charles Johnson's

A General History of the Lives and Adventures of the Most Famous
Highwaymen, Murderers, Street-Robbers, &c. To which is added, a genuine account
of the voyages and plunders of the most notorious pyrates . . .

Printed in 1734, this is far more than a collection of fascinating stories about highwaymen, pirates and rogues, however; it is a volume that raises questions that go to the very heart of what we know about the past . . . and the present.

Captain Charles Johnson was something of a literary phenomenon in the first half of the eighteenth century. He first roared onto the London publishing scene in a cloud of gunsmoke and cursing a full decade before the 1734 edition was published, with the first-ever published collection of pirates' lives, *A General History of the Robberies and Murders of the most notorious Pyrates*, which came out in the spring of 1724. By the end of that summer – just three months later – he had issued a second, longer and more detailed edition. A third followed the subsequent year and then a fourth, now further extended and split into two volumes, in 1726. Although it is impossible to recreate sales figures for this period, it is generally considered that these volumes sold well, and we can say with confidence that, by 1734, both Johnson and his pirates were already famous.

Johnson did not create a market in criminal biography: in 1724 that market was already long-established. In the same year that Johnson made his first literary appearance, four other criminal biographies were published, each of them a life of Jack Sheppard, a notorious thief who was executed that winter at Tyburn, the 600-year-old, central-London location for public hangings. Two biographies had been published the year before, one on the highwayman Rob Roy, and the other on John Stanley, a murderous 'Knight-Errant'; five had been published the preceding year and so on. In fact, the phenomenon of criminal biography can easily be traced back to the reign of the Tudor queen Elizabeth I: in 1592 five such biographies were published – that is, 132 years before Johnson published his collection of pirates' lives.

Throughout these centuries criminals were celebrities and these books gave the public a glimpse into their lives. Indeed, if you change the words in the title 'highwaymen, murderers, street-robbers' for 'celebrities' you have '*A General History of the Lives and Adventures of Celebrities*' – and *that* is something we can all relate to: it's the very essence of Instagram.

Jack Sheppard captured by Mr Austin.

Johnson was also building on the publishing entrepreneurialism of another man, Captain Alexander Smith, who had already done what Johnson did with pirates, but with highwaymen. In 1713 Smith published

The History of the lives, of the most noted Highwaymen, foot-pads, shop-lifts and cheats of both sexes, in and about London and other places . . . for fifty years last past.

Just like Johnson's book, Smith's was very popular and two new editions had appeared by 1714. By 1734, therefore, not only were Johnson and his pirates famous, so too were Smith and his highwaymen. In that year Charles Johnson decided to combine these two literary sensations and create what we would describe today as a mash-up: in his new book Smith's highwaymen and rogues would sit alongside his pirates, but the book would be issued under his name alone.

Considering the fame of both Smith and Johnson, it is perhaps surprising that we don't know who either of these people were – though considerable effort has been made to unravel their identities. It has been assumed by all historians who have written on the subject that both are men, but there is no proof that this is the case. It has also been assumed that both Smith and Johnson were pen names for individual people, but there is no proof of that either and there remains every possibility that both were names that could have disguised two or more writers working together in a team. There is also the assumption that the Captain Johnson who wrote the book on pirates in 1724 was *the same person* who wrote the book in 1734, again, with no proof. Indeed, when considering the authorship of the first edition and its related volumes, one does well to consider that any explanation is still possible.

Smith, it has been argued from hints in the introduction to the second volume of his 1714 edition, may have been the satirist Ned Ward (1667–1731), the author of the well-known periodical about London life *The London Spy*. Johnson, it was once believed, was none other than the author Daniel Defoe (1660–1731) but the argument has now lost weight. A more recent suggestion is that Johnson was the newspaper owner, printer and journalist Nathaniel Mist (d. 1737) (for whom Defoe worked), a proposal that is supported by some – albeit indefinite – written evidence. Part of the attraction of both Defoe and

3

Jos. Nicholls Delin.   *J. Basire Sc.*

Captain Teach commonly call'd Black Beard.

Mist as possible authors is that these men, at different times of their lives, were imprisoned. Defoe was accused of Seditious Libel which led to the pillory and a sentence in Newgate. Mist, a known Jacobite, was in trouble with the authorities on no fewer than fourteen occasions with several prison sentences and also a visit to the pillory. And so, yes, they were authors, but they were also criminals: if they did write the book, to some extent they had a vested, and insider know-ledge of their subject matter as well as access to criminals for material.

Part of the charm of the 1734 volume, therefore, is that the identity of its author/s remains a mystery. Perhaps the only secure facts we have are that Johnson was a man of the sea – his accounts of the pirates are littered with convincing and accurate descriptions of the realities of life at sea; that he had intimate and accurate knowledge of the West Indies; and that he had access to incoming reports about pirates in the same way that a good fishmonger has access to fresh fish: he had his ear to the sea, perhaps a network of informers from whom he could accurately take the pulse of the maritime news. We also know that whoever wrote the 1734 book was more than happy to freely take material from Smith's book to make a few sovereigns of his own – this book itself is a brazen act of literary robbery – an activity we might describe now, particularly in relation to music, as piracy.

This question of authorship hobbles us as historians, but so too does the material in the 1734 book itself. It is an unpredictable mixture of fact and fiction – but presented as fact. Some of the characters – not least the first, which is a life of Shakespeare's John Falstaff – are entirely fictional, plucked from myth or lite-rary works. But others are real, even though their crimes, appearance or beha-viour *seem* unreal. What is the attraction of the pirate Blackbeard – who ignites fireworks in his beard and hair to scare off his enemies and impress his victims as the incarnation of Lucifer himself – if not that he is something so fantastical that you *couldn't* make it up? Some of the actions of those who are real, however, we also know to have been fabricated.

The result of all of this is that the book is a challenge as much as it is a source of entertainment; to read it is to be entertained and informed but it is also to play a game with – and perhaps even to *spar* with – an author who lived 285 years ago but who is now joined directly to you through the words of this new edition. As you read this, know that you are in the hands of a master storyteller as well as a consummate historian, who deliberately weaves truth and lies together, at once telling us that we can 'depend' on the 'authenticity' of his tale and then suddenly pulling away the rug by including the implausible. In our modern world beset with fake news, such a challenge as is posed by this text is one that we must all be able meet, and to learn these skills of the historian our only recourse.

But with this challenge in mind, the 1734 book opens up a world of entertainment and historical enquiry. As a contemporary document it is a political satire and a commentary on crime; as a popular literary work it is a precursor to the novel as much as it is to popular biography and more general popular history; as an *object*, the British Library's First Edition – from which this particular edition on the Highwaymen comes – is evidence of publishing and printing techniques and its healthy size and impressive engravings suggestive of a target audience with a disposable income and the desire to be seen as well-read – it is an early coffee-table book made for display as much as for reading; as a source of artwork it is an important contribution to what we know about the development of illustration; as an historical source it is unparalleled in what it tells us about certain types of crime; as an anonymous work it is a contribution to our understanding of the use of pen names, a fascinating history of its own which includes Charlotte Brontë, Agatha Christie, Stephen King and J.K. Rowling. The list of themes in the book ripe for exploration goes on and on. The more you look, the more you discover; the more you discover, the more questions you raise.

To read it is to be entertained and intrigued, shocked and bewildered. As you read it and experience those emotions, consider the bridge across time that this book has created, and know that thousands of people have similarly been lured by its title to pick it up, lured by its introduction to look inside, and lured by these lives into a world where innocence and evil, truth and lies, and past and present, all lie side by side. So read this new edition, but as you do so give half a thought to your historical shadow, that person who has picked it up, thumbed through the pages, and is now reading it in 1734.

Publishing this extraordinary volume now will, hopefully, bring it to the large audience it deserves, lead to further research to help us understand it, and engage people with the very stuff of history and with the skills of *being* a historian: read it and let me know which bits *you* believe.

@DrSamWillis

A GENERAL HISTORY OF HIGHWAYMEN

Occasionally a fact leaps out from history and makes you realise that something you have taken for granted was not always so: it is as if you have been beset on your comfortable modern journey by history itself acting as highwayman. You are stopped abruptly and left shaken, disoriented. The history of the British road system is a fine example. Nowadays roads are a simple way of getting from A to B; the only danger we might consider on a journey by road comes from traffic accidents, but for *centuries* before the Industrial Revolution – which brought turnpikes, gates and patrols to Britain's road network – roads were a source of anxiety and a reason for fear. Robbers lurked in hedgerows and brazenly blocked the way.

Settlements of all types were far smaller and more spread out; the landscape was utterly dominated by woodland, moorland, heath and fields. Travelling was isolated and wild. The few roads that linked villages, towns and cities together also made journeys predictable and, for the would-be robber, provided a ready-made and quick escape route. There was no formal police force with the exception of watchmen in towns and cities until the Metropolitan Police force was established in London in 1822. Other cities followed in the subsequent decades.

Even roads just beyond the outskirts of major cities could feel utterly remote. In London, Shooter's Hill in Greenwich and Hyde Park were both notorious places for highway robbery: in 1749 the MP Horace Walpole was set upon by two highwaymen in Hyde Park, one of whom was the notorious James Maclaine. The *London Evening Post* subsequently ran a story:

> He was stopt in Hyde-Park by Two Men on Horseback, mask'd, one of which held a Blunderbuss to the Coachman, while the other came up to the Chariot, and, thrusting a Pistol into it, demanded Mr. Walpole's Money and Watch; he gave the Fellow his Purse, and as he was giving him the Watch, the Pistol, which was held close to his Cheek, went off; but, tho' it was so near that the Force struck Mr. Walpole backwards, the ball luckily miss'd him, and went thro' the Corner of the Chariot just above his Head, only scorching his Face, and leaving several marks of Powder.

As you read through these highwaymen's lives it is particularly important to keep in mind the fear that attacks like these created. In our contemporary world, so profound is the experience of being robbed that an entire academic discipline has arisen whose sole purpose is to understand the post-traumatic psychological effects of robbery. The many and varied symptoms can be utterly debilitating, and yet these rough edges are often lost in the history of highwaymen – when a violent act becomes a story about a violent act.

Moreover, from the 1660s the image of the highwayman, as represented in literature, underwent a lengthy and complex process of change from the desperate and violent robber to a 'Knight of the Road', or 'Gentleman Thief', a man pungent with charm, humour and the skill of the horseman. He is proud. He is free. This process of change reached its apogee in William Harrison Ainsworth's novel *Rookwood* (1834). Ainsworth introduces to us the highwayman Dick Turpin as a lively, adventurous gallant. In reality, Turpin (1705–1739) was a murderer, poacher and burglar, hanged for horse theft in York in 1739. It is this romantic version of the highwayman that has given us the fable of a dashing Claude Du Vall dancing at the side of the road with his female victims, and of 'Sixteen-String Jack' so named for the colourful strings he wore on his silk breeches while, with wit and charm, he would relieve his often obliging victims of their portable wealth.

The highwaymen's lives that are featured in this book played an important part in that romanticising process. They are a mixture of fact and fiction. The meat of the

John Cottington *alias Mul-Sack, Robbing ye Oxford Waggon Wherein he found four Thousand Pounds in money.*

stories was taken by Captain Charles Johnson from Alexander Smith's *The History of the lives, of the most noted Highwaymen, foot-pads, shop-lifts and cheats of both sexes, in and about London and other places . . . for fifty years last past.* (1713) and Smith had taken his material from published trial accounts, criminal biographies and interviews with condemned criminals held by the chaplain at Newgate prison. With a salacious audience in mind and a tangible (and rather charming) troublemaking streak, Smith then added a little spice to the mix, often glorifying in unpleasant detail. His looseness with the truth led to one contemporary rival, the author of a 1723 biography of the Scottish outlaw Rob Roy, exploding that Smith's book was, a confus'd Lump of absurd Lies, gross Obscenity, aukward Cant, and dull Profaneness. If you find a Story, or but one Sentence in all his Scribling, that is even tolerable, depend upon it he stole it; he has the most unlucky Talent at Invention of any Man breathing, for he's as great a Stranger to Fable as to Truth; he's so far from writing Probabilities, (without which even a Romance be monstrous) that he tells you of things that are entirely impossible; Lies, that Sir John Mandevile would have been asham'd of;— and yet the Fool diverts the Populace—and so does a Monkey—but much more agreably.

Johnson himself makes a handful of fleeting mentions of Smith's contribution to his own work, and he is never complimentary. 'Most of his stories', claims Johnson, 'are such barefac'd inventions, that we are confident those who have ever seen his Books will pardon us for omitting them.' True to his word, Johnson omits some of Smith's highwaymen. Where, for example, is William Coe, famed by Smith for killing his wife by farting into her mouth? He also subtly changes some of the stories he takes, toning down Smith's extravagances but freely toying with the facts in his own way. In Smith's original Claude Du Vall story, for example, Du Vall steals a silver baby's bottle right from the baby's mouth; but in Johnson's version it is one of Du Vall's men. Similarly, a shockingly violent gang rape and murder in the life of Patrick O-Bryan is more lightly sketched over in Johnson's book, though still powerful: 'This young lady they severally forced after one another to their brutal Pleasure, and when they had done, most inhumanely stabb'd her.'

The way in which these stories were massaged by Johnson is made most clear when you notice that two stories in the chapter on Robin Hood are also attributed to other highwaymen: the unforgettable story involving a dog dressed in a cow's hide being lowered down a chimney appears again in the chapter on Claude Du Vall, and another involving the robbery of a mean landlord in the chapter on Ned Wickes.

This work, therefore, is just one layer – though a crucially important one – in the way that highwaymen's lives were altered by successive generations over two centuries of literary attention. There is still a healthy and unresolved scholarly debate over the reasons *why* these stories were so manipulated, told, sold, read, and enjoyed. As you read, think particularly of the social background of the highwaymen and of their victims, for there is often a hidden message: who, actually is the robber here? Is it the highwayman or his 'victim' – the sly lawyer, grasping politician, crooked tradesman, or quack doctor – who are parasites on everyone's lives? If so, is the 'robbery' not just? Johnson himself hints at his politics in the introduction:

> We presume it will be some credit to this work to have a dignified Plunderer at the Head of it; but we would by no Means have Readers expect an Account of all the Plunderers that have been dignified; unless they are willing to buy fifteen hundred sheets instead of an hundred and fifty

He goes on to argue that 'A Great Villain may commit more Depredations in a short time, than a hundred little ones can in a long Course of Years' and yet again makes the point 'It is not unprecedented for a very great Knight to be a very great Robber'. Johnson then unmasks both male and female citizens as rogues themselves, scolding them publicly as hypocrites: this is Johnson's world turned upside down.

Beyond this, it has been argued convincingly that the text hints at contemporary politics as well as contemporary perceptions of crime, punishment and morals: consider that highwaymen were publicly executed for their crimes – primarily theft – which was a crime against *property*. Indeed, we might say nowadays that they were executed for *nothing more* than crimes against property. Were the contemporary readers comfortable with that, and also with the popularity of watching public executions? By telling the criminals' stories in this fanciful way, did it make this legal system somehow more palatable? Or the actual threat of robbery less intimidating? What *is* certain is that Johnson's book is proof that a line has been crossed by a culture that has become happy not to discriminate between fame and infamy.

Of all of the themes raised in this book, however, perhaps it is most important to embrace the idea that these stories stand testament to an acute public interest in history, almost 300 years old. They are proof of a fundamental desire to understand how things *came to be* – in this case how a man was brought up, took to the road and ended up on the scaffold – and that restless desire to understand our world is a human trait which can most certainly be admired and learned from. As Johnson himself says:

> We shall take care that every one who reads our collection may be diverted, and that as many as will, may be instructed.

J. Nicholls delin.   _J. Basire sculp._

Sr JOHN FALSTAFF and his Companions at GAD'S HILL.

THE LIFE OF
SIR JOHN
FALSTAFF

W e begin this history with the life of Sir John Falstaff, who flourished in the reigns of Henry IV and V Kings of England; and we cannot help wishing that we were able to draw his character in this place as beautifully as it is drawn by Shakespear in several of his plays, which are indeed almost the only materials that remain for our purpose. It is proper to say this to prevent the reader's wondering at our method, and at the several dialogues which we shall intersperse, or rather only connect in this essay.

Sir John Falstaff then was born at a place called Potten in Bedfordshire, which is all we know concerning his birth; and indeed if history had been as silent in this article of place as it is in that of the time when, it had signified little, there being no remarkable action, as we know of, to be settled by this piece of chronology. By the courses he took, we may supppose his estate was not very large; for the first time he is mentioned, it is in company with thieves; tho' you may be sure it was none of your poor pick-pocket gangs, forasmuch as Henry Prince of Wales (afterwards King Henry V) appears among them: Poins, Bardolph, Gads-Hill, and Peto, were the names of the rest. As we shall transcribe a great many of Shakespear's inimitable speeches, it would be a folly to say any thing in general of Sir John's person and temper, besides what is contained in them. 'When I was about thy years, Hal,' (says Sir John to the Prince) 'I was not an eagle's talon in the waste; I could have crept into an alder-man's thumb-ring: A plague of sighing and grief, it blows a man up like a bladder!' For Sir John, you must know, when he said this, was not such a skeleton as he describes: no, he was 'a tun of man', 'a trunk of humours', a 'boulting-hutch of beastliness', a 'swoln parcel of dropsies', a 'huge bombard of sack', a 'stuft clock-bag of guts, a 'rosted manning-tree ox, with a pudding in his belly', &c.' as Prince Henry humorously draws his picture.

The first scene between these two pleasant companions gives us such a sketch of our hero, that I can't forbear transcribing some of it. He addresses himself to the Prince in this merry manner: 'Hal, what time of day is it, lad?' [Prince Henry.] 'Thou art so fat-witted with drinking of old sack, and unbuttoning thee after supper, and sleeping upon benches in the afternoon, that thou hast forgotten to demand that truly which thou wouldst truly know. What a Devil hast thou to do with the time of the day? unless hours were cups of sack, and minutes capons, and clocks the tongues of bawds, and dials the signs of leaping-houses, and the blessed Sun himself a fair hot wench, in flame-colour'd taffata, I see no reason why thou shouldst be so superfluous to demand the time of the day.' [Falstaff.] 'Indeed you come near me now, Hal. For we that take purses, go by the Moon and seven stars, and not by Phoebus, he, that wandering knight so fair; but I pr'ythee, sweet wag, when thou art King,—as God save thy Grace, (Majesty I should say, for Grace thou wilt never have so much as will serve as a prologue to as egg and butter) marry, I say, sweet wag, when thou art King, let not us that are squires of the night's body, be call'd thieves of the day's beauty: let us be Diana's foresters, gentlemen of the shade, minions of the Moon; and let men say, we be men of good government, being govern'd as the sea is, by our noble and chast mistress the Moon, under whose countenance we—steal.—But I pr'ythee, sweet wag, shall there be gallows standing in England when thou art King? and shall resolution be thus fobb'd as it is, with the rusty curb of old Father Antick, the law? Do not thou when thou art King hang a thief.'

Immediately after this Sir John falls into a strain of repentance, and cries out, 'thou art indeed, able to corrupt a saint: Thou hast done much harm to me, Hal, God forgive thee for it: Before I knew thee, Hal, I knew nothing, and now I am, if a man should speak truly, little better than one of the wicked: I must give over this life, and I will give it over by the Lord; and I do not I am a villain. I'll be damn'd for never a King's son in Christendom.' Hereupon the Prince asking him where he should take a purse the next day, Sir John answered, 'Where thou wilt, lad, I'll make one; an I do not, call me villain, and baffle me.' And when the Prince told him, he saw a good amendment in him, from praying to purse-taking, 'Why Hal,' says Sir John, ' 'tis my vocation, Hal: 'Tis no sin for a man to labour in his vocation.'

Poins, the bravest of all the gang next to the Prince, understanding that there were pilgrims going to St Thomas Becket's tomb at Canterbury, with rich presents, and that at the same time there were several wealthy traders riding to London, he entered into an agreement with his Highness, that Falstaff, Harvey, Rossil, and Gads-Hill (so called from the place where they used to rob) should take the booty from them; and that afterwards they (Poins and the Prince) should rob the robbers in disguise. This design was accordingly executed; for the four that were appointed having got possession of the shining metal, which was the piety of the pilgrims, and the life of the tradesmen, our two heroes fell upon them as they were dividing the prey, put them all to flight, and went off undiscovered, and sufficiently pleas'd. Some time after this, Falstaff and his stout-hearted companions in the exploit, meeting the Prince and Poins at a tavern in Eastcheap, which they all frequented, the knight began, after his usual manner, to extol his own valour, exclaiming bitterly against all cowards, and professing that good manhood was forgot upon the face of the earth. 'There live not,' quoth he, 'three good Men unhang'd in England, and one of them (meaning himself) is fat, and grows old. God help the while a bad world, I say!' His Highness asking the occasion of this bravado, 'Why,' says Sir John, 'here are four of us have taken a thousand pounds this morning; but a hundred, a full hundred! fell upon us, and took it away again. I am a rogue, if I was not at half-sword with a dozen of them two hours together. I have escap'd by a miracle; I am eight times thrust through the doublet, four thro' the hose, my buckler cut through and through, my sword hack'd like a hand-saw; here, look at it! I never dealt better since I was a man; all would not do: A plague of all cowards, I say still.' The Prince and Poins upon this, burst out a laughing, and told the whole story. Harvey, Rossil, and Gads-Hill, Falstaff's companions, confess'd that he had hack'd his sword with his dagger, and said, he would swear truth out of England, but he would make Harry believe it was done in fight, and that he had perswaded them to tickle their noses with spear-grass to make them bleed, and then beslabber their garments with it, and swear it was the blood of true men. This instance of his Worship's cowardice exposed him to the ridicule of the whole gang; but Sir John was not to be laugh'd out of countenance; he had a salve for every sore. 'By the Lord,' says he, 'I knew ye as well as he that made ye; but hark ye, my masters, was it for me to kill the heir apparent? Should I turn upon the true Prince? Why, thou knowest, I am as valiant as Hercules; but beware instinct.—The lion will not touch the true Prince.—Instinct is a great matter: I was a coward on instinct: I shall think the better of myself and thee during my life: I for a valiant lion, and thou for a true Prince.' An excellent way of coming off!

Sir John however, seems, contrary to his usual custom, to have taken this disgrace a little to heart; for the next time he meets Bardolph, he accosts him in this manner: 'Bardolph, am I not fallen away vilely since this last action? Do I not bate? Do not I dwindle? Why, my skin hangs about me like an old lady's loose gown: I am wither'd like an old apple-john. Well, I'll repent, and that suddenly, while I am in some liking: I shall be out of heart shortly, and then I shall have no strenght to repent. An I have not forget what the inside of a church is made of, I am a pepper-corn, a brewer's horse: the inside of a church! Company, villainous company has been the ruin of me!' Upon this Bardolph telling him he was fretful, and could not live long, 'Why there it is' (quoth the knight) 'come sing me a bawdy song to make me merry: I was as virtuously given as a gentleman need be; I swore little; diced not above seven times a week; went to a bawdy-house not above once in a quarter of an hour; paid money that I borrowed—three or four times; liv'd well, and in good compass; but now I live out of all order, out of all compass.' This may serve for another sketch of Sir John's manner of repenting.

Some time after this, the civil wars breaking out between the Houses of York and Lancaster, Prince Henry was sent for to court to defend the throne of his father. Being unwilling to desert his humorous old squab companion, he made him captain of a company of soldiers, with orders to march down to Shrewsbury, to meet the enemy. But before we give an account of our knight's behaviour in the field of battle, hear him describe his company. 'If I be not asham'd of my soldiers, I am a sous'd gurnet: I have misus'd the King's press damnably; I have got, in exchange of a hundred and fifty soldiers, three hundred and odd pounds. I press me none but good house-holders, yeomens sons; enquire me out contracted batchellors, such as have been ask'd twice upon the banns: such a commodity of warm slaves, as had as lieve hear the Devil as a drum; such as fear the report of a culverin worse than a struck fowl, or a hurt wild duck. I press me none but such toasts and butter, with hearts in their bellies no bigger than pins heads, and they have bought out their services; and now my whole charge consists of antients, corporals, lieutenants, gentlemen of companies, slaves as ragged as Lazarus in the painted cloth, when the glutton's dogs lick'd his sores, and such as indeed were never soldiers, but discarded unjust servingmen, younger sons of younger brothers; revolted tapsters, and hostlers trade fall'n, the cankers of a calm world and long peace, ten times more dishonourably ragged than an old-fac'd antient; and such have I to fill up the rooms of those that have bought out their services, that you would think I had an hundred and fifty tatter'd prodigals, lately come from swine-keeping, from eating draff and husks. A mad fellow met me on the way, and told me I had unloaded all the gibbets, and press'd the dead bodies. No eye hath seen such scare-crows: I'll not march thro' Coventry with them, that's flat. Nay, and the villains march wide between the legs, as if they had shackles on! for indeed, I had the most of them out of prison. There's but a shirt and a half in all my company; and the half is two napkins tack'd together, and thrown over the shoulders like a herald's coat without sleeves; and the shirt, to say the truth, stollen from my host of St Alban's, or the red-nos'd inn-keeper of Daintry; but that's all one, they'll find linnen enough on every hedge.'

The forces of Henry IV and Hot-spur Piercy being met at Shrewsbury, the place of action, the morning before the battle Falstaff desires the Prince to get astride him, and defend him, if he should happen to fall, telling him, that it would be a point of friendship to do so: to which the Prince pleasantly replying, that nothing but a collossus could do him that service, and that he ow'd Heaven a death, bidding him withal say his prayers, and take his leave, we have the following humourous speech of the knight's upon record, which he made in answer to his Highness. 'The debt to Heaven which you speak of is not due yet, and I should be loth to pay him before his day. What need I be so forward with him that calls not on me? Well, 'tis no matter, honour pricks me on: but how if honour pricks me off, when I come on? How then? Can honour set a leg? No. Or an arm? No. Or take away the grief of a wound? No. Honour hath no skill in surgery then? No. What is honour, a word. What is that word honour? Air, a trim reckoning. Who hath it? He that died on Wednesday. Doth he feel it? No. Doth be hear it? No. It is insensible then? Yes, to the dead. But will it not live with the living? No. Why? Detraction will not suffer it? Therefore I'll none of it. Honour is a mere scutcheon, and so ends my catechism.' During the battle, we find the valourous Sir John getting as far as he can out of the way, and making this soliloquy: 'Tho' I could 'scape shot-free at London, I fear the shot here; here's no scoring; but upon the pate. Well, I am as hot as melted lead, and as heavy too; Heaven keep lead out of me: I need no more weight than mine own bowels.' The Prince coming up, and chiding him for being idle at such an important time: 'O Hal! pr'ythee give me leave to breathe,' says he, 'Turk Gregory never did such deeds in arms as I have done this day. I have paid Piercy; I have made him sure.' The Prince telling him Piercy was alive, and so leaving him, Sir John goes on with the soliloquy thus: 'If Piercy be alive, I'll pierce him, if he come in my way: if he do not, if I come in his, willingly, let him make a carbonado of me: I like not such grinning honour as Sir Walter hath,' (seeing the dead body of Sir Walter Blunt, a brave old commander.) 'Give me life, which if I can save, I will; if not, honour comes unsought, and there's an end on't.' Immediately after this the Prince and Hot-Spur meet, and a terrible encounter ensues; Douglas, a Scots nobleman, and friend to Hotspur, falls at the same time on Sir John, and Sir John falls on the ground, to prevent any farther mischief. The Prince kills Hotspur, and laments his old friend Jack, whom he fancies to be dead: talks of having him imbowelled, and so departs. Sir John, who all this while had received no hurt, rises at the word imbowel, and speaks as follows: 'Imbowell'd! if you imbowel me to-day, I'll give you leave to powder me, and eat me to morrow: 'Sblood! 'twas time to counterfeit, or that hot termagant Scot had paid me Scot and Lot too. Counterfeit? I lie, I am no counterfeit; to die is to be a counterfeit; for he is but the counterfeit of a man who hath not the life of a man; but to counterfeit dying, when a man thereby liveth, is to be no counterfeit, but the true and perfect image of life indeed. The better part of valour is discretion, in the which better part I have saved my life. But I am afraid yet of this gunpowder Peircy,

18

though he be dead. How if he should counterfeit too, and rise? I am afraid he would prove the better counterfeit? therefore I'll make him sure, yea, and I'll swear I kill'd him. Why may not he rise as well as I? Nothing confutes me but eyes, and no body sees me; therefore Sirrah, with a new wound in your thigh, come along with me.' Upon this, he very manfully ran the dead general through the thigh, and taking him upon his back, went to find out the King, that he might claim the honour of killing him. He was met by the Prince, who almost fancied he saw the ghost of his old crony: but Sir John soon convinc'd him that he was the same individual John Falstaff, safe and sound; and throwing down the body, 'There' says he, 'is Peircy; if your father will do me any honour, let him; if not, he may kill the next Peircy himself: I look to be either Earl or Duke, I assure you.' The Prince told him he kill'd Peircy himself, and saw him lie, as he thought, dead. 'Didst thou,' quoth Falstaff? 'Lord, Lord, see how the world is given to lying: I grant I was down, and so was he; but we rose both at an instant, and fought a long hour by Shrewsbury clock: I'll take't on my death, I gave him that wound in the thigh: if the man were alive, and would deny it, I would make him eat a piece of my sword.'

One would have thought the Prince, after this, should have had no more employment for Sir John in a martial capacity; and by what has been said, there is good reason to think that Sir John would have been very well satisfied at home in quiet; but whether his Highness was willing to cross the capricious old fellow, or whatsoever else was the cause, it is certain, that a fresh insurrection was no sooner heard of, but Captain Falstaff was again ordered to appear in arms. When the Lord Chief Justice told him of it, 'Well,' says the knight, 'all you that kiss my Lady Peace at home, pray that our armies join not in a hot day; for I take but two shirts out with me, and I mean not to sweat extraordinarily. If it be a hot day, if I brandish any thing but a bottle, would I may never spit white again. There is not a dangerous action can peep out his head, but I am thrust upon it. Well, I cannot last ever:—But it was always the trick of our nation if they have a good thing, to make it too common. I would to God my name were not so terrible to the enemy as it is! I were better to be eaten to death with a rust, than to be scour'd to nothing with perpetual motion.' Sir John took as much care this time in the choice of his men as he had done before, and was particularly cautious that he did not get into the field of battle too soon; so that the action was pretty well over when he made his appearance. However, he had the good fortune to meet a knight of the enemy's party, called Sir John Coleville of the Dale, who was endeavouring to make his escape from the victorious Henry. Falstaff bid him surrender, and Sir John Coleville, tho' otherwise a brave man, did not think proper to dispute at this time. By this accident our bully knight got into his possession one of the noblest prisoners that were taken in the whole engagement. He soon met the Prince, who began to call him to account for his delays. 'I should be sorry, my Lord,' says Falstaff, 'if it were not thus; I never knew yet but rebuke and check were the reward of valour. Do you think me a swallow, an arrow or a bullet? Have I in my poor old motion the expedition of thought? I speeded hither with the very extremest inch of possibility: I have founder'd nine score and odd posts; and here, travel-tainted as I am, in my pure and immaculate valour, taken Sir John Coleville of the Dale, a most furious knight, and valorous enemy: but what of that? he saw me, and yielded: that I may justly say with the hook-nos'd fellow of Rome, "I came, I saw, I overcame".' Here the Prince telling him it was more out of Sir John Coleville's courtesy than his deserving, 'I know not that,' quoth Sir John, 'but here he is, and here I yield him; and I beseech your Grace, let it be book'd with the rest of this day's deeds; or, by the Lord, I will have it in a particular ballad else, with mine own picture at the top of it, and Coleville kissing my foot; to the which course if I be enforced, if you do not all shew like gilt two-pences to me, and I, in the clear sky of fame, o'ershine you as much as the full Moon doth the cinders of the element, which shew like pins heads to her, believe not the word of the noble; therefore let me have my right, and let desert mount.' We have no account what reward Sir John met with for this exemplary piece of valour.

The reader, by this time, may have heard enough of Sir John Falstaff's courage, it may be proper, therefore, to relieve him a little with some of our knight's gallantry, which was altogether as singular as the former; at least, in the instance we are going to produce. Two wealthy inhabitants of Windsor, call'd Mr Ford and Mr Page, liv'd in very good friendship. The wives were as great cronies as the husbands, and were besides, the wittest, merriest women in the whole town. The gay easy temper of the dames made Sir John fancy they were both in love with him, and in this opinion, he writes each of them a very amorous epistle, and sends 'em at the same time: the consequence of this, was a visit between the two women, when they laid their heads together, how to be reveng'd upon the leachrous old load of iniquity. It was agreed, that Mrs Ford should give him encouragement, and appoint a time for him to come and see her. A servant of Sir John's in the mean time, goes and informs Mr Ford who was before inclin'd to jealousy, of the whole affair. Ford goes to Sir John in disguise, tells him his name is Broom, and that he is in love with Mrs Ford, offering him a large reward, if he could help him to the enjoying of her. Falstaff hereupon discovers the hour of assignation, and promises to introduce Mr Broom, who went away fully satisfied of a terrible plot against his head, which seemed already loaded with horns.

At the time appointed, Falstaff goes to Ford's house, and the good natur'd gentlewoman received him in the best manner imaginable; but they had not long enjoy'd their transport, before they were alarm'd by Mrs Page, who was conceal'd in the next rooms for that purpose: she seemed to come from the street, and told Sir John that Mr Ford was coming with a great many neighbours, vowing revenge. A basket of foul linnen stood by, and Sir John without ceremony desired to be put into it, and sent to the washer-woman's, or any whether, to escape the fury of the injur'd good man. The basket was placed there for this very purpose, and the servants had their lessons beforehand: so the knight was stuff'd in and covered, and the two men went away with the burden, who carried all together, threw it into a shallow place in the Thames, and went their way. Sir John made a shift to scrabble out, and get home. Hear him give a description of this misfortune to one of his servants 'Go fetch me a quart of sack, put a toast in it. Have I lived to be carried in a basket, like a barrow of butcher's offal, and to be thrown into the Thames? Well, if I be served such another trick, I'll have my brains taken out and butter'd, and give them to a dog for a New-Year's-gift. The rogues slighted me into the river with as little remorse as they would have drowned a blind bitch's puppies, fifteen in the litter; and you may know by the size, that I have a kind of alacrity in sinking: if the bottom were as deep as Hell, I should down. I had been drowned, but that the shore was shelvy and shallow; a death that I abhor; for the water swells a man: and what a thing should I have been when I had been swelled? I should have been a mountain of Mummy. Come, let me pour in some sack to the Thames water; for my belly is as cold as if I had swallow'd snowballs, for pills to cool the reins.'

The two gossips, who knew nothing of the information Mr Ford had received, were amaz'd to see him come home in a real fury: they could not so much as guess at the cause; however, they were resolved to have another bout with Sir John, come what would of it: to this end, their former go between was again employ'd. The knight was at first refractory, because of his late ill usage; but so well did the hag tell her story, that at last he yielded to come to Mrs Ford's again the next morning between eight and nine. No sooner was the emissary gone, but in comes the sham Mr Broom. Falstaff tells him how he had succeeded with Mrs Ford; how the peaking cornuto her husband had came home at the prologue of their comedy, with a rabble of his companions; how he was cramm'd into a buck-basket, with foul shirts, smocks, socks, stockings, and greasy napkins, and carried out; how he was met by Ford, and frighten'd terribly; in short, how he was thrown hissing hot into the Thames. 'And think, Master Broom,' says he, 'how all this must be to a man of my kidney! but I am to meet her again this morning, her husband is gone a birding; and then, Mr Broom, for you!' Ford, who having searched all the house over before, and found no body, was almost reconcil'd to his rib, now went away more uneasy than ever; all the circumstances agreed, and 'twas plain he was a dupe.—Well, the hour came, and Falstaff went, but was no sooner there, than he was again surpriz'd with Ford's coming. The women were very officious to dress him in the cloaths of a fat woman, who pass'd for a witch, and whom Ford had forbid his house. Sir John, by this means escaped unknown, but was heartily bang'd in his quality of an old woman for presuming to come there; and Ford and his friends search'd the house over again to no purpose.

Mrs Ford thought it was now high time to set her husband at ease; so she and Mrs Page produce their letters, and tell the whole story to all the company. The man was satisfied, the women applauded, and a fresh revenge was resolved on. Mrs Quickly, the former messenger, was sent again, who informed Sir John she was come from the parties. 'The Devil take one party, and his dam the other,' says he, 'and so they shall be both bestow'd: I have suffer'd more for their sakes than the villainous inconstancy of man's disposition is able to bear. I was beaten into all the colours of the rain-bow, and like to be apprehended for the Witch of Brainford: But that my admirable dexterity of wit deliver'd me, I had been set in the stocks, in the common stocks, for a witch!'—'Well,' says the cunning old hag,

22

'but to prevent all danger, sh'll meet you to night in the forest, where you may pass for Herne the Hunter, who, they say, walks with a great pair of horns on his head: put on the horns, and fear nothing!' Falstaff consented, the woman went her way, and Mr Broom came again, not now to entrap his wife, but only to catch the knight, who tells another lamentable story of his being beaten grievously in the shape of a woman: 'For in the shape of a man, Master Broom,' says he, 'I fear not Goliah, with a weaver's beam. But meet me at night, and all shall be well.' So he recited the whole story of his new assignation. This was the worst punishment of all; for Ford, Page, their wives, children, and friends, were ready against the appointed hour, all dress'd like fairies. Sir John, as before, went to the place in time, big with the hopes of enjoying what he had sought so long, and suffered so much for. A huge pair of stags horns were upon his head, which he esteem'd as emblematical of those he was to fix upon the head of poor Ford. In a word, the fairies came, and pinched him almost to death; which done, they all discovered themselves: and from this time poor Falstaff became a laughing-stock to all the good people in Windsor. He has humorously described this disposition of mankind towards him in these words: 'Men of all sorts take a pride to gird at me. The brain of this foolish compounded clay, man, is not able to invent any thing that tends to laughter more than I invent, or is invented on me. I am not only witty in myself, but the cause that wit is in other men.'

How much of the foregoing stories we owe to the fruitful invention of Shakespear, we shall not pretend to determine. 'Tis certain the whole character of Sir John Falstaff, as he has drawn it, whether it be entirely founded upon truth or no, is one of the most beautiful pieces in our language; which my be a sufficient excuse for our inserting so much of it. Those who are acquainted with the plays from which the foregoing is extracted, will see we have bestowed a pretty deal of labour, and, we hope, some judgment in what we have done, which is all we shall say concerning ourselves. Give us leave, however, to add, that the late celebrated Duke of Buckingham, after he has discoursed very finely upon the humour of our plays, uses these words: 'But Falstaff seems inimitable yet.'

We now proceed to give a less poetical account of some of the merry pranks which are recorded of our hero; and indeed a very different account from the foregoing. Instead of making him a coward, a glutton, and a drunkard, all other authors that mention him say, he was a very brave commander; and that, on the account of his valour against the York faction, King Henry IV knighted him, and gave him a pension of four hundred marks per annum, which was a great income in those days. Be this as it will, his revenue was not sufficient to support his extravagancies; for all agree, he took up the occupation of a gentleman highwayman.

He first set out upon this unlawful design by himself; but as man need never want a companion in wickedness, several other dissolute and disorderly gentle-men quickly enter'd themselves into his service: their names were the same as before recited, and the robberies they committed were almost innumerable. They were completely mounted and armed, and having been lately in the service of the House of Lancaster, they wanted not for skill to make use of those advan-tages. Scarce could a traveller be safe for them upon any road for a hundred miles round London, tho' the place which Sir John himself commonly collected at was Gads-Hill in Kent.

It was here that he one day met a country farmer, and demanding what money he had about him, the farmer replied, 'None'; adding, that he did not use to carry money about him for fear of robbing. Sir John hereupon, commanded him to kneel down, and fall to prayers; and at the same time he pullled a little manual out of his pocket, and kneeled down by him. The countryman did not know what to make of this unseasonable piece of devotion, and would willingly have taken another time and place to make his orisons. But there was no resi-sting necessity: Sir John was inclined to be pious, and the farmer must be so too, at least must appear so; for very probably his fear might abate the fervour which he might else have shewn. The knight mumbled over some words between his teeth with a great deal of seeming devotion, and then enquir'd of his fellow Christian how it fared with him; 'For Heaven,' he said, 'would not be deaf to the pious addresses of those that were sincerely devout; wherefore, pr'ythee feel in thy pockets, that we may see what God hath sent thee.' The countryman did so, but pretended he could find nothing: upon which Sir John feeling in his own pockets, pulls out a nine-penny piece, telling him withal, 'that for certain he pray'd not heartily; therefore 'twas necessary for him to pray again. If you look,' says he, 'directly towards Heaven, it cannot be but you must get somewhat as well as I.' With that, putting his hand into his pocket again, he pulls out a thirteen-pence half-penny piece. Still the other poor man had no success: he could not find a single farthing, and doubtless he pray'd, that no body else might find any thing upon him. He produces now no less than a noble, six shillings and eight-pence! The countryman continued firmly in the negative: upon which, Sir John told him plainly, 'that either he did not pray with devotion, or else he would not let him see how liberal Heaven had been to him? For,' says he, 'how comes it to pass, that my prayers should be heard, and not yours? If you pray with as much spiritual zeal, as you outwardly make shew of, it must needs be, that by this time you have gained very considerably. Therefore I am resolved to examine into the truth of this matter.' He did so, and found in the country-man's pockets twenty broad-pieces of gold, at which they were both amaz'd, Sir John seemingly at the liberality of Heaven, and the the other really at the loss of his money. Falstaff, however, dealt better with the farmer, than he expected: for he gave him the money, which he had at several times taken out of his own pocket, adding this severe reprimand, 'What a hypocrytical rogue are you to endeavour to cheat me, your companion, at this rate! Is this the agreement we made before we went to prayers? Good Lord! how few people are just upon Earth! Well, to punish you for your wickedness, I shall keep what Heaven has sent into your pocket; but that you may not want upon the road, take what I have got by praying; and when you are got home, acquaint your neighbours with what an honest gentleman you met, who gave you eight shillings and six-pence, when you endeavoured to cheat him of twenty broad-pieces.'

A little after this religious enterprize Sir John, and some of his comrades, met the common hangman coming from an execution at Kingston upon Thames: they robb'd him of what little money he had, and then dragged him out of the road, into an adjacent wood, and hang'd him upon a tree, as a dangerous fellow to their profession, which, in their opinion, was a very honourable one.

On the same day that the executioner was executed Sir John received notice of the return of a certain rich merchant, who had been at a fair at Guilford. Upon this he dressed himself in woman's apparel, and rode along 'till he came in sight of his intended prey. He then alighted; and lying down, after he had tied his horse in a wood, he filled the road with loud cries and lamentations; accusing Heaven and Earth as conspiring in his misfortunes. The merchant, being a man of a brisk and airy temper, and one who well understood the delights of a female conversation, was not a little mov'd with joy at this happy surprizal, imagining himself in the easy possession of a jolly young woman; for indeed Sir John, though something of the thickest, did not make a disagreeable figure in his female habit: there appeared so much delicacy and softness in his skin, (at least what was seen of it, for he was mask'd,) that not a few women would have been proud to have possest the like. The honest man, therefore, very generously a-lights from his horse, and enquires of the fair charmer (for so he called Sir John) what was the cause of her complaints? She, poor soul, for her part tells him a long story of her piteous adventures; as that she had been to visit some relations along with a barbarous inhuman brother, who had left her in this unknown place, upon a very small difference that had arisen. 'Twas impossible for the tender-hearted merchant to help pitying her misfortunes, which he looked upon to be real, and joining with her in lamenting her condition, and cursing the cruelty of her brother. Pity, it has been observ'd, frequently tunes the soul to love; and thus it was with our merchant: he sate himself down, and spoke a great many soft things; and, in short almost brought matters to the last extremity. Sir John, who was still covered with his mask, made but a feeble resistance, only crying, 'I am undone, lost, ruin'd forever! Alas, dear Sir, what do you mean? What would you do with me? Is this your Compassion? This your kindness to a poor, distressed, miserable creature? What! rob me of my honour, dearer to me than my life? For Heaven's sake, Sir, forbear!' The merchant was not to be repulsed with such a weak opposition as this; he thought it was only virgin modesty that would presently be overcome; and therefore, comforted his dear soul with all the kind words, and fair promises he could invent, taking her by the hand, and leading her to the entrance of the wood; Sir John, feeing it was now time to draw towards a conclusion, told him, 'that since her misfortunes had· so ordered it, that she was fallen into his hands, she entreated he would do her the favour to advance farther into the wood, that she might not be openly prostituted'. Still our excellent droll sobbed, and cried, and called upon death a thousand times to come and succour her, before she was eternally disgrac'd. The merchant complied with this last reasonable request, and went with her into the most solitary part of the wood; where being just about to work his wicked will upon the poor unhappy yielding creature, to his great surprize, as well as pain, she drew a poignard out of her bosom, and thrust him through one of his arms: the amorous gallant being hereby disabled, his supposed female beauty rifled his pockets, took out three or four purses of gold, and immediately rode off with the booty.

Another time, Sir John, in company with but one of his companions, met a couple of friars, belonging to a monastery, which, in those times of popery, was at Dartford in Kent: our thieving knight stripped them of their religious habits, which was much against the will of his companion, 'till he gave him the following reason for his so doing. 'You know,' says he, 'that we are not far from Lewisham, where there is a noble large golden chalice, belonging to the Church, and you ought to know as well, that there is no habit which a man can rob in so safely as a religious one. My advice then is, that we assume the sheeps clothing, and make the best of our way to the curate's house. Never doubt of success, and leave the conduct of the affair to me.' Falstaff's comrade was now very well pleased with the contrivance, and consented to assist in the putting it forthwith in practice. Away march our two friars, and the generous curate, believing them to be what they appeared, received them, in a manner so very kindly as gave them fresh hopes of succeeding in their design. At night, as they lay together, they were a considerable time consulting how they should carry on the affair: but they at last concluded to both their satisfactions, and went to sleep. The morning being come, they got up very early, and went to the curate's chamber, telling him, 'it was their custom to say Mass always at that time; and therefore they desired he would join with them'. The good man, without mistrusting any thing, arose and opened the door; which he had no sooner done, but our two ruffians rushed in upon him, knocked him down, gagged him, and tied him neck and heels; after which, they broke open his trunks, and took away all his money; and not contented with this, they took the keys of the church, and carried away not only the chalice, but all the other ornaments that were portable, and so they marched off.

One day as Sir John was riding along the road by himself, he met with two of his own profession, who, not knowing him, and seeing he made a good appearance, thought they had found a prize. With this confidence they rode up to him, who did not endeavour to avoid 'em, and bid him stand; swearing, damn 'em, and sink 'em, he was a dead man, if he did not immediately deliver his money. Sir John being accustomed not to give, but to take, could not heartily relish this demand; and therefore, very boldly told them, he had none; at the same instant laying his hand suddenly upon one of their swords, he wrenched it out of his hand, and gave him such a blow with it on his arm, that the pain took away all sense. Having done this, he set upon the other very furiously, who, being less valiant than his companion, betook himself to the swiftness of his horse's heels. But Sir John pursued him so closely, that he made him yield himself to his mercy: upon which he generously gave him his life, after reprimanding him severely for attempting to meddle with one who was his master at his own trade. Returning after this to the other, whom he had first struck, he threaten'd him with death, if he deliver'd not his money: the poor thief would willingly have excus'd himself by pretending he had none: but Falstaff was not to be put off in that manner, being well satisfied there was no credit to be given to persons of that vocation. He very orderly therefore applied to his pockets, where he found a large quantity of gold and silver, the spoils of a great many honest people. To be more completely revenged of his antagonist, Sir John bound him strongly neck and heels, wrote his crime upon a paper, and pinned it to his breast; then placed him where he might be exposed to the view of all passengers. The unfortunate highwayman had not lain long in this position, before some whom he had lately robbed came by, who looking at the paper, and at the same time examining his face, knew him to be the man: upon this they carried him before a magistrate, who committed him to prison, where he remained till the next assizes, when he was convicted, sentenc'd, and shortly after executed. Thus was Sir John the means of bringing one of his brethren to justice, while in the height of his own crimes; but the action was honourable, and in his own defence; for the soul of our knight was above submitting to the detested office of a mercenary thief-catcher.

Sir John followed this disorderly course of life a great many years; and what made him the more daring in his unlawful enterprizes, was the having a no less man than the eldest son of King Henry IV in his wicked fraternity, with whom he was very familiar, as we have before observed. This Prince being prompted on by his own vicious inclinations, and the fire of youth, and encouraged by a set of debauched and abandoned courtiers, committed such extravagancies as are almost incredible: for he not only frequently robbed upon the highway, in company with Falstaff and others, whom we have mentioned, but went so far as to set upon his father, and several times put him in fear of some design against his person: for kings went not guarded in those days as they do at present. He attempted also to rescue a prisoner from the face of justice, in the court of King's-Bench, Westminster; for which he was himself committed a prisoner by the Lord Chief Justice, whom he struck on the seat of judgment. The Justice was admir'd and applauded for this action; and the Prince, notwithstanding his ungovernable temper, submitted to the sentence, seemingly without reluctance. And indeed it apears this Prince, who had a prodigious natural genius, often disaprov'd his own extravances when he came to reflect seriously. Shakespear has given us a speech, or rather soliloquy of his, suppos'd to be spoken at the place of haunt in Eastcheap, immediately upon parting with his scandalous company. 'Tis in these words: 'I know you all, and will uphold your humour a little; yet in this will I imitate the Sun, who permits the base contagious clouds to hide his beauty sometimes from the world, that when he pleases to be himself again, at a time when he is very much wanted, he may be the more wonder'd at, by breaking thro' the foul and ugly mists and vapours that seemed almost to smother and strangle him. If all the year were holidays, it would be as tedious to sport as to work; but when play-days come seldom, they come wish'd for, and nothing pleases but what is rare: so when I throw off this base behaviour, and pay the debt I never promis'd, by how much I am better than my word, by so much shall I falsify men's hopes: and my reformation glittering over my fault, like bright metal upon a sullen ground, shall shew more goodly, and attract more eyes than that which has no foil to set it off.' And we find this illustrious person was not at all worse than his word, especially in the case of the Lord Chief Justice. This good man, upon the death of Henry IV was under terrible apprehensions of severity from the hands of his new master: the young King put on a sullen coun-tenance, and reprehended him with a great deal of seeming warmth; and the judge defended himself as nobly as he had acted before, by telling him, that upon the bench he represented his father, who was insulted in his person; and desiring him to make the case his own, and consider whether, now he was King, he would suffer his dignity to be profan'd in a chief magistrate, by a disobedient son. But how agreeably was this venerable person surpriz'd, when his Majesty returned him this answer: 'You are right, Justice, and you weigh the matter well; therefore still bear the ballance and the sword, and I wish your honours may increase till you live to see a son of mine offend you, and obey you as I did: so shall I live to speak the words of my father, happy am I, that I have a magistrate

29

so bold as to dare to do justice upon my own son; and no less happy in having a son that would deliver up his greatness into the hand of justice. You committed me; for which I commit into your hand the unstain'd sword that you used to bear, remembring you still to use the same with the like bold, just, and impartial spirit as you have done against me. There is my hand; you shall be a father to my youth, and I will humble myself to your wise directions: I will mock the expectations of the world, and frustrate the prophesies of the vulgar: my tide of blood, that has proudly flow'd in vanity till now, shall turn back to the sea, from whence it shall henceforth flow in state and formal majesty. The wisest of our nation shall form our council, of which you, father, shall be the chief, and I will mingle in your solemn debates 'till peace and war become familiar to me, and England is own'd the best-govern'd nation in the world.' It is further reported of this Prince, that he was wont every day after dinner to set apart two hours to receive petitions, and redress grievances, which he would do with wonderful equity; and that he sent to Rome to be absolved from the death of King Richard II (of which it is thought his father was guilty) tho' 'tis certain he had no hand in it.

This account of the reformation of King Henry V is doing justice to the memory of one of the greatest and best monarchs that ever sate upon the English Throne: besides, it is not altogether foreign to our design, as it makes way for another story of our hero, Sir John Falstaff. The knight was in the country, at the house of one Justice Shallow, an old acquaintance of his, when the news was brought by Pistol of his friend Hal's advancement. He was unable to contain his joy, and summoning all his own gang and the Justice's family about him, he made this harangue: 'Away Bardolph, saddle my horses.—Master Robert Shallow, chuse what office thou wilt in the land, 'tis thine—Pistol, I will double charge thee with dignities—Carry Master Silence to bed—Master Shallow, my Lord Shallow, be what thou wilt; I am fortune's steward. Get on thy boots; we'll ride all night— Oh! sweet Pistol, utter more to me; and withal devise something to do thyself good.—Boot, Boot, Master Shallow, I know the young King is sick for me—Let us take any man's horses; the laws of England are at my commandment—Happy are they who have been my friends; and wo to my Lord Justice.' Accordingly they all got ready, and Mr Shallow lent Sir John a thousand pounds to maintain his dignity, 'till the King loaded him with riches. They rode post to London, and came just time enough to see the coronation. The whole company got among the mob, and Sir John addressed himself to the Justice in this manner: 'Stand here by me, Master Robert Shallow, I will make the King do you grace: I will lear upon him as he comes by; and do but mark the countenance that he will give me. O if I had time to have made new liveries, I would have bestow'd the thousand pounds I borrowed of you. But it is no matter, this poor shew doth better; it infers the zeal I had to see him; it shews my earnestness of affection; my devotion, as it were, to ride day and night, and not to deliberate, not to remember, not to have patience to shift me, but to stand stained with travel, and sweating with desire to see him, thinking of nothing else, putting all affairs in oblivion, as if there were nothing else to be done but to see him.'

Thus did Sir John run on in a lofty strain, indulging his own vanity, and the hopes of all that were with him, till the Royal Person appear'd in all the splendour and magnificence that was suitable to the occasion. 'God save thy Grace, King Hal, my sweet boy, my love, my heart!' said Sir John with his wonted air: but how was he disappointed, when, instead of the warmth he expected to be receiv'd with, his Majesty, with a forbidding countenance, deliver'd these words! 'I know thee not, old man, what is thy meaning? Do these white hairs become a buffon and a jester? I have long dream'd indeed of such a man as thou art, so surfeit-swell'd, so old, and so prophane: but being awake, I despise my dream— Make thy body less, and thy grace more; for the grave gapes for thee three times wider than for other men.—Do not reply to me with a foolish jest, nor be so presumptuous as to think me the thing that I was: Heaven knows, and the world shall perceive, that I have turned away my former self; so will I those that have kept me company. When thou shalt hear that I am what I have been, approach me, and be what thou wast, the tutor and feeder of my riots; 'till then, I banish thee from my presence, as I have done the rest of my misleaders;—dare not henceforth, on pain of death to come within ten miles of our person: I will allow you a competence for life, that want may not induce you to evil; and as we hear of your amendment, we will advance you according to your strength and qualities.' The King did according to his word in every particular, and conquer'd himself in a manner that won the hearts of all his people.

Habits of vice are very difficult to be worn off, even tho' the occasions that first produc'd them cease; Henry's extravagancies were only the sallies of a great and violent soul, not yet subjected to the government of reason; but Sir John was grown grey in iniquity, he acted his crimes with coolness and deliberation; neither the example, the severity, nor the promises of his Sovereign, could have any effect upon him. He continued his dissolute courses 'till he was apprehended, and committed to Maidstone gaol for a robbery at Gad's-Hill. At the next assizes he was capitally convicted, but the King unwilling he should suffer death, order'd him only to transport himself in a month's time out of the English dominions. It was thought this sentance, tho' very mild, broke the knight's heart, for he died before the time allow'd him was expir'd.

THE LIFE OF
SIR GOSSELIN
DENVILLE

T he gentleman we are going to give an account of, was descended of very honourable parents at Northallerton, a market town in the North-Riding of Yorkshire. The family was very ancient, and came into England with William the Conqueror, who assign'd 'em lands for the services done him in the north of England, where they lived in great esteem, and the sucessors after them, for several ages, till the time of Sir Gosselin.

The father of this gentleman being a pious and devout man, sent his son to Peter-Colledge in Cambridge, where, for some time, he prosecuted his studies with great warmth; and, to outward appearance, gave signs of making a fine man. This gave the ancient father extreme joy, who began to think of placing his son in the priesthood; but it seems Gosselin sat at his books purely to amuse his father, and to gain some advantage he had in view by it. It was found out afterwards that a religious life, as his Father had design'd for him, was not the thing he relished; but that the prosecution of amours and love intriegues, had the greatest ascendant over his mind; nay, he began now to display his natural propensity to a luxurious and profligate life.

These steps creating great discontent in the breast of the father, he took the violent courses of his son so much to heart, that 'twas not long before he died leaving our gentleman in full possession both of the dignity of the family, and his estate, valued at twelve hundred pounds per annum, a considerable fortune in those days. Thus our gentleman becomes a knight, rolls in a plentiful fortune, and gives a loose, more extravagant than ever, to his ill courses. He associates a brother of his, named Robert, with him, and they two together, by their profuseness, soon made an end of the estate.

Being now out of the reach of maintaining themselves as usual, and finding the poverty of their circumstances still increasing upon them, they perceived there was no other way of supporting themselves, than by raising contributions on the highway. To this end, being men of extraordinary valour and courage, they ecquipt themselves out for a daring enterprize, which was to rob two cardinals, sent into his kingdom by the Pope, to mediate a peace between England and Scotland, and terminate the differences then on foot, between Edward II and the Earl of Lancaster.

One Middleton and Selby, two robbers of these times, having heard of Denville's design, came and join'd him with all the forces under their command, which were no inconsiderable number. In short, the cardinals were robbed, and a very large booty taken from them, which put our bravo into a tolerable way of subsistence for some time; but there happening some difference between Middleton and him, with regard to the sharing of this booty, the former left the association, and went some time on the road by himself; but being soon apprehended, was brought up to London, and there executed.

All this while, Sir Gosselin pursued his illegal practices; the valour of his arm, and the continual preys he and his men made on all travellers, put the whole country into a terrible pannic; for there was no such thing as travelling with any safety; and the great number of persons, of whom his gang was composed, plainly shewed, that they defied the laws, and every thing else. What they could not obtain on the highway, they sought for in houses, monasteries, churches, and nunneries, which were rifled without any distinction; and the most valuable and sacred things carried off. The men under Sir Gosselin's conduct led a most licentious life; and, like their master, committed the worst of villainies and barbarities. Persons were murdered in their houses, when their goods might have been taken without using bloodshed: so that killing and doing havock, rather looked like sport or pastime with these desperadoes. Our countryman Tom Shadwell seems to point at our knight, in his play,

34

called *The Libertine*; nay, to have founded the main plot of that piece upon his barbarous and licentious conduct. They who have a mind to be further informed in this particular, may, by perusing that dramatic performance, see how near the whole conduct of the *Libertine* squares with that of the person we are speaking of.

A while after our knight and his associates marching on the road between Marlow in Buckinghamshire, and Henley upon Thames, met with a Dominican monk, named Andrew Symson, who not only was obliged to deliver what little gold he had, to them, but also to climb into a tree, and preach them a sermon, which he did with a great deal of judgment and good sense, though pronounced extempore.

This sermon being at this very time recorded in the Bodleian Library, as a piece containing sound divinity, and a great deal of wit, we shall make no apology to our readers for inserting it, but give it an immediate place here. Mr Sympson having got into the tree, chose for his text the following words:

LUKE, Chap. x. Ver. 30.

'A certain Man went down from Jerusalem to Jericho, and fell among Thieves, which stript him of his Rayment, and wounded him, and departed, leaving him half dead.'

Our Blessed Saviour himself pronounced these Words to a Lawyer by Way of Parable, who came with a View to tempt him, by putting this Question to him, 'Master, What shall I do to inherit eternal Life?' Luke 10. 30. The Lawyer is taught by our Lord in the Context both before and after these Words, on which I lay the Foundation of my ensuing Discourse; That, in order to obtain Life Eternal, he was to esteem every Man his Neighbour, that stood in need of his Assistance; after which, the good Samaritan is introduced to shew the Love to one's Neighbour; for this Person, though a Priest and Levite, had before past by this poor Man spoken of in my Text, who was fallen among Thieves, had Compassion on him, went and bound up his Wounds, placed him on his own Beast, carried him to an Inn, and giving Orders to the Host to let him have any Thing he wanted, promised to defray all Expences, so the poor Man but recovered.

Having thus explained the Meaning of my Text, I shall now go on to a farther Illustration of it, by Discoursing on the three following Heads:

I.   The Hazard or Danger of taking a Journey.
II. Who it is that may bring this Danger.
III. What the Danger is, which is two fold, either the Loss of Goods, or Loss of Life; and sometimes Loss of both.

First then, I shall discourse on the first of these Heads, namely, the Hazard or Danger of taking a Journey. Now, this is when a Man leaves the City to go into the Country; in the former of which a Person need not be much apprehensive of himself, because the Numbers of Inhabitants are a sufficient Guard to protect him; but it is quite otherwise in the Country, I mean on the Road, where an honest Man, thro' the few People passing and repassing, and perhaps through the Obscurity of the Place, is exposed to the Insults of such abandon'd Wretches, whose Actions we should by no Means imitate or agree with. For the Royal Psalmist seems to allude to this Doctrine: 'When thou sawest a Thief, then thou consentedst with him', Psal. i. 18. And I observe again, that if a Man but goes a few Miles from his Habitation, he cannot assure himself that he shall return unrobbed; for it seems that the Person here spoken of in the Evangelical Parable, went but to Jericho, which was only six Miles South Eastward from Jerusalem. And what added to the Opportunity of the Thieves robbing him, was the Desart that lay between the two Places, which the Inhabitants call Quarentem, where great Thieving and egregious Robberies are committed to this Day.

Secondly, Who it is that may bring this Danger. They who willfully give themselves over to an indolent and lazy Life, and to covetous Pursuits, or they who abandon themselves to Drunkenness, to Gaming, or following lewd Women; for such as these turning Thieves, through their profligate Life, put honest Men into great Disorder, and commit great Damage upon them. Judas thus for Example, coloured over his Actions, with a specious Pretence of loving the Poor, and with pretending to extraordinary Charity; when, on the contrary, he was neither a charitable Man, nor a Lover of the Poor, but a Thief, and a very covetous Wretch.

This was his Hypocrisy; and one of the Evangelists witnesses thus much. 'Why was not this Ointment sold for Three Hundred Pence, and given to the Poor?' John xii. 5, 6. I cannot but say, that depriving even a Man of an Advantage is a great Injustice, tho' robbing us of Things we hold the most considerable is much superior to this. But where both Life and Goods too are in the Case, then 'tis a most dismal Consideration; for not only the Laws of Man, but those of God likewise have made it a Capital Crime to take away any Thing unjustly from a Man, or to detain what of Right belongs to another; now this taking away which I am speaking of, is branched out into the three following Denominations; First, simple Theft, which means a private taking away of that which is another Man's. Secondly, Rapine, by which Word is implied a forcible or compulsive Way of taking away of that which appertains to another Body's Right; And Thirdly, Sacriledge, which imports the taking away of Things dedicated to holy Uses, or in sacred Places. Now the First and Last of these Kinds, are, for the Generality put in Execution in the Night-time, that being the most convenient Season to accomplish the Ends design'd by them. 'If' (says the Prophet) 'Thieves comes to thee, if Robbers by Night, how art thou cut off; would not they have stollen till they had enough.' Obad. v. 5. And our Saviour himself compares his coming on Earth to a Thief in the Night. 'The Day of the Lord so cometh as a Thief in the Night', I Thess. v. 2. Says St Paul.—Agreeable to which is the following Passage of St John the Divine. 'Behold I come as a Thief', Revel. xvi. 15. Which Words, if they were paraphrased, import thus much. Behold I come when you know nothing of it. But the other Kind of taking away is generally put in force (as you have now done) in the Day-time, putting Men and Women into terrible Frights, and vast bodily Fears.

But I must beg Leave to acquaint you, Gentlemen, by the way, that you are not the only Thieves in the World, for a great many others come under the Denomination; such as Kings and Princes, when they lay unnecessary Taxes and Excises upon their Subjects; Subjects when they do not pay the customary Tribute to their Princes; Tradesmen, when they use deceitful Weights and Measures, and unjustly enhance the Price of Commodities; Masters, when they defraud Servants of their Wages;

and Servants when they embezzle the Goods of their Masters: Nay, Apothecaries, and Taylors, when they make unconscionable Bills; Butchers, when they blow their Veil; Millers, for taking double Toll; Shoemakers, for stretching their Leather larger than their Consciences; Surgeons, for prolonging a Cure; Physicians, for taking away the Lives of their Patients; and Lawyers, for taking Bribes on both Sides: I say, that all these are no better than Thieves, and such as they, nor Covetous, nor Drunkards, nor Revilers, nor Extortioners, shall inherit the Kingdom of God, I Corinth. vi. 10. Now what I have already observed brings me to the following Inferences. 'Thou shalt not steal.' This is a positive Precept delivered to us by the Hand of God himself, who has also declared his avenging Hand on those that infringe it; yet this is so far from deterring Mankind from the Commission of it, that rather than not indulge your Headstrong Inclinations this Way, you will cut, hack, maim, wound, tie Hand and Foot, Neck and Heels together; you will rob, pilfer, and plunder any one, so this vicious Desire is but served. What a melancholy Thing is this, and astonishing Considerations does it present to an honest and virtuous Mind! But, lack-a-day, why should I talk at this Rate; will not Courtiers rob People that solicit them for Favours? Will not Judges pervert the Laws and administer Justice partially? These are shocking Reflections, and yet they are no more shocking than true. I confess they are hard, but true, Instances of Injustice and Thieving. But considering the Age we live in, 'tis not to be wondered at; for if Arts and Sciences are suffer'd to augment, much less is it to be admired why Vices and Immorality in all Shapes increase; Satan being industrious to plant his Schools of Wickedness, as much as our best Instructors their's, of good Learning and Morality.

Now they who relinquish the Paths of Virtue, and will voluntarily pursue the Road of Iniquity and Thieving, Robbing, and Plundering, every one they meet, without any Distinction either of Sex or Person, expose themselves to an untimely Fate, which not only proves a miserable Exit to themselves, but also involves their Families, Friends, and Relations, in a great Deal of Scandal. And supposing they who pursue this profligate Course of Life, do not meet with the Gallows for their Rewards, yet ten to one, they die no natural Death, for, 'tis possible, that one Time or other, meeting with a Prey, as they imagine, they may find some obstinate Resistance from the Person they attack, as may at last over-power them, and in the End take away one or other of their Lives; then pray what's the Consequence? Why, being thus cut off in their Sin, they tumble Headlong into Perdition, where endless Torments wait for them. Probably you are dispatched and sent out of the World some Years before your appointed Time, whilst he that sent you packing out of this World, enjoys his Quiet, without being accountable to the Laws of his Country for what he did; and besides, we have the Levitical Law justifying the killing of a Thief. 'If a Thief be found breaking up, and be smitten that he die, there shall no Blood be shed for him', Exod. xxii. 2. And indeed all honest Men look upon Theft with such Detestation, that on a Thief's being apprehended, they are ready to massacre him, before he is carried to Gaol. And under the Denomination of Theft we may justly place Usury, Bribery, and Cheating in Gaming. Let us now suppose that the Thief may run on in his Villainous Course of Life several Years, without either being taken from his Roguery, or paying his Recompence to the Laws, yet what's this to the Purpose? All this Time he has something within him called Conscience, which incessantly tells him of his Ways; his Mind presents to itself terrifying Ideas; nor can he purchase one Night's sound Sleep he's haunted in every Corner, nor will Conscience suffer him to be at rest; possibly his pleasing Sins may delude his Thoughts with Gaiety and Mirth for a while, but this Scene lasteth not long, before a Vulture gnaweth his Heart, and eternally racks him: For ill Actions are constantly attended with Perturbations; and the Punishment that follows is a thousand Times Worse than all the Delight such Actions produced. Ill-acquired Gains are far more detrimental than all the Losses of an adverse Fortune. These latter but disturb us once; the first are perpetually teazing us. And indeed that Man can never think of adding to his Contentment, who pursues Ways diametrically against it, still fixing his Eyes on the Beginning of Things, but has never once the Sense to consider where the End will reach. Now, Gentlemen, if you are ignorant to this Particular, I will make bold to tell you, that the Beginning of Theft is an Entrance into Prison, where your chiefest Companions are Hunger, Thirst, Shackles, Bolts, Irons, and Vermin; and the End Hanging, unless you have the good Fortune to meet with an Adversary as favourably as King Edward the Confessor. I will produce the Instance for your Informations. It Seems this Prince one Morning lying in Bed with his Curtains drawn, saw a poor Courtier come into his Chamber, and, going up directly to his Coffer, take as much Money away as he was able to carry, and came again, and was suffered to convey his second Booty off without being spoke to, but King Edward finding him advance thither the third Time, reproved him for his Covetousness, and commanded him to be gone; for if Hugoline his Treasurer, came and caught him in the Fact, he would certainly have a Rope for his Deserts; Now it seems he was scarce got out of the Chamber, but the Treasurer who had left open the Coffer, came and seemed in a vast Surprize at the Loss, but the King bid him not concern himself, for he had most Occasion for the Money, that had taken the Opportunity to convey it away.

40

Now I shall infer once more from this Discourse, that Persons of your Profession, let your Lives be never so flagitious and enormous, may probably be of Opinion, that the same Mercy is laid up in Store for you, which the penitent Thief on the Cross found and enjoyed: But let me tell you, and be you assured, that you are far from it, unless you can bring yourselves to repent as he did. But pray what Man in his Senses would run the Risque of Damnation by suffering a reproachful Death, 'When cursed is everyone that hangeth on a Tree', Gal. xiii. 21. Nay he that is hanged is accursed of God. Alas! no Man always sins unpunished, Deut. xxi. 23. Is it not a common Thing for us to see the Son punish'd for the Vices and profligate Life of the Father? I am very well assured that there are but few Vices of any Magnitude, which are not punished in this World. God, let me tell you, Gentlemen, doth not bless or punish all at once, but by Degrees and Warnings. So much Knavery possesses the World at this Time of Day, that to be an honest Man is reputed Vice, and so many Mutations are hourly observed, that 'tis very rare to see the compleated Race of another. Our lives are too short to take exact Notice how the most just God dispenses his Judgments, and how he strikes pernicious

Mortals. Some of his Corrections are performed in the Dark, nor does every notorious Act meet with its just Punishment, notwithstanding (as I have observed in the foregoing) private Punishments sometimes give a Man vast Uneasiness within, while Mankind observing only the Superficies of Things, see not how he Smarts in secret.

Having proceeded thus far, I shall now come to some few Exhortations, and then close my Discourse. I must take the Freedom to acquaint you Gentlemen, that the Sin of Theft is Obligatory, that is, that you are obliged if you are able to restore back the Things you steal, or forcibly take from another, otherwise, let me tell you, your Sins are not forgiven. I speak not this for the Sake of myself, but for the Benefit of your precious Souls; entertaining so favourable an Opinion of you, that I believe you to be good-humour'd, generous tenderhearted Gentlemen, and such who, without being spurred on, have the Sense to shew a compassionate Honesty. All Things whatsoever you would that Men should do unto you, do ye even so to them: For this is the Law and the Prophets. Some of you probably may object, and say, that it is impossible to keep the Commandments. I answer to this; that it is because you have no Inclination to oblige yourselves to the Observance of them, but are more willing that God should be thought the Author of Sin, which is exceedingly blasphemous and wicked. Possibly too you may endeavour to justify your Iniquities and scandalous Lives, by alledging you cannot restrain yourselves, liking this Evasion much better than acknowledging your Iniquities, and confessing your Sins in order to amend, by engraving the Law of God upon your Hearts.

It is my sincere Hope that the Words and Doctrine I have already deli-vered, will have the same Influence on you, as the Advice once had on the Thief which the Apostle St John gave him, which reclaimed him from his wicked Courses. The Narrative is not very long, and for your Information, I will acquaint you with it. St John, as soon as the Tyrant was dead, who had banish'd him to the Isle of Pathmos, returning to Ephesus, and being importuned to visit the Countries adjacent, to put the Churches in Order, when he was come into a certain City, and seeing a young Man of goodly Body, handsome Face, and fervent Mind, among the Brethren, he turned his Face to him, who was appointed chief over all the Bishops, and said, 'I commend this young Man unto thy Custody, with an earnest Desire to take Care of him, as Christ and the Church bear me witness.' The Bishop having received his Charge, carried the young Man Home, and took extraordinary Care of him. But it seems that this young Convert, in spite of the Bishop's Precepts and Admonitions soon abandon'd himself to lewd and dissolute Courses, and associated with young Men of his Years, who were Idle, Debauch'd, and acquainted with all Manner of Vice and Immorality. The first Step these evil Counsellors take with their Pupil, is to bring him to costly Entertainments; afterwards to Steal and Pilfer in the Night, and commit a great many other offences. Thus our Convert soon became acquainted with all manner of Wickedness; he plunges himself into a Bottomless Pit of all Disorder and Outrage, and in the End, Despairs of the Saving Grace that cometh of God. He is past all Hopes of Mercy; and therefore being quite regardless of the Consequences of his irregular Life, he proceedeth onward in his Impieties, and takes his Lot in common with the rest of his Companions. It seems that a Gang of Thieves being gather'd together, he puts himself at their Head, and conducts them in the Execution of their Enterprizes. His Mind is now entirely bent to Robbing, extream Cruelty and Murder. A while after this the Bishop, being under some Necessity, sent for St John, who having declared the Cause of his sending for him, the Apostle addressed him in the following Manner: 'O Bishop! I require the young Man and the Soul of our Brother, whom I committed to thy Custody.' The Bishop hearing this, with a dejected Countenance, and sobbing and sighing, told him that he was dead. 'Dead,' said St John; 'how? by what kind of Death?' The Bishop replied, 'he is dead to God; for he is become a very wicked and pernicious Wretch; nay, a Thief, keeping this Mountain over-against the Church, in Company with his Associates.' St John immediately rent his Garments, and beat his Head saying to the Bishop, 'I have left a wise Keeper of our Brother's Soul; prepare me a Horse, and let me have a Guide.' He hasten'd out of the Church, and rode Post to the Place he intended, but was immediately apprehended by the thievish Watch; yet he makes no Resistance, but exclaims aloud, and says, 'Bring me hither your

Captain,' who, in the mean time, as he was arm'd, saw him coming. As soon as the Captain saw the Apostle's Face, knowing it to be St John's, he was stricken with Shame, and ran away. The old Man, unmindful of his great Age, pursues him flying, and cries, 'My Son, why turnest thou away from me thy Father, unarm'd, and old? Be not any way daunted, as there are Hopes of Salvation remaining; I will plead for thee with Chirst; nay, I will expose my Life to Death for thee, if there be Occasion, as Christ exposed his for our Redemption; believe me, that I too will even hazard my Soul for thee and thine, for Christ sent me.' Our Thief hearing this warm Expostulation, stood some Time stock still, with his Countenance fix'd on the Ground, trembling like an Aspin Leaf, and all the while shed a Flood of Tears. He took St John in his Arms, and, with great Emotion, embraced him, making him as pertinent Answers as he could for his weeping; so that to outward Appearance he look'd as tho' he had been baptiz'd again with Tears. After St John had promis'd and assured him to obtain his Pardon with our Saviour, and pray'd, and fell on his Knees, and kissed his Right Hand, which Repentance had now purified; he conducted him to the Church again, where rectifying his late fallen Soul with abundance of Prayers and Fastings, and confirming his Mind with several excellent Sermons, he left him fully restored to the Church, a great Example of true Repentance, a brave Trial of a new Birth unto Righteousness, and a singular Pledge of a visible Resurrection from mortal Sin.

Wherefore, Gentlemen, if your Inclinations are to imitate the Examples of this great Convert, and to put on the new Man, by being good Christians, associate yourselves with honest and good Company; for there is nothing more prejudicial than to keep that which is bad: Our Fame and our Souls are utterly ruined by it; we receive Wounds by it which are incurable and past Remedy; besides, consider the Disgrace: Was a Man a King, he would lose his Majesty and Dignity by it; for pray tell me, who would pay Obedience to his Commands or Government, when, in imitation of Nero, he would waste his Time at Taverns with the lewd and debauched, play with Minstrels in his Chariot, and frolick with common Players on the Stage? Bad Company may be compared very justly to the new Trimming of a Ship; wheresoever you but touch it, you are all bedaub'd; and supposing you are clean when you go aboard, yet the smallest Motion in the World will soon discover the Blotches you have received. How many hundreds could I enumerate, who, going to perform the last Scene of an ignominious Death, have blamed ill Company as the Original of all the Failings they have made, as though some Witch had enchanted them into their Follies? Bad Company is an Engine which the Devil always is putting in Play to remove Man from the Pursuit of virtuous Ways: Bad Company is the spiritual Whore, that by fond Dalliances and Arts betrays a Man into his Destruction: Bad Company is certainly a Delilah, if there be one under Heaven; But not to tire you with more of this Nature, I shall conclude my Discourse with this Admonition in Scripture, 'Let him that stole, steal no more.'

This sermon was vastly well received by Sir Gosselin and his associates, who returned the monk their extraordinary thanks for the excellent sermon he had made; in short, they gave back not only the gold they had taken from him, but making a collection among themselves presented him a purse (above his money) by Sir Gosselin their spokesmen, who, after a few ceremonies on either side, left the monk to descend out of the tree quietly: and go home in peace.

One would have thought that the doctor's impartial handling of his subject, and the open manner in which he exposed thieving, and the direful conse-quences that waited upon it after this life, would have awaked our adventurers to a better sense of themselves: but, it seems they were too far plunged in their iniquitous course of life, to retreat back and reform. Which will be proved in the sequel. Nay, if accounts be true that are transmitted down to us concerning this knight and his confederates, whole parties of horse and foot sent out to suppress their career, were several times defeated; at which the whole kingdon was put into so much terror and amazement, that none durst take a journey, or appear on the roads. The King then reigning having acquainted his nobles of his intention to make a progress through the north of England, Sir Gosselin came timely to hear of it, and accordingly put himself and his whole gang in priests habits. Now the King being on his progress and near Norwich, our adventurers, being a considerable number, drew up to him in their venerable habits; which making the King halt to observe them a little more closely, Sir Gosselin closed up with him. The King upon this seemed desirous to hear what he had to say, which Sir Gosselin observing, after a low obeisance made to his Majesty, he told him that he was not come to discourse about religious matters, but secular affairs, which was to lend him and his needy brothers what money he had about him, otherwise not all the indulgences he could obtain from the Pope should save him from being exposed to a very hard and rigid penance. The King having but about forty to attend him, found it impossible to get clear of his adversary, or save his money, but was obliged to surrender all; nay look on while his noblemens pockets were searched; after which Sir Gosselin and his associates left them to perform the remaining part of their progress.

This attempt upon the King was highly resented; and several proclamations with considerable rewards inserted, issued to apprehend any of the persons concerned in this robbery, alive or dead. In less than six months above sixty were treacherously taken by people, in order to obtain the præmium. Notwithstanding, this change of fortune was so far from working any reformation in our knight, that he and his brother robbed with greater boldness; so that those noblemen and gentlemen who had seats in the county, were afraid to reside at them, and were obliged to secure themselves and their effects in the fortified cities and towns of the kingdom.

The last adventure which we have on record of this knight was this: Sir Gosselin and the remaining part of his associates being in the north of England, were determined to see what the rich Bishop of Durham could afford them; accordingly they got into his palace, which they rifled from top to bottom of all the valuable things in it; and, not content with the spoil they found, bound the reverend prelate and his servants hand and foot, while they went down into the cellar, drank as much wine as they could well digest, and then let the rest run out of the barrels; after which they departed, leaving the ecclesiastick to call upon God to deliver him in his necessities.

But fortune now weighs down the scale of our knight's iniquities: it seems a man kept a publick house in a by-place in Yorkshire, where Sir Gosselin frequently went, not so much for the liquors there, as the beauty of the woman of the house: a freer acquaintance than consisted with decency had been kept up very openly some time between the knight and the landlady; which the husband

45

at first connived at, through a notion his dignified customer, and the company he brought to his house, would be of considerable advantage to his trade: but Sir Gosselin and his wife pursuing their love intrigues in broad daylight, to the no small scandal of his family, and he beginning too late to think himself injured, found no other resourse to repair the ill name thrown upon him by the people in the neighbourhood, than by removing the knight out of the way: to which end he goes to the sheriff of the county, and acquaints him how Sir Gosselin might be apprehended with little difficulty at his house provided he came that night. The sheriff rejoyced at the opportunity, but considered that the knight and his associates were men of desperate fortunes, vast courage, and resolved to hazard the last, rather than surrender or be taken; upon which he muster'd up between five or six hundred men at arms, came privately at night with them to the house, which they vigorously attacked as our knight and his company were revelling over their cups. Now or never was an important battle, or rather siege, to be determined. The persons within resolutely defended themselves for some time, and the men at arms without were not less valiant. Good fortune seemed to incline to our knight's side, who, in conjunction with his men, laid two hundred of his adversaries dead on the spot; but being tired with the slaughter, and fresh enemies pouring in upon him, he was presently hemmed in on every side, and obliged to surrender, tho' not without fighting to the last. The sheriff exasperated to think at losing so many men, took care to put the captive knight, and three and twenty of his comrades, who were made prisoners at the same time, under a very strong guard, who safely conducted them to York, where, without any trial, or other proceedings had upon them, they were executed, to the joy of thousands; the satisfaction of the great, and the desire of the common people, who waited upon them to the gallows, triumphing at their ignominious exit.

THE LIFE OF
ROBIN HOOD

The accounts of this man's genealogy are exceeding various, and the stories of him as fictitious among the country people, as the theft of mercury among the heathens, the one being accounted a god for his dexterity of pilfering, and the other being generally reputed a nobleman. I shall only confine myself to two, out of the several accounts we have of this man. In the first he is said to be the Earl of Huntington, that his father was head-ranger in the north of England, that his mother was a daughter of the Earl of Warwick, that he had an uncle named Gamwell of Gamwell-hall there, that his father and mother lived at a small village called Loocy, near the forest of Sherwood, and that he himself was born in Henry the Second's Time.★ But in the second he is said to derive his family *ab origine*, from no higher persons than shepherds, who for some time had inhabited in Nottinghamshire, in which county, at a small village adjacent to the forest of Sherwood, he was born in the reign of King Henry the Second, and bred up a butcher; but being of a licentious and wicked inclination, left his trade, and associating himself with several robbers and outlaws, put himself at their head, because he was a man of extraordinary courage, and wou'd never entertain any in his fraternity, but such as had been sufficiently tried both as to their stoutness and dexterity in handling their arms.

⋆But we are acquainted from the former of these two accounts, that Robin was put to school, where he made a surprizing progress in his books, and could answer to any question put to him by his master with wonderful facility and wit, which gave his parents no small joy: and that one Christmas he went to see his Uncle Gamwell, at whose house, in company with Little John (who was a servant there) he performed very unusual tricks with cups and balls; which won the heart of the aged gentleman so much, that, dying not long after, he left Robin his sole heir, who now began to be very beneficent and hospitable to all that came to see him; relieved the poor, and did a thousand other meritorious actions, which gained him the good-will and esteem of all about him; but that this open and free way of living did not last long, for, by his profusion and too great liberality having run thro' the estate, he was obliged to support himself as well as he could. That he had abundance of deep reflection within himself how to maintain his usual grandeur and hospitality, which at length turned upon robbing the rich, and always shewing kind to the poor, who were always sending up their prayers to heaven for his prosperity and long life, because, if he met any of them, he would not only restrain from injuring or robbing them, but give them money; nay, wheresoever he heard that any were sick or in want, he was sure to send his succour and assistance to relieve them in their necessitous circumstances.⋆

By this time he and Little John (so called, tho' otherwise of lofty stature) were become sworn brothers. They were together in all parties of pleasure, of robbing, or otherwise. And the first adventure of theirs which we have on record was performed by them, and fifteen more, on the Bishop of Carlisle, who had fifty in his retinue. The account of this matter stands thus: Robin having intelligence that the Prelate was in his way to London, met him on the south-side of Ferrybridge in Yorkshire, and, notwithstanding his retinue was so numerous, attacked him with his much inferior number, took from him eight hundred marks, and then tying him to a tree, made him sing Mass; after which he unty'd him, set him on his horse again with his face to the tail, and in that condition obliged him to ride to London, where he made heavy complaint to the King of the indignity that had been offered him, who issued out a proclamation for his being apprehended; but all endeavours were ineffectual.

Some time after this the King having proposed a shooting-match in Finsbury-fields, Robin and his gang, notwithstanding their late insulting the Bishop, had a mind to be spectators of this diversion, nay, to make parties in it, and accordingly having disguised themselves, they came up to London, and mixed incognito among the company assembled on this occasion. Great commendations were given to the King's archers, who, to say the worst of them, shot exceeding well, and large betts moving about, Robin steps up, and offers to lay an hundred marks, that he singled out three men who should shoot better than any three others that could be produced to oppose them; the King takes up our adventurer, and the Queen, admiring the resolution of the strangers, as she thought them, was incited to lay a thousand pounds on their heads against the King, which example was followed by several of the nobility. Robin now bent his bow and shot almost into the middle of the clout, beating his adversary above a span; Little John hit the black mark in it, and overcame his antagonist, but Midge the Miller pinn'd up the basket, by cleaving with his arrow the pin in two which was in the middle of the black, so that the Queen, and all those that laid on her side won the betts, but when the King came to know afterwards that it was Robin Hood and part of his gang, that had beaten his archers, he swore that he should be hanged whenever he was caught, and, in order thereto, sent out several detachments of soldiers into the forest of Sherwood after him, which Robin having private notice of, made him withdraw into Yorkshire, thence to Newcastle, Cumberland, Lancashire, and Cheshire, and last of all to London till the heat of the hue and cry was over, and then he returned to his old place of rendezvous, to the no small joy of his companions, who had been from him full eight months.

Robin having a mind to make a progress by himself, put into a bye-sort of a house, a little out of the road, in which he found no body put a poor old woman, who was weeping very bitterly, and in a flood of tears. Robin, moved at her extraordinary crying, desired her to acquaint him with the cause of her sorrow, to which she answered, that she was a poor woman and a widow, and being somewhat indebted to her landlord for rent, she expected him every moment to come and seize what few goods she had, which would be her utter ruin. This news filling Robin's breast with compassion, he bad her rest herself contented, and he would make things easy; so pulling off his rich laced cloaths, and putting on an old coat, which the old woman lent him, and having likewise secured his horse in an old barn, in a little time came the old miserly landlord, and demanded his rent: upon this Robin rises out of the chimney-corner with a short stick in his hand; and says, 'I understand, Sir, that my sister here (poor woman) is behind hand for rent, and that you design to seize her goods; but, she being a desolate widow, and having nothing wherewithal to satisfy you at present, I hope you will take so much pity and compassion on her mean circumstances, as not to be so severe upon her; pray, Sir, let me perswade you to have a little forbearance', to which the Landlord reply'd, 'Don't tell me of forbearance, I'll not pity people to the ruin of myself; I'll have my money, I want my rent, and if I am not paid now, I'll seize her goods forthwith, and turn her out of my house.' When Robin found that no intreaties nor perswasions would prevail with the old miserly cuss, to have patience with the poor woman, he pulled a leathern bag out of his pocket, and said, 'Come, let's see a receipt in full, and I'll pay it'; so accordingly a receipt was given, and the rent paid: then the landlord being upon going away, says Robin, ' 'tis drawing towards night Sir, and there's great robbing abroad, therefore I would advise you to stay here till tomorrow morning, and take the day before you.' 'No, no,' replied the landlord, 'I'll go home now, I shall reach seven miles before 'tis dark.' 'Pray, Sir,' says Robin to him again, 'Let me perswade you to tarry here, for indeed there's great robbing abroad': 'I don't care,' answered the landlord, 'what robbing there is abroad; I'll go home now, besides, I don't fear being robbed by any one man, let him be what he will': so taking his horse, away he rode, and Robin after him; drest then in his fine cloaths, and meeting him at a pond where he knew he must pass by, bid him stand and fight, or deliver his money: which words so terrified him, that he delivered all the money he had received for rent, and as much more to it. Then Robin riding back to the old woman again, and disguising himself as before, it was not long before the landlord came back to the house again, and knocked at the door; upon which Robin asks who was there? The landlord answers, ''Tis I': 'What I?' says Robin; 'Why 'tis I', answered the landlord again. At these words the old woman cry'd, 'O dear: it is my landlord': so letting him in, he told his grievance with a great deal of sorrow, as how he was robbed by a rogue in a lac'd coat, who swore a thousand oaths at him, and had certainly knocked his brains out had he not given him all his money: 'Ay,' says Robin, 'I told you there was great robbing abroad, but you would not take my advice; now I hope you'll stay here till morning': however he did not; for, having given an account of his misfortune, he made the best of his way homeward.

The King having determined to make a progress into the north of England, Robin came to hear of it, and was resolved to rob him. Accordingly taking sixty of his followers, determined to rob him, and with that view put himself and his associates in very rich cloaths, with each man his white horse, well harnassed and accoutred. They met the King at a small village, with about thirty in his retinue (for the kings of England in those days were not wont to be attended with horse-guards as now) whereupon Robin, the foremost of his comrades, stept up to the King, and addrest him in a very handsome manner, 'My Liege,' says he, 'by our extraordinary garb and dress we should seem to be persons of dignity and fortune, but I must crave leave to be so sincere with you, as to inform you we are of a quite different stamp and condition to that which probably you and your retinue may take us to be. For my part, having been descended of honourable parents, and left, when very young, in possession of a considerable estate, which for several years supported me in a generous and gay manner, I reckon my self among the number of those of your countrymen (for subject is too harsh a word for a gentleman to pronounce) who think themselves the happiest persons living, by having lost all thro' generous and polite living!' 'What mean you Sir, by this mysterious way of discourse?' answered the King. 'Explain your self, for really I am at a loss to understand you.' To which Robin replies, 'My Liege, my actions are already so much divulged throughout this land, that there's no need of making enquiry about me; I am only to inform you, that, having run thro' all that I was born to, and double the quantity, I made myself captain over these brave fellows whom you see before you. Our employment is to collect tribute (not as you do, to satiate the hungry appetites of ministers of state and pensioners) of every one that travels thro' these counties, which I have some time ago annexed to my dominions. I constantly take from the rich to give to the poor, for those share my benevolence hourly, and I cannot think but your generosity will look upon me as a person deserving. What I want Sir, is your money, which will give you a free passport to the place you are going to.' The King finding by the number of Robin's attendance, that there was no such thing as resisting his demand, voluntarily pulled out a purse and gave it him, who found it, by the weight, sufficient to answer his present occasions, without having recourse to the noblemens pockets who waited upon the King to increase the booty.

Our readers are to be acquainted, that it was no difficulty to rob our kings at that time of day: several of our nobility of the present age appear more splendid

W.^m fell delin.   J. Basire Sculp.^t

WILLIAM STUTELY making his Complaint to ROBIN HOOD.

and numerous in their attendance than they did. Kings formerly used to make frequent progresses to different parts of the kingdom, to diffuse among their country subjects their riches, and see how matters went among them; but now the custom is quite varied, and nothing but large bodies of life guards are seen waiting upon our kings, though it be but for three or four miles, which makes it seem rather a clog upon majesty than an augmentation of it.

Robin, happening to be out one morning by himself, observed a young man, of a genteel aspect, and well drest, sitting under the shade of a tree in a very melancholly and dejected mood: the sight presently made our adventurer step up to him, and ask the reason of his sitting so disconsolately there. The young man, after many sobs and tears, broke out very fervently into an exclamation against womankind, who, he said, were the most perfidious wretches in the world. 'I this morning,' said he, 'had got all things ready in order to be married to the gentleman's daughter of that house; but money being a stronger perswasive than the truest love, another person in the neighbourhood has supplanted me by the young woman's own appointment, tho' she's mine by all the sacred oaths under heaven.' 'Ay, ay,' says Robin, 'is your case so? Never be afraid man, but put on a more chearful look, and I'll warrant you success; you shall not only have the woman, but her fortune too.' Having thus said, he took the young man along with him to his comrades, who went back to the church together, and meeting the bishop, Robin began to discourse him on some points in religion, till a wealthy knight, and the young man's mistress came in to be married. Upon which Robin said, ''Tis a great shame that such a young beautiful woman should be married to such a fumbling old man as this, to lie grunting by her side, and to make a nurse of her all the days of her life: no, no, she shall have her own bride-groom, and he his right mistress.' With that he blew a blast, and straightway appeared the young man, and twenty yeomen. 'Now,' said Robin, 'you shall enjoy the woman you love, this very day.' 'No, hold,' said the bishop, 'that's against the laws of our church, to marry any person that has not been ask'd three times.' Robin hearing this, immediately pulled off the bishop's robes, and put them on Little John, who went up directly into the choir, and asked them seven times before all the people; but the young gentlewoman absolutely refused to make any response, till menaces and high words forced her into a compliance, when away they carried her to Sherwood, where they kept the wedding.

53

Another time Robin being at Coventry, and having a mind to play a prank, which he mightily delighted in doing; and understanding that a certain lord was to set out for London the next day on horseback, with a great retinue, he put himself in woman's apparel; and overtaking his lordship on the road, having a tolerable good face, and young, the noble peer was pleased to scrape acquaintance with this young damsel, as he suppos'd her; so after a great deal of chat together, his lordship, being amorously inclined, was for fulfilling the primary command, 'encrease and multiply'; and putting the question to her, this masculine, feminine creature pretending great modesty, said, 'It became her sex never to permit dishonesty to come nearer than their ears, and then, to save virtue the labour, wonder and detestation ought to stop it.' However, his lordship pursuing his inclination very close, it made her simper at the conceit of it; and at last giving way to her enamarato's courtship, she told his lordship, that if they had been in any place of privacy, she should have been very ready to gratify his desire; but to expose herself before all his men, she would not for the world. His lordship being very joyful at her condescension to his embraces, they had not rid above half a mile further, before a wood presented itself to their sight, where he ordered his servants to halt till he came to them: so he and his dear masculine mistress rid into the wood, and there alighting with an intention of having a full enjoyment of his supposed lady, when his lordship taking up her petticoats, found under them a pair of breeches; and said, 'What's the meaning of your wearing breeches, Madam?' 'Nothing,' replied our adventurer, 'but to put your money in, and now you must pay for your peeping'; with that he beat his lordship, and took away above an hundred marks from him, and then tied him to a tree, to cool his courage, and so bid my lord farewel till the next meeting. The servants mean time waiting the return of their master, wondred, having staid an hour, at his long absence; but at last they determined to seek him out, and so entring the wood, they heard a voice crying out for help; they followed the sound as fast as they could, till at length they found his lordship fast; he bad them untye him, and said, that the villain whom he had taken for a woman, proved to be neither better nor worse than an highwayman and a robber, and had taken all he had from him, that was valuable, but that for the future he would be hang'd, if ever he trusted himself alone with any thing in the shape of a woman.

Another time Robin disguised himself in a friar's habit, and travelling from his companions, had not gone far before he met a couple of priests, and he

54

making a pitiful moan to them, begg'd their charity, and that they would relieve one of their function, for the Virgin Mary's sake: that we would willingly do, said they, was it in our power, 'but we have lately met with a gang of villains, who have robbed us of all our money, and left us nothing to relieve our selves.' 'I am afraid,' said Robin, 'you are all so addicted to lying, that an honest man cannot take your words: therefore let us all down on our knees, and pray to the Virgin Mary to send us some money to defray our charges.' Upon which they offered to run away, but Robin soon put a stop to their career, and made them go to prayers. They had not been long at their supplications, before Robin bad one of the priests feel in his pockets what the Virgin Mary had sent; upon which both, to obey the word of command, put their hands in their pockets and pulled out nothing. Robin upon this fell into a great passion, and told them, that he believed they were nothing but a parcel of lying deceitful knaves, to make him believe that the Virgin had sent them nothing, when they had all prayed so heartily; therefore, don't deceive one another, but each of you stand a search: so Robin began, and search'd their pockets, and soon found five hundred pieces of gold. When he saw this glorious sight, he could not forbear calling them lying and deceitful knaves. Soon after this they rose up to go, but Robin stopt them and made them take an oath never to tell lies to a friar again, nor to tempt young virgins, nor to lie with other men's wives. After which he mounted his horse and returned to Sherwood.

Another time a gentleman as he was riding from Coventry to London, happened to meet with Robin Hood, and thinking him to be honest gentleman, desired him to turn back, and go some other way, or else he would certainly meet with highwaymen, and be robb'd for he had narrowly escaped them himself, and so advised him, if he had any charge about him, not to venture that way. 'I have no great charge about me, Sir,' said Robin; 'however, I'll take your advice for fear of the worst': so as they were riding along, said Robin, 'perhaps we may meet with some rogues of the gang, by the way, for this is an ugly robbing road, therefore I'll secure that little I have: which is but ten guineas, by putting it into my mouth.' Now the gentleman, not in the least suspecting him to be of that profession, told him, that in case he should be set upon, he had secured his gold in the feet of his stockings which he said was no small quantity, and that he had receiv'd it that day of his tenants for rent. Discoursing thus together they had not gone above half a mile further, before they came into a very by-place, where Robin bad the gentleman stand and deliver his money. The gentleman was in a great surprize, and told him, he took him for a very honest and worthy person. However there was no remedy for the loss of his money, which was about fourscore and ten marks. So Robin left the gentleman cursing his folly for telling him where he had hid his money.

Some time after this Robin, meeting with a butcher going to market to sell his meat, bought his whole cargo, and his mare with it, which came together to about twenty pounds: with these Robin immediately goes to the market, and sells his bargain presently, making such good pennyworths, that all the people thought he had stole the meat; which now being converted into money, he puts into an inn at Nottingham, and treats all his customers to the value of five pounds, which coming to the sheriff of the county's ears, who was at the same time in the inn, and taking him to be some prodigal spark, of whom he might make a penny, intrudes into his company, and after some short discourse, ask'd him if he had any more meat to sell. 'Not ready dress'd,' said Robin; 'but I have two or three hundred head of cattle at home, and a hundred acres of land to keep them on, which, if you'll buy, I'll sell you them a Pennyworth.' The sheriff snapt at the proffer, and took four hundred pounds in gold along with him. Away they rid together; but he was very much surpriz'd at the malancholy place that Robin had brought him to. He told him, he wish'd they did not meet with a man call'd Robin Hood, and began to wish himself back again, but 'twas then too late; for Robin winding his horn, presently came Little John with fifty of his companions, who were commanded by their Captain Robin to take the sheriff to dinner with them assuring them he had money enough to pay his share. Accordingly, they got a collation ready for the sheriff, and after dinner was over, they led him into the forest, and there took all his gold from him, good part of which he had borrow'd of the inn-keeper, where he met with Robin Hood.

Our adventurer being another time at Wigton in Yorkshire, and hearing how barbarously the hostlers would cheat the horses of their provender, privately went into the stable, and hid himself under the manger: a little time after came the hostler into the stable, under pretence of feeding Robin's horse; no sooner had he put the oats and beans into the manger, and laid down his sieve, but he sweeps them all into a canvas bag fix'd under one corner of the manger, and so away he went. Robin all this while kept himself secretly hid under the manger, and saw how the hostler manag'd his matters; upon which he got up from his private recess, and went into the kitchen again. After dinner he seem'd to be for going, and calling for his reckoning, ask'd the hostler what corn he had given his horse? He said he had given him what corn he had order'd him, and that the gentleman who din'd with him, saw him bring it through the kitchen. To which Robin answered, 'Don't tell me a lye, for I shall ask my horse presently.' This saying put all the strange gentlemen that were with him into admiration; but above all, the inn-keeper ask'd him if his horse could speak. 'Yes,' said Robin. 'That's impossible,' reply'd the landlord. 'Not at all,' said Robin; 'for my horse is taught by art magic; so fetch him hither, and you'll soon see whether the hostler has done him justice or not.' Accordingly, the horse was fetched, and Robin striking him on the belly, he laid his mouth to his master's ear (by custom) just as the pidgeon did to Mahomet. 'Look you there now,' said Robin, 'did not I tell you that the hostler had cheated him of his corn.' 'Why' said the landlord, 'What does he say?' 'Say,' quoth Robin; 'why he says your hostler has flung all the corn into a bag placed at one corner of the manger'; upon which the landlord and his guest went into the stable, and searching narrowly about the manger, found the bag of corn at one corner of it; for which cruel villainy he immediately turn'd away his hostler.

It was customary for our adventurer to go frequently in disguise; so one time he pulled off his fine cloaths, and dress'd himself like an old shoemaker, and put an old leather apron about him, the better to colour his being one of the gentle craft. In this disguise he set out to travel, and coming to a lone inn in the road to Newcastle, it being near night, he put in there; and being pretty liberal in his expences, the landlord lik'd him, and provided him a good lodging; and Robin went to bed betimes. The house, it seems, was full of guests, so that all the lodgings were taken up; and a friar coming in very late, they had no lodging for him: the friar, rather than go farther, chose to accept of a bed-fellow; but there was none that cared to be disturbed at that time of night; but Robin (whom they took for a shoemaker) was well enough pleas'd to have such a bedfellow. Well, matters being thus accommodated, and the friar in bed, he soon fell asleep, and slept very heartily, being tired with the fatigue of his day's journey; but Robin having got a pretty good nap before, had no mind to sleep any more that

57

night, but to lie awake and meditate mischief for he never lov'd any of that function: so he studied how he should contrive to change breeches with the friar, and after having resolved upon what he would do, he gets up at dawn of day, and puts on not only the friar's breeches, but also his sacerdotal or canonical garment. Now Robin finding these sacred habiliments fitted him very well, and being thus rigg'd, down stairs he goes and calls the hostler, bidding him bring his boots, and make ready his horse. The hostler not in the least mistrusting, but that it was really the friar, brought him his boots, and ask'd him what corn his horse must have: 'Half a peck of oats,' says Robin, which was accordingly given him, Robin all this while being extremely uneasy till the horse had eat them; but that he might be the sooner ready to go, he call'd for the reckoning, and was answer'd that he had paid all last night, but for his horse. The horse having eat up his corn, he mounted him with all the expedition imaginable, having paid for his corn, and given the hostler something to drink his health. Away he rid as fast as the friar's horse would carry him, resolving to make himself merry at the first convenient place he came to. The friar mean time not dreaming what had happen'd, kept close within his bed; but about seven in the morning (it being in the month of June) he rose out of his sleep, and going to bid his bedfellow good morrow, soon found not only that the bird was flown, but also that he was flown away with his feathers; for he saw nothing but a parcel of old cloaths, which he supposed belong'd to his bedfellow. Upon this the friar in a great surprize knocks and calls for some body to come up; but the servants, who supposed it to be only the old shoemaker, ask'd him, what a pox ail'd him to make such a noise, and bade him be quiet, or else they'd make him so. This vex'd the friar, and made him knock the harder; upon which the chamberlain went up, and threaten'd to thrash him if he made any more noise. The friar not understanding the meaning of this rude treatment, was amaz'd, and ask'd where his cloaths were? The chamberlain taking him for Sir Hugh, replied, 'Where a plague should they be, but upon the chair where you left them? Who the Devil do you think would meddle with your nasty cloaths? They an't so much worth, that you need be afraid of anybody's stealing them.' 'The man's mad,' replied the friar; 'do you know who you speak to?' 'Yes, I do,' says the chamberlain. 'If you did,' answer'd the friar, 'you'd use better language.' 'Better language,' replied the chamberlain; 'my language is good enough for a pitiful drunken shoemaker.' 'What do you mean by a drunken shoemaker? Why, I am the friar,' said he, 'who came in here late last night.' 'The Devil you are,' replied the chamberlain, 'I am sure the friar went away soon after three o'clock this morning.' With that the friar jumpt out of bed in his shirt, and taking fast hold of the chamberlain, 'Sirrah,' says he, 'produce me my cloaths and money, or I'll break your neck down the stairs.' With this noise and scuffle up comes the landlord of the inn, and some of the servants, who presently discover'd that this was the person they had taken for the shoemaker; and upon a little enquiry into the matter, found that Sir Hugh had made an exchange with the friar; upon which the master of the inn furnish'd him with a suit of his own cloaths, and money to bear his charges through his journey.

Robin Hood another time was riding towards London, and being on Dunsmore Heath, met with William Longchamp, then Bishop of Ely, with a small retinue of about four or five in number. Immediately he rides up on one of the bishop's servants, whom he pretended to know; 'Ah! Tom,' says he, 'I'm glad with all my heart that I am come up with you, for there's whipping doings abroad; there's nothing but robbing go where one will; I have got a great charge of money about me myself; but since I have the good luck to get up with these honest gentlemen, I'm not in fear of losing it; 'egad let the rogues come now if they dare, I'm resolved to have a slap at them myself.' This discourse which Robin had with the man, made his Lordship and his retinue think him to be a very honest man, and they held a great deal of chat with him on the road, till at last an opportunity favouring his intention, says he to the bishop's attendance, 'I'm very dry, and since you are pleased to give me protection from danger as far as I shall go your way, I'll ride before, and see if I can get any good liquor, to treat you for your civility, and shall be glad to find any worth your acceptance.' Accordingly Robin set spurs to his horse, and rid away as fast as if it had been for some wager, when being out of sight, he quickly tied his horse to a tree in a thick wood, which was on one side of the road, through which the bishop was to pass; and Robin making what haste he could back again to the company, says he, 'O gentlemen! I am ruin'd and undone, for in younder's lane, meeting with two rogues, they have robb'd me of all I had; they have taken above forty marks from me, but the villains being but indifferently mounted, I don't doubt but that if you were to persue them, you'd soon take them.' This news put them into a consternation, and the bishop pitying Robin's loss, as he pretended, said to his servants, 'Let the poor fellow shew you which way the rogues took, and go all of you after them as fast as you can, and take them if possible.' They obeyed the bishop's command, taking Robin along with them; and when they came into a narrow lane, he gave them the necessary direction for persuing the highwaymen, and away they rid as fast as the horses could carry them, to catch the rogues. But Robin's business was with the bishop, and back he goes immediately, and says to him, 'Sir, my time is but very short, and very precious too; therefore you must deliver what money you have, or expect the worst of usage.' The bishop was very much surpriz'd at his impudence; but not knowing how to help himself, was forced to give him two hundred and fifty marks, and then Robin making all the expedition he could to the wood, there mounted his horse, and rid off with his prize. Soon after the bishop being met by his servants, they told him they could not hear of the rogues high nor low: 'Ah!' answer'd the bishop, 'the greatest rogue has been with me, for he that pretended to be robb'd of forty marks, hath just now made up the loss by robbing me of six times the money; but for his sake I shall never put confidence in a man who pretends to too much honesty.'

Robin, after coming into an inn near Buckingham, heard a great singing and dancing; he enquired the reason thereof, and found it was a country wake; at which were present most of the young men and maids for several miles round about. Robin, pleased at the adventure, set up his horse at the same inn; and as he was drinking in the kitchen, an old rich farmer came with an hundred marks ty'd up in a bag under his arm, which he had just received. The farmer, it seems must needs step into this inn, to see their mirth and pastime, instead of going directly home with his money, which was not above a quarter of a mile from the town. Robin seeing him admitted in the room where the wake was kept, ask'd the landlord whether he might be permitted to see the country diversion without any offence to the company. The landlord told him he might and welcome; so he enter'd the room likewise; but Robin's eyes were more fix'd upon on the farmer's bag of money than the young folks dancing; and observing in the room where they were, that there was a chimney with a large funnel, he went out and communicated his design to the hostler, who, for a reward, drest up a great mastiff dog in a cow's hide that he had in the stable, placing the horns just on the forehead, when, in the height of their jollity, by the help of a ladder and a rope, he let him hastily down the chimney into the room where they were all assembled: Robin was returned before the acting of this scene; the dog howled hideously as he descended, and rushing among them in that frightful form, turn'd all into a hurry and confusion: the musick was immediately silenced, the tables overthrown, the drink spilt, the people screaming and crowding to get down stairs as fast as they could, every one striving to be foremost, lest the Devil (as they supposed this to be) should take the hindmost: their heels flew up, the womens coats over their heads and tails, whilst their back-strings loosing, gave full flushes, and made them in a very unsavoury condition: all the musical instruments were trod under foot, and broken to pieces, and the supposed Devil making his way over all, got into the stable, whither the hostler hasten'd to uncase him. Some time after, coming a little to their senses, looking about them, and seeing no more of this supposed Devil, they all concluded he was vanished into the air: but during this hurly-burly, the old farmer being in as dreadful a fright as any of them, and his breeches as well befoul'd, dropt his hundred marks, and fled for safety: the mean time Robin securing the money under his cloak, immediately took horse, and made the best of his way; but as soon as all things were in a little order again, there was a sad outcry for the hundred marks, which being not to be found, the company supposed the late Devil had taken them away, and imputed the loss as a judgment inflicted on the farmer, who was a covetous wretch; one whose study was how to cozen his tenants, beggar the widow, or undo the orphan, or any body else, so he could but obtain their money.

Another time Robin having been riding for his pleasure, as he was returning home in the evening, very well mounted, and drest like a gentleman, coming near Turnton-Bridge in Yorkshire, he perceived from a rising ground a gentleman walking in his gardens, which were indeed very fine, and of a large extent: then Robin rode up to the gardiner, who was standing at a back-door, and enquired of him whether a gentleman, whose curiosity had led him to see those famous gardens, might not have the liberty of taking a walk in them? The gardiner, knowing his master was willing that any person appearing in good fashion, might walk therein, gave him admittance: then Robin alighting, he gave the gardiner his horse to hold; and seeing the gentleman in the walks, Robin paid his respects to him in a very submissive manner; at the same time desiring he would pardon his presumption of coming into the gardens when his Worship was there recreating himself. The gentleman told him he was very welcome, and invited him to see his wilderness; where sitting down in an arbour, they began to talk very merrily together; and at the latter end of their discourse, Robin told him, 'That he heard he was a very charitable gentleman, and that he must now make bold with him to borrow that little money he had about him; for he had but little himself, and that he had a long way to travel.' At these words the gentleman began to startle, and was very much surpriz'd at his impudence. But Robin told him 'he was a dead man if he made any resistance'. Then he tied him to a tree, and went away with a large booty; but he bad the gentleman be of good cheer, for he would send one presently to relieve him. And accordingly going to the gardiner, who held his horse all this while, giving him a ninepenny piece; says Robin, 'Honest friend, your master wants to speak with you'; then mounting, he rode off the ground, whilst the gardiner made haste to his master, and was very much surprized to find him bound in that manner; but he immediately loosed him, and the gentleman returned his servant many thanks for sending a rogue to rob him in his own gardens.

Our adventurer was a man of great courage, and a noble daring and resolute temper, and would often seek out for some new adventures by himself. He had not gone far before he met the Lord Longshamp, near Nottingham, with three servants. His first words were these: 'Sir, I have a great occasion for a little money at this time; so deliver what you have, or expect a knock on the pate.' Says his Lordship, 'how dare you, Sirrah, have the impudence to stop a nobleman? Let me get off my horse, and I'll fight you at quarter-staff.' 'Why truly,' replied Robin, 'my Lord, that's a fair challenge, and I should be very willing to accept of it, but I doubt when you are off your horse, instead of fighting, you'll run away, as you did when you betray'd the poor Duke of — I won't put it into your power to run away; so pray, Sir, don't stand prating, but deliver what you have presently.' Says his Lordship, 'What the Devil are my servants doing there? What! three great cowardly dogs of you, and all stand still, to let me be robb'd by one poor Thief?' 'Thief! Scoundrel,' replied Robin, 'I am a gentleman bred and born, and you see I live by my sword and staff; therefore don't rely on your servants assistance; for the first of them that offers to lay his hand on his sword, is a dead man, as you are, if you make any more words,' offering as if he would strike him. His Lordship cried out for quarter, and gave him a brace of hundred pounds, which he had in his portmanteau, and then Robin returned to Sherwood, to make merry with his companions.

Our adventurer being endued with a great deal of love and charity for the poor, insomuch that he would relieve any poor family in distress, was, on the contrary, a mortal enemy to misers and engrossers of corn; for he would often take from these to relieve the necessitous. One time being at Wantage, a great market for corn, he happened to fall into a person's company at an inn there, whom he knew to be a great engrosser of corn, and who had bought as much corn in the market as cost him fourscore marks, which Robin bought of him again, and paid him an hundred marks ready money for it, liking it, as he pretended far beyond any he had seen that day. The corn he immediately sent to be distributed amongst the poor of the country. Robin understanding which way his corn-merchant went, was soon at his heels, and demanded his money again, and what he had besides. The countryman was in a great surprize, shaking and trembling very much, asking him, 'whether he thought it justice to take from him his goods and money too?' Says Robin, 'why han't I, you villain, paid you for your corn honestly, and can you assume the impudence to talk of justice, when there's none in the world acts more injustice than an engrosser of corn? Sirrah, there's no vermin in the land like you, who slanders both heaven and earth with pretended dearths, when there is no scarcity at all: So talk no more of your justice and honesty, but immediately deliver your money, or I shall crack your crown for you.' Upon this he deliver'd him a bag, in which Robin found his own money, and as much more to it; so away he went with a great deal of satisfaction.

As Robin was going one morning to Nottingham, he met with a tinker, and civilly ask'd him where he lived, for he heard there was nothing but bad news abroad: 'What bad news is it?' answer'd the tinker, 'for I live at Banbury, and am a tinker by trade, and as I came along I heard no bad news. 'Yes,' says Robin, 'the news that I heard was bad, but true; for it was only two tinkers in the stocks for drinking.' 'Your news,' says the tinker, 'is not worth a fart, and had they look'd in your face, they would have put you in to bear them company; for I dare say you love beer as well as any tinker in town.' 'So I do,' answered Robin, 'but pray tell me what news abroad; for you that came from town must needs hear some news.' 'Why,' replied the tinker, 'I hear no other news than of taking Robin Hood; and I have a warrant in my pocket for apprehending him, wheresoever I

63

find him; and if you can tell me where he is, I'll make a man of you for your pains': 'Let me see the warrant,' says Robin, 'whether it be made strong and good, and I'll go with you and take him this night, for I know a house that he uses at Nottingham.' 'No,' answered the tinker, 'I'll let no man see my warrant, and if you won't help me take him, I'll go and apprehend him myself.' So Robin perceiving how the game went, ask'd him to go with him to Nottingham, for, he said he was sure to meet with Robin Hood there; they were not long before they arrived at Nottingham, where they went into an inn, and drank so plentifully, that the tinker got drunk, and fell asleep; then Robin took away the tinkers money, and the King's Warrant, and left him ten shillings to pay; but when he awak'd it would have made any one laugh to have beheld the poor tinker's fright at the loss of his money and warrant; he called up his landlord, and told him what a mischance had befallen him; that the stranger who was drinking with him was run away, and had robbed him of all his money, and had took a warrant out of his pocket, which he had from the King to apprehend Robin Hood: the landlord told him, that was Robin Hood who had been drinking with him all that day; then the tinker rav'd and fretted like a madman, and swore what he would have done, had he but known it had been him. In fine, the tinker was obliged to leave his budget to answer the reckoning.

The above recited stories are some of the great number told of this adventurer, and were we to give an account of all, it would swell his history to too immoderate a length; let it suffice to say, that Robin Hood was a very bold man, of a charitable disposition, generous and open to the last degree. The long distance of time he lived in from these our days, make the generality of people look upon his actions as fabulous. It may be so, for we are at no certainty about them, because, in several books I have been obliged to peruse, I find the very same stories attributed to him which are reported to be done by Falstaff and Glanville. These I have purposely omitted, not to give my readers the same things in two different places. But I might have inserted the story about our adventurer and the Pinner of Wakefield, this having as much veracity in it, as any thing that Captain Alexander Smith (who is too concise) says about him; but I have thought fit to omit it, as I am come to a length large enough already, and shall only add, that Robin Hood having pursued his licentious courses of living above twenty years, when falling sick, was struck with remorse of conscience for his past mispent life, and unlawful practices, which made him privately withdraw to a monastery in Yorkshire, where being let blood by a monk, he bled to death; aged forty three years, and was interred in Kingsley, with this epitaph on his grave-stone.

> Here underneath this Marble Stone,
> Through Death's Assault, now lieth one,
> Known by the Name of Robin Hood,
> Who was a Thief and Archer good;
> Full twenty Years or somewhat more,
> He robbed the Rich to feed the Poor,
> Therefore his Grave bedew with Tears,
> And offer for his Soul your Pray'rs.

THE LIFE OF
THOMAS DUN

This person was of very mean extraction, and born in a little village between Kempston and Elstow in Bedfordshire. 'Tis said he had contracted thieving so much from his childhood, that every thing he touch'd stuck to his fingers like birdlime, and that the better to carry on his villanies, he chang'd himself into as many shapes as Proteus, being a man who understood the world so well, I mean the tricks and fallacies of it, that there was nothing which he could not humour, nor any part of villainy that came amiss to him. To day he was a merchant, to morrow a soldier, the next day a gentleman, and the day following a beggar: in short, he was every day what he pleased himself.

When he had committed any remarkable roguery, his usual custom was to cover his body all over with nauseous and stinking sear-cloths and ointments, and his face with plaisters, so that his own mother could not know him. He would be a blind harper to commit one villany, and a cripple with crutches to bring about another; nay, he would hang artificial arms to his body: besides, his natural barbarity and cruel temper was such, that two or three men together durst scarcely meet him; for one day being upon the road, he saw a waggoner driving his waggon full of corn to Bedford, which was drawn by five good horses, the sight of which inflamed him to put the driver to death; accordingly, without making any reflection on the event, he falls on the waggoner, and with two stabs killing him on the spot, boldly took so much time as to bury him, not out of any compassion for the deceased, for he never had any, but the better to conceal his design: and then mounting the waggon, drives it to Bedford, where he sells it, horses and all, and marched off with the money.

Dun at first thought it the best way to commit his robberies by himself, but finding, upon trial, the method not so safe, as where they were a company together, he betook himself to the woods, where he was soon joined by gangs of thieves as wicked as himself. These woods served them as a retreat on all occasions, and the caverns and hollow rocks for hiding places, from whence night and day they committed a thousand villanies. The report of their barbarity diffusing it self round about, caus'd all the country to keep off from them, and more especially to avoid the road leading from St Alban's to Tocester, betwixt which they every day acted insupportable mischiefs, murdering and robbing all travellers they met, insomuch that King Henry the First built the town of Dunstable in Bedfordshire, to bridle the outrageousness of this Dun, who gave name to the aforesaid place.

However, this precaution of the King was no impediment to Dun's designs, who still pursued his old courses, and tho' the age he lived in was not so ripe for all manner of villainy as it is now, yet the gang under his command consisted of several sorts of artists, who were made to serve different purposes and uses, just as he observed which way every man's particular genius directed him. Some of these being very expert in making false keys and betties, he never suffered them to remain idle or without business. Others were ingenious at wrenching off locks, and making deaf files, which wasted the iron without noise, making the strongest bolts give way for their passage. His fraternity being thus composed of lifters, pickpockets and filers, he refines, corrects, augments and establishes their laws, and one day having read to them some few comments on the art and mystery of robbing on the highway, he for a while leaves them, but in a short time returns, and begins a pleasant adventure; for being informed that a company of lawyers were to dine at a certain inn at Bedford, he hastens directly to the place appointed, where entering puffing and blowing, as a man in extraordinary haste, he gives orders, as if deputed by the company, to make ready a dinner for ten or twelve persons; which he had no sooner done, but the company comes to the house, and Dun bustles about as if a principal servant of the inn, and was indeed believed so to be by the lawyers, so notably did he bestir himself in the business; when being about the middle of their dinner, he packs up the best of their cloaks, and so marches off. Scarcely had they made an end, but they began to miss them, demanding where they were; but they might look long enough before they found them, for Dun having done his work, was got too far for the lawyers to overtake him, or their cloaks either.

After this adventure, Dun, with some of his associates, marches some miles from whence they were known, and puts in at the first inn he came at, where asking for a chamber, the mistress of the house, supposing them honest men, shews them up stairs, and perceiving her alone, they intended to force her, and in effect were ready to put their intention into practice, when the master of the house just enter'd; upon which they were forced to wait a more favourable opportunity. Accordingly about midnight one of Dun's comrades feigns himself to be extraordinary ill, and raises the master and mistress of the house; but it happening as he stept out of bed, that he espied a neighbour of his in the chamber, upon which the host, being transported with jealousy, runs after the man, while in the mean time these rascals laid hands on his wife, who had gotten up stairs in the dark into Dun's chamber, where they began to truss her up like a woman of her profession; but presently after the husband coming to his chamber, and missing his wife, goes up to them, and finding her with them, would have put her to death, but by a strange kind of perfidiousness, she caused him to be murder'd by one of these villains, thinking to come off well enough herself; but Dun would not be contented; for having understood of a long time that there was money in the house, he comes up to her, claps a dagger to her breast, (for there was no pistols nor use of gunpowder in those days), and tells her, 'that if she shew'd him not where the money lay, there was an end of her life'; but she making resistance when there was a demand for the money, was immediately dispatch'd, and her house rifled of all the money and plate which Dun and his confederates could find.

Some time after this, Dun, being very well drest, went to an eminent lawyer's house near Bedford, and demanded of the lawyer a hundred pounds, which, as he pretended, he had lent him on bond. The barrister was surpriz'd at his demand, as not knowing him, and looking on the bond, his hand was so exactly counterfeited, that he could not in a manner deny it to be his own hand writing, but that he knew his circumstances were such that he was never in any necessity of borrowing so much money in all his life of any man; therefore as he could not be indebted in any such sum upon the account of borowing, he acquainted Dun that he would not pay a hundred pounds in his wrong: upon this Dun taking leave of him, told him, he must expect speedy trouble; and in the mean the lawyer, expecting the same, sent for another, to whom opening the matter, they concluded it was a forged bond; upon which the lawyer having got a general release forged for the payment of this hundred pounds; and when issue was joined, and the cause came to be tried, the witnesses to Dun's bond swore so heartily to his lending the money to the defendant, that he was in a very fair way of being cast, till the lawyer's council moving the court in behalf of his client, acquainted the judge that they did not deny the borrowing the hundred pounds of the plaintiff, but it had been paid for above three months. 'Three months,' said the judge, 'and why did not the defendant then take up his bond, or see it cancelled?' To this his council replied, 'That when they paid the money, the bond could not be found, whereupon the defendant took a general release for the payment of it'; which being produced in court, and two knights of the post swearing to it, the plaintiff was cast, which putting Dun into a great passion, he cried to his companions, as he was coming from the court, 'Was ever such rogues seen in this world before, to swear they paid that which was never borrowed?'

This very story is related by Captain Smith, in the 'Life' of one Tom Sharp, who lived some hundred of years after our adventurer. We shall make no remarks on it, but proceed to somewhat else.

Dun having intelligence that the sheriff of Bedford with his men were in search of him, and that they had determined to beset the wood, where he then was, obliged him to be upon his defence, which however did not make him lose his usual courage; wherefore, to prevent any danger that might happen, he musters up his company of grand rogues, and retires into the thickest part of the wood, to a place, in his opinion, the most advantageous; where having left necessary orders, he sent out scouts; but judging it not safe to put his confidence in spies in case of such importance, he puts on a canvas doublet, and breeches, old boots without spurs, and a steeple-crown'd hat on his head, and so draws near them, where taking notice that they were unequal to him both in number and strength, he comes back to his companions, makes them stand to their arms, and so encourages them by words and example, that in setting upon them, as they did immediately, they were presently routed; and pursuing them closely, they took eleven prisoners, whom they stript of their liveries, and hanged them on several trees in the wood; after which they made their coats serve them to commit several robberies in: for Dun going one night to a castle near this wood, order'd, in the King's name, the gates to be open'd, pretending that Dun and his companions had hid themselves there. Accordingly the gates were open'd, without the least suspicion of what afterwards fell out. Dun made a pretence of searching into every corner for thieves, bustling every where throughout the castle with the greatest eagerness imaginable; but happening to find none, he would needs perswade the waiters that they had concealed themselves in the trunks. Upon this he gave orders for the keys to be immediately brought him, when opening the trunks, and having loaded himself and companions with every thing that was any way valuable, he returns back to the wood. Mean time the lord of the castle was extremely enraged at this proceeding, and could not brook to think that he should be thus robb'd, concluding that the sheriff's men, under colour of searching for thieves, had thus pillag'd him. Upon this he addresses the King and Parliament, giving an account by whom he thought he was thus robb'd, who immediately issued out an order for examining the sheriff's men, one of whom was hang'd to see what influence it would have on the other; but they persisting (as well they might) on their innocency, and discovering how eleven of their companions had been used by Dun and his associates, were set at liberty.

A very rich knight living in the neighbourhood, Dun was determined to ask his benevolence, and accordingly went and knock'd at the house door. The maid coming and opening it, Dun ask'd her if her master was within, who told him he was. Upon this he acquainted her he had earnest business, and must needs speak with him. The maid taking Dun for a gentleman by his mien and dress, admits him within the house, and conducts him up stairs to her master's chamber, into which Dun enters without any concern; and after having complimented the gentleman, sits down in a chair, and begins a hotch-potch discourse, which the knight admiring at, Dun steps up and demands a word or two in his ear. 'Sir,' says he, 'my necessities come pretty thick upon me at present, and I am obliged to keep even with my creditors for fear of cracking my fame, and fortune too. Now having been directed to you, by some of the heads of this parish, as a very considerate and liberal person, I am come to petition you in a modest manner for the lending me a thousand marks (which are thirteen shilling and four pence a piece) which will just answer all the demands upon me at present.' 'A thousand marks!' answer'd the knight, 'why man that's a capital sum; and where's the reason to lend you so much money, who are a perfect stranger to me; for to my eyes and knowledge, I never saw you before all the days of my life.' 'Lord, Sir, you must be mistaken, I am the honest grocer at Bedford, who has shared so often your favours.' 'Really, friend, I do not know you, nor shall I part with my money but on a good bottom': 'Pray what security have you?' 'Why this dagger (says Dun, pulling it out of his breast) is my constant security; and unless you let me have a thousand marks instantly, I shall drive it into your heart.' This terrible menace so frighted the knight, that rather than expose his life to any danger, he thought it safer to deliver his money, and get rid of his audacious visiter.

Another time Dun, having a mind to make a journey some miles off to see an old aunt of his who was still alive, took horse and set forward; but unluckily mistaking his way, and the night coming upon him, he was obliged to put in at the first house he came to. Accordingly seeing a light at a considerable distance from him (for it was quite dark now) he made the best of his way thither over hedge and ditch. When he came to the house, he observed a great bustle in the stables and court before the house; and enquiring of some of the servants, who he saw were busied in rubbing down several horses, as though lately come off a journey, 'if he could lodge there that night, having lost his way, and being benighted, so that he could not pursue his journey any farther till the morning', he was answered, 'that they believed their master would not turn away at that time of night a person of his condition, but they would go and ask'. In consequence hereof, the gentleman of the house was acquainted with our adventurer's being in his court, who immediately came to the door, and after mutual respects paid on both sides, told Dun, 'that he was sorry to think he had not a bed to spare to entertain a gentleman, but that really his house was taken up from top to bottom by some acquaintance and relations who were come to honour him with their presence at his daughter's marriage, which was design'd to be solemniz'd the next day. However,' he said, 'there was one room in his house which his family from time to time told him was haunted; but he looked upon such a thing as ridiculous, and could not for his part be ever brought to come into such a notion: that if he pleased, the room was at his service, and if he required it, persons should be appointed to sit up with him.' 'No,' replied Dun, 'I have so little faith, Sir, as to stories of haunting houses, or walks of spirits, that I chuse to be entertained in such places before any others.' Upon this Dun dismounts, and is conducted by the gentleman of the house into the apartment where his guests were, who receive him with extraordinary civility; and all strive to banish out of his mind the thoughts of fear. But Dun is above vain apprehensions, and looks on tales of this nature as the produce of a romantick brain. He, on his part, strives to divert to company with several humourous relations, which gain wounderful approbation. He sat over-against the gentleman's daughter, who was designed for marriage, and eyed her with eager looks; nor could all the reason he was master of restrain him from wishing that she was his. The clock strikes twelve, and all are immediately desirous of going to rest. They rise up, and with hearty zeal wish our adventurer all the quiet in the world, nor would they leave him till they had seen him in bed. The house is now in a profound rest, and Dun by himself to reflect on his adventure. Two large tapers and a good fire burn by him; he waits, every moment for something to appear, which he could not well tell how to devise. An hour or more is past, but his curiosity is disappointed; wherefore he is resolved to compose himself to rest, and leave the consequence to fate; but soon he is charm'd by the appearance of the finest woman his eyes ever saw. The gentleman's daughter comes into the room, (for he had not lock'd the door,) and stalks slowly to the bed-side. Dun was in amaze, and could not tell what to think: sometimes he thought 'twas a ghost he saw; sometimes he consider'd the young gentlewoman might be addicted to dreaming, and walk in her sleep, (as thousands have been known to do) and a thousand to one but that might be the real cause of the house being thought to be haunted: but he was resolved to find the truth of the matter, and accordingly reaching his hand softly to her, he gently touch'd her shift, and then found how matters went. She seem'd earnestly to look upon him; but after some time turn'd about, went to the farther side of the bed, and got in. Here's an adventure worth notice: if ever man hugg'd himself on his good fortune, certainly Dun did now. He was in a thousand doubts what to do, but his surprize was at length prodigiously heighten'd, by seeing the young lady go to the farther side of the bed, gently turn up the cloaths, and lay herself down by him. She had not lain above six or seven minutes, before she pulled off her finger a diamond ring, which Dun no sooner cast his eyes on, but transporting wishes prevailed within his breast to seize it. However, being determined within himself to see the issue of the adventure, he lay quietly, without offering either to take the ring or incommode the lady. But this surprize now vanishes; the lady rises up, leaves the ring on the pillow, and goes out of the room with the same silent steps as she came in. Now our adventurer is convinced of the reality of the gentleman's house being haunted; he forms pleasing ideas in his mind about it, and cannot compose himself to rest for a long time, without having a thousand thoughts about his good fortune. However, at last he falls asleep, and dreams that the same gentlewoman comes to him again; and, enquiring for her ring, seems solicitous about it. She acquaints him that she is going to be married to a person that she can never love, and if he does not assist her in the critical conjuncture she was in, she was lost to the sense of all pleasure and satisfaction for ever; and then with a sigh departs. The morning now appears, and Dun awakes; his dream sits fresh on his mind, and he is at a loss what to determine, whether to stay and see the conclusion of the intended nuptials, or get himself ready, and ride off with the extraordinary prize he had made. After some deliberation, the latter expedient seems best and fastest. 'What have I to do,' says he, 'with matrimony, or the copulation of fools; I have got sufficient in my hands to defray my expences homewards, and that's the sole affair I came about: my aunt now may go to the Devil if she will, for what I care': and so saying, he rises up, dresses himself, and, without once taking leave of the gentleman his benefactor, or so much as staying to gratify the company with an account of his night's transactions, leaves them to animadvert on his sudden departure, and the lady to look after her ring.

I believe this same story has been fixed on ten other persons of modern date; but as I find a very grave author seriously attribute it to Dun, I shall make use of his authority, and let our adventurer go with it.

By this time the person we are speaking of was become formidable to all; for not only the peers and other great personages of the kingdom stood in awe of him, but also those of the lower rank durst not frequent the roads as usual. What a melancholy circumstance in his conduct was, his generally committing murder; and we find but one instance, among the several particulars of his life, in which he refrained from this barbarity, and that was in the case above recited.

73

We shall draw now to his last period, and only endeavour to shew the extraordinary struggles he made to obtain his usual liberty, and preserve his life, without being called to give an account of his actions, or answer the laws of his country what he was indebted to them for the many villanies and barbarities he had committed. He had continued in his wild and infamous course of life for above twenty years, and about the River Ouse in Yorkshire, was the general scene where he play'd his pernicious and destructive pranks, where men, women and children fell a prey to his attempts, for he went constantly attended with fifty horse, and the men of the country round about were so much terrified at his inhuman cruelties, and the number of his partizans, that very few had the courage, or even durst venture to attack him, in order to apprehend and bring him to justice. We may venture to affirm, that if his life contained many unaccountable and strange exploits, yet that his death was as remarkable: for having transacted things beyond imagination, his fame, or rather infamy, encreased every day, so that the country were determined to put up with his insolencies no longer. It seems threatnings against him came from all parts; but these, instead of working a reformation, or making him reflect on his past conduct, only the more inflamed his audacious and villainous temper. A stout fellow, we are told, about Dunstable, had made five or six of the sheriff's officers to come to his house, with a design to apprehend Dun, who sometimes would venture to walk out by himself. But Dun having got previous information of this design against him, came in the night time with his partizans to the man's house, and filled it with a thousand oaths and curses, which presently got wind throughout the town, and among the sheriff's men, who came and pursued him with all their forces. The fellows, his partizans, finding they were closely pursued, divided themselves into separate companies, and fled away to what places they could come to, but Dun got into a certain village, where he took up his quarters for that time. However, the pursuit still continued very warm, and his adversaries arriving at the house where he had concealed himself, asked where he was hid, and at last found that he was concealed there. Immediately, on this report, the people, in crowds, gathered together about the house, and two especially posted themselves in the threshold of the door to apprehend him; but Dun, with an insurmountable courage, started up, with his dagger in his hand, from the table, and laid one dead that instant, and then dispatched his companion, who ventur'd to oppose him. But what was the most surprizing, he had the boldness to bridle his horse in the very midst of this confused uproar, mount, and force his way out of the inn. The people no sooner saw this, but they fell upon him to the number of one hundred and fifty, armed with clubs, forks, rakes, and what else they could next come at. With these weapons they forced him from his horse, but this was so far from dismaying our adventurer, that he mounted again in spite of all opposition, and made his way clear thro' the crowd that opposed him, with his sword. The countrymen, upon this found there was more difficulty than they at first apprehended in taking him; but fresh supplies coming in to their assistance, they gave him chase still. Our adventurer, now finding the last period of his life drawing on, made all the haste he was able, and got among the standing corn, and then taking to his heels (for by this time he was forced to quit his horse) outstript his pursuers a matter of two miles, a circumstance that seems almost incredible. Dun having procured this advantage, as he thought, would have lain him down to rest, and composed himself a while, but was presently, to his exceeding surprize, hemmed in with no less a number than 300 men. Thus was he brought into as great a dilemma as before, but resuming his wonted courage, he push'd valiantly through them, and got to some vallies, where, considering there was but one expedient left to save himself, he presently undrest himself, and then taking his sword between his teeth, plunged into the river below, and fell to swimming. Instantly were all the banks covered with multitudes of people, some of whom were drawn together merely out of curiosity to be eye-witnesses of the event; while others got ready boats with a design to give him chase, and try if they could take him. 'Twas an astonishing sight to behold him with the sword all the time between his teeth, and swimming so many cross and various ways, as still to elude his pursuers. At length he got upon a little island which was in the river, where he sat down to get breath a while; but his adversaries having determined not to let him have any rest, follow'd him in their boats, but were forced to return back wounded in the attempt. After this he jumps in again, falls to swimming, and tries to gain the shore at another place; but ill fortune attends him; and the people crouding thither, make at him with all their oars, when they found it no way possible to take him without blows: several times they struck him on the head, and the blows stunning him, it was no hard matter then to apprehend him, which they did, and conveyed him to a surgeon, in order to have his wounds cured, and care taken of him.

75

When his wounds were drest, he was conducted before a magistrate, who, with very little examination, sent him to Bedford gaol, under a strong guard, to hinder his being rescued by his companions. Within a fortnight after this, being tolerably well cured, he was brought into the market-place at Bedford, without being put to the trouble of undergoing a formal trial, where a stage was erected for his execution, and two executioners appointed to finish his last scene of life. Dun, on beholding these dreadful men, was so far from giving into the least concern or dismay, that he warned them, with an unconcerned air, not to approach him for fear of the consequences, telling them he would never suffer himself to undergo the punishment determined him from their hands. Accordingly, to convince the spectators round him, that his usual intrepidity and greatness of mind had not left him, he grasped both the executioners, and strugled so long with them, that he was seen nine times successively upon the scaffold, and the men upon him. However, he had still strength to rise up from them, and taking his solemn walks from one end of the stage to the other, all which time he cursed the day of his birth, and vented a thousand imprecations on those who had been the cause of his being apprehended, but chiefly on him who had been the first to beset him. But his cruel destiny is determined not to leave him; he finds his strength diminish, and that he cannot, in spite of himself, defend himself any longer. He yields, and the executioners chopping off his hands at the wrists, then cut off his arms at the elbows, and all above next, within an inch or two of his shoulders; next his feet were cut off beneath the ankles, his legs chopt off at the knees, and his thighs cut off about five inches from his trunk, which, after severing his head from it, was burnt to ashes. So after a long struggle with death, as dying by piece-meal, he put a period to his wicked and abominable life; and the several members cut off from his body, being twelve in all, besides his head, were fix'd up in those of the principal places in Bedfordshire, to be a terror to such villains as survived him.

Here ends the life of Thomas Dun, one of the most profligate wretches that ever lived, and had not so many murders stained his actions, our censures of him might somewhat be abated, but where blood was so plentifully spilled, and his robberies attended with such miserable catastrophes of the persons he committed his depredations on, we have no room left for pity, notwithstanding the infamous and extraodinary cruel death he was put to. But waving more about this point, we shall proceed to another equally as flagitious.

THE LIFE OF
SAWNEY
CUNNINGHAM

This person had no reason to say he was come of mean parents, or that good education or tuition was denied him, whereby he might have avoided the several pernicious actions and villanies he committed, as will presently be shewn in the sequel. His family lived in tolerable good repute at Glasgow in Scotland, where he was born; but, in spite of all the learning his parents had given him, or good examples they had set before him, to regulate his passions and direct his conduct right, he abandoned himself, from his earliest acquaintance with the world, to little shuffling and pilfering tricks; which growing habitual to him, as he advanced in age, he increased in his wicked practices, till at last he became a monster of prophaneness and wicked living. However, these (which one would take to be) great disadvantages, hindred him not from making a very honourable match in wedlock; as his parents could not be blamed with any misconduct, but still kept up an honest and genteel character in the neighbourhood where they lived; and as it would have been infamous to have reproach'd them for those miscarriages in the son which they had strove all they could to root out of his mind, and could not help, so an old gentleman, who had preserved for a long time an inviolable friendship for the family, entered into an alliance with Mr Cunningham the Elder, which at last terminated in giving his daughter to Sawney, and an estate in portion with her of above one hundred and forty pounds per annum, thinking that marriage might be a means to reclaim our adventurer from his ill course of life, and at last settle his mind, to the mutual satisfaction of both families, for which he thought his daughter's portion would be a good purchase, and well laid out. But how are mankind deceived, and, in short, all our foresight and consultation. Sawney no sooner found himself in possession of an estate able to support his extravagancies, but he immediately gave a more violent loose to his passions, than he had hitherto done. He made taverns and alehouses the frequent places of his resort; and, not content idly to waste the day in debauches and drunkenness, the night too must come in to make up the reckoning. These destructive steps could not be attended but with hurtful consequences, and he was too soon as eye-witness of some of them: for not having always wherewithal to indulge his usual expences and method of living, he was forced to have recourse to indirect measures, which ended in pawning every thing he had, not only of his wife's but of his own. Melancholy things were unavoidably to follow, if some redress or care was not taken to put a restraint on this destructive course. Sawney laughed at his follies, and could not bring himself to believe he should ever want, while he had either hands or heart to support him. He was determined to enter upon business as soon as possible, I mean such business as generally brings so many unhappy men to the gallows. His wife, who was vastly beautiful and handsome, saw this, but, with a prudence that became her sex, stifled her uneasiness so long, till no longer able to bear the torment upon her mind, she first began with kind entreaties, since all they had in the world was gone, to fall into some honest way of livelihood, to support themselves, for 'twas much and more commendable to do so, than for him to give his countrymen every day so many instances of his riotous and profuse living. Had Sawney been so good to himself as to have given ear to this remonstrance, without doubt things had succeeded well, and we should never have read the miserable end he suffered. But all admonition was lost on a man abandoned to wickedness, and determined to support his usual extravagancies at any rate. The poor young gentlewoman, instead of being answer'd civilly for her love and affection to him, met with nothing but harsh and terrifying words, attended with a thousand oaths and imprecations. The parents on both sides observing this, were in extreme grief and concern; and determined, after a serious consultation, to dissolve the couple, but the young and handsome wife would never consent to part from her husband, tho' so base to her.

Before we enter upon the first remarkable transaction of Sawney's life, we think ourselves under an obligation to lay before our readers some account of this young bride's rare qualifications. In the first place, as I have taken notice above, she was extreamly beautiful, not only in a perfect symmetry of features, but likewise to these were joined an exquisite person. She was tall, finely shap'd, full-breasted, and had all the other exterior ornaments of her sex. For her temper and the qualifications of her interior part or soul, she was sincere in her love to the last, ever patient under the greatest difficulties, and ready at all times to extricate her husband out of the misfortunes he involved himself in, by lawful and justifiable methods; she had a nice conduct, and an extraordinary restraint upon every passion that might betray her into unforeseen miscarriages. In Glasgow, where an university was, and consequently young gentlemen in fortune and address, it was impossible for Mrs Cunningham to hide the charms of her face and person, so as not to be taken notice of. Several immediately offer'd their respects, and money was not wanting to promote their suits; but all were below the prudent sentiments of her mind: she could not endure to think of dishonouring the bed of her husband, by a base compliance with the richest man in the kingdom, and always she put off her suitor with a frown, and a seemingly disdainful air. But this only served to animate her lovers the more, who now seemed to attack her with a resolution not to quit the siege till she had either capitulated or surrender'd herself. Amongst the rest was a certain lawyer, who was so frequent in his importunities, that she was quite tir'd out. However, she was so discreet all the while, as to conceal from her husband Sawney the importunities of her several lovers; but their sollicitations increasing, and being determin'd to be deliver'd of them as soon as possible, she, one night, as she lay in bed with her husband, began to discourse him in words to the following effect: 'You are sensible, my dear, of the inviolable love I have, from the first day of my marriage to you, preserved for you, which shall still, let whatever will happen, be as chastely maintained; for the infernal regions shall sooner open and receive me alive, than I will dare to break the laws of your bed, or bring dishonour to my person, by a shameless prostitution of my person in the embraces of any man alive. As a proof of what I tell you, you need only be acquainted, that for these several months I have been strongly importuned by Mr Hamilton the lawyer to consent to his embraces, but still I have warded off from his addresses, yet cannot be free from him; which makes me now discourse thus, in order to hear your opinions in the matter, and see which will be the safest and best expedient to be delivered of his company.' Here she ended, and Sawney being thoroughly convinced of his wife's loyalty and fidelity, first answered her with a 'desire she should forget all his irregularities, confessing their present poverty had been the immediate consequences of his too liberal and profuse living, but that for the future she should see a good alteration in his conduct, and he would make one of the best of husbands'. As for Mr Hamilton, said he, 'it is my advice that you do not give him an absolute refusal, but pretending a kind of love at a distance, make him think that a considerable sum of money will finish his expectations, and gain him what he so much longs for; you have youth and beauty on your side, and you may, consequently, command him as you please; for I am not so much a stranger to Mr Hamilton's temper, and inclination, but that I know love will influence him to perform generous things: my dear, I have no occasion to acquaint you with our poverty at this time, which, to my extreme grief, has been the consequence of my irregular and profane living; but our wants and necessities may be amply made up by dexterously managing this adventure, the prosecution of which I leave to your own prudence and conduct; and for my part I shall take effectual care to extricate you and myself out of any consequences that may happen upon it.'

Mrs Cunningham, after this conference with her husband, had a thousand thoughts in her head, how to manage this scheme, so as to make the most advantage of it: she saw that the want of money in her family must oblige her to it, tho' never so much against the bent of her inclination to the contrary, and therefore determining to put it in execution as soon as possible, she composed herself to rest for that night. The next day Sawney got purposely out of the way, but not without a longing expectation of receiving extraordinary matters from his wife's conduct. Hamilton appeared as usual; and, protesting his love for her was the sincerest in the world, said, 'that it was impossible for him to enjoy a moment's rest without tasting those joys she could so easily afford him.' Mrs Cunningham, at first, reproved him for such a bare declaration of his desires, and said, 'that so long as her husband liv'd, she could not, without the most manifest breach of conjugal fidelity, and an eternal infamy to herself, give way to comply with his demands. Your person, Mr Hamilton,' said she, 'is none of the worst, neither is your sense to be despis'd; but alas! Heaven has decreed it, that I am already another man's wife, and therefore deprived from gratifying you as I would were the case otherwise. And I have apprehensions of my husband, who is a choleric person, and presently urged into a passion upon the most trifling affair, which either he doth not like, or squares not with his happiness or interest.' 'Interest,' reply'd Hamilton, 'Why, if that be the case, neither your husband nor you shall have any reason to complain: for, let me tell you for once and all, I do not require a gratification from any one, without making a suitable return; your circumstances, Madam, are not unknown to me, and I am sorry to think that after having brought Mr Cunningham so plentiful a fortune, I should have a just occasion to say that you are poor; but mistake me not, I scorn to make a handle of your circumstances, neither do I believe Mrs Cunningham would ever consent to my desires on such servile terms.' Upon this madam answer'd him with a great deal of prudence and art; she told him, 'that he pleaded handsomely for himself, and if she was not a married woman, there should be nothing to obstruct their desires.' Mr Hamilton finding this, gave her long harangue, in which he endeavour'd to shew how weak her objection was, with respect to her husband, concluding, that what they did might be so artfully contrived, that neither Mr Cunningham nor the world should know any thing of it. In fine, the lawyer pleaded as if it were for life, for her consent, which madam observing, and not caring to prolong the time too far, but dispatch a great deal of business in a little time, she artfully told him, 'That since her stars had so directed the actions of her life, that she had no power of herself to contradict them, she resign'd herself to him, and said, that it was to no purpose to stifle her inclinations for him any longer; for, to be plain with him, she had lov'd him from their first acquaintance together, before all the men she had ever seen, and that she hop'd there was no transgression in an affair which her destiny over-ruled, and if the world proved censorious, she did not care, and left her cause to be determined by the stars, who, together with Mr Hamilton's fine person, had influenced her to it.' To be short, an assignation was made, and a porch of one of the churches in Glasgow designed to be the place where these two lovers were to meet. Nothing in the world gave the lawyer so much satisfaction as the

81

thoughts of having obtained the consent of his fair mistress, who had declared her love to him, and resigned herself up to his arms. Hamilton promised to make her a present of a purse of a hundred pounds sterling before any thing was done, and she on her side assured him she would please him to the utmost, and acquainted him, that he might expect all the kindness she was able to afford him. Here they parted, and the lawyer thought the time contained a thousand days till the hour appointed was come, and he in the arms of his mistress. It arrives, and both appear in the porch; they caress and toy, but no farther than the laws of modesty permitted. Hamilton wants to know where Mr Cunningham her husband is, and is acquainted that he was gone a short journey into the country, which however would take him up eight days; whereas madam had posted him, or he had done it himself, in a private place in his chamber at home. Hamilton seems extraordinarily pleased at his success, and the repose he should find in humouring his appetite, now his antagonist was out of the way as he thought. In a little time both these lovers came to Sawney's house, and having entered his bed-chamber, where he was concealed, and a good fire burning, Mr Hamilton pulls out two purses of gold and gives them to her, and then going to undress himself, Sawney springs out from his secret place, and with one stroke lays Mr Hamilton flat on the floor with a club he had in his hand; for, not contented with his wife's having received the two purses of gold, he must have the lawyer's cloaths too; and therefore to make sure of them, he redoubles his blows, till the poor gentleman gave up the ghost at Mrs Cunningham's feet. This was a sacrifice to love with a witness: the lawyer had contributed handsomely before for a night's lodging, and must he give his life into the bargain? I know not how mankind may think on't, but the affair was carried to a desperate length. Now Mrs Cunningham not dreaming her husband would have carried matters to such an issue, seemed frighted to the last extreme at what had been done; but Sawney endeavour'd to give her ease, by telling her, that he would work himself out of the scrape immediately, and so saying, hoisted the body on his shoulders, and went out at a back-door which led directly to Hamilton's house, which easily opening, as a profound sleep in the family, and the darkness of the night favoured him, he carried the lawyer to the vault, and placed him upright on the seat, to the end that the first who found him there might conclude he had died in that place and posture.

Now it seems Mr Hamilton the day before had acquainted a particular friend who lived in his house, with his success, and how he was to have a meeting with Mrs Cunningham that night. This friend had had the gripes upon him for three or four days, which made him have a very violent looseness, and being obliged to untruss a point about mid-night, rises in his night-gown, and steps down to the vault, where opening the door, he spies Mr Hamilton sitting, as he supposed, and taking it that he was come there on the very same errand as himself, stays without a while to let him have quiet play; but finding he made no motion to stir, after having waited a considerable time, to his own uneasiness, he opens the door again, and taking him by the sleeve of his coat, was surprized to find him fall down. He stoops to take him up, but finds him dead; at which being in a thousand perplexities, and fearing to be thought the murderer, he brings to mind his acquainting him with the assignation between him and Mrs Cunningham; upon which he concludes his friend had found no fair play there, knowing the husband to be none of the easiest of men. What should this lodger do in this case? Why he takes up the body, throws it upon his shoulders, and carries it to Sawney's house door, where he sets it down. Madam, a little after midnight, having occasion to discharge, gets out of bed, and opening the door, lets the body of her late lover tumble into the house, which putting her into a fright, she runs up stairs into the chamber, and tells Sawney how that the lawyer was come back: 'Ay, ay,' says he, (just waking out of his sleep) 'I'll warrant he shall come back no more, I'll secure him presently'; and so saying, gets immediately out of bed, puts on his cloaths, and hoists the dead lawyer once more on his shoulders, with a design to carry him to the river and throw him in, but seeing some persons at some distance coming towards him, he steps up to the side of the street, till they were got by, fearing his design might be discovered, and consequences were dangerous. But what should these persons be but half a dozen thieves, who were returning from a plunder they had made, of two large flitches of bacon, out of a cheesemonger's shop: and as they came along were talking of a vintner hard by, who sold a bottle of extraordinary wine? Sawney was somewhat reliev'd from his fears (for fears he could not miss from having) at hearing this conversation. He had not been in his post long, before he had the satisfaction of seeing this company put their bacon, which was in a sack, into an empty cellar, and knock the master of the tavern up to let them in. The coast

83

being now clear, Sawney conveys the dead lawyer into the cellar, and taking out the purloined goods, put his uneasy cargo in the room, and then marcht home. Mean while the thieves were carousing, little dreaming what a change they should presently find in their sack. Little or no money was found amongst them, and the flitches were to answer the full reckoning, so that they continued drinking till they thought the bacon was become an equivalent for the wine they had drank. One of them, who pretended to be spokesman, addressing the landlord, told him, 'That he must excuse him and his comrades for bringing no money in their pockets to defray what they had expended, especially at such an unseasonable time of night, when he had been called out of his bed to let them in; but landlord, in saying this, we have no design of doing you any wrong, or drinking your wine for nothing. For if we cannot answer the shot with the ready cole, we will make it up by an exchange of goods. Now we have got two flitches of bacon in a cellar hard by, which will more than answer our expences, and if you care to have them, they are at your service, otherwise we must be obliged to leave word with you where we live, or you lay under a necessity of trusting us till the morning, when, on sending any body along with us, you may depend on receiving the money.' 'Gentlemen,' says the vintner, 'you are all meer strangers to me, for to my eyes and knowledge, I cannot say I ever saw one of you before; but we will avoid making any uneasiness about my reckoning: I do not care to purchase a commodity I never saw, or, as the saying is, to buy a pig in a poke: if the flitches of bacon, you say you have, are good, I'll take them off your hands, and quit scores with you, so they but answer my demands.' Immediately one of them, who had drunk plentifuller than the rest, said he would go and fetch them, and accordingly coming into the cellar, strove to hoist the sack up; 'Zounds,' says he, 'why I think the bacon's multiplied, or I am damnably deceived. What a pox of a load is here to gaul a man's shoulder's? Tom might well complain they were heavy, and by Gad, heavy and large ones they are, and the vintner will have a rare bargain of them; much good go along with them,' and so saying, he lugs, the corpse on his shoulders to the tavern. On coming to open the mouth of the sack, Lord, what a surprize were all in to see a man's head peep out. Mr Dash presently knew the lineaments of the deceased's face, and cried out, 'You eternal dogs, did you think to impose a dead corpse on me for two flitches of bacon? Why, you rascals, this is the body of Mr Hamilton the lawyer, and you have murther'd him, have you, you miscreants; but your merits shall soon be soundly rewarded, I'll warrant you.' At this all the six were in the saddest plight that could be imagined, nothing but horror and dismay sat on their looks, and they really appeared as the guilty persons. But the vintner, observing them bustling to get away, made such a thundering noise of murtherers, murtherers, murtherers, that immediately all the family were out of their beds, and the watch at the house door to know the reason of such an alarm. The thieves were instantly convey'd to a place of durance for that night, and in the morning were sent to the main prison, when after a little time, they took their trials, were found guilty (though innocent) of Mr Hamilton's death, and executed accordingly.

Sawney came off very wonderfully from this matter, though neither his wife's admonitions, nor his own frequent asseverations to her to leave off his irregular course of life, were of any force to make him abandon it; the bent of doing ill, and living extravagantly, was too deeply rooted within him, ever to suppose now that any amendment would come; nay, he began to shew himself a monster in iniquity, and committed every wickedness that could exaggerate the character of a most prophane wretch. For 'tis impossible to enumerate, much more to describe, the quantity and qualities of his villanies, they being a series of such horrid and incredible actions, that the very inserting them here would only make the reader think an imposition were put upon him, in transmitting accounts so shocking, and glaring. The money he had obtained of Mr Hamilton was a dear purchase; it was soon play'd away with and consumed, which made him throw himself on other shifts to support his pockets; to which end he visited the highway, and put those to death who offered to oppose him. His character was too well known in the west of Scotland, to want any further information about him, which obliged him to retract towards Edinburgh, where meeting with a gang of his profession, who knew him to be most accomplish'd in their way, he was constituted generalissimo of their body, and each man had his particular lodging in the city. But Sawney, who ever chose to act the principal part in all encounters, industriously took lodgings at a house noted for entertaining strangers, where he was not long in insinuating himself into their acquaintance, by making them believe, that he was a stranger as well as they, and was come to Edinburgh on no other account than purely to see the city, and make his observations upon its publick buildings, and other curiosities; and that his ambition had been always to procure honest and genteel acquaintance. Sawney, indeed had a most artful method to conceal the real sentiments of his mind, and hide his actions, which in a little time so gained upon the belief of these strangers, that they could not help taking him for one of the sincerest men breathing: for it was his custom sometimes to take them along with him two or three miles out of the city to partake of some handsome dinner or supper, when he was sure never to let them be at a farthing expence, but generously discharge the reckoning himself: the design of all this was to make his advantage of them, and force them to pay an extravagant interest for the money he had been out of pocket in treating them: for constantly were persons planted in one place or other of the road by his immediate direction, who fell upon them as they returned to the city, and robbed them of what they had: but the cream of all was, that to avoid suspicion they always made Sawney their first prize, and rifled him, who was sure in the morning to obtain his own loss back again, and a considerable share of the other booty into the bargain.

Some time after this, our adventurer, with two of his companions, meeting on the road with three citizens of Edinburgh, affronted them in a very audacious manner, and threw such language at them as plainly discovered that either death or bloodshed was near at hand. He had the impudence to tell the person who seemed the genteelest and best drest of the three, that the horse he rode on was his, and had been lately stolen from him, and that he must return it him; or else the sword he wore should do him right. Sawney's companions began with the others after the same manner, and would needs force them to believe that the horses they rid upon were theirs; the citizens, astonisht at this gross piece of impudence, endeavour'd to convince them the horses they rode on were their own, and they had paid for them, and wondered how they durst pretend to dispute an affair which was so essentially wrong; but these words were far from having any effect on Cunningham, and the citizens, in the conclusion were forced to dismount and give them their horses and money into the bargain, being somewhat satisfied they had suffered no worse consequences, for Sawney, by this time was drenched in all manner of villany, and bloodshed was now accounted a trifle, so little value did he set on the lives of any persons.

Sawney having run a merry course of roguery and villany in and about Edinburgh for some time, where he made a considerable advantage to himself, so that fortune seem'd to have requited him for all the poverty and want he had before endured, determined now to go home to his wife, and spend the remainder of his days agreeably with her, on the acquisitions and plunder he had made on his countrymen. Accordingly he came to Glasgow, where, among a few acquaintance he conversed with, for he did not care to make himself too publick, he gave signs of amendment, which struck those that knew him with such astonishment, that at first they could hardly be brought to believe it. One night being in bed with his wife, they had a close discourse together on all their foregoing life, and the good woman expressed an extraordinary emotion of joy at the seeming alteration and change in her husband; she could not imagine what reason to impute it to; for she had been so much terrified from time to time with his barbarities, that she had no room to think his conversion was real; neither, on reflecting on the many robberies and murthers he had committed, could she perswade herself, that he could so soon abandon his licentious and wicked courses; for she supposed, if his alter'd conduct (as she thought) was real, it was miraculous, and an original piece of goodness hardly to be met with. The sequel will prove that this woman had better notions of her husband, than the rest of his acquaintance, and those that knew him, and that she built all her fears on a solid and good foundation. The proverb says, 'What is bred in the bone will never be out of the flesh'; and this will be remarkably verified in Cunningham, as we shall endeavour to shew in its proper place. For all the signs he gave of an alter'd conduct, and all the plausible hints to rectify his former mistaken steps, were no other than only to amuse the world into a good opinion of him, that so he might make his advantage, through this pretended conversion, with the greater freedom and impunity. And he was not out in his aim; for it seems, whenever he committed any thing sinister, or to the disadvantage of any of his countrymen, and he was pitch'd on as the transgressor, the town would say, 'It could not be, for Mr Cunningham was too much reclaimed from his former courses ever to give into them again.' I shall insert a very notable adventure Sawney had with a conjurer, or fortune-teller; to which end I shall trace it up from the fountain-head, and give my readers the first cause that induced him to it. When Sawney was an infant, he was put out to nurse to a poor countrywoman in a little village a mile or two out of Glasgow; the woman, as the boy grew up, could not help increasing in her love for him, and he being an exceeding snotty child, would

87

S. CUNNINGHAM'S *Adventure with his* Old Nurse *and* ASTROLOGER.

often say to her neighbours, 'Oh! I shall see this lad a rich man one day.' This saying coming to the ears of his parents, they would frequently make themselves merry with it, and thought no more of it, than as a pure result of the nurse's fondling. Sawney having enrich'd himself with the spoils about Edinburgh, actually thought his old nurse's words were verified, and sent for her to give her a gratification for her prediction. She came, but Sawney had chang'd his cloathes, so that the poor woman did not know him at first. He told her that he was an acquaintance of Mr Cunningham's, who, on her coming, had order'd him to carry her to Mr Peterson the astrologer's, where she would be sure to see and speak to him; for he was gone there to get some information about an affair that nearly concerned him. The nurse and her pretended conductor go to the fortune-teller's, where desiring admittance, Peterson thought they were persons that wanted his assistance, and bad them sit down, when Sawney taking a freedom with the reverend old gentleman, as he was known to use with all mankind, began to give an harangue about astrology, and the laudable practice of it. 'I and this old woman,' said he, 'are two of the most accomplish'd astrologers or fortune-tellers in Scotland; but I would not, Reverend Sir, by so saying, seem to depreciate from your knowledge and understanding in so venerable a science: I came to communicate a small affair to you, to the end, that not relying on my judgment and this woman's, I might partake of yours. You are to know, Sir, that from six years of age I have led a very untoward life, and been guilty of many egregious sins, too numerous to tell you at present, and what your ears would not care to hear; for my employment has been to lay with other mens wives, make a sharer of other people's money, bilk my lodging, and ruin the vintners; for a whore and a bottle I have sold the twelve signs in the zodiack, and all the houses in a horoscope; neither sextile, quartile, or trine ever had power over me to keep my hands out of my neighbours pockets; and if I had not a profound respect for the persons of my venerable order and profession, I should call Mercury the ascendant in the Fourth House at this minute, to lug half a score pieces of yours. By my exceeding deep knowledge in astrology, I can perfectly acquaint all manner of persons, except myself, with every occurrence of their lives, and were it not to frighten yourself, I would conclude from the appearance and conjunction of Saturn and Vulcan, that your worship would be hanged for your profession. But Sir, though destiny hangs this unfortunate death over your head, it is at some distance from it, and may be

89

some years before it strikes you. Is it not surprising that a man shall be able to read the fates of mankind, and not have any pre-knowledge of his own? and is it not extremely afflicting to think, that one who has done so much good in his generation, and assisted so many thousands to the recovery of things, that would have been inevitably lost, without his advice, should come at last to meet with an ignominious halter, as a fit recompence for his services? Good heavens! where is the equity of all this? Certainly, Sir, if we are to measure the justice of things, by the laws of reason, we must naturally conclude that laudable and good actions deserve a laudable and good recompence; but can hanging be said to be this good recompence? No, but the stars will have it so, and how can mankind say to the contrary?' Cunningham paused here a while, and the astrologer and old nurse wonder'd who in the Devil's name they had got in company with. Mr Peterson could not help staring, and well he might, at the physiogminy of our adventurer, and, in spight of himself, began to be in a pannick at his words, which so terribly frighten'd him. The nurse was in expectation of seeing Sawney come in every minute, little dreaming the person she was so near was the man she wanted. Cunningham's harangue was a medley of inconsistencies and downright banter: 'tis true the man had received tolerable education in his youth, and consequently might obtain a jingle in several sciences, as is evinced from the foregoing. 'Well, venerable Sir,' says he, 'do not be terrified at my words; for what cannot be avoided must be submitted to. To put you out of your pain, I'll tell you a story: a gentleman had a son who was his darling, and consequently trained up in all the virtuous ways that either money could purchase, or good examples teach. The youth, it seems, took to a kind and laudable course of life, and gave promising signs of making a fine man; nor indeed were their expectations deceived; for he led a very exemplary life of prudence, excellent conduct, and good manners, which pleased the parents so much, that they thought everything they could do for him too little. But the mother, out of an inexpressible fondness for him, must needs go to an astrologer, and enquire how the remaining part of his life must succeed. Accordingly the horoscope is drawn, but a dismal appearance results from it; it acquaints the mother that her son shall remain virtuous for two and thirty years, and then be hanged. Monstrous and incredible, says she, but I'll take care to secure him in the right way; or all my care will be to no purpose. Well, the family are all soon acquainted with this threatning warning. The person determined to be the sacrifice, is already nine and twenty years old, and surely they suppose they can easily get the other three years, when all shall go well with their kinsman. But what avails all the precaution of mankind; this same son obtains a commission of a ship, goes to sea, and, acting quite contrary to his orders, turns pyrate, and, in an encounter happens to kill a man, for which, on his return to his native country, he is try'd, condemn'd and hang'd. What think you of this, venerable brother? Is not he a sad instance of an over-ruling influence of the stars? But not to prolong too much time on a discourse of this nature, let us come to the purpose. You are now, as I cannot do it myself, to tell me my fortune, and this old woman is to confront you if you tell me a lie: there is no excuse to be made in the matter; for by heavens, on your refusal, I'll ease this room of your damnable trumpery, and send you packing to the Devil after them.' These words were enough to frighten any man out of his senses, nor could Peterson well discover the intention or drift of his talkative and uneasy visitant. 'What would you be at,' says the astrologer? 'Why, do not you see, what a terror you have put that good woman into, who trembles like an aspen leaf? I am not used, friend, to have persons come into my house, and tell me to my face, that I am to be hanged, and then to confirm it, as you pretend, tell me an old woman's story of a cock and a bull, of a young man that went to sea, and was hanged for robbing, for which he certainly deserved the punishment he met with: as for telling your fortune, I'll be so plainly with you, that you'll swing in a halter as sure as your name is Sawney Cunningham'—'Sawney Cunningham', quoth the mawke, who straightway throwing her arms about his neck, began to kiss him very eagerly, and then, looking earnestly in his face, cry'd aloud, 'O Laird! And art thou Sawney Cunningham! Why, I thought thou come to be a great man, thou was such a "Scotty" lad?' 'Do you see now,' says Sawney, 'what a damnable lie you have told me, in impudently acquainting me that I shall be hanged, when my good prophetess here tells me, I am a great man, for great men never can be hanged.' 'I do not care for what she says nor you neither, for hanged you'll be, and that in a month's time, or else there never was a dog hanged in Scotland.' 'Pray, brother, how came you to know this without consulting my horoscope?'—'Know it, why your very condition tells me you have deserved hanging these dozen years, but the laws have been too favourable to you, else Mr Hamilton's death had been revenged before this time of day. Now to convince you of my superior knowledge in astrology, I mean, in telling how far their influence extends over any man's actions, I will point to you the very action and persons that will bring you to the gallows. This very day month you shall go (in spite of all your foresight and endeavours to the contrary) to pay a visit to Mr William Bean, your uncle by the mother's side, who is a man of an unblameable character and conversation. Him shall you kill, and assuredly be hang'd.' Was there ever such a prophetick or divining tongue, especially in these modern days, heard of? For the sequel will presently discover how every circumstance of this prediction fell out accordingly. Sawney, having observed the air of gravity wherewith Mr Peterson delivered his words, could not help falling into a serious reflection about them, and thinking the place he was in not convenient enough to indulge the thoughts he found rising within him, abruptly left the fortune-teller, and giving his old nurse five shillings, returned home.

But what does he determine on now? After having seriously weighed on the several particulars of Peterson's words, he could not for his heart but think, that the old man, in order to be even with him for telling him of being hanged, had only served him in his own coin; so that after a few hours every syllable was vanished out of his mind, and he resolved to keep up to his usual course of life.

King James I sitting on the throne of Scotland at this time, and keeping his court at Edenburgh, the greatest part of the Scotish nobility resided there, when our adventurer used frequently to go to make the best hand he could of what spoil he found there. The Earl of Inchequin, having a considerable post under the King, and several valuable matters being under his care, had a centinel assigned, who constantly kept guard at this lord's lodgings door. Guards were not much in fashion at this time, and about two or three hundred in the same livery were kept only on the establishment. Cunningham having a desire of breaking into this minister's lodgings, and having no way so likely to succeed by, as to put on a soldier's livery, went in that dress to the centinel, and after some little talk together, they dropt accidentally into some military duty and exercise, which Cunningham so well display'd, that the centinel, seeming to like his brother's notions, and smile extraordinarily, it made Cunningham stay a considerable time, till in the end he ask'd the centinel to partake of two mugs of ale, and put six-pence into his hand to fetch them from an alehouse, at some distance from his post, giving some reason for it, that it was the best drink in the city, and none else could please his palate half so well as that. Hereupon the centinel acquainted him, that he could not but know the consequences that attended leaving his post, and that he had rather enjoy his company without the ale, than run any risque by fetching it. 'Oh!' says our adventurer, 'I am not a stranger to the penalties we incur on such an action, but there can no harm come of it, if I stand in your place while you are gone.' And with that the centinel gives Cunningham his musket, and goes to the place directed for the drink; but, on returning, he must needs fetch a pennyworth of tobacco from the same place, during which, some of our adventurer's companions were broke into the lord's apartments, and had rifled the same of three hundred pounds value. Cunningham was, however, so generous as to leave the centinel his musket. The poor soldier returns in expectation of drinking with his friend, and enjoying his company some time longer; but alas! the bird is fled, and he is taken up to answer for his forth coming, and committed to the Talbooth Prison, where he was kept nine months in very heavy irons, and had only bread and water all the while allowed him to subsist on. At length he is tried, condemned and hanged. Thus did several innocent persons suffer death for that which ought to have been the portion of our adventurer. We draw on to his last scene now, which shall be dispatch'd with all the brevity we are masters of. Sawney having thus escaped so many dangers, and run through so many villanies with impunity, must needs go to his Uncle Bean's house, who was a very good Christian, and a reputable man, as we have before observed, to pay him a visit, with no other design than to boast to him of his late successes, and how fortune had repaired the injuries his former misconduct and remissness had done him. He went, and his uncle with his moral frankness, bade him sit down, and call for any thing his house could afford him. 'Nephew,' says he, 'I have desired a long time to see an alteration in your conduct, that I might say I had a nephew worthy of my acquaintance, and one to whom I might leave my estate, as deserving of it; but I am acquainted, from all hands, that you go on worse and worse, and rather than produce an amendment, abandon yourself to the worst of crimes. I am always willing to put the best interpretation I can upon people's conduct; but when so many fresh reports come every day to alarm my ears of your extravagances and profuse living, I cannot help concluding but that the greatest part of them are true. I will not go about to enumerate what I have heard, the discovery of mistakes only serving to increase one's uneasiness and concern. But methinks if a good education, and handsome fortune, and a beautiful and loving wife could have done any service with respect to the reclaiming you, I should have seen it before now. Your wife has been an indulgent and faithful friend to you in all your misfortunes, and the lowest employment in life, could you but have confin'd yourself, would have proved more beneficial, and secured your character, and the esteem of your family and friend, better than the ways you now tread in. I am sensible my advice is insignificant, and men of my declining years are little valued or thought of by the younger sort, who, in this degenerate age think none wiser than themselves, and are above correction or reproof. Come, nephew, Providence may allot you a great many years more to run, but let them not be such as those already past, if heaven should grant you the indulgence. If I could build any hopes on a good foundation, that you would yet repent, methinks I could wish to have vigour and strength to live to see it; for what my satisfaction would be then, none are able to declare, but such only as are in the like case with myself. Our family has maintain'd an unspotted character in this city for some hundreds of years, and should you be the first to cast a stain upon it, what will mankind or the world say. You may depend that the load of infamy will be thrown on your back, for all who know, or have heard the least of us, will clear us of the dishonour, as knowing how well you were educated, how handsomely fitted out for the world, and how well you might have done. If fame says true, you are to be charged with Mr Hamilton's death; but I cannot bring myself to think, you would ever be guilty of so monstrous an impiety. It seems he had been your benefactor, and several considerable sums of money he had given you, in order to retrieve your lost circumstances; but was to give him his death the way to recompence him for his kindness? Fie on't. Not pagans or the worst of infidels would repay their benefactors with such usage; and shall we Christians, who boast so much above them, dare to do that which they abhor from their souls? It cannot be, nephew, but all thoughts of humanity and goodness are banish'd from your mind, otherwise some tincture would still have remained of Christian principles, that would have told you, you were highly indebted to that good and eminent lawyer's bounty. I am more diffusive on this head, because it requires a particular disquisition; neither mistake me in this matter, for I am not determin'd to reap up things to the world, in order to blacken your character more than 'tis already, nor to bring you under condemnation; only repent and lead a soberer life for the time to come, and all the wishes and expectations of your friends and family are then fully answered. First endeavour to reconcile your passions to the standard of reason, and let that divine emanation conduct you in every action of your future life, so will you retrieve the time you have lost, patch up your broken reputation, be a comfort to your family, and a joy to all who know you. Ill actions seem pleasing in their commission, because the persons that pursue them have some aim of advantage in doing them; but let me tell you there is nothing in the world like a virtuous pursuit, though the road is beset with thorns and briars, but there are inexpressible delights and pleasures in that wilderness which not all the vices in the world can balance. This exhortation probably may be the last that may come from my lips; but indeed you have need of advice every moment, and want the leading-strings of a child, yet neither want you sense or understanding: how comes it then you make such bad use of them? Are not all the miserable catastrophes of profuse and wicked livers, sufficient to deter you from your licentious course of life? If gibbets and gallows could have any influence on a mind, unless lost to all sense of goodness, certainly the melancholy ends so many monthly make here, should be a means of opening your eyes and reclaiming you. But, alas! the wound I fear is too deep, and no medicines can now prevail; your enormities are of such an egregious dye, that no water can wash it out. Well, if neither the cruel consequences of an iniquitous and mispent life, nor all the advice which either your friends and relations can give you; if good examples, terrors or death cannot awaken you from your profound lethargy and inactivity of mind, I may well say your case is exceedingly deplorable, and what for my part I would not be involved in for ten thousand worlds. You cannot surely but know what you have to depend on now your friends and relations abandon you, for you are stiled a murderer; and a man that has once dipt his hands in blood, can never expect enjoyment of any felicity either in this or the next world; for there is an internal sensation called conscience, which brings an everlasting sting along with it, when the deeds of the body are heinous and black. Indeed some may pretend to stifle their iniquities for a considerable time, but the pause is but short; conscience breaks thro' all the barriers, and presents before the eyes of the guilty person his wickedness in frightful colours. What would not some give to be relieved of their racking nights and painful moments? when freed from the amusements of the day, they lie down to rest, but cannot. 'Tis then that

Providence thinks fit to give them a foretaste of those severities even in this life, which will be millions of times increased in the next.' Here the good old man issued a flood of tears, which pity and compassion had forced from his eyes, nor could Sawney forbear shedding a tear or two at hearing; but it was all pretence, and an imitation of the crocodile; for he was determin'd to take this reverend old gentleman out of the world to get possession of his estate, which, for want of male issue, was unavoidably to devolve upon him after his death. With this view, after he had made an end of his exhortation, he steps up, and without once spea-king, thrusts a dagger to his heart, and so ended his life. Thus fell a venerable old uncle for pronouncing a little seasonable advice to a monster of a nephew, who finding the servant-maid come into the room at the noise of her master's falling on the floor, cut her throat from ear to ear, and then to avoid a discovery being made, sets fire to the house, after he had rifled it of all the valuable things in it; but the divine vengeance was resolved not to let this barbarous act go unpunish'd: for the neighbourhood observing a more than ordinary smoke issuing out of the house, concluded it was on fire, and accordingly unanimously joined to extinguish it; which they effectually did, and then going into the house, found Mr Bean and his maid inhumanly murther'd. Our adventurer was got out of the way, and no one could be found to fix these cruelties upon; but it was not long before justice overtook Cunningham, who, being impeach'd by a gang of thieves that had been apprehended, and were privy to several of his villainies, he was taken up and committed a close prisoner to the Talbooth, where so many witnesses appeared against him, that he was condemn'd and hang'd for his tricks at Leith, in company with the same robbers that had sworn against him.

This was the catastrophe of this man, who deserved the fate he suffered long before it happened. We have not given our readers a great many adventures of his, because they were commonly attended with bloodshed, an account of which only presents several melancholy ideas to the reader: but we have this to say, that we have far exceeded Capt. Smith's narrative of him. When he went to the place of execution, he betray'd no signs of fear, nor seemed any way daunted at his approaching fate: as he lived, so he died, valiantly and obstinately to the last, unwilling to have it said, that he, whose hand had been the instrument of so many murthers, proved pusillanimous at the last.

THE LIFE OF
WALTER TRACEY

This person was the younger son of a gentleman, worth nine hundred pounds per annum, in the county of Norfolk. He was sent to the university to qualify him for Divinity, and had a hundred and twenty pounds left him by his father when he died: but his studies not having a relish pleasing enough to his mind, and his estate being too little to support his extravagancies, he, to uphold himself in his profuse expences, would now and then appear well accoutred on the highway, and make his collections. But happening once to rob some persons who knew him, he was obliged to leave the college, and directly went down into Cheshire, where he put himself into the service of a wealthy grasier in the country. Tracey, having an excellently well-shaped body, and a face that had power to draw a thousand admirers after it, soon found the country a pleasanter scene of life, than the wrangling and dull college. He had a genteel air and mien, and a hundred liberties were given him by his master, which the other servants in the family were not allowed to take: the old farmer and his wife, with their daughters (for sons they had none) would divert themselves, after the labour of the day, with hearing our rustick gentleman play on the violin, which he did with admirable skill and sweetness. His fine person and face soon gain'd him followers, and Tracey was not insensible to love, for if ever man had opportunity of indulging his passion that way, certainly he had; for whenever he took his musical instrument into the meadows or pastures, he was sure to be surrounded with a crowd of buxom lasses, among whom some had beauty enough to make his wishes rise. There was a sprightly brown girl, who was his constant hearer, that seem'd to touch his heart more than the rest; she would walk by his side from field to field, nay, accompany him into caves and solitudes, where she would listen with admiration of his musick. Tracey employ'd these moments to promote his suit; for the lass was none of the fairest, yet had a charming body, and a delicacy in the plain delivery of her words that was irresistible. Tracey durst not make an open discovery of the real intention of his mind, for fear of spoiling all the adventure; he was convinced she admired his musick, and nothing but the notion of musick, he thought, would gain upon her. So he tells her he has another instrument that would afford the sweetest melody upon earth, and that his violin was no more to stand in competition with it, than a Jew's harp with the organ of their church. The girl is ravish'd till she hears it, and begs him a thousand times to bring it to-morrow to the cave they were in, which Tracey complies with, and so they part for that night. The female lover, you may besure, had little rest till the time appointed came; nothing but harmony, and melody, and enchantment fill'd her thoughts; she longs to see Tracey and his new instrument, which shall not be long before she has her satisfaction accomplish'd. Both meet in the cave, and both have different views; the one is at loss still how to behave in so critical a minute, and the other importunes him to produce the instrument and play upon it. I've brought the instrument, my dear, along with me, which for its silent melody exceeds every thing you ever saw or heard of: but I must acquaint you, before I shew it, that it is no composition either of wood or horn, but that its harmony proceeds from the members of my body. The unpractised girl was so simple as to imagine, that from gestures and movements of the bones of his body, some agreeable harmony would proceed, or that his hand by striking on the other parts of his body will raise a transporting sound. 'Come, my dear girl,' says he, 'the harmony that proceeds from my new instrument, cannot be raised without your assistance, and therefore if you have a desire of receiving pleasure, you must necessarily be at some pains yourself; for 'tis a task beyond my single reach to perform, and I beg you'll give me aid in it'—'If it is so,' reply'd she, let us see what it is, and instruct me in the manner I am to act.' Upon this, Tracey clasped her in his arms, and with great eagerness embraced her, and then offered to accomplish the rest. 'Oh fie,' says she, 'you are going to wrong me, let me alone, I cannot suffer such usage; you press my breast too close; fie upon it, then, what's this you mean?'—'Do not be fearful, my girl, there's no harm, I'll assure you in the case;—for the harmony and melody is so conceiv'd; and the ending will be much more pleasing than the beginning'—She feels the tingling pleasure, and swoons away, but soon recovering her raptur'd senses, and seeing Tracey rising up, she asked him, 'What? have you done already? you have but just this minute begun; fie, you baulk a body of the pleasure I expected'—'Indeed,' says Tracey, 'I imagined the thing would do you no damage, but that you would have such a longing appetite, once you had found the melody out, as to wish for it again'—'Ay, truly,' said she, ' 'tis the best musick in the world, and I'll come hither any night to enjoy it from you, but 'tis so short, and though I could not hear it, yet I felt an unaccountable sweetness that warm'd all my blood; pry'thee, what cannot you begin it again'—'I can do that,' answered he, 'but I had a mind to give you a taste before-hand, to see how you liked it; such extraordinary things as this are rare, very rare, my dear, and too much repetition but cloys us: and, besides, sweet meat is not always so laid on the stomach; you are sensible, my dear, that the musick and harmony of our own two bodies moving together, are inexpressible, and that during the raptures which they afforded, all our senses were lost'—'That's very true,' says she, 'but methinks I've a longing desire to taste once more of this divine pleasure'— and saying, they fell to it again, which Tracey performed with more vigour than at first.

The young woman having had a foretaste of this new instrument of our adventurer's, returned home exceedingly well pleased, and could not help the next night she got among some of her female acquaintance, to take one of them aside, and acquaint her with the satisfaction Mr Blundel the grasier's man had given her, by his pleasing words, but more pleasing harmony, which flowed from a new instrument different to his violin. Upon this, both seem'd earnest together, and the acquaintance ask'd her, if she might not be allowed to enjoy the same liberty as herself, which the other said she might do, and accordingly both determined to meet our adventurer at the cave, who was previously acquainted with their design. Tracey was pleased to think his humour should be so variously gratified, and rather than not keep touch with his inamorates, would have sacrific'd all he had in the world. Every one met at the cave at the appointed time, but, Heavens! What a difference appeared between the two country girls. The new acquaintance had nothing to set her off, which might stand in competition with the brown maid, and Tracey was so far from admiring, that he entertained at first view, an utter aversion not only to her person, but the enjoyment of her body. But how to be rid of this inconvenience was the question; and absolutely to reject one or the other might endanger his happiness with the brown maid. Betwixt these he was in some perplexity, but to extricate himself out of the snare, he acquainted them he was sorry he could not gratify them according to their expectations, but really he was indispos'd, and the parts of his body to compose the harmony wisht for, were so much out of order with the fatigues of the day, that he was obliged to desire them they would forbear making any more importunities about it then, and he would certainly crown their satisfaction the next night; the girls could not forbear murmuring, and seem'd extraordinary uneasy; but at last, striving to combat their disorder at his seeming refusal, returned home, and left Tracey to go another way. As the girls returned, the acquaintance began to importune her, what, in the name of the stars, this harmony was she had brought her to hear, that Tracey was so fond of, not to let her hear it. Upon this the brown girl, out of her native simplicity, acquainted her as well as she could, with the manner of our adventurer's playing; concluding, that in all her life, she had never experienced such a pleasing and enchanting piece of diversion. The acquaintance, from the language and discovery of her companion, drawing a right judgment how matters had gone, told her, that she was sorry to think she had betrayed so much ignorance and folly; for what Tracey had done was no more than any other man could, and it was too much to extol him for it, because she herself, about four years before, had received as much, or more pleasure in the same way, from her father's man Arthur, and therefore she need not think she had obliged her in bringing her to Tracey's cave, since he had no better capacity that way than their man Arthur; for had she known the errand had been only about that, she would have got Arthur to perform his musick with her, in order to see the difference, who, she assured her, would have gratified her without making scruples, or pretending indisposition. 'And the next time you see him, let me advise you to tell him, that he has wronged your virginity, and, unless he will make some reparation for it, convince him by threats and menaces, that your father shall know his villainous designs, and that you can tell how to revenge an injury. For if you do not follow my direction herein, I myself will do his business, and shew him that a neglected woman, when rouz'd up to resentment, can execute uncommon things. What,' added she, 'my person was not so lovely as yours, nor had my face an equality of charms, but I'll make him quit scores with me, or I'll know why. You, my dear, may please yourself with as extraordinary notions as you please, but, for my part, I cannot help entertaining such an aversion to his baseness and ingratitude, that, of all men living, he least sets in my thoughts. He's handsome, you'll probably say, and has a delicate face, what's this to the purpose? There are more such in the world, and, observe, he's a great deal inferior to you. But why should I name inferiority, when I myself have been guilty of the same indulgence, at a far younger age than you.' Such was the discourse as these two went home together, and a thorough resentment seemed to be working up for what Tracey had done, who was out of the way of hearing; or else he had reconciled the uneasy parties by proffering to them the utmost submission. 'Lord,' says the brown girl, 'what a work you make? If Tracey had no desire of making his pleasing harmony with you, and that I obtained the preference, can you blame the man, let every person exercise his faculties as he thinks proper, for I take it, where the humour or inclination is obstructed, there can be no enjoyment of happiness, and it would be a pity to make a man of Tracey's good nature do a thing which is against his appetite.' 'You may defend him as you please, but observe by the way, that e're ten months are past, you may probably have an harmonist of your own to play with, and then say how will it stand with you'—'Why,' answer'd the other, 'exceeding well, for were it to be done over again, I'd rather be thus pleasingly deceived again by Tracey, than all other men in the world. For it can be no scandal to bear a child by an handsome fellow, and all the country lasses about us will agree with me in this, and supposing people should censure, I'll never disturb myself, or break my repose about it, but rather impute it to envy, because the same good fortune has not happened to them. As to your objecting to me an harmonist before ten months are past, I hope I shall see myself another long before that time, which will not only be extreme satisfaction to myself, but to my parents also, and rather than be deprived of Tracey's pleasing company, I'll promote a better understanding between him and me, with my antient father, whom I'll bring over to a consent of giving me in marriage to him; when all the expectations I have a long time entertained in my breast will be amply rewarded, and then the brown lass will be accounted the happiest woman and wife in the whole parish. For Tracey, I am told for certain, is a gentleman, though at present only in the capacity of a menial servant to my father.' The discourse ending here, they both went home, and on the brown girl's returning to her father's, she found Tracey sitting under an arbour with her father and mother, and diverting them with several comick tales and stories. This made her make one of the company, but soon she discovered an extraordinay pleasure in her countenance, which the parents attributed to the influence of Tracey's discourse, in which they were no bad prophets. All that night the girl could take no sleep, but her head ran on the great pleasure Tracey had given her. As soon as it was morning she took him aside, and blamed him heavily for refusing to yield the same harmony to her acquaintance as he had done to her; which he endeavoured to excuse, by telling her how impossible it was to give to another the same satisfaction as he had done her, considering the vast inequality of persons betwixt them; that the charms of her face were as superior to those of her acquaintance, as the radiance of a star excelled the flame of a candle; that he had too long been in love with her person, to let another share his affection; and how could the other expect, who was so much uglier than her, to be gratified in the same manner? 'Let me advise you,' says he, 'for the future, to confine yourself to me; who will constantly use you in the same extraordinary manner as I have already done. And though the secret place of our meeting has been discovered by your means, yet, never fear, I'll find another more suitable for our turn, where we may heighten this harmony a great deal more.' These words revived the brown girl extremely, who could not but admire the winning words of our adventurer, and fix her love upon him.

It was necessary to think now that the acquaintance must be discarded, who saw it, and consequently was violently enraged. At first she began to spread reports no way to our adventurer's advantage, and got it divulged in his master's family that his designs were dishonourable, and only calculated to ruin the reputation and chastity of her daughter. But this was the worst way in the world to proceed with Rusticus, who was too much a lover of our adventurer, to form in his breast a sudden aversion to him; neither had he any reason to raise a mis-understanding between them; for Tracey had managed his cards with great dexterity, and always took care so to contrive his matters, that no bad conse-quences might be gather'd from them. The old man was entirely devoted to him on account of his gay and humourous disposition, which served to ease his mind and body after the fatigues of the day were over; nor was the grasier's wife (who was a considerable number of years younger than her husband, being his second wife) less taken with the handsome mien and winning conversation of our adventurer: we shall have occasion to mention a very comic adventure between Tracey and this woman presently.

Tracey finding the inclination of the grasier his master so much attach'd to his advantage, that all the reports spread to ruin his credit with him, were not able to prevail, and that his mistress join'd in the same friendship for him, was extremely pleased, and thought one opportunity or other would soon be thrown into his hands, to make a further benefit of his journey to Cheshire, than the obtaining the good-will of a score of country girls. But he soon found himself involved in a very troublesome affair, which sensibly touch'd him, and out of which he had a great deal of work to extricate himself.

The second wife of the grasier, on weighing in her mind the difference there was between the old fumbling husband and our adventurer, who was young and sprightly, could not, after she had receiv'd a foretaste of pleasure from him, be reconciled to leave him, but fondly betrayed an excessive desire for him. Her conjugal affection began by degrees to turn off from the old grasier, who was too good-natur'd a man to impute any dishonesty to his wife, for fear of creating jealousies and alarms in his family, which he naturally abhorr'd, being a man who loved peace, and had liv'd quietly till then. Tracey had still generosity enough left not to violate the bed of his master any longer, for what he had already done, was at the earnest importunities of the wife, who was always teazing him to a compliance. But the mistress had too little beauty to inspire a man of our adventurer's gaiety and temper with love; and, besides, her frequent intreaties and fulsome dalliancies with him, when her husband was out of the way, made him quite averse and nauseate her. However, though it was plain by his conduct, that he had not that affection for her which she wanted, yet she would not desist, but seemed rather the more enclined to win him over. One

Saturday her husband being gone to market, she finding all the family at their employments, except Tracey, she took him to task, and ask'd the reason of his seeming coldness. 'What,' says she, 'do you despise my person, who can be of so much advantage to you? What think you? Supposing the old man should die, of which there is some probability, would not this farm and the stock upon it, and my person into the bargain, be an equal recompence for your love. I'm sorry, Tracey, to think I should humble myself thus far to make declarations of love to one so much beneath me; but it is the misfortune of some women, and they cannot help it. You have given me a foretaste of enjoyment, and now decline gratifying me any further, which makes me long the more. Had I never seen your person, or been so much acquainted with your conversation, I had never been the fool I now make myself; but the remedy is past cure unless you apply the medicine, for 'tis you alone that can heal me, and recover all my lost hopes.' Tracey was confounded at this speech, and knew not what to answer. Here were circumstances that both pointed at his advancement, and yet threatned him with consequences prejudicial to his repose. The farm and the stock upon it were

worth a considerable sum of money, which laid out prudently, might answer all the purposes of his life; but then his mistress cool'd his pursuit; he could see nothing in her that was either amiable or pleasing, for besides her temper, which was none of the best, she had several defects in her body, which together made him utterly hate her: yet that the correspondence between them might not be broke, he endeavoured to insinuate a seeming kindness, though in reality, he had much ado to comply with himself to perform it. He told her, 'that he should from that time, owe her infinite thanks, for making a declaration of love to him, which his ambition could never have flattered him with: that he had nothing to object against satisfying their mutual desires, but her husband, who, while alive, would be an eternal impediment to their wishes: that he look'd on violating his bed as the grossest abuse in the world, and could not, considering the respect he bore him, be brought to consent to so notorious an injury, that he hoped she would think on his conduct in this respect as praise-worthy, and not to be blamed, since, after his decease, he was ready to join hands with her, and be her partner in her pleasures and pains: that, to confess his mind, her daughter-in-law would make a more suitable match, not that he, by so saying, endeavoured to depretiate from her, but their years were more conformable, and it was more

natural, that like and like should by link'd together. However, rather than dis-
oblige her by an absolute refusal, he would consent to embrace her once more,
and would be ready to receive her that night in his chamber.' If any thing in the
world ever gave woman pleasure, these words certainly did the grasier's wife,
who was so much transported with Tracey's pleasing offer, that she had great
difficulty to contain herself till the time of assignation came, till when every
moment seem'd an hour. But madam will dearly pay for this appointment; for
Tracey, acquainting in the mean time, the goatherd and swineherd, how that
every night a spirit tormented him, desired them to watch that night in his room
to bear him company: the fellows were terrified at the relation, and by no means
could be brought to consent, till Tracey telling them they should come to no
harm, and ordering each to bring a bundle of rods to whip the ghost, they gave
their consent, and said they would come; the fellows concluded from Tracey's
words about the rods, that there was some sport on foot that would give them
entertainment enough, which made them ready to embrace going. Tracey told
them, that as soon as the spirit appeared, they were to fall to exercising their rods,
which would make it retire, and probably never haunt his chamber more. All
things were now in a right preparation, Tracey in bed, and the other two servants
posted behind it: it was not long before the mistress came in, in her smock,
having double lock'd the door of her husband's chamber, who was fast asleep, to
prevent his sudden surprizing them together, provided he wak'd and found her
missing. As soon as she was entred, the two men rusht out with the rods in their
hands from their post, and scourged the poor woman unmercifully; who durst
not make any noise lest her husband should over-hear, and alarm the house; but
when she found them so far from desisting from their stripes, that they laid on
the heavier, she could not restrain her tongue any longer, but calling out murder,
so alarmed the family, that the old man immediately waking out of his sleep,
wondered what was the matter: he put on his cloaths to go and see what it was
that made such a noise; but fortune at first directed him into the yard; still he
listned, and still he heard the noise, and at last found that it came from Tracey's
chamber. Up stairs he goes directly, but his wife, in the interim, got to bed. On
coming into the chamber the fellows hid themselves as before, and he asking our
adventurer what was the meaning of all that noise, was answer'd, 'that he might
take his house to himself; for he would not be hamper'd and beat about by spirits

105

as he had been, for the best place in England'. 'Spirits,' says the old man! 'Ay, dear master, spirits,' and so saying, the fellows came suddenly upon him, and pulling down his breeches, gave him the same lecture as they had done his wife. But the grasier was not contented with this usage, but lifting up his hands, he poured such heavy blows about the shoulders of the fellows, that they no more imagin'd them the cuffs of a mortal man, but of an hobgoblin, and so, being terrified, ran again underneath the bed. At this the old man in a violent rage call'd out to Tracey, and ask'd him where he was, who told him in bed. 'Ah, my dear master,' says he, 'these are the spirits that continually teaze me; I've suffered such usage as this a long time, but being unwilling to put your house into any fears on my account, have submitted to it with a great deal of patience. For God's sake go to bed, for I'd rather endure their blows, than you should endure any harm.' The wife, all this time, notwithstanding the severe smart she felt, was extremely rejoiced to think that her husband had shared with her in the same punishment, and when he came to bed, seem'd to condole him in a very piteous manner. 'What o' pox,' says he, 'are you in bed, where was you just now? What! are you a ghost too? Egad I have a handsome house on't, indeed'; and with that he got to bed, and rested pretty well the remainder of the night. In the morning the grasier could not help bringing to his thoughts what had happened to Tracey; he was very fond of the man, and wanted to know the particulars that had befallen him. Tracey, having a ready and copious invention, made a thousand things more of the story than it realy contain'd; and, by exaggerating it with abundance of falsities, so terrified the old man, that he could not forbear compassionating him, and shewing a great deal of concern. But, all the while, the wife took the notion of spirits for a meer whim, and concluded within herself that it had been all Tracey's doing; for she observed a more than ordinary coolness in his behaviour, and, if at any time she but spoke to him at dinner or otherwise, was answered with a plain negligence and disrespect, which so exasperated her, that she was resolved to be even with him for his inconcern and indolence. She had a thousand thoughts what expedient to make use of, in order to accomplish her design in the surest manner, and, on long deliberation, found the only way to ruin him, was to discharge him before her husband, with a design upon her honour, which she was not long before she put in execution. Tracey was not a stranger to her ill temper, but was determined to see the upshot of the whole affair; so one evening seeing the old man walking in his orchard alone, he goes to him, and, after some chat on indifferent matters, begins to lay open his birth, parentage and education, by acquainting him, that he had been master of a small estate of sixscore pounds per annum, but, living too profusely, had run it thro', which he was sorry for, because, had he known the same frugality then as now, he had still been master of it, or more; that his father had sent him to the university to qualify him for the Ministry, but he had frustrated the expectations of his parents, who reposed all their hopes in him: that his former extravagancies had obliged him to commit actions he was now sorry for, and, to keep up his usual way of life, he was forced to support himself by indirect means; but, that his coming to his house had entirely wiped out of his mind the desire of committing the like follies, and thought that heaven had favour'd him, in giving him the grace, after having been brought up so well, and lived so liberally, to take to such an honest, painful, and laborious life: that he esteemed the happiness of the country much above that of the city, the extravagancies of which he had seen and the ways the men there pursued to support themselves; that the hard bed he laid upon, was more soft to him than all the down ones at his father's house, and that to rise by peep of day, and go to his daily employment, was more healthful and satisfactory, than to sleep snoring till noon, and have no other business than poring over a parcel of wrangling books;—'I beg,' continued he, 'that you would mind my discourse, because I have something to say that may be to your advantage—Now, Sir, you are to know, that after I had spent my estate, I came into this country with no other mind than to do penance for my former miscarriages, by hiring myself to be a menial servant to any gentleman that wanted one. Fortune has favour'd me in throwing me into your family, among whom I take it, I have behaved with some degree of modesty, honesty, and diligence; my conversation, Sir, has already drawn several persons to covet my acquaintance, and, if I may be indulged the expression, the lasses round about are ready to run mad for me; and I am sorry to have the obligation to say, that your wife, is not the least among them that sollicits my favour' 'Hold that, not a word more—My wife run mad after thee! Blood and wounds—I'll cure her of her itching, Wat'—'Why, Sir, that would do exceeding well, but give me leave to make a conclusion of my discourse, and then say and object what you please. Your wife, indeed, Sir, has more than once desired the favour of my bed, and to

107

convince you that what I speak is true, she was the person who raised the spirit the night you came into my room; 'twas she her own self who walk'd, which may be verified by your goatherd and swineherd, who saw her in her smock. For my part, I have hitherto refrained violating your bed, for reasons which all mankind ought to allow the justest in the world. But if you don't restrain her, flesh may be frail, though I had rather quit your service a thousand times over than commit so much ingratitude against my master and benefactor. But what is the real occasion of all these words of mine, is, that my mistress is determined at supper-time to charge me with several high crimes against her chastity, which are entirely groundless, and which I hope you'll give no credit to. And there is but one thing more, which is, that as I was born a gentleman to an estate, and trained up at the university, and through my own default, am now descended to the low condition you see me in, you would bless me with an alliance with your daughter, who is a deserving young woman, and one whom I have tenderly loved, ever since my first coming here. There will be no scandal in this match, for, was I not convinced of her sincere affection for me, I would never presume on what I have said; and with her, to be a servant, to be a slave, nay, to be the worst of mankind, I mean, in the lowest degree, will be the greatest joy, happiness, and contentment.' What could be more surprizing than these words to the old grasier, who was so far from imputing any kind of impudence to our adventurer, that he seem'd vastly rejoic'd at the tidings he had given him, and told him, that he thank'd him a thousand times for the discovery he had made both of his wife's villainy and himself; adding thus, 'Wat, I have a long time consider'd you in a very promising light, and been determin'd to put the question to you several times, to know if you entertain'd any thoughts of marriage; judging that a wife with a little money would be no unacceptable thing in your present condition, which I have frequently wish'd for the better; but now, wat, for the timely service you have done me, perhaps it may be in my power shortly to recompence you handsomely, and repay your extraordinary care and industry, suitably for your consulting my repose, and for your surprizing modesty and self-denial, in resisting such temptations as might have ensnared others; but my wife's conduct is no more than usual long before you came into my service; and whenever I am told of it, the consideration gauls me in the most sensible manner, as a man in the like case would, you know, fret and fume: but,

108

lack-a-day, wat, my wife is not the only thing that disturbs my quiet, and molests my slumbers; I have other causes of disturbance, which time and another oppor- tunity, if you and I hit in joining horses together, may make you acquainted with. Never mind all she can either say or invent againt you; I am master of my family, I believe, and who, tell me, dare pretend a superiority in it, besides myself? Zounds, wat, I heartily love you; and had you been so free with me a quarter of a year ago, you had been a better man behalf than you are now: but, however, I'll endeavour to requite you as you deserve, and my daughter, with three hundred pounds, shall be yours, man, in spite of all the second wives in Christendom—If I say it, who's the other to controul me? Here's my hand, that she's yours before eleven o'clock to-morrow morning: but, methinks, good wat, I have a mind to restore you in some degree to what you have lost. I do not question but your former extravagancies have set all your relations and friends you have entirely against you; to reconcile whom, and make up the breach between them and you, I take the best expedient to be, to send to the most considerable amongst them a very submissive letter, worded dextrously, but above all, containing your hearty repentance for the omissions you have formerly been guilty of, and acquainting them, that having from a gentleman's life descended to the low condition of a peasant, you have forced yourself to a very hard and laborious penance for your misdeeds, which you now suppose you have justly perform'd; and that fortune smiling upon your endeavours, has, to reward your extraordinary humility, made your master to think well of you, nay, to offer you his daughter in marriage, provided they will answer three hundred pounds he designs to give you in portion with her: this, wat, I take for a tolerable good beginning to succeed; and if you hear of no answer soon, you and I will then take horse, go and negociate the whole affair with them ourselves. Let me tell you, six hundred pounds will purchase a pretty farm for you two, and answer all necessaries so long as your wife remains without children; but when those come on, and I find you diligent, 'tis very likely I may add to your estate, and gratify you with a present of thirty or forty acres more, which with effectually do your business. Oh! metkinks, I congratulate you now on the felicity you'll enjoy, so you mind yourself, prove an endearing husband, and a laborious father.' Here the old grasier ended greatly to the satisfaction of our adventurer, who began to entertain a great many different thoughts in his head, how he should contrive to make the most advantage to himself, and still keep a steddy harmony in the family: he had frequent thoughts how to accomplish his ends; sometimes he was determin'd to throw for ever away his desire of making plunder on his countrymen, and to embrace the generous offer which his master the grasier had made him; thinking if he did so, his life would be made easy, provided he could but conform himself to the rules of wedlock, and preserve the same good thoughts he had all along entertain'd during his abode in Cheshire. Vast was his desire to be reconcil'd to his mistress, whom he look'd on now as his implacable enemy; but he had so much faith in his master, that he could not, without doing him an injustice, think he would act against his interest. Supper-time now comes, and nothing but anger and resentment glare in the countenance of the grasier's wife, who seem'd resolv'd to do as she had determin'd, tho' to her own disadvantage, and even ruin. Tracey endeavour'd by all the external signs he was master of, to convince her that he had still left a dutiful respect for her, and that she might expect to win him, provided the old man was out of the way. But resentment rooted in the breast of a woman whose love has been rejected, admits of no bounds, nor had our adventurer any room to hope for success: he drank to her, but she return'd the compliment with a disregard that plainly discover'd he was distasteful to her. 'No,' said she, 'if my husband is the fool to humour you, it shall never be seen that I will; you are an ungrateful man, nay, a villain, Tracey, (now I am forc'd to open my mind) after all the civilities you have receiv'd in this family, to use me, who ought to have some sway in my own house, in the manner you have done. Was not the receiving you poor, mean, and admitting you to such privileges as few servants can boast of, a kindness deserving of some acknowledgement? Was not preferring you to be the first of our servants, when another, who had serv'd under us several years, and better deserv'd it, a favour which any one but you would have required? But it seems our kindness and generosity turn'd your brain, and made you giddy-headed, so that forgetting the obligations you were under to us, you have had the presumption not only of keeping up a close communication with our daughter, but also to address me with your fulsome speeches, which my virtue hath constantly guarded against; thinking that the fame you so much boast of, could find no refusal, and that I, as I fear my daughter-in-law has already, should fall a sacrifice to your inordinate desires. Had not my husband's peace and tranquility been struck; had not my honour and chastity been openly attack'd by you, and an infamy endeavour'd to be laid on our family, I would have scorn'd to have made this discovery; but as I am tied by the solemn rites of religion to obey another man, I was forc'd, even tho' against myself, to publish the injustice that has a long time been design'd him: for it is not once or twice that is enough to exaggerate your crime so as to deprive you of the favours you enjoy as present; but, Tracey, you know how often have been the times of this insulting and dishonourable way of yours; had a thousand other miscarriages proclaim'd your conduct disrespectful to me, I should have put up with every one of them; but an open attack against my honour, my modesty and fame, has no excuses, nor ever shall with me.' Tracey, who heard this all the while with an attentive ear, was surpriz'd at the woman's presumption and boldness; he could not help staring upon her with an eye full of resentment, equal to that which she had in her own breast: he could have crush'd all she had avanc'd in a minute or two, had he been so minded; but he was in expectation to hear his master speak first, who, he depended on, was to vindicate him: nor, indeed, was he long before he did; for putting the tankard he was drinking out, out of his hands, he began to question his wife about her insincerity and baseness in taxing Tracey, whom he look'd upon as one of the best friends he had, with a crime he was no way guilty of, and which properly was her own fault, but he need not be any way surpriz'd about it, since he had for some years past receiv'd so many complaints, which he had been unwilling to give ear to, purely because he loved his ease and quiet: but now there was no longer room to distrust her perfidy, since Tracey, who was so bashful a man, had brought all things to light: that for the future he would make himself very contented, and only desir'd her to return back to her friends, for stay with him she should not, and all the money she brought him was at her service, to carry and dispose of just as she pleas'd.—Here the old grasier stopp'd, and then Tracey took his turn to speak, saying, the calling the goatherd and swineherd would soon put an end to the dispute, 'who would swear they saw her come into my bed-chamber in her shift, with a design of procuring me to do that which you ought to perform; but far be it from me to create any misunderstanding in a family unjustly, to which I lay under so many obligations'—'Misunderstanding,' reply'd the old grasier, 'none at all, for you shall be my son, and I your father'; and having so said, the dispute broke up, and in a little time the family retired to bed.

All this time the grasier's daughter, who was the brown lass above-mention'd, was full of joy and gladness at the good fortune of Tracey, whom she look'd upon now as her real husband: she found herself with child by him, and was glad her father was so considerate to join them together, in order to wipe off her disgrace; but the old man little thought of the intercourse that had been betwixt his daughter and his man; else 'tis very probably all his intended kindness had vanish'd to air. In short, the morning came, and the old man, to make sure of a son-in-law, rode to the next rural dean, and got a marriage-licence; when about 11 o'clock they were join'd together. The remaining part of the day was dedicated to mirth and jollity, the neighbourhood being invited to partake of the mirth.

Tracey was now in the possession of a bride already with child by him; and what made more to his happiness, was, the old father's putting him immediately into part of his own estate; out of which he reserv'd, a small annual rent as an acknowledgment: a stock sufficient to live upon it was bought, and every thing manag'd according to Tracey's wish, who finding himself at liberty to do and act just as he thought fit, had several serious reflections within himself, how to make the best advantage of all under his care, and make the father believe him a laborious and pains-taking man: after he and his wife had liv'd about two months together, he often intimated to her, that 'twas true, the country was a very pleasant place, and a life spent there vastly agreeable; but nevertheless, society, to which he had always been used, was wanting, which made it not so recreating; that a walk into the meadows, or by the side of some river, was a delightful way to wipe off the mind its gloomy and melancholy ideas; and that murmuring streams, rising hills, and shady woods, were the recreation of philosophic and contemplative minds; but that they two, who were very young, had brisker notions, and lov'd gaity and an humourous way of living; and that the plough, rake, and sickle were too vulgar things for such as they, and that the means of obtaining what both earnestly desired, was to see London, where all the pleasure which the world afforded, was to be found: that in order to this, they were to get their father to a consent of selling their farm, and with the purchase-money buy some place or other of profit, able to maintain them in a genteeler way than at present, which he knew he would soon comply with, as he himself advised him to write to his friends to obtain an equivalent for the three hundred pounds he had given him with her. That his relations liv'd in Norfork, and would comply with any reasonable request, and would be so glad to see him, after so many years absence, that they would not know how to do too much for him: that he mention'd this with no manner of view, to leave his father-in-law desolate, after he had, on his account, sent his second wife back to her relations; but that he might see his desire was no other than to honour his family, by being preferr'd to a post of life more agreeable and profitable than the maintaining of a farm.—The wife having all her life-time been used to a rural life, had little thoughts of the pleasures of a city so numerous and populous as London was, so that she was at a loss how to answer her husband. However, Tracey's importunities, and the thousand charms he told her was in a city life, soon won her over, insomuch that nothing but London ran in her mind; nothing now but gaity and pleasure; nothing but dress and acquaintance; nothing but tea-tables and plays; nothing but gallantry and appointments; and nothing but Madam and Madam could now please her. Hence arose an aversion to the country; no more the pastures and meadows; no more the woods and hills; no more the rivers and fountains; no more the shades and haycocks; no more wakes and rural dances; and no more the inhabitants in Cheshire delighted her. She is determin'd, the first opportunity, to lay open her and her husband's mind with regard to their seeing London, and sollicit him to take a journey into Norfolk to see his relations. Tracey approves well of his wife's conduct, and strives to heighten it; and it was not long e're she found a seasonable conjuncture one Saturday evening, when the old man retired from market somewhat fuller with liquor than ordinary: she laid open the whole affair with a great deal of perswasion and address; the father readily granted all, and a day was appointed for their journey. Mean time, Tracey made all the advantage secretly he could of his effects, and the old grasier in about a fortnight's time got a purchaser for Tracey's farm, who gave bills in the room of money. Every thing was now got ready, and our adventurer, wife, and father-in-law on the road. When they came to Trentum in Straffordshire, they put up at an inn there, in order to stay two or three days to refresh the old man, who was already weary with his journey. During their abode they happened to have a good deal of company, among whom Tracey always found admittance; for having a smooth tongue, and a tolerable voice for singing, every one were glad to get into his company. 'Twas here that Tracey was determin'd to put a finishing stroke to his long adventure with the grasier; he was resolved not only to leave him his daughter with child by him to keep, but also to make himself master of the bills e're the morning, and to that end, getting his father to carouze that night a little freer than ordinary (his wife being already gone to bed) he dextrously conveyed the old man's pocket-book, wherein the bills were, out of his pocket, and then to colour over his villainy with some pretence, wrote the following letter, and left it in the room of the pocket-book.

> Dear Sir,
>
> I Make no Wonder of your being surpriz'd at finding the Inclos'd; but I have innumerable Reasons for my doing thus, which I shall wave at this Time, and acquaint you with at my Return. When my Wife and you read this in the Morning, be sure to think that I have done both of you the best Action in the World, which I could prove, were it not that I was in too much Haste when I wrote this: For finding you fatigued with your Journey before we had got half Way, I thought I could not do a better Deed than leave you where you were, with your Money in your Pocket, and in the midst of Plenty and good Company. As for the Bills, I take them to be properly mine, as they stand in the room of the Purchase-Money for the Estate which came to me by right of Marriage, and I humbly conceive I can make as right a Use of them as any Man living. As for going into Norfolk, I apprehend the Journey is useless, till I have made myself certain of a Place in London, when probably they may do something for me; till which Time adieu.
>
> W. TRACEY.

Mean time the old man and his daughter were fast asleep in separate beds, and our adventurer, to make sure of what he had, got up early in the morning; and, under a pretence of riding out half a dozen miles till breakfast-time, got his horse saddled, mounted, and rode off. About seven o'clock the father and daughter rise, and missing Tracey, enquire of the people in the inn if they had seen him, who are told by the hostler that he went on horse-back at three, and would return by breakfast-time. But no Tracey appears at that time, nor all that day. This astonishes the old man; but more the daughter, who began to lament his absence. They have different thoughts about him, but all are in vain. Sometimes they are afraid that some mischance has befallen him; at other times, that having a mind to view the country, he had rode out for that day; but at length, the old man finding no signs of his returning, goes and sees how things stand about him. The first that presents itself is the letter, which being perused, put the old man into a violent fit of trembling, which ended in a kind of convulsive pangs. Drops are applied, which soon recovering the old gentleman, every one are desirous to know the cause of his uneasiness. They are acquainted from the beginning to the end, and all seemed concerned at his sorrow. What should the old man do in this case? Why, he is determin'd this minute to travel after him, the next to return home; but before he does that, he gets it proclaimed round about, that such a man and such a horse was missing, and if any one could inform him where they were, he, she or they making such information, should receive from him the sum of five pounds. This was a tolerable good way of proceeding; for the money induced several to make enquiry; but in short all was to no purpose, for our adventurer was by this time got to Coventry; and the old man and his daughter, after a week's stay at Trentum, thought best to return home to Cheshire, to save more expences, and wait there the return of their hopeful son-in-law.

Tracey, in the mean time, was got to Coventry, where he put up at the Rose and Crown, one of the best inns in that city. On his going into the inn, he observed a more than usual stillness, which he could not tell well what to attribute to. He placed his horse in the stable, and then going into the house, he heard a dispute carrying on in the room over his head, which raising his curiosity to know what all meant, he went directly up stairs into the chamber. On his entring, the people within were somewhat astonish'd: he look'd about him, and saw in the bed a man with only a sheet over him, and near the fire-side a woman, the mistress of the inn, and a young man. Tracey ask'd them what made them take so little care about the house; for had he been an ill-disposed person, he might have run away with half the things in the kitchen. Upon this the man in the bed, whom he took for dead, (being laid out as dead men are) started up on his backside, and address'd him in the following manner: 'Sir, I'm heartily glad you are come in, since, you being an impartial man, I may venture to lay open my case without offence. You are to know then that the woman sitting there is my wife, which word I wish I had never known; for from the time the matrimonial knot was tied between us, I may safely say I have not had a day's rest, put all together, and now we have lived together seven years wanting but a single month. I believe I may alledge, without any injustice, that during that time I have been one of the most affectionate husbands to her; for I have never debarr'd her from any thing, nor has she had the least pretence for complaint, occasion'd by me; whenever she wanted, I readily gave her more than she ask'd for: whenever she was willing to go abroad, a servant and a chaise was at her command, nay, whenever any new costly fashion came up, I was the first to promote it, I mean in shewing it upon her; and yet all these favours and considerations would not do. My life upon this became uneasy; and I had a thousand restless moments about it. I communicated my uneasiness to a particular friend, who told me that she did not love me, and the only way to discover it was to feign myself dead. Accordingly I pretended myself dead, and presently this wretch brought that old woman, who together with her laid me out, as you saw me at your first coming in. During my dead penance, I had an opportunity of hearing how the case went, and soon found that love, or rather lust, was the real cause of all my late miseries. The young rascal there is her gallant, who I am sure has handled above five hundred pounds of my substance, which from time to time I have found missing. This is a miserable case, Sir, and deserves compassion. But this not all, she has already given orders for my funeral, for making of mourning cloaths and rings.'—Tracey all this while stood gazing with due attention, and could not but reflect on the inconstancy, profusion, and artifice of some women. He told the person in bed he was extremely sorry for his misfortune in being wedded to such a she-devil, who was a thousand times worse to him than all his money; but he would give him a seasonable relief by-and-by. The husband hereupon thank'd him, and express'd his gladness for his coming into his chamber so opportunely. 'But Sir,' says he, 'this wretch held a pretty long consultation with the other two how she should behave in so nice a circumstance; "for," said she, "I cannot weep, and the town will admire at my not shedding a tear over his grave, who, they know was so tender and loving a husband. Oh!" added she, "I'll put onions into my handkerchief, and by that means I shall deceive the world with a forc'd lamentation."' 'Ay, ay,' replied Tracey, 'this is worse than all; but I'll spoil her of her artifices presently,' and so saying, he pulls a loaded pistol out of his breast, and commanded, on pain of death, every one of them, not excepting the man in bed, to deliver what money they had; 'for,' said he, 'it is money that has made this confusion, and I'm resolv'd to ease you of it, in order to make you live together more quiet for the future.'—Upon this going up to the wife, he received from her fifty guineas, from the gallant thirty, and from the old woman five.—'An handsome spoil i'faith,' says he, 'and pray, landlord, what can you afford me?' 'Nothing in the world,' reply'd he, 'for I humbly conceive I have given you eighty five guineas already, which is a tolerable good fee for your advice, Sir'—'Say you so, Mr Buffler—Well, I shall call this day se'n-night again to see how affairs go, and if I do not find your wife reconciled by the loss of this money, I'll then remove double the sum, and so every week in proportion, till I have made a thorough cure', and with that he bad them farewel.

Tracey, after this adventure, made his way to Ware, where taking up his lodgings for that night, he got into the company of a young Oxonian, who had brought a large portmanteau behind him. The student seemed very well pleased at his friend's conversation, as he thought, and, to encrease a better understanding betwixt them, they supped together, and drank a couple of bottles of wine afterwards. They lay together in the same bed, and, an hour or two before they went to sleep, had a great deal of conversation about the ways of mankind, which terminated at last about the university, which Tracey pretended to be an entire stranger to. In the morning both drank sack posset, mounted and pursued their journey together. Tracey endeavour'd to amuse his fellow traveller with a series of foreign adventures, which he had never perform'd; the scholar, on his part, laid open the wicked practices of the colleges, so that both seem'd to be fit and choice companions for each other. Tracey would now and then take hold of the student's portmanteau, and tell him 'twas very heavy, and wonder'd he did not bring a servant along with him, so much undervaluing his profession, by being master and man himself. The student constantly answered, that the times were exceeding hard, and he travelled by himself to save charges. 'How,' replies the other, 'charges! Why, the charges of a servant are vastly insignificant in compa-rison of the loss you may probably sustain on the road for want of one: I hope, Sir, you have not got any great charge of money within your portmanteau, for I think you act a very unwise part, if you carry much about you, without having some one or other in company with you': the student told him, he had no less than threescore pounds within it, which he was carrying to the universtiy to defray the customary fees for taking up his degree of Master of Arts. 'Ah,' says

117

Tracey, 'that's a round sum, o' my word, and 'tis a thousand pities so much should be given away to persons that no way deserve a farthing of it. If I had known of your having threescore pounds about you, when we were at the inn, I could have procured you a chap that would have sold you a place for it much more beneficial than any thing you hope for, by being a Master of Arts, but as we are too far a distance off from Ware to return in time, you shall be eas'd of your money and portmanteau presently; for I have an occasion at this very conjuncture for such a quantity of money, and there's no better person than myself you can lend it to'; after which words Tracey unlooses the straps, takes the portmanteau, and puts it on his own horse—The student observing this, immediately cried aloud, 'Oh dear Sir, I hope your design is not to rob me; I shall lose a pretty good parsonage that is offered me in Essex, if you take away my money from me. Pray, Sir, consider the crime you are going to act, for the loss of my threescore pounds will not only deprive me of a competent means of livelihood, but also the Almighty will lose a Minister of his word. And for the sake of heaven, I beseech you to be compassionate, and not so severe on a poor man that was obliged to borrow this money of several persons, who would not have lent it, but through a view of being soon repaid. Sir, you commit a thing against the laws of your country, and the precepts of humanity, to wrest thus by force what belongs to another man, and I dare say you are not so much a stranger to the injustice of it, but you know 'tis an error, and a great one. The sin too is vastly enlarged, when a specious pretence of friendship is made use of for such a dishonourable deed; for how will any man know he is safe in travelling, if every one he meets with on the road, converses with him in the sincere manner (I mean outwardly) as you have pretended to me. But, Sir, not to enlarge further, let me intreat you over and over again, not to take my all from me, for if so, I am inevitably ruin'd, and am an undone man for ever.' Tracey seemed to mind the student's desire of having his portmanteau again with a grave attention, but the thought of having obtain'd such a considerable booty, made him banish every compassionate sentiment out of his breast, till no longer able to bear with the tedious importunities of the scholar, he pulled out of his breeches pockets a leathern purse with four pounds odd money in it, and gave it the collegian, saying, 'Friend, I am not yet so much lost to the sense of compassion, but I can extend my charity and generosity; 'tis not customary for a gentleman of my fortune to give money, but your intercession has won me over to it. Here are four pounds odd money to bear your expences to the university, so that you will not be all the loser, and when you come in the college, acquaint all those whom it may concern, that you have paid your Master of Arts fees already to a collector on the road, who had a thousand times more occasion for the money than a parcel of old mollies, that live by whoring, and stealing out of other authors works.' And so saying, he bad the poor collegian farewel, leaving him to pursue his journey, and obtain his degree as well as he could, while himself made the nearest way to the next village, where opening the portmanteau, he found nothing but two old shirts, half a dozen dirty bands, a thread bare student's torn gown, a pair of stockings without feet, a pair of shoes, but with one heel to them, some other old trumpery, and a great ham of bacon, but not one farthing of money; which set him a swearing and cursing like a devil, to think he should be such a preposterous ass, to give four pounds and more for that which was not worth forty shillings.

We have but two adventures more of Tracey which we find on record; the first relating to a robbery he committed on the famour poet Ben Johnson; the other to another on the Duke of Buckingham, who was slain by Felton, as he was going to embark at Portsmouth; for which he was hanged, both which we shall be very brief in.

Ben Johnson had been down in Buckinghamshire to transact some business, but in returning to London happened to meet with Tracey, who knowing the poet, bad him stand and deliver his money. But Ben putting on a courageous look, spoke to him thus:

> Fly villain hence, or by thy Coat of Steel,
> I'll make thy Heart my leaden Bullet feel,
> And send that thrice as thievish Soul of thine
> To Hell, to wean the Devil's Valentine.

Upon which Tracey make this Answer:

> Art thou, great Ben? or the revived Ghost
> Of famous Shakespear? or some drunken Host?
> Who being tipsy with thy muddy Beer,

> Dost think thy Rhimes will daunt my Soul with Fear;
> Nay, know, base Slave, that I am one of those,
> Can take a Purse, as well in Verse, as Prose,
> And when thou art dead, write this upon thy Herse,
> Here lies a Poet who was robb'd in Verse.

These words alarmed Johnson, who found he had met with a resolute fellow; he endeavoured to save his money, but to no purpose, and was obliged to give our adventurer ten jacobus's. But the loss of these was not the only misfortune he met with in this journey; for coming within two or three miles of London, it was his ill chance to fall into the hands of worse rogues, who knock'd him off his horse, stript him, and tied him neck and heels in a field, wherein some other passengers were enduring the same hard fate, having been also robbed. One of them crying out, that he, his wife and children were all undone, while another, who was bound, over-hearing, said, 'pray, if you are all of you undone, come and undo me'. This made Ben, though under his misfortunes, burst out into a loud laugh, who being delivered in the morning from his bands by some reapers, made the following verses:

> Both robb'd and bound, as I one Night did ride,
> With two Men more, their Arms behind them ty'd,
> The one lamenting what did them befal,
> Cry'd, I'm undone, my Wife, and Children all;
> The other hearing it, aloud did cry,
> Undo me then, let me no longer lie;
> But to be plain, those Men laid on the Ground,
> Were both undone, indeed, but both fast bound.

The last robbery he committed was on the Duke of Buckingham above-mention'd; but some say, he only endeavoured to commit one. Now as we have neither the place, nor in what manner this attempt was made, nor how much he took from his Grace, nor any other circumstances to help us to a discovery of this adventure, we are obliged to be silent, and only say that he suffered for it at Winchester.

Tracey might have made a good man, had he turned those talents Providence had given him to better uses than he made of them. For he had a fine way of delivery, a volubility of speech, extensive memory, and was well versed in the books of the antients. We may very well say, that his irregular life was owing to the first immoderate courses he learnt at the college, where so many young gentlemen, by running beyond their salaries, are forc'd on dishonourable artifices to support themselves. And Tracey happened to be one of these. While he remain'd in Cheshire, he gave signs of being a frugal and provident young man, and to descend so low as to hire himself, who had been born a gentleman, to drudge in the fields and meadows, was what ten thousand, except himself, would have scorn'd to have done; but this heightens his character, as it argues a real sign of humility, which, had our adventurer continued in the country with his father, had made him one of the happiest of men.

Tracey had amassed together in money and goods sufficient to support him handsomely during life, and determining with himself to take up betimes, and live peaceably on what he had got, he placed his money in a friend's hand, who made off with it, and left our adventurer to pursue his old trade towards obtaining more. He was heard to speak the following words on this occasion, ' 'Tis true that at this time we are almost grown a nation of cheats; but that which is worst of all is, that men will not cheat upon the square; one engrosses more knavery than the other, for if it went round equally, there would be nothing lost.'

I shall conclude what I have to say concerning this person, with a short, but merry adventure, which, according to method, ought to have been inserted a good while ago.

Our adventurer, while in Cheshire, was thought to be conversant with familiar spirits; for naturally being a lover of solitude, he would repeat verses frequently under shades and in caves, which the peasants would sometimes chance to over-hear; but Tracey uttering some poetick phrases, which were above the country-mens apprehensions, they concluded the Devil must be his school-master. They imagined he had the gift of prophecy, and could divine. It happened, that he went one day to Chester, where, getting amongst some citizens daughters, he told them he'd lay a wager, that he acquainted them which among them was not a maid. This speech raising a loud laughter amongst the girls, one of them said immediately, 'Why, friend, your knowledge will be employed in vain, for you may well say there is not one in all this company that has lost her honour.' These words did not hinder Tracey from pursuing his design, but least he might give offence, he said he would not make all the world privy to it, and would only disclose to one of her acquaintance then present, who amongst them it was that had lost her maidenhead. In consequence of this he took the acquaintance aside, and spoke thus in her ear, 'my art informs me, that she, amongst all these maids, who has committed the act of fornication, is the very person who spoke last to me'. This discovery was kept a secret from the rest for the space of eight days, when the abovesaid girl, and a gardiner, an inhabitant in the village, where Tracey then dwelt, were married together. As she was in bed, it was not long before she was seized with child-bearing pains, and at length delivered of a fine boy— The maid who had receiv'd the secret from Tracey, published it as a miracle the same hour; upon which our adventurer's reputation was vastly increas'd and nois'd about. Every one were extremely fond to see him after this prediction, as admiring his profound knowledge and experience. But what made the case not quite so bad as it would have been, was, that the husband swore, 'That the child was his own, and that his wife would not take a husband, without having first made trial of him, for having seen a pattern of the cloth, she might try whether it were good or not, and if it did not please her, she might leave it to other customers.' This made abundance of people speak pleasantly, that the bridegroom was an able workman, to have a child the first week; but they who were more serious, were amazed how his wife could carry her great belly so well, so as not to be found out; but 'tis beyond question she used some artifice to hide it.

THE LIFE OF
THOMAS RUMBOLD

T his Thomas Rumbold was descended from honest and creditable parents at Ipswich in Suffolk. In his youth he was put apprentice to a bricklayer, but evil inclinations having an ascendant over his mind, he went from his master before he had well served two thirds of his time. This elopement obliged him to pursue some irregularities to support himself: he absconded from his father's house, and having a desire of seeing London, he came up to town, where getting into the company of a notorious gang of robbers, he went on the highway, and frequently took a purse. This course he continued some time, in conjunction with confederates; but having a mind to make prizes by himself, he ventured by himself, committing several depredations on his countrymen; the following whereof have come to our hands.

★The Archbishop of Canterbury being to go from Lambeth to Canterbury, Rumbold was determin'd to way-lay him; and accordingly getting sight of him between Rochester and Sittingborn in Kent, he gets into a field, and spreading a large tablecloth on the grass, on which he had placed several handfuls of gold, he then takes a box and dice out of his pocket, and falls a playing at hazard by himself. His Grace riding by that place, and espying a man shaking his elbows by himself, sent one of his footmen to know the meaning of it. The man was no sooner come up to Rumbold, who was still playing very eagerly, swearing and staring like a fury at his losses, but he returns to the Reverend Prelate, and telling him what he had seen, his Grace stept out of his coach to him, and seeing none but him, ask'd him who he was at play with? 'Damn it,' said Rumbold, 'there's five hundred pounds gone: pray, Sir, be silent.' His Grace going to speak again, 'Ay,' said Rumbold, 'there's a hundred pounds more lost.' 'Prithee,' said the Archbishop, 'who art thou at play with?' Rumbold reply'd with —; 'And how will you send the Money to him?'—'By,' said Rumbold, 'his Ambassadors; and therefore looking upon your Grace to be one of them extraordinary, I shall beg the favour of you to carry it him': according, giving his Grace about six hundred pounds in gold and silver, he put it into the seat of his coach, and away he rid to Sittingborn to bait. Rumbold rid thither also to bait in another inn; and riding some short while before his Grace, as soon as he had sight of him again, he had planted himself in another field in the same playing posture as he had before; which his Grace seeing as riding by, went again to see this strange gamester, whom he then took to be really a madman. No sooner was his Grace approaching Rumbold, who then had little or no money upon his cloth, but he cry'd out—'Six hundred pounds'—'What,' said the Archbishop, 'lost again.' 'No,' reply'd Rumbold, 'won, by Gad; I'll play this hand out, and then leave off. So, eight hundred pounds more, Sir, won; I'll leave off while I'm well.' 'And who have you won of,' said his Grace? 'Of the same person,' reply'd Rumbold 'that I left the six hundred pounds with you for before you went to dinner.' 'And how,' said his Grace, 'will you get your winnings?' Says Rumbold, 'of his Ambassador too': so riding up with sword and pistol in hand to his Grace's coach, he took fourteen hundred pounds out of the seat thereof over and above his own money, which he had entrusted in his hands to give to — and rid off.*

When Rumbold had got this large booty by playing, whose happiness it was never to see, without becoming a very great convert indeed, he bought him a place, but did not leave off robbing on the road; and in order for his better advantages, he kept in fee with most of the hostlers and chamberlains of the chiefest inns in the country for forty miles about London: so that having one day a blow set him at Colebrook, that is to say, being inform'd that a couple of travellers lay at a certain inn in the abovesaid town, he rose early the next morning, and way-laid them in their journey to Reading, so went before them to surprize them at Maidenhead-Thicket; but the travellers being cunning, they had given out in publick the wrong road they were to go; for instead of riding to Reading, they went to Windsor, so that Rumbold missing of his prey, rode back again very melancholy; when meeting with the Earl of Oxford, who was attended only with one groom and a footman, he clapt his hair into his mouth to disguise himself for his intended design, and attack'd his lordship with the terrifying words, 'Stand and deliver', withal swearing, that if he made any resistance he was a dead man. The expostulations the earl used to save what he had, were in vain; however he swore too, that since he must lose what he had, Rumbold should search his pockets himself, for he would not be at that trouble. Upon this our adventurer commanding his lordship's servants to keep at above a hundred foot distance upon pain of death, he took the pains of searching the earl; when finding nothing but boxes and dice in the pockets of his coat and waistcoat, he began to rend the skies with many first-rate oaths, swearing also, that he believ'd he was the groom-porter, else some gaming sharper going to bite the poor country people at their fairs and markets, till searching his breeches, he found within a good gold watch and six guineas; he changed his angry countenance into smiling features, and giving his lordship eighteen pence, bad him be of good cheer, go up to his regiment then at London as fast as he could, and do his duty as he ought, and when he next met with him, he would give him better encouragement.

Rumbold and an acquaintance of his being one day at Canterbury, in the dress of a country fellow, they went to a tavern to drink a quart of wine. It seems the master of the house was a complete sharper, who, taking his two guests for ignorant fellows, was determined to put the chouse upon them, as he call'd it; accordingly he brought them a wine quart pot, but it was little more than half full: he intended they should have it raw, but it being a cold morning, they bad him roast it, that is, put it to the fire and burn it: the vintner was at a loss in filling out the first glass, but not knowing how to help it, he set it down before the fire, and, as was suppos'd, intended to fill it up afterwards; but he forgetting that, and our adventurer and his acquaintance being busy in discourse, forgot to look after the pot; when on a sudden they look'd, and the pot was melted above half way down, which was as far as there was no wine in it: the maid observing the pot melted, call'd out to them, 'What? Honest men, do you melt your pot?'

'Not we,' said they, 'it was the fire': 'But you are like to pay for it,' reply'd the wench. 'That is when we do,' said they. Upon this, the master of the tavern appears, to whom the maid tells how the two fools had been telling their Canterbury tales together till the pot was melted.—'Then they must pay for it,' answers the vintner, 'for it was given into their charge and custody, and that therefore they ought to look after it, and since it was damag'd to pay for it.' They reply'd, they took no charge of it, neither did they touch it, but only order'd him to burn the wine well. The vintner insisted to be paid for his pot. They told him, they would not. Upon this he threaten'd them with a Justice of Peace's warrant. This menace somewhat troubling them, and unwilling to have any dispute in the affair, they told the vintner they were content to pay for the wine, and allow sixpence more for mending the pot. The vintner told them that would not do, for it could not be mended, and he must have a new one. Our adventurer and his companion seeing the vintner so unreasonable, were content to have the Justice determine the controversy, wherefore before his Worship they went, and the vintner made his complaint, how that those two men had melted his quart-pot, and refused to pay for it. The Justice perceiving how the matter lay, and that he told his tale wrong, desired the men to speak, who, in plain terms, told him they took no charge of the pot, but only desir'd the drawer to cause the wine to burnt; that he had accordingly set it down by the fire, and that without their handling or touching it, the pot was melted. 'So,' said the Justice, 'and did neither of you drink of the wine?' 'No, not one drop,' reply'd our adventurer, 'and yet we offer'd to pay for the wine, and give six-pence towards mending the pot.' 'This is more than you shall need to do,' answer'd the Justice, and then he thus proceeded with the vintner.

'Friend, with what confidence can you demand any money of these men, who had nothing of you? Since you will not do them justice, I will. I do hereby acquit them from paying any thing for wine, because they never had any, and for the melting the pot, how did they do it? It was not they, but your servant who drew wine, who, had he fill'd the pot full of wine, the fire could not have melted it; for I very well understand that the pot was melted no farther than it was empty; and farther,' continu'd the Justice, 'this shall not serve your turn, for I shall fine you for not filling your pot: your crime is very apparent and evident, and so shall your punishment be; and I order you, as a fine, to pay down twenty shillings for your misdemeanour, or else I shall make your mittimus, and send you to prison.' Thus was the case alter'd, and the tale now was of another hog, for the vintner, who expected satisfaction, was forc'd to give it, and that immediately, or else go to prison. This went against the hair, but necessity has no law, and therefore down he paid the money, and came home heartily vexed, not so much for the money he had paid, as for the disgrace he receiv'd, for he was now become the town-talk.

As Rumbold was riding along the road he met with a young girl with a milk-pail on her head, but was amaz'd to see so much perfection in her face; he rode up pretty close to her, purposely to entertain some discourse with her, introductory to a new acquaintance: the first questions he put to her were frivolous and indifferent, which she seem'd to answer with abundance of modesty. Rumbold seeing her open a gate to milk a cow, followed her, and tying his horse to a hedge, desir'd her pardon for his rudeness, and begg'd her to entertain a favourable opinion of his actions, for he would not offer the least injury or prejudice to her chastity. Being over persuaded with his protestations and vows to that purpose, she admitted him to sit down and discourse with her, whilst she perform'd the office of a milk-maid. Rumbold had much ado to contain his hands within bounds when he viewed her stroking the cow's dugs, which so heighten'd his amorous passion, that the vows and protestations he had so lately made soon vanish'd out of his memory. In short, after some dalliances, intreaties and love-persuasions, and using corporal strength, he obtain'd his desires. After this they grew more familiar together, but the burthen of the song was, that Rumbold had undone her; but let the reader judge the truth of this. It was concluded that she should go home to her father's house, and that towards night our adventurer would come thither likewise according to the time appointed, as if he had never seen her before, and that he accidentally rode that way in order to be inform'd what course he was to take to pursue his journey right.

The maid went cunningly in, and acquainted her father and mother, that there was a gentleman without, who appear'd such by his countenance, garb and dress, that fearing to travel farther, being night, and not knowing the way, he desir'd to rest himself until the morning. The parents of the young woman had more respect for our adventurer than to let him travel farther, whereby he might be expos'd to difficulties, civilly admitted him into their house. Rumbold being

127

handsomely entertain'd, was resolv'd to dedicate that night to the charms of his fair and young mistress; but Heaven cross'd his amorous design, and all the stars were against him.

Next morning our adventurer feign'd himself very ill, purely to have a pretence of staying, which he acquainted the daughter with. The old people were vastly loving and courteous, so that as soon as they heard of it, they came to see Rumbold in his chamber, and express'd extraordinary compassion and pity for him. They provided every thing they thought necessary for him. Our adventurer offer'd them money for their services, but they absolutely refused it; and to make them entertain the better opinion of him, he shew'd a great quantity of gold.

Rumbold lay at the farmer's house at least a fortnight in this pretended ill state of health; several doctors had been with him, but not one of them all had knowledge enough to dive into his distemper. During this time he had the charming daughter every night, who, contrary to the custom of most women, did not seem coy and nice in gratifying that passion which was the centre of her hopes. Rumbold fearing too long as illness might give the old people some uneasiness, or cause 'em to suspect him, left off counterfeiting any longer indispositions, and shew'd them some recovery of his strength. When the old people at any time came into his chamber, the main subject of our adventurer's discourse commonly turn'd on the many signal favours he had receiv'd, and that if he liv'd he would gratefully repay them. Being restor'd to his usual strength, he told them that he could never well enough recompence the care and love they had had over him, unless it were by marrying their daughter, who had already won his heart. The parents made many excuses upon this article: the first objection was, that she was but a poor country girl, and the like. However, Rumbold was not so backward to himself but he made several enquiries in a neighbouring town about the circumstances of the farmer, whom he found by the report of every body to be a very wealthy person; and that time had not been more careful in furnishing his head with silver hairs, than he industrious to maintain them by the procuration of a plentiful estate. The girl he pretended to love was the only darling of the good old people; for the father furrow'd the surface of the earth, and chose rather to sell than to eat his better sort of provision, in order to augment and increase her portion. The old farmer thought he had bestow'd his labour to a good purpose, since he had met with a blest opportunity, wherein he should add gentility to his daughter's riches. O! the slaughter of pigs, geese and capons, which, as to some idol, were sacrificed daily to procure our adventurer's favour. As he was not sparing of his food, so was he liberal enough in sending for wine, which he did at the quantity of six bottles at a time; so that the old man was brought to this pass, that he car'd not whether he spent his estate on Rumbold or gave it him; and the daughter was so pleas'd with the person and embraces of our adventurer, that above all other satisfactions in the world she lov'd his company the best. The endearments Rumbold and the daughter had together are inexpressible, and the old parents were never more pleas'd than when they saw them together, which gave our adventurer more opportunities of being with his mistress than he could reasonably hope for or expect. Rumbold's main design was to sift the young woman in relation to the quantity of money her father had, and where it lay. She told him that he had not above five pounds in the house, having two or three days past laid out all his ready money in a purchase. This was no small mortification to our gentleman, who thought it labour lost to stay any longer, when he could not glean the father's harvest, tho' he had cropt the mother's labour, and so resolv'd to be going, but not without one solemn night's taking leave of her. The night being come, she purposely staid up till all the rest were gone to bed. But fortune now had a mind to play our adventurer an ill turn; for he and his mistress being too imprudently hasty in the kitchen, both of them stumbled against two barrels piled one on the other, and fell, and both were so entangled that they could not disengage themselves so soon, but that her father came out crying—'In the name of goodness what is the matter?' And groping about, caught Rumbold by the naked breech. Seeing there was no remedy, he desir'd him to be silent, and not spread his daughter's disgrace; if so, he would shortly make her a recompence. The old man was very much perplex'd, and could not forbear telling his wife of what had past. They both cry'd out, that their daughter was undone; and the daughter was in the same tone unless Rumbold would marry her.

Rumbold, to colour the matter, stay'd about three or four days longer, and at last march'd off incognito, sending her twenty pieces of gold, and a copy of verses, which, as too plain and pertinent to the sweet treatment that had pass'd between them, we shall at present here omit.

Rumbold taking his leave thus abruptly of the farmer and his loving daughter, rode a long time, but met with no body worthy of his notice: being weary, he struck into an inn, and by the time he had thoroughly refresh'd himself, the evening began to approach. Upon this he mounted, and so put on. Passing by a small coppice in a bottom between two hills, a gentleman (as our adventurer suppos'd him) well armed, and handsomely accoutred, started out upon him, and bad him deliver instantly. Rumbold hearing him say so, told him, if he would but have patience he would, and with that drew out a pocket-pistol, and fir'd at him without doing any execution. 'If you are for a little sport,' reply'd the gentleman, 'I'll shew you some instantly'; whereupon drawing a pistol he shot our adventurer into the leg; having so done, with his sword, that hung ready at his wrist, he neatly cut at one blow the reins of Rumbold's bridle, so that he was not able to manage his horse; but he being good at command, and used to the charge, he gave him to understand with the winding of his body what he was to do.—'Come, Sir,' said the adversary, 'have you enough yet?' 'In faith, Sir,' answer'd our adventurer, 'I'll exchange but one pistol more, and if that proves unsuccessful, I'll then submit to your mercy.' Upon this he shot but miss'd his mark, however he kill'd his horse, which instantly fell. The gentleman, notwithstanding this loss, was so nimble, that, before Rumbold could think what to do, he had sheathed his sword in his horse's belly, which made our adventurer come tumbling down too. 'Once more,' said my antagonist, 'we are upon equal terms, and since the obscurity of the place gives us freedom, let us try our courage, one must fall': and upon that with his sword, which was made for cut and thrust, he made a full pass at his body, but he putting it by, closed in with him, and upon the hug threw him with much facility. Our adventurer was surpriz'd at first, which he needed not have done, since his nature (as he understood afterwards) was so prone to it. Having him down, 'Sir,' said he, 'I shall teach you for the future to be careful on whom you set; wherefore now yield, Sir, or I shall compel you.' With much reluctance he did, and ty'd his hands and feet with cords he had for that purpose, and so fell to rifling him. Unbuttoning his coat to find if there was no gold quilted therein, he wonder'd to see a pair of breasts so unexpectedly greater and whiter than any man's; but being intent upon his business, his amazement soon vanish'd out of his thoughts. Coming, after this, to his breeches, which he laid open, his curious search omitted not any place, in which he might suspect the concealment of money; at last, offering to remove his shirt from between his legs, he suddenly cry'd out, and strove to lay his hand there, but could not.—'I

beseech you, Sir, to be civil,' said he. Rumbold imagined that some notable treasure lay conceal'd there, and therefore he pull'd away his shirt, (alias smock) and
found himself not much mistaken.

This unexpected sight so surpriz'd him, that he look'd as if he had been
converted into a statue by the head of some gorgon; but after a little pause he
hastily unbound her, and taking her into his arms, said, 'Pardon me most courageous Amazon, for thus rudely dealing with you; it was nothing but ignorance
that caused this error, for could my dim-sighted soul have distinguish'd what
you were, the great love and respect I bear your sex would have deterr'd me
from contending with you, but I esteem this ignorance of mine as the greatest
happiness, since knowledge in this vase would have depriv'd me of the benefit of
knowing there could be so much valour in a woman. For your sake I shall for
ever retain a very good esteem for the worst of females.' Here our adventurer
paused, upon which she begg'd him not to be too tedious in his expressions, nor
pump for eloquent phrases, alledging where they were, was no proper place to
make orations in: 'But if you will declare yourself,' said she, 'let us go into a place
not far distant from this, better known but to few besides myself.' Rumbold
approv'd well of her advice, and returning what he had taken from her, follow'd
her through several obscure passages, till they came to a wood, where in a place
the sun had not seen since the deluge, stood an house. At our first approach the
servants were all in a hurry who should obey Mrs Virago's commands, for they
all knew her, being no strangers to her disguise, but wonder'd to see St George
and his trusty esquire on foot, neither durst they show themselves inquisitive
presently.

After some short time they were conducted into a very fine apartment,
where embracing one another, they nit an indissoluable tie of friendship. Having
refresh'd themselves with what the house afforded, they began to discourse
together with the same familiarity as if they had been born together. Rumbold
observing her frankness, press'd her to tell him what she was, and what manner
of life she led. 'Sir,' said she, 'I cannot deny your request, wherefore to satisfy you,
know that I was the daughter of a sword-cutler: in my younger days my mother
would have taught me to handle a needle, but my martial spirit gainsaid all
persuasions to that purpose; I could never endure to be among utensils of the
kitchen, but spent most of my time in my father's shop, taking wonderful delight

131

in handling the war-like instruments he made: to take a sword in my hand well mounted and brandish it, was reckon'd by me among the chief of my recreations. Being about a dozen years of age, I studied by all ways imaginable how I might make myself acquainted with a fencing-master. Time brought my desires to their compliment; for such a one as I wish'd for accidentally came into my father's shop to have his blade furbished; and fortune so order'd it, there was none to answer but myself. Having given him that satisfaction he desired, tho' not expecting it from me, among other questions, I ask'd him, whether he was not a professor of that noble science? (for I guest so much by his postures, looks, and expressions.) He told me, he was a well-wisher to it. Being glad of this opportunity, desiring him to conceal my intentions, I begg'd the favour of him to give me some instructions how I should manage a sword. At first he seem'd amaz'd at my proposal; but perceiving I was in earnest, he granted my petition, allotting me such a time to come to him as was most convenient. I became so expert at back-sword and single rapier in a little time, that I needed not his assistance any longer, my parents not in the least mistrusting any such thing.

132   'I shall wave what exploits I did by the help of my disguise, and only tell you, that when I arriv'd to the age of fifteen years, an inn-keeper married me, and carried me into the country. For two years we liv'd very peaceably and comfortably together, but at length the violent and imperious temper of my husband made me shew my natural humour. Once a week we seldom miss'd of a combat betwixt us, which frequently prov'd so sharp, that it was a wonder if my husband came off with a single broken pate; by which the gaping wounds of our discontents and differences being not presently salved up, they became in a manner incurable. I was not much inclin'd to love him, because he was of a mean darstardly spirit, and ever hated that a dunghill cock should tread a hen of the game. Being stinted likewise of money, my life grew altogether comfortless, and I look'd on my condition as insupportable; wherefore as the only remedy or expedient to mitigate my vexatious troubles, I contriv'd a way how I might sometimes take a purse. I judged this resolution safe enough, if I were not taken in the very fact, for who could suspect me to be a robber, wearing abroad mens apparel upon such designs, but at home that which was more agreeable and suitable to my sex; besides, no one could have better encouragement and conveniency than myself, for, keeping an inn, who is more proper to have in custody

what charge my guests brought into my house than myself? Or if committed to my husband's tutelage, I could not fail to inform myself of the richness of the booty: besides, the landlady is the person whose company is most desired, before whom they are no ways scrupulous to relate which way they are a going, and frequently what the affair was that led them that way.

'Courage, I knew, I wanted not (be you my impartial judge, Sir) what then could hinder me from being successful in such an enterprize? Being thus resolv'd, I soon provided my necessary habiliments for these my contrivances, and never miscarried in any of them till now: instead of riding to market, or travelling five or fix miles about such a business, (the usual pretences with which I blinded my husband) I would, when out of sight, take a contrary road to this house (in which we now are) and metamorphose myself, and being fitted at all points, pad incontroulably, coming off always victoriously. Not long since my husband had about one hundred pounds due to him about some twenty miles from his habitation, and design'd such a day for receiving it. Glad I was to hear of this, resolving now to be reveng'd on him for all those injuries and churlish outrages he had committed against me: I knew very well which way he went, and understood the time of his coming home: upon which I way-laid him at his return; and fortunately, as I would have it, he did not make me wait above three hours for him. I let him pass by me, knowing that by the swiftness of my horse I cou'd easily overtake him; and so I did, riding with him a mile or two before I cou'd do my intended business. At last looking about me, I saw the coast clear on every side, wherefore riding up close to him, and taking hold on his bridle, I clapt a pistol to his breast, commanding him to deliver, or he was a dead man. This imperious don seeing death before his face, had like to have sav'd me the labour, by dying voluntarily without compulsion, and so amaz'd was he at his being so suddenly surpriz'd, that he look'd like an apparition, or one lately risen from the dead. "Sirrah," said I, "be expeditious"; but a dead palsy had so seiz'd every part of him, that his eyes were incapable of directing his hands to his pockets; but I soon recall'd his spirits by two or three blows with the flat of my sword, which so awaken'd him out of the deep lethargy he was in, that, with much submission, he deliver'd all his money. After I had dismounted him, and cut the reins of his bridle and girts, I baisted him so soundly, till I had made almost jelly of his bones, and Egyptian mummy of his flesh. "Now you rogue," said I, "I am even with you, have a care the next time how you strike a woman, (your wife I mean) for none but such as dare not fight a man will lift up his hand against the weaker vessel. Now you see what it is to provoke them, for if irritated too much, they are restless till they accomplish their revenge to satisfaction; I have a good mind to end your wicked courses with your life, inhuman varlet, but that I am loth to be hang'd for nothing, I mean for such a worthless man. Farewel, this money shall serve me to purchase wine to drink. Healths to the confusion of such rascally and mean-spirited things." And so I left him.'

She was about to proceed on farther with her rencounters and exploits, when word was brought her up, that two gentlemen below desired to speak with her; and so begging our adventurer's excuse, she went down, and in a little time return'd with them: she made an apology to me for doing so, adding, that if she had committed a crime herein, my future knowledge of those persons wou'd extenuate it: by their effeminate countenances I cou'd not miss of judging who they were, I mean females.

What the female warrior had advanc'd was too true, for having discoursed to her some time, Rumbold grew so well-pleas'd with his new acquaintance, that he resolv'd to spend some time in their conversation and company. At the time of going to bed they were all conducted into one chamber, where two beds were; but what satisfaction they enjoy'd there, we leave to the thoughts of our candid readers, who, we hope, can construe as well as we. In fine, our adventurer rising betimes in the morning, and finding his three females fast asleep, examin'd the pockets of the two last, out of which taking a dozen guineas, the very sum he had return'd to the first, he got his horse, and rode off.

Rumbold was a very merry, facetious and comical sort of a fellow, as appears by the following relation. Being one time at an inn in Buckinghamshire, and hearing how unmercifully the hostlers would cheat the poor horses of their provender, he privately went into the stable, and hid himself under the manger. A little while after the hostler came also into the stable to feed Rumbold's mare, and no sooner had he put the oats and beans into the manger, and laid down his sieve, but he sweeps them into a canvass-bag fix'd under one corner of the manger, just like a net-bag hanging under a billiard-table, and went his way. Rumbold comes from his private recess, and went into the kitchen again, when after dinner, seeming to go away, and calling for the reckoning, he ask'd the

134

hostler, 'what corn he had given his mare?' He reply'd, 'All which he had order'd him, nay, the gentleman he din'd with saw him bring it through the kitchen.' Rumbold said to him, 'Do not tell me a lie, for I shall ask my mare presently.' This saying put all the strange gentlemen with him into admiration; but above all, the inn-keeper ask'd him, 'if his mare could speak?' 'Yes,' said Rumbold.—''Tis,' reply'd the landlord, 'impossible'.—'Not at all,' answer'd Rumbold, 'for when I was at the University of Leyden in Holland, I studied magick, or the black-art, and afterwards it being my misfortune to marry a most prodigious scolding wife, I led such an uneasy life with her, that to be rid of her vexatious company, I, by my great skill in the said art, transform'd her into a mare. So fetch my mare hither, and you shall see whether the hostler has done her justice.' Accordingly the mare was fetch'd, when Rumbold striking her on the belly, she laid her mouth to his ear through custom, just as the pigeon did to Mahomet's.—'Why, there now,' says Rumbold, 'did not I tell you, Sir, that the hostler had cheated her.'—'Why,' said the landlord, 'what does she say?' 'Say?' answer'd Rumbold, 'Why, she says that your hostler has flung it into a bag plac'd at one corner of the manger.' Hereupon the landlord and his guests went into the stable, and searching the manger, found the bag of corn at one corner of it, for which he begg'd a thousand pardons, and presently turn'd the hostler away. But you must understand, that the inn-keeper's wife likewise being a very scolding woman, and asking Rumbold, 'whether he could turn her into a mare too?' Upon assuring him he cou'd, he gave him fifty guineas. The operation was immediately put in execution, with this caution, that the landlord, whatever he saw transacted, must not speak a word, for if he did he would spoil all. So bringing the woman into a large room above stairs, Rumbold with a piece of chalk, drew a large circle on the floor; in which placing himself, and the person to be metamorphosed, or transform'd into a beast of carriage, he made her strip to the skin, then making her lie on her hands and knees, he went to copulate with her backwards; at which the husband crying out, (but wou'd not venture his carcass into the circle, because several large and strange figures and characters were chalk'd round it) 'Damn you, Sir, hold, what a plague are you going to cuckold me before my face?' 'Why,' says Rumbold, 'look there now, you have broke the power of my charm by untimely speaking.' So the landlord was contented to lose his money rather than his wife transform'd by grafting a pair of horns on his head.

135

Something like the former part of the foregoing paragraph occurs in Robin Hood's 'Life'; the reader, by comparing them together may observe the variation: however, 'tis not impossible for two persons at different times to put a like scheme in execution, which is the reason that has induc'd us to insert it here, with the appendix of the inn-keeper's wife's transfiguration, as pretended to be done by our adventurer, which, however, improbable, we ask pardon for placing here, as Captain Smith and other biographers, of the low class, have inserted it in their accounts.

Rumbold having a long time observ'd a goldsmith in Lombard-Street to be very intent in counting several bags of money, was resolved to have a share out of some of them; but, having tried several essays, still came off disappointed. He had several rings about him which he had got by robbing, one of which had a very fine diamond set in it. Money being wanting, and so many disappointments crossing his desires, he went to the goldsmith's to sell him the ring, in company with a servant he kept. On entring the shop, he pull'd the ring off his finger, and ask'd him what it was worth? The goldsmith looking on him, and then on the ring, hop'd to make the ring his own for a small matter; and seeing our adventurer (who had disguis'd himself in a plain country dress) believ'd that he had little skill in diamonds, and that this came accidentally into his possession, and that he might purchase it very easily, wherefore being doubtful what to answer as to the price, told the countryman that the worth of it was uncertain, for he could not directly tell whether it was a right or a counterfeit one. 'As for that,' said our pretended countryman, 'I believe it is a right one, and dare warrant it; and indeed I intend to sell it, and therefore would know what you intend to give me for it.' 'Truly,' reply'd the goldsmith, 'it may be worth ten pounds'; 'yes, and more money,' said the countryman; 'not much more,' answered the goldsmith, 'for look you here,' said he, 'here is a ring, which I will warrant is much better than your's, and I will also warrant it to be a good diamond, and I will sell it you for twenty pounds.' This the goldsmith said supposing that the countryman, who came to sell, had no skill, inclination, or money to buy; but our pretended countryman believing that the goldsmith only said this, thinking to draw him on to part with his own ring the more easily, and by that means cheat him, resolved if he could to be too wise for the goldsmith, wherefore taking both the rings into his hands through a pretence of comparing them together, he thus said, 'I am sure mine is a right diamond,' 'and so is mine' replied the goldsmith, and said the countryman 'shall I have it for twenty pound?' 'yes,' replied the goldsmith: 'But' said he, 'I suppose you came to sell and not to buy; and since you shall see I will be a good customer, I will give you fifteen pounds for yours': 'Nay,' replied the countryman, 'since I have the choice to buy or sell, I will never refuse a good pennyworth, as I think this is, therefore master goldsmith I will keep my own, and give you money for your's,' 'where is it,' said the goldsmith hastily? and endeavouring then to seize on his ring, 'hold a blow there' said Rumbold, 'here's your money, but the ring I will keep': the goldsmith seeing himself thus caught, fluttered and flounced like a madman, and Rumbold pulling out a little purse, told down twenty pieces of gold, and said, 'here shopkeeper, here's your money, but I hope you will allow me eighteen pence a piece in exchange for my gold.' 'Tell not me of exchange, but give me my ring,' said the goldsmith. 'It is mine,' said the countryman, 'for I have bought it, and paid for it, and have witness of my bargain.' All this would not serve the goldsmith's turn, but he curs'd and swore that Rumbold, the pretended countryman, came to cheat him, and his ring he would have, and at the noise several people came about the shop, but he was so perplex'd that he could not tell his tale, and at length a constable came, and although the goldsmith knew not to what purpose, yet before a Justice he would go. Rumbold seem'd content, and therefore before a Justice they went together; when they came there, the goldsmith, who was the plaintiff, began his tale, and said, that the countryman had taken a diamond ring from him worth one hundred pounds, and would give him but twenty pounds for it. 'Have a care,' replied Rumbold, 'for if you charge me with taking a ring from you, I suppose that is stealing, and if you say so, I shall vex you more than I have yet done'; and then he told the Justice the whole story as here related, which was then a very plain case, and for proof of the matter, our pretended country gentleman's man was a witness. The goldsmith hearing this, alledged, that he believed the country gentleman and his man were both impostors and cheats. To this our adventurer reply'd as before, that he had best have a care he did not make his case worse, and bring an old house over his head by slandering him thus; for it was well known that he was a gentleman of three hundred pounds per annum, and lived at a place not above twenty miles from London, and that he being desirous to sell a ring, came to his shop for that purpose, but he would have cheated him, but it prov'd that he only made a rod

137

for his own breech, and what he intended to him was fallen upon himself: thus did our adventurer make good his case and the Justice seeing there was no injustice done, dismiss'd him, but order'd that his neighbour the goldsmith should have the twenty pieces of gold for twenty pound, though they were worth more in exchange, and this was all the satisfaction he had.

Rumbold had a mighty itching after the goldsmith's money in Lombard-Street; he would not pass through that street, and hear those tradesmen telling their sums, but his hands longed to be feeling of them. He had a boy that constantly attended him, who, every time his master had a mind to make some advantage to himself, went into a goldsmith's shop, took up an handful of money, and then letting it all fall down on the counter, ran out. Once on a time this boy performed this trick, the servants in the shop ran after him, and taxed him with stealing some of the money. Rumbold, who always vindicated his youngster, bad them take care what they said, and positively affirm'd that his boy had not taken a farthing, and must be so plain with them, as to tell them, that the goldsmith should pay for it. Hereupon they fell to hot words, and the goldsmith calling our adventurer a shirking fellow, said, he would have both him and the boy sent to Newgate for robbing him, and that in conclusion, he must, and should pay for it. At first our adventurer desired to know with what sum they pretended to charge the boy; they said they knew not, but that he had taken money from a heap they were telling, and which was a hundred pounds. Rumbold hearing them say thus, told them, that he would stay the telling of it, and then they might judge who had the abuse. They were content with it, and accordingly went to telling. Half an hour had dispatch'd that matter, and then they found all their money was right to a farthing; the goldsmith seeing this, ask'd our adventurer's pardon for the affront they had done him, saying it was a mistake. Rumbold answered to this, that he must pay for his prating; and that being a person of quality, he would not put up with the affront, and that he must expect to hear further from him. The goldsmith seeing our adventurer hot, was as cholerick as he, and so they parted for that time. Rumbold, the next day got the goldsmith to be arrested in an action of defamation, and the serjeant who arrested him being well feed by our adventurer, told the goldsmith, that he had better by far compound the matter, for the gentleman he had injured was a person of quality, and would not put it up, but make him pay soundly for it, if he proceeded any farther. The goldsmith being desirous of quiet, hearkened to his counsel, and agreed to give ten pounds; but that would not be taken, but twenty pounds was given to our adventurer, and so the business was made up for the present.

Rumbold having got some of the goldsmith's money, was determined to have more, or venture hard for it; wherefore having again given instructions to his boy what to do, he made several journeys to the goldsmith's, walking by his door to watch an opportunity; at length he found one; for seeing the servants telling a considerable quantity of gold, he gave the sign to his boy, who presently went in, and clapping his hand on the heap, took up, and brought away a full handful, and coming to his master, gave it him; neither did the boy make so much haste out of the shop, but that he could hear a stranger who was in the shop receiving of money, say to the apprentice, 'Why do not you stop the boy?' 'No,' said the apprentice, 'I do not mean it, I know him well enough, my master paid sauce lately for stopping of him'; and so they continued telling of their money.

Rumbold being intimately acquainted with a jeweller in Foster-Lane, whom he often helped to the sale of rings and jewels, which made his credit good with him, went one time into his work-room, and chancing to spy a very rich jewel, he told him, that he could help him to the sale thereof. 'My Lady such an one having spoke to me,' said he, 'about such a thing.' The jeweller, glad of the opportunity, delivered it to our adventurer at such a price to sell for him. But Rumbold only carried it to another workman, to have another made like it with counterfeit stones. Before he went, he ask'd if the lady dislik'd it, whether he might leave it with his wife or servant: 'Ay, ay,' says he, 'either will be sufficient.' Rumbold was forced to watch a whole day to see when he went out, and being gone, presently went to the shop, and enquired of the wife for her husband, she answered him that he was but just gone. 'Well, Madam,' said he, 'you can do my business as well as he, it is only to deliver these stones into your custody,' and so he went his way. Not long after, Rumbold met the jeweller in the street with displeasing looks. 'Sir,' said he, 'I thought a friend would not have served me so,' but our adventurer deny'd it stifly; whereupon he was very angry, and told him he would prosecute him. Rumbold seem'd not to value his threats, and so left him. Rumbold was not gone many paces before he met with a friend, who complain'd to him, that he had lost a very valuable locket of his wife's, it being stolen from her. Rumbold was glad to hear of such a circumstance that had fallen out so favourably to his present purpose, he ask'd him to give him a description of it, which he did punctually. 'Now,' said Rumbold, 'what will you give me, if I tell you where it is.' 'Any thing in reason.' 'Then go to such a shop in Foster Lane (the same shop where he had cheated the man of his ring) and there ask'd peremptorily for it, for I was there at such a time, and saw it; nay, he would have had me help'd him to a customer for it: mean time, I'll stay at the Star tavern for you.' Away he went and demanded his locket. The jeweller deny'd he had any such thing (as well he might.) Upon this, Rumbold advised him to have a warrant for him, and to fetch him before a Justice of the Peace; and that he, and the person who was with him, would swear it. The goldsmith was instantly seized on by a constable, and as soon as he saw who they were that would swear against him, desired the gentleman to drink a glass of wine, and then ordered him satisfaction. But Rumbold had so ordered the business that it would not be taken, unless he would give all three general releases. The goldsmith knowing the danger that might ensue to life and estate if he persisted, consented to the proposal.

Rumbold walking one time in the fields with an attendant or two, who should be constantly bare before him, if in company with any person of quality, but otherwise, 'kind fellow well met': he was got as far as Hackney before he knew he was, for his thoughts were busied in forming designs, and his wit was contriving how to put them into execution. Casting his eye on one side of him, he saw the prettiest built and well situated house that ever his eyes beheld. He had immediately a covetous desire to be master thereof; he was then, as fortune would have it, in a very handsome dress. He walk'd but a little way farther before he found out a plot to accomplish his desires; and thus it was: he return'd and knock'd at the gate, and demanded of the servant whether his master was within? He understood he was, and thereupon desir'd to speak with him. The gentleman came out to him himself, and desir'd him to walk in. After Rumbold had made a general apology, he told him his business, which was only to request the favour of him, that he might have the privilege to bring a workman to survey his house, and to take his dimensions thereof, because he was so well pleas'd with the building, that he earnestly desir'd to have another built exactly after that pattern. The gentleman could do no less than grant him so much civility. Coming home, he went to a carpenter, telling him he was about buying a house at Hackney, and that he would have him go along with him, to give him (in private) the estimate. Accordingly they went and found the gentleman at home; who entertain'd our adventurer kindly as a stranger. In the mean time the carpenter took an exact account of the buts and bounds of the house on paper, which was as much as he desired at that time.

Paying the carpenter well, he dismiss'd, him and by that paper had a lease drawn with a very great fine (mentioned to have been paid) at a small rent. Witnesses he could not want to his deed; and shortly after he demanded posses-sion. The gentleman thinking our adventurer out of his wits, only laugh'd at him. Rumbold commenced a suit of law against him, and produc'd his creatures to swear to his sealing and delivery of the lease, and the carpenter's evidence, with many other probable circumstances to corroborate his cause; whereupon he had a verdict. The gentleman by this time understanding who our adventurer was, thought it safer to compound with him, and lose something rather than all.

Another time putting on one of the best suits of cloaths he had, he went to a scrivener in Bow-Lane, and acquainted him how he had a present occasion for an hundred pounds. He demanded the names of his securities. Rumbold told him where they liv'd, being persons of eminent worth, (but our adventurer knew they were out of town at that juncture) and desir'd to make enquiry, but to be private in managing of it. The scrivener accordingly went as he had desired him, and found them by report to be what they were, really able and sufficient men. Two or three days after Rumbold call'd upon him to know whether he might have the money upon the security propounded? He told him that he might on bringing the persons, and fix'd a day for meeting. According to the day he came with two of his accomplices, dress'd like rich citizens, who personated such persons to the life, that the scrivener could not entertain the least suspicion. The money being ready, he told it over, and put it into a bag; upon which our adven-turer and his insignificant bonds-men sealed the writing, leaving the scrivener to another enquiry after them, whom, if he did not mean, 'twas very confidently to be believ'd that he could never find them, by reason of the several names they went by. It chanced that Rumbold's forged name was the same with that of a gentleman's in Surrey, who was a great purchaser, which our adventurer came to know by being accidentally in his company the next night after he had cheated the credulous scrivener, understanding likewise the exact place of his abode, and as the D—l would have it his Christian name was the same as well as his sirname with that of our adventurer's, which he had borrowed. Upon this he went to the scrivener again, and told him that now he had a fair opportunity of benefiting himself very much by a purchase, provided he wou'd assist him two hundred pounds more: 'But, Sir,' said he, 'take notice (in a careless and generous frankness) that it is out of a particular regard and respect to you that you might profit by me, that I come again, neither will I give you any other security than my own bond, tho' I did otherwise before; but if you will be satisfy'd as to my estate, pray let your servant go to such a place in Surrey, there is a piece of gold to bear his charges, and I will satisfy you farther for the loss of time occasion'd by sending him.' He being very greedy of gain, very officiously promised to do what I requir'd, and would speedily give me an answer. Imagining what time his servent would return, Rumbold repaired to him again, and understood from him by the sequel, that he had receiv'd as much satisfaction as in reason any man wou'd desire. Upon this he procured the two hundred pounds upon his own bond; which was accordingly paid him.

Rumbold supported himself by these cheats a considerable time, tho' unlike his companions, he was never known to be very extravagant. He had amassed together a matter of eight hundred pounds clear, and resolving to leave off in time, put the money into the hand of a banker a friend of his, in order to live the remainder of his days comfortably on the interest thereof; he had the mortification, within a month or two, to hear that his trustee was march'd off not only with his money, but a great many thousand pounds more of other peoples; so that being reduc'd to an impoverish'd state, he was forc'd, tho' somewhat against his inclination, to betake himself again to his former irregular courses, several merry pranks of whom the sequel will soon discover.

Rumbold having a design a robbing a gentleman's house near Uxbridge, put up at an inn in that town, in order, on the first opportunity, to put his scheme in practice. Several companies were in the house, and lodg'd there; and it being the time of long nights, much of that tedious time was spent in gaming and merry conversation with one another. All companies join'd with pastime; but it growing late, they that were weary and sleepy dropp'd away to bed; among the rest, a man who had a very handsome wife went to bed, and his lodging was in a chamber where there was another bed. The man being in bed laid his wearing cloaths upon him, and putting out the candle went to sleep. A little time after our adventurer, who were to lie in the bed in the same chamber, came up, and walking about, a conceit came into his head, that it was probable he might have a she-bedfellow, and in order thereto he thus carry'd on his device; he put off his own cloaths, and laid them very orderly on the bed where the man was asleep, first taking off those of his chamber-fellows, and when he had done, he very fairly spread them on the bed he was to lie in; having done thus, he went to bed and put out his candle, and expecting the event, which fell out according to his hopes, for not long after up came the woman intending to go to bed to her husband, undress'd herself, and seeing, and very well knowing her husband's cloaths, believing that to be a sufficient sign of her husband's being there, not looking on the face, which was purposely hid, she put out the candle and went to bed to our adventurer; who altho' he pretended to be then asleep, yet he did her right before morning, for she still supposing it was her husband, gave him free liberty to do what he would. Her bedfellow, tho' he had taken much pains, and was weary, yet towards morning, considering that if this matter was disco-ver'd, he might have sower sauce to his sweet meat, studied and contrived how to come off as well as he had come on, and therefore turning to his bedfellow and kissing her, &c. as a farewel, he, pretending to rise and make water, went out of the bed; he soon found his way to his chamber-fellow's bed's-side, and there took off his cloaths, dress'd himself and departed. The woman missing her bedfellow, whom all the while she had took for her husband, wonder'd much what was become of him, and lay and studied in great confusion without knowing either what to do or say; at length she began to mistrust she had wrong'd her bedfellow, especially when she began to consider with herself that her husband was not wont to be so kind: when she was partly sensible of the mistake, she could not tell how to think of a remedy; if she should arise and go into the other bed, she might chance to be mistaken again; and therefore in this confusion she knew not what to do. While she was in these thoughts, a maid with a candle appear'd, who passing through the room, gave her a clear view that her husband was in the other bed; accordingly she resolv'd to take her cloaths and go to bed to her husband; but he who had slept hard all night, was now awaken'd with the noise of the maid's passing through the chamber, and there-fore he crept out of bed, and felt for a chamber-pot; at length having found one,

143

and us'd it, and going to return to bed where he had lain, his wife then took the opportunity to call to him, saying, 'My Dear, whither are you going? You mistake your bed.' 'No, sure,' said the man, 'Where are you?' 'Here,' reply'd she. He hearing her voice, soon found out where she was, but could not presently be persuaded that he had lain there all night. 'You shall see that by and by,' said she, 'when you can see your cloaths on this bed.' 'If it be so, then you are in the right,' answer'd he. In fine, getting him to sleep again, she, in the interim, got his cloaths laid on the bed; and daylight coming on, and he seeing them there, was satisfy'd. Thus was this Christmas adventure ended. She, towards one in the morning, made great enquiry after her bedfellow, but no tidings could be given of him.

Another time Rumbold coming early one morning to an inn in the country, called for a flaggon of beer, and desir'd a private room, 'for,' said he, 'I have company coming to me, and we have business together.' The tapster accordingly shows him a room, and brings him a flaggon of beer, and with it a silver cup worth three pounds. Rumbold drank off his beer, and call'd for another flaggon, and at the same time desir'd the landlord to bear him company. The landlord seeing him alone, sat and talk'd with him about state affairs till they were both weary, and the landlord was ready to leave him. 'Well,' said our adventurer, 'I see my company will not come, and therefore I will not stay any longer.' Neither did he; but having drank up his beer, he call'd to pay: 'Fourpence,' said the tapster; 'There it is,' answer'd our adventurer, laying it down, and so he went out of the room. The tapster staid behind to bring away the flaggon and silver cup; yet tho' he found the flaggon, the cup was not to be found; wherefore running hastily out of the room, he cry'd 'Stop the man.' Rumbold was not in such haste but that he quickly stopt of himself; he was not quite gone out of the doors, and therefore soon return'd to the bar; where when he was come: 'Well,' said he, 'what is the matter? What would you have?' 'The cup,' answer'd the tapster, 'that I brought to you.' 'I left it in the room,' reply'd Rumbold. 'I cannot find it,' answer'd the tapster; and at this noise the landlord appear'd, who hearing what was the matter, said, 'I am sure the cup was there but just now, for I drank out of it.' 'Ay, and it is there for me,' reply'd our adventurer. 'Look then farther,' said the landlord. The tapster did so, but neither high nor low could he find the cup. 'Well then,' said the landlord, 'if it be gone you must pay for it, countryman, for you must either have it or know of its going, and therefore you must pay for it.' 'Not I indeed,' reply'd our adventurer, 'you see I have none of it, I have not been out of your house, nor no body has been with me, how then can I have it? You may search me.' The landlord immediately caus'd him to be search'd, but there was no cup to be found: however the landlord was resolved not to lose his cup so, and therefore he sent for a constable, and charged him with our adventurer, and threaten'd him with the Justice. All this would not do, and Rumbold told him, 'that threaten'd folks live long,' and if he would go before a Justice, he was ready to bear him company to him. The landlord was more and more perplex'd at this, and seeing he could not have his cup, 'nor nothing confess'd,' before the Justice they went: when they came, the landlord told the story as truly as it was, and our pretended countryman made the same answer there as he had done before to the landlord: the Justice was perplex'd, not knowing how to do justice: here was a cup lost, and Rumbold did not deny but he had it, but gone it was, and although Rumbold was pursued, yet he did not fly; he had no body with him, and therefore it could not be convey'd away by confederacy; and for his own part he had been, and was again searched, but no such thing found about him, and he in all respect pleaded innocency.—This tho' consider'd, and weighed in the balance of justice, he could not think that our adventurer had it, and therefore to commit him would be injustice: he consider'd all he cou'd, and was inclin'd to favour the countryman, who was altogether a stranger, and he believed innocent, especially when he consider'd what a kind of person the landlord was, of whose life and conversation he had both heard and known enough, and cause him to believe that it might be possible that all this might be a trick of the landlord's to cheat our adventurer, and therefore he gave his judgement, that he did not believe by the evidence that was given that the countryman had the cup, and that he would not commit him, unless the landlord would lay and swear point-blank felony to his charge, and of that he desir'd the landlord to beware. The landlord seeing how the affair was like to go, said no more, but that he left it to Mr Justice, who being of the opinion above-mention'd, discharg'd Rumbold, and advised the landlord to let him hear no more of such matters, and if he could not secure his plate, and know what company he had deliver'd it to, then to keep it up. The landlord thank'd the Justice for his advice, and so departed, our pretended countryman going about his business, and he returning home being heartily vex'd at his loss, and the carriage of the whole affair, which was neither for his profit nor credit, but he was forc'd to sit down

145

with the loss, being extremely uneasy at thinking which way he should lose the cup. He threw away some money upon a cunning-man to know what was become of it, but all he could tell him was, that he would hear of it again, and so he did shortly after, tho' it was to his further cost, and to little purpose.

He had some occasion to go to the market-town during the time of the assizes, and there seeing the prisoners brought to their trials, among others he espied Rumbold, whom he had charged with the silver cup. He enquired what was his crime, and was told it was for picking of a pocket. 'Nay then,' said the landlord, 'probably I may hear of my cup again'; and therefore, when the trial was over, and the prisoners carried back to the gaol, he went and enquired for our adventurer, to whose presence he was soon brought. 'Oh Lord, Master! How do you do? Who thought to have seen you here? I believe you have not met with so good friends in this country as you did at our town of our justice, but let that pass.—Come, let us drink together.' Hereupon a jug of ale was call'd for and some tobacco, which they very lovingly drank off, and smok'd together; which done, said the landlord to our adventurer, 'I would gladly be resolv'd in one point, which I question not but you can do.' 'I suppose you mean,' said Rumbold, 'about the old business of the silver cup you lost.'—'Yes,' said the Landlord; 'and the losing of it does not so much vex me, as the manner how it was lost, and therefore,' continued he, 'if you would do me the kindness to give me satisfaction what became of it, I do protest I will acquit you altho' you are directly guilty.' 'No, that will not do,' reply'd Rumbold, 'there is somewhat else in the case.' 'Well then,' said the Landlord, 'if you will tell me, I will give you ten shillings to drink.' 'Ready money does very well in a prison,' said our adventurer, 'and will prevail much; but how shall I be assured that you will not prosecute me, if I should chance to be concern'd': 'For that,' reply'd the landlord, 'I can give you no other warrant than my oath, which I will inviolably keep.' 'Well then,' said Rumbold, 'down with the merry grigs, let me handle the money, and I'll be very true to you, and as for your charging me with it I fear you not.' The landlord being big with expectation to know how this clean conveyance was wrought, soon laid down the ten shillings, and then our countryman thus proceeded: 'I must confess that I know which way your cup went, but when you charg'd me with it I had it not, neither was it out of the room, and I must tell you thus, that if you had sought narrowly you might have found it, but it was not there long after. We who live by our wits must act by policy more than down-right strength, and this cannot be done without confederates, and I had such in the management of this affair, for I left the cup fastned with soft wax under the middle of the board of the table where I drank; which place of the table, by reason it was cover'd with a cloth, as you may remember it was, it could not well be seen, and and therefore you and your servants miss'd it: you know that very willingly I went with you to the Justice; and whilst we were gone, those friends and confederates of mine, whom I had appointed, and who knew the room and every thing else, went into the house, and into the same room, where they found the silver cup, and without the least suspicion went fairly off with it; and at a place appointed we met, and there acquainted one another with our adven-tures, and what purchases we had made; we equally shared them between us.' The landlord at the hearing this discourse was extremely surpriz'd, altho' fully satisfy'd; 'but yet,' said he, 'I would be resolv'd one question, which is this; how, if we had found it where you had put it whilst you were there?' 'Why, truly,' said Rumbold, 'then you would have charg'd me with nothing, and I would have put it off with a jest; and if that would not have done, the most you could have done would have been only to have kick'd and beaten me, and those things we of our quality must venture: you know the old proverb, "Nothing venture, nothing have"; and, "faint heart never won fair lady". And we have this other proverb to help us; "Fortune favours the bold", as it commonly does those of our quality, and she did me, I thank her, in that attempt.' Rumbold thus descanted upon his actions, and the landlord finding no likelihood of getting his cup or any thing else of our adventurer, return'd home.

147

We shall give our readers now the last adventure of Rumbold which he perform'd upon this mortal stage. It is this:

Our adventurer in company with two or three more cheats going together, saw a countryman who had a purse of money in his hand; they had observ'd him to draw it to pay for some gingerbread he had bought on the road; wherefore they clos'd with him, and endeavour'd to nip his bung, pick his pocket, but could not, for he knowing he was in a dangerous place, and among as dangerous company, put his purse of money into his breeches, which being close at the knees, secur'd it from falling out, and besides he was very sly in having any body come too near him. Our practitioners in the art of thieving seeing this would not do, set their wits to working farther, and having all their tools ready about them, taking a convenient time and place, one of them goes before and drops a letter; another of our adventurers who had joined himself to the countryman, seeing it lie fairly for the purpose, says to him, 'Look you, what is here?' But altho' the countryman did stoop to take it up, yet our adventurer was too nimble for him in that, and, having it in hand, said, 'Here is somewhat else besides a letter': 'I cry half,' said the countryman. 'Well,' said Rumbold, 'you stoop indeed as well as I, but I have it; but however I'll be fair with you, let us see what it is, and whether it is worth the dividing'; and thereupon he breaks open the letter, and there sees a fair chain or necklace of gold. 'Good fortune,' says Rumbold, 'if this be right gold.' 'How shall we know that,' reply'd the countryman, 'let us see what the letter says'; which being short, and to the purpose, spoke thus:

> Brother John,
>
> I have here sent you back this Necklace of Gold you have sent me, not for any Dislike I have to it, but my Wife is covetous, and would have a bigger; this comes not to above seven Pounds, and she would have one of ten Pounds, therefore pray get it chang'd for one of that Price, and send it by the Bearer to your loving Brother,
>
> Jacob Thornton.

'Nay then, we have good luck,' said the cheating dog our adventurer; 'but I hope,' continued he to the countryman, 'you will not expect a full share, for you know I found it, and besides, if we should divide it, I know not how to break it in pieces but I doubt it would spoil it, therefore I had rather have my share in money.' 'Well,' said the countryman, 'I'll give you your share in money, provided I may have a full share.' 'That you shall,' said Rumbold, 'and therefore I must have of you three pounds ten shillings, the price in all being as you see seven pounds.' 'Ay,' but said the countryman, (thinking to be too cunning for our adventurer) 'it may be worth seven pound in money in all, fashion and all, but we must not value that, but only the gold, therefore I think three pounds in money is better than half the chain, and so much I'll give you if you'll let me have it.' 'Well, I'm contented' said Rumbold, but then you shall give me a pint of wine over and above.' To this the countryman also agreed, and to a tavern they went, where

Rumbold receiv'd the three pounds, and the countryman the chain, who believ'd he had risen that day with his arse upwards, because he had met with so good fortune. They drank off their wine, and were going away, but Rumbold having not yet done with him, intended to get the rest of the money from him, offered him his pint of wine, which the countryman accepted of; but before they had drank it off, in comes another of the same tribe, who asked whether such a man, naming one, were there? 'No,' said the bar-keeper. Rumbold and the countryman sitting near the other cheat all the while, asked of the enquirer, 'Did not you enquire for such a man?' 'Yes,' said the enquirer. 'Why,' said Rumbold, 'I can tell you this news of him, that it will not be long before he comes hither, for I met him as I came in, and he appointed me to come in here and stay for him.' 'Well, then 'tis best for me to stay,' said the enquirer; 'but,' continued he, 'it would be more proper for us to take a larger room, for we cannot stir ourselves in this.' 'Agreed,' said Rumbold; so the reckoning was paid, and they agreed to take a larger room, leaving word at the bar, that if any enquiry should be made for them, there they should find them; accordingly they went into another room, and the countryman having done his business, gave signs of going away. 'No,' said Rumbold, 'I beg you would stay and keep us company, it shall not cost you any thing.' 'Well then,' said the countryman, 'I am content to stay a little.' They being now entred into their room, called for a quart of wine, and drank it off. 'What shall we do to spend time,' said the last cheat? 'for I am weary of staying for this man, are you sure you are not mistaken?' 'No,' said the other. One of them upon this pretended to walk a turn round the room, and coming to the window, behind a cushion, finds a pack of cards, which indeed he himself had laid there: 'Look you here,' said he to the countryman, and the others, 'I have found some tools, now we may go to work and spend our time, if you will play.' 'Not I,' said the countryman, 'I'll not play'; 'then I will,' said Rumbold, 'but not for money.' 'Why then,' said the other, 'for sixpence to be spent, and the game shall be Putt.' They being agreed, and the countryman being made overseer of the game, fell to playing, and the countryman's first acquaintance had the better of it, winning twelve games to the other's four. 'Come,' said he, 'what shall we do with all this drink? We will play twopence wet, and fourpence dry.' To this the other agreed, and so they play'd; and at this low gaming Rumbold had, in short, won of his confederate ten shillings in money. The looser seem'd to be angry, and therefore proposed to play for all money, hoping to make himself whole again. 'Nay,' said the other, 'I shall not refuse your proposition, because I have won your money'; and therefore to it they went, and Rumbold had still the same luck, and won ten shillings more. Then the other would play for twelvepence a game. 'No,' said Rumbold, 'I am not willing to exceed sixpence a game; I will not alter what I have began, lest I change my fortune, unless this honest countryman will go my halves.' 'I have no mind to gaming,' reply'd the countryman. 'You need not play,' said the other; 'I'll do that, and you see my fortune is good; venture a crown with me, you know we have both had fortune, which I hope will continue propitious to us still.' 'Well, content,' said the countryman, and so they proceeded; still Rumbold had good fortune, and he and the countryman won ten shillings apiece more of the others, which made them merry, and and the other was extremely enraged; he therefore told them, 'he would either win the horse or lose the saddle, and venture all now'; and drawing out about thirty shillings, 'Come, take it all, win it and wear it', and so they play'd; but they had now drawn the countryman in sufficiently, and he was flush, but it lasted not long thus before he was taken down a button-hole lower, for the fortune chang'd, and that he had won was lost, and forty shillings more. He was now angry, but to no purpose, for he did not discover their foul play; and he, in hopes of his good fortune, ventur'd, and lost the other forty shillings, and then he said he would go halves no longer, for he thought he would be merry and wise, and if he could not make a winning, he would be sure to make a secure bargain; which he reckon'd he should do, because altho' he had lost four pounds in money, and given Rumbold three pounds for his share of the chain, that yet he should make seven pounds of the chain, and so be no loser. They seeing he would not play, left off, and he that had won the money, was content to give a collation, which was called for; but Rumbold pretending much anger at his loss, was resolv'd to venture more, and to playing again he went, and in a short time he recover'd a great deal of his losses. This vexed the countryman, that he had not join'd with him; and, in the end, seeing his good fortune continue, and that he won, he again went halves, but it was not long that they thrived: the countryman was obliged to draw his purse, and in the end lost all his money, which was near twenty pounds. He did not think his condition to be so bad as it was, because he believed he had a chain worth seven pounds in his pocket, and therefore he reckoned he had not lost all. By this time several other confederates (having been abroad, employ'd on the same acount, couzening and cheating of others) came into the tavern, which was the place appointed for their rendezvous, then they acquainted one another of their several gains and prizes, afterwards fell to drinking, which they did very plentifully, and the countryman for anger called up the landlord to make one of the company. He soon understood what kind of guests he had in his house, and how they had cheated the poor countryman, and therefore he was resolved to serve them in the same sort: accordingly he put forward the affair of drinking; and some being hungred, called for victuals: he told them he would get them what they pleas'd; and they being determin'd to take up their quarters there for that night, a supper was bespoke for all the company, such as the master of the house in his discretion should think fit: he told them they should have it, and accordingly went down to provide supper: he soon return'd, and helped them off with their liquor till supper-time; by this time they were all perfectly drunk; he then commands up supper, and they fall to with a shoulder of mutton and two capons; 'Eat and drink hard, and call for more,' he tells them; 'it's coming': but they now having set still a while, were all fallen asleep; he makes use of this opportuntiy, and brings up half a dozen empty foul dishes, or at leastwise, full of bones of several fowls, as pigeons, partridges, pheasants, and all the remains of victuals that had been left in the house that day, which he strewed and placed on their plates, and so left them. Some of them sleeping, and sitting uneasily, fell from their chairs, and so waked themselves, and their companions being thoroughly awak'd, they again fell to eating and drinking, some turning over the bones that were brought, said, 'How came these here? I do not remember that I eat any such victuals': 'Not I,' said another; upon which the master of the house was call'd, and the question was ask'd him: 'Why, surely, gentlemen, you have forgot yourselves,' said he, 'you have slept sound and fair indeed, I believe you will forget the collar of brawn you had too, that cost me six shillings out of my pocket.' 'How, brawn,' said one. 'Ay, brawn,' answer'd the landlord, 'you had it, and are like to pay for it; you'll remember nothing presently, this is a fine drunken bout indeed.' 'So it is,' reply'd one of the company, 'sure we have been in a dream, but it signifies nothing, my Landlord, you must and shall be paid; give us another dozen bottles and bring us a bill, that we pay the reckoning we have run up.' This order was presently obeyed, and a bill brought, which in all came to seven pounds; in which 'tis taken for granted, that he misreckon'd them above one half, tho' he acquainted them, that he had used them very kindly; they were bound to believe him, and therefore every man was call'd for to pay his share: the countryman shrunk behind, intending to escape; which one of the company seeing, call'd him forwards, and said, 'Come, let us tell noses, and every man pay alike.' The countryman desired to be excused, and said he had no money; which they knowing well enough, at length they agreed to acquit him: this done, they went to several lodgings to bed, and it was time, for it was past midnight; they all slept better than the countryman, who could hardly sleep a wink for thinking on his misfortunes, and having such good fortune in the morning, it should prove so bad before night. But morning being come, he and they all arose, and the countryman's money being all spent, he knew it was to no purpose for him to stay there, wherefore he resolv'd to go to a goldsmith in the city, and sell, or pawn his chain, that he might have some money to carry him home: being come to the goldsmith's, he produced the chain, which tho' at first sight he took to be gold, yet upon trial he found it otherwise, and that it was but brass gilt; he told the countryman the same, who, at this heavy news was like to break his heart. The goldsmith seeing the countryman in such a melancholy taking, he enquired of him how he came by it. He soon acquainted him with the manner, and every circumstance; the goldsmith, as soon as he understood the cheat, advised him to go to a Justice, and get a warrant for him that had thus cheated him; and the countryman telling him that he had no money, nor friend, being a stranger, he himself went with him to the Justice, who, soon understanding the matter, granted his warrant, and the goldsmith procured a constable to go with him to the tavern or nighthouse, where Rumbold was apprehended, but he found means some way or other to make his escape out of the house, as did the rest by main force.

After Rumbold had lost the money he had put in his friend the banker's hands, he was forc'd to shift after this manner, cheating and cozening any one whom he took for a prey. He narrowly escap'd being apprehended at his lodging in Golden-Lane near Barbican; but at length, still pursuing his courses of iniquity, he was taken, and sent to Newgate; when, after five or six days imprisonment, he receiv'd his trial at the Old Bailey, was condemned, and executed at Tyburn.

THE LIFE OF
CAPT. JAMES HIND

The father of Capt. Hind was a sadler, an inhabitant of Chipping-Norton in Oxfordshire, where the captain was born. The old man lived there many years in very good reputation among his neighbours, was an honest companion, and a constant churchman. As James was his only son, he was willing to give him the best education he was able, and to that purpose sent him to school till he was fifteen years of age, in which time he learned to read and write very well, and knew arithmetick enough to make him capable of any common business.

After this he was put apprentice to a butcher in his native town, where he served about two years of his time, and then ran away from his master, who was a very morose man, and continually finding something or another to quarrel with him about.

When he made this elopement, he applied immediately to his mother for money to carry him up to London, telling her a lamentable story of the hardships he suffer'd from his master's severity. Mothers are generally easily wrought upon with stories of that kind; she therefore very tenderly supplied him with three pounds for his expences, and sent him away with tears in her eyes.

He had not been long in London before he got a relish of the pleasures of the place (pleasures I call them in compliance with the opinion of gentlemen of the captain's taste) I mean, the enjoyment of his bottle and his mistress; both which, as far as his circumstances would allow, he pursued very earnestly. One Night he was taken in company with a woman of the town, who had just before picked a gentleman's pocket of five guineas, and sent with her to the Poultry Compter till morning, when he was released for want of any evidence against him, he having, in reality, no hand in the affair. The woman was committed to Newgate, but what became of her afterwards we are not certain, nor does it at all concern us. The captain by this accident fell into company with one Thomas Allen, a noted highwayman, who had been put into the Compter upon suspicion of some robbery, and was released at the same time with Hind, and for the same reason. These two men going to drink together, after their confinement, they contracted a friendship which was the ruin of them both, as the reader will observe in the perusal of these pages.

Their first adventure was at Shooters-Hill, where they met with a gentleman and his servant. Hind being perfectly raw and unexperienced, his companion was willing to have a proof of his courage; and therefore staid at some distance while the captain rode up, and singly took from them fifteen pounds; but returned the gentleman twenty shillings to bear his expences on the road, with such a pleasant air, that the gentleman protested he would never hurt a hair of his head, if it should at any time be in his power. Allen was prodigiously pleased both with the bravery and generosity of his new comrade, and they mutually swore to stand by one another to the utmost of their power.

It was much about the time that the inhuman and unnatural murder of King Charles I was perpetrated at his own palace gate, by the fanaticks of that time, when our two adventurers began their progress on the road. One part of their engagement together was like Capt. Stafford's resolution, never to spare any of the regicides that came in their way. It was not long before they met the grand usurper Cromwell, as he was coming from Huntingdon, the place of his nativity, to London. Oliver had no less than seven men in his train, who all came immediately upon their stopping the coach, and over-power'd our two heroes; so that poor Tom Allen was taken on the spot, and soon after executed, and it was with a great deal of difficulty that Hind made his escape, who resolved from this time, to act with a little more caution. He could not, however, think of quitting a course of life which he had just begun to taste, and which he found so profitable.

The captain rode so hard to get out of danger, after this adventure with Cromwell, that he killed his horse, and he had not at that time money enough to buy another. He resolved, therefore, to procure one as soon as possible; and to this purpose tramped it along the road on foot. It was not long before he saw a horse hung to a hedge with a brace of pistols before him; and looking round him, he observed, on the other side of the hedge, a gentleman untrussing a point: 'This is my horse,' says the captain, and immediately vaults into the saddle. The gentleman calling to him, and telling him, that the horse was his: 'Sir,' says Hind, 'you may think yourself well off, that I have left you all the money in your pockets to buy another, which you had best lay out before I meet you again, lest you should be worse used'; so he rode away in search of new adventures.

There is another story of the captain's getting himself remounted, which I have seen in a printed account of his life. Whether it be only the same action otherwise related, or another of our adventurers pranks, I shall leave the reader to determine, and proceed.

Being reduced to the humble capacity of a foot-pad, he hired a common hack of a man who made it his business to let out horses, and took the road on his back. He was overtaken (for he was not able to overtake any body) by a gentleman well mounted, with a portmanteau behind him. They fell into discourse upon such topicks as are common to travellers, and Hind was very particular in praising the gentleman's horse, 'till the gentleman repeated every thing his horse could do. There was upon the side of the road a wall, over which was another way, and the gentleman told Hind, that his horse could leap that wall. Hind offer'd to lay a bottle of it; upon which the gentleman attempted and accomplished what he proposed. The captain confessed he had lost his wager, but desired the gentleman to let him try if he would do the same with him upon his back, which the gentleman consenting to, the captain rode away with his portmanteau, and left him to return his horse to the owner.

Another time Captain Hind met the celebrated regicide, Hugh Peters in Enfield-Chase, and commanded him to deliver his money. Hugh, who had his share of confidence, began to lay about him with texts of scripture, and to cudgel our bold robber with the eighth commandment. 'It is written in the law,' says he, 'that thou shalt not steal. And furthermore Solomon, who was surely a very wise man, speaketh in this manner: Rob not the poor, because he is poor.' Hind was willing to answer the finished old cant in his own strain; and for that end, began to rub up his memory for some of the scraps of the Bible, which he had learned by heart in his minority. 'Verily,' said Hind, 'if thou hadst regarded the divine precepts as thou oughtest to have done, thou wouldest not have wrested them to such an abominable and wicked sense as thou didst the words of the Prophet, when he saith, Bind their kings with chains, and their nobles with fetters of iron. Didst thou not, thou detestable hypocrite, endeavour from these words to aggravate the misfortunes of thy royal master, whom thy accursed Republican Party, unjustly murdered before the door of his own palace?' Here Hugh Peters began to extenuate that horrid crime, and to alledge other parts of scripture in his defence, and in order to preserve his money: 'Pray Sir,' replied Hind, 'make no reflections on my profession; for Solomon plainly says, Do not despise a thief; but it is to little purpose for us to dispute: the substance of what I have to say, is this, deliver thy money presently, or else I shall send thee out of the world to thy master in an instant.'

These terrible words of the captain frighted the old Presbyterian in such a manner, that he gave him thirty broad pieces of gold, and then they parted. But Hind was not thoroughly satisfied with letting such a notorious enemy to the Royal Cause depart in so easy a manner. He, therefore, rode after him, full speed, and overtaking him, spoke as follows: 'Sir, now I think of it, I am convinced that this misfortune has happened to you, because you did not obey the words of the scripture, which say expressly, Provide neither gold, nor silver, nor brass in your purses for your journey. Whereas it is evident that you had provided a pretty deal of gold: however, as it is now in my power to make you fulfil another command, I would by no means slip the opportunity. Therefore, pray give me your cloak.' Peters was so surprized, that he neither stood to dispute, nor to examine what was the drift of Hind's demand; but Hind soon let him understand his meaning, when he added, 'You know, Sir, our Saviour has commanded, That if any man take away thy cloak, thou must not refuse they coat also; therefore, I cannot suppose you will act in direct contradiction to such an express direction, especially now you can't pretend you have forgot it, because I have reminded you of your duty.' The old Puritan shrugged his shoulders for some time, before he proceeded to uncase them; but Hind told him his delay would do him no service; for he would be punctually obey'd, because he was sure what he requested was consonant to the scripture: accordingly Hugh Peters delivered his coat, and Hind carried all off.

Next Sunday when Hugh came to preach, he chose an invective against theft for the subject of his sermon, and took his text in the Canticles, Chap. v. Ver. 3. 'I have put off my coat, how shall I put it on.' An honest Cavalier who was present, and knew the occasion of his chusing those words, cry'd out aloud: 'Upon my word, Sir, I believe there is no body here can tell you, unless Capt. Hind was here!' Which ready answer to Hugh Peters scriptural question, put the congregation into such an excessive fit of laughter, that the fanatick parson was ashamed of himself, and descended from his pratling box, without proceeding any further in his harangue.

It has been observed before, that Hind was a professed enemy to all the regicides; and, indeed, fortune was so favourable to his desires, as to put one or other of those celebrated villains often into his power.

He met one day with that arch-traytor, Sergeant Bradshaw, who had some time before the insolence to sit as judge of his lawful Sovereign, and to pass sentence of death upon Majesty. The place where this rencounter happened, was, upon the road between Sherbourn and Shaftsbury, in Dorsetshire. Hind rode up to the coach side, and demanded the sergeant's money; who, supposing his name would carry terror with it, told him who he was. Quoth Hind, 'I fear neither you, nor any king-killing son of a whore alive. I have now as much power over you, as you lately had over the King, and I should do God and my country good service, if I made the same use of it; but live, villain, to suffer the pangs of thine own conscience, till justice shall lay her iron hand upon thee, and require an answer for thy crimes, in a way more proper for such a monster, who art unworthy to die by any hands, but those of the common hangman, and at any other place than Tyburn. Nevertheless, though I spare thy life as a regicide, be assured, that unless thou deliverest thy money immediately, thou shalt die for thy obstinacy.'

Bradshaw began to be sensible that the case was not now with him, as it had been when he sate at Westminster-Hall, attended with the whole strength of the rebellion. A horror naturally arising from a mind conscious of the blackest villainies, took possession of his soul, upon the apprehensions of death, which the pistol gave him, and discovered itself in his countenance. He put his trembling hand into his pocket, and pulled out about forty shillings in silver, which he presented to the captain, who swore he would that minute shoot him through the heart, if he did not find coin of another species. The sergeant at last, to save a miserable life, pulled out that which he valued next to it, as of two evils all men chuse the least, and gave the captain a purse full of jacobuses.

Hind, having thus got possession of the cash, he made Bradshaw yet wait a considerable time longer, while he made the following eulogium on money; which, though in the nature of it, it be something different from the harangues, which the sergeant generally heard on a Sunday, contains, nevertheless, as much truth, and might have been altogether as pleasing, had it come from another mouth.

'This, Sir, is the metal that wins my heart for ever! O precious gold, I admire and adore thee as much as either Bradshaw, Pryn, or any other villain of the same stamp, who, for the sake of thee, would sell their Redeemer again, were he now upon earth. This is that incomparable medicament which the Republican physicans call the wonder-working plaister: it is truly Catholick in operation, and somewhat of a kin to the Jesuits powder, but more effectual. The virtues of it are strange and various; it makes justice deaf as well as blind, and takes out spots of the deepest treason, as easily as castle-soap does common stains; it alters a man's constitution in two or three days, more than the virtuoso's transfusion of blood can do in seven years. 'Tis a great Alexiopharmick, and helps poisonous principles of rebellion, and those that use them. It miraculously exalts and purifies the eye-sight, and makes traytors behold nothing but innocence in the blackest malefactors. It is a mighty cordial for a declining cause; it stifles faction and schism as certainly as the itch is destroy'd by butter and brimstone. In a word, it makes fools wise men, and wise men fools; and both of them knaves. The very colour of this precious balm is bright and dazling. If it be properly applied to the fist, that is, in a decent manner, and a competent dose, it infallibly performs all the abovesaid cures, and many others too numerous to be here mentioned.'

The captain having finished his panegyrick, he pulled out his pistol, and said farther:

'You and your infernal crew have a long while run on, like Jehu, in a career of blood and impiety, pretending that zeal for the Lord of Hosts has been your only motive. How long you may be suffered to continue in the same course, God only knows. I will, however, for this time, stop your race in a literal sense of the words.' With that he shot all the six horses which were in the sergeant's coach, and then rode off in pursuit of another booty.

Sometime after, Hind met a coach on the road between Petersfield and Portsmouth, filled with gentlewomen: he went up to them in a gentile manner, told them, that he was a patron of the fair-sex; and that it was purely to win the favour of a hard-hearted mistress, that he travelled the country: 'But Ladies,' added he, 'I am at this time reduced to the necessity of asking relief, having nothing to carry me on in my intended prosecution of adventures': the young ladies, who had most of them read a pretty many romances, could not help conceiting they had met with some Quixot or Amadis de Gaul, who was saluting them in the strain of knight-errantry: 'Sir Knight', said one of the pleasantest among them, 'we heartily commiserate your condition, and are very much troubled that we cannot contribute towards your support; but we have nothing about us but a sacred depositum, which the laws of your order will not suffer you to violate.' Hind was pleased to think he had met with such agreeable gentlewomen, and, for the sake of the jest, could freely have let them pass unmolested, if his necessities at this time had not been very pressing. 'May I, bright Ladies, be favoured with the knowledge of what this sacred depositum, which you speak of, is, that so I may employ my utmost abilities in its defence, as the laws of knight-errantry require?' The lady who spoke before and who suspected the least of any one in company told him, that the depositum she had spoken of, was 3000 *l.* the portion of one of the company, who was going to bestow it upon the knight who had won her good-will by his many past services. 'My humble duty be presented to the knight,' said he, 'and be pleased to tell him, that my name is Capt. Hind; that out of mere necessity I have made bold to borrow part of what, for his sake, I wish were twice as much; that I promise to expend the sum in defence of injured lovers, and the support of gentlemen who profess knight-errantry.' At the name of Capt. Hind, they were sufficiently startled, there being no-body then living in England who had not heard of him: Hind however bid them not be affrighted, for he would not do them the least hurt, and desired no more than one thousand pound, out of the three. This the ladies very thankfully gave in an instant (for the money was ty'd up in separate bags) and the captain wish'd them all a good journey, and much joy to the bride.

We must leave the captain a little, to display the corruption of human nature, in an instance, which the captain has often protested was a great trouble to him. The young lady, when she met her intended husband, told him all that had past upon the road, and the mercenary wretch, as soon as he heard of the money that was lost adjourned the marriage, till he had sent to her father to ask whether or no he would make up the original sum agreed upon, which he refusing (partly because he had sufficiently exhausted his substance before, and partly because he resented the sordid proposal) our fervent lover entirely broke through all his vows, and the unfortunate young lady died of grief and indignation. This account sufficiently demonstrates the truth of what is advanced in the two lines of Mr Cowley's translation of one of the Odes of Anacreon.

160

Gold alone does Passion move;
Gold monopolizes Love.

Another time Hind was obliged to abscond for a considerable time in the country, there being great inquiries made after him; during this interval, his money began to run short, and he was a great while before he could think of a way to replenish his purse. He would have taken another turn or two on the high-way; but he had lived so long here that he had spent his very horse. While he was in this extremity, a noted doctor in his neighbourhood went to receive a large sum of money, for a cure which he had performed, and our captain had got information of the time. It was in the doctor's way home to ride directly by Hind's door, who had hired a little house on the side of a common. Our adventurer took care to be ready at the hour the doctor was to return, and when he was riding by the house, he addressed himself to him in the most submissive stile he was master of, telling him, 'That he had a wife within who was violent bad with a flux, so that she could not live without present help; intreating him to come in but two or three minutes, and he would shew his gratitude as soon as he was able'. The doctor was moved with compassion at the poor man's request, and immediately alighted, and accompanied him in, assuring him that he should be very glad if it was in his power to do him any service. Hind conducted him up stairs; and, as soon as they were got into the chamber, shut the door, and pulled out a loaded pistol, and an empty purse, while the doctor was looking round for his patient. 'This,' quoth Hind, holding up the purse, 'is my wife; she has had a flux so long, that there is now nothing at all within her. I know, Sir, you have a sovereign remedy in your pocket for her distemper, and if you do not apply it without a word, this pistol shall make the day shine into your body.' The doctor would have been glad to have lost a considerable fee, provided he might have had nothing to do with the patient; but when he saw there was no getting off, he took forty guineas out of his pocket, and emptied them out of his own purse into the captain's, which now seemed to be in pretty good health. Hind then told the doctor, that he would leave him in full possession of his house, to make amends for the money he had taken from him. Upon which he went out, and locked the door upon poor Galen, mounting his horse, and riding away as fast as he was able, to find another country to live in, well knowing that this would now be too hot to hold him.

161

Hind has been often celebrated for his generosity to all sorts of people; more especially for his kindness to the poor, which it is reported was so extraordinary, that he never injured the property of any person, who had not a compleat share of riches. We shall give one instance, instead of a great many, which we could produce, which will sufficiently confirm this general opinion of his tenderness for those that were needy.

At a time when he was out of cash (as he frequently was, by reason of his extravagancy,) and had been upon the watch a pretty while, without seeing any worth his notice, he at last espied an old man jogging along the road upon an ass. He rides up to meet him, and asked him very courteously where he was going. 'To the market,' said the old Man, 'at Wantage, to buy me a cow that I may have some milk for my children.'—'How many children', quoth Hind, 'may you have?' The old man answered 'Ten'.—'And how much do you think to give for a cow,' said Hind?—'I have but forty shillings, master, and that I have been saving together these two years,' says the poor Wretch.—Hind's heart asked for the

Capt. Hind Robbing Col: Harrison in Maidenhead-Thicket.

poor man's condition, at the same time that he could not help admiring his simplicity; but being in so great a strait as I have intimated, he thought of an expedient, which would both serve him, and the old man too. 'Father,' said he, 'the money you have got about you, I must have at this time; but I will not wrong your children of their milk. My name is Hind, and if you will give me your forty shillings quietly, and meet me again this day se'ennight at this place, I promise to make the sum double. Only be cautious that you never mention a word of the matter to any body between this and that.' At the day appointed the old man came, and Hind was a good as his word, bidding him buy two cows, instead of one, and adding twenty shillings to the sum promised, that he might purchase the best in the market.

Never was highwayman more careful than Hind to avoid blood-shed, yet we have one instance in his life, that proves how hard it is for a man to engage in such an occupation, without being exposed to a sort of wretched necessity some time or other, to take away the life of another man, in order to preserve his own; and in such a case, the argument of self-defence can be of no service to extenuate the crime, because he is only pursued by justice; so that a highwayman, who kills another man, upon whatever pretence, is as actually guilty of murder, as a man who destroys another in cold blood without being able to give a reason for his so doing.

Hind had one morning committed several robberies in and about Maidenhead-Thicket; and, among others, had stopped Col. Harrison, a celebrated regicide, in his coach and six, and taken from him seventy odd pounds. The colonel immediately procured a hue-and-cry for taking him, which was come into that country before the captain was aware of it. However he heard at a house of intelligence which he always had upon every road he used, of the danger he was in; and thereupon, he instantly thought of making his escape, by riding as fast as he could from the pursuers, 'till he could find some safer way of concealing himself.

In this condition, any one would imagine, the captain was apprehensive of every man he saw. He had got no farther than a place called Knole-Hill, which is but a little way of the thicket, before he heard a man riding behind him full speed. It was a gentleman's servant, endeavouring to overtake his master who was gone before, with something that he had forgot. Hind, just now thought of nothing but his own preservation; and therefore resolved either to ride off, or fire at the man, who he concluded was pursuing him. As the other horse was fresh, and Hind had pretty well tir'd his, he soon perceived the man got ground of him; upon which he pulls out a pistol, and just as the unfortunate countryman was at his horse's heels, he turns about and shoots him through the head, so that he fell down dead on the spot. The captain, after the fact, got entirely off; but it was for this that he was afterwards condemn'd at Reading.

There have been a great many more stories related of this celebrated highwayman, which were either the actions of other men, or so improbable in themselves, that we did not think them worth rehearsing. Any man who has excelled in his way will be always loaded with so much praise as to make his whole history seem a fable. Whether this be occasion'd by the partiality of writers, or by a fate common to such men, I shall not determine. The Hercules of Greece was the most famous of all that bore that name; therefore the actions of all the rest that bore that name are attributed to him; almost the same may be said of Captain Hind. One relation more, which is universally known to be authentick, and redounds to the honour of our hero, shall close our account of his life.

After King Charles I was beheaded, the Scots received and acknowledged his son King Charles II and resolved to maintain his right against the reigning usurpation. To this end they raised an army, and marched towards England, which they entered with great precipitation. Abundance of gentry, and others who were loyal in their principles, flocked to the Standard of their Sovereign, and resolved to lose their lives in his service, or restore him to his dignity. Among these Hind, who had as much natural bravery as almost any man that ever lived, resolved to try his fortune. Cromwell was sent by the Parliament into the north to intercept the royal army, but in spite of that vigilant traytor's expedition, the King advanced as far as Worcester, where he waited the enemies coming.

Oliver came to Worcester soon after, and the consequence of the two armies meeting was a very fierce and bloody battle, in which the Royalists were defeated. Hind had the good-fortune to escape at that time, and came to London, where he lodged with one Mr Denzie, a barber, over against St Dunstan's Church in Fleet-Street, and went by the name of Brown. But Providence had now ordered, that he should no longer pursue his extravagancies;

for he was discover'd by a very intimate acquaintance. It must be granted, that he had sufficiently deserved the stroke of justice; but there yet appears something so shocking in a breach of friendship, that we cannot help wishing somebody else had been the instrument.

As soon as he was apprehended, he was carried before the Speaker of the House of Commons, who then lived in Chancery-Lane, and, after a long examination was committed to Newgate, and loaded with irons. He was convey'd to prison by one Capt. Compton, under a strong guard; and the warrant for his commitment commanded that he should be kept in close confinement; and that no body should be admitted to see him without orders.

On Friday the 12th of December, 1651 Captain James Hind was brought to the bar of the Sessions-House in the Old-Bailey, and indicted for several crimes; but nothing being proved against him that could reach his life, he was conveyed in a coach from Newgate to Reading in Berkshire, where on the 1st of March, 1651 he was arraigned before Judge Warberton for killing one George Sympson at Knole, a small village in that county. The evidence here was very plain against him, and he was found Guilty of Wilful Murder; but an Act of Oblivion being issued out the next day, to forgive all former offences but those against the state, he was in great hopes of saving his life; 'till by an order of council he was removed by habeas corpus to Worcester jail.

At the beginning of September, 1652 he was condemn'd for high-treason, and on the 24th of the same month, he was drawn, hang'd, and quartered, in pursuance of the same sentence, being thirty-four years of age. At the place of execution, he declared that most of the robberies which he had ever committed, were upon the Republican Party, of whose principles he professed he always had an utter abhorrence. He added, that nothing troubled him so much as to die before he saw his royal master established on his throne, from which he was most unjustly and illegally excluded by a rebellious and disloyal crew, who deserved hanging more than him.

After he was executed, his head was set upon the bridge gate, over the River Severn, from whence it was privately taken down, and buried within a week afterwards. His quarters were put upon the other gates of the city, where they remained 'till they were destroy'd by wind and weather.

To the Memory of Capt. HIND.

By a poet of his own time.

I.

Whenever Death attacks a Throne,
Nature thro' all her Parts must groan,
The mighty Monarch to bemoan.

II.

He must be wise, and just, and good;
Tho' nor the State he understood,
Nor ever spared a Subject's Blood.

III.

And shall no friendly Poet find,
A monumental Verse for Hind?
In Fortune less, as great in Mind.

IV.

Hind made our Wealth one common Store;
He robb'd the Rich to feed the Poor:
What did immortal Cæsar more?

V.

Nay, 'twere not difficult to prove,
That meaner Views did Cæsar move:
His was Ambition, Hind's was Love.

VI.

Our English Hero sought no Crown,
Nor that more pleasing Bait, Renown:
But just to keep off Fortune's Frown.

VII.

Yet when his Country's Cause invites,
See him assert a Nation's Rights!
A Robber for a Monarch fights!

VIII.

If in due Light his Deeds we scan,
As Nature points us out the Plan,
Hind was an honourable Man.

IX.

Honour, the Virtue of the Brave,
To Hind that Turn of Genius gave,
Which made him scorn to be a Slave.

X.

This, had his Stars conspir'd to raise,
His natal Hour, This Virtue's Praise
Had shone with an uncommon Blaze.

XI.

Some new Epocha had begun,
From ev'ry Action he had done;
A City built, a Battle won.

XII.

If one's a Subject, one at Helm,
'Tis the same Violence, says Anselm,
To rob a House, or waste a Realm.

XIII.

Be henceforth then forever join'd,
The Names of Cæsar, and of Hind,
In Fortune different, one in Mind.

THE LIFE OF
CLAUDE DU VALL

S ome have affimed that this very celebrated highwayman was born in Smock-Alley, without Bishopsgate; but this is without ground, for he really received his first breath at a place called Damfront in Normandy. His father was a miller, and his mother the daughter of a taylor: by these parents he was brought up strictly in the Roman Catholick religion, and his promising genius was cultivated with as much learning as qualified him for a footman.

But though the father was so careful, as to see that his son had some religion, we have good reason to think, that he had none himself. He used to talk much more of good chear, than of the Church; and of great feasts, than great faith; good wine was to him better than good works; and a sound courtezan was far more agreeable than a sound Christian. Being once so very sick, there was great hopes of his dying a natural death, a ghostly father came to him with his *corpus domini*; and told him, that hearing of the extremity he was in, he had brought him his saviour to comfort him before his departure. Old Du Vall, upon this, drew aside the curtain, and beheld a goodly fat friar with the Host in his hand. 'I know,' said he, 'that it is our Saviour, because he came to me in the same manner as he went to Jerusalem, *c'est un asne que le porte*: it is an ass that carries him.

Whether the old man departed at this time, or lived to dishonour his family by some more ignominious death is still very uncertain, nor shall we trouble ourselves about it. This we are credibly informed, neither father nor mother took any notice of young Claude, after he was about thirteen years of age. Perhaps their circumstances might then oblige them to send him abroad to seek his fortune. His first stage was at Rouen, the capital city of Normandy, where he fortunately met with post-horses to be returned to Paris; upon one of which he got leave to ride, by promising to help dress them at night. At the same time falling in with some English gentlemen, who were going to the same place, he got his expences discharged by those generous travellers.

They arriv'd at Paris in the usual time, and the gentlemen took lodgings in the Faux-bourg St Germain, where the English generally quarter. Du Vall was willing to be as near as possible to his benefactors, and by their intercession he was admitted to run on errands, and do the meanest offices at the St Esprit in the Rue de Bourchiere; a house of general entertainment, something between a tavern and an alehouse, a cook's shop and a bawdy-house. In this condition he continued till the Restauration of King Charles II in 1660 at which time multitudes of all nations flocking into England, among them came Du Vall, in the capacity of a footman to a person of quality.

The universal joy upon the return of the Royal Family, made the whole nation almost mad: every one ran into extravagances; and Du Vall, whose inclinations were as vicious as any man's, soon became an extraordinary proficient in gaming, whoring, drunkenness, and all manner of debauchery. The natural effect of these courses is want of money; this our adventurer experienced in a very little time; and as he could not think of labouring he took to the highway to support his irregularities. In this profession he was within a little while so famous, as to have the honour of being named first in a proclamation for apprehending several notorious highwaymen. And here we have reason to complain that our informations are too short for our assistance, in writing the life of such a celebrated offender. However, such stories as have been delivered down to us, we shall give our readers faithfully, and in the best manner we are able.

He had one day received intelligence of a knight and his lady that were travelling with four hundred pound in their coach. Upon this he takes four or five more along with him, and overtakes them on the road. The gentry soon perceived they were like to be beset, when they beheld several horsemen riding backwards and forwards, and whispering one another; whereupon the lady, who was a young sprightly creature, pulls out a flagelet, and begins to play very briskly. Du Vall takes the hint, and plays excellently well upon a flagelet of his own, in answer to the lady, and in this posture rides up to the coach door. 'Sir,' says he to the knight, 'your lady plays excellently, and I make no doubt but she dances as well: will you please to step out of the coach, and let me have the honour to dance one courant with her on the heath?' 'I dare not deny any thing, Sir,' the knight readily replied, 'to a gentleman of your quality, and good behaviour: you seem a man of generosity, and your request is perfectly reasonable.' Immediately the footman opens the door, and the knight comes out; Du Vall leaps lightly off his horse, and hands the lady down. It was surprizing to see how gracefully he moved upon the grass; scarce a dancing master in London, but would have been proud to have shewn such agility in a pair of pumps, as Du Vall shewed in a great pair of French riding boots. As soon as the dance was over, he waits on the lady back to the coach, without offering her the least affront; but just as the knight was stepping in, 'Sir,' says he, 'you have forgot to pay the music.' His Worship replied, that he never forgot such things; and instantly put his hand under the seat of the coach, and pulled out a hundred pound in a bag, which he delivered to Du Vall, who received it with a very good grace, and courteously answered: 'Sir, you are liberal, and shall have no cause to repent your being so: this hundred pound given so generously, is better than ten times the sum taken by force. Your noble behaviour has excused you the other three hundred pound, which you have in the coach with you.' After this he gave him the word that he might pass undisturbed, if he met any more of their crew, and then very civily wished them a good journey.

Another time, as Du Vall with some of his companions were patrolling upon Blackheath, they met with a coach full of ladies. One of them had a young child in her arms, with a silver sucking-bottle. The person appointed to act in this adventure, robbed them very rudely, taking away their money, watches, rings, and even the poor baby's sucking-bottle. The infant cried, as was natural on such an occasion; and the ladies intreated him only to return the bottle; but the surly thief refused to give any ear to their request, 'till Du Vall, observing he staid longer than ordinary, rode up, and demanded what was the matter. The ladies, hereupon, renewed their petition in behalf of the child, and Du Vall threaten'd to shoot his companion, unless he restored what they required, adding these words: 'Sirrah, can't you behave like a gentleman, and raise a contribution, without stripping people; but, perhaps, you had some occasion for the sucking bottle; for by your actions one would imagine, you were hardly weaned': this sharp reproof had the desired effect; and Du Vall took his leave of the ladies in a courteous manner.

Capt. Smith has been guilty of an unpardonable blunder in his account of this robbery; for he tells us, that it was Du Vall himself, who behaved in this rustic manner, and who was compelled by one of his comrades to restore the sucking-bottle; but the reader need only reflect on Du Vall's general character, to convince him of the captain's error.

A little after the above-mentioned action, another lucky turn in Du Vall's favour happened, as much as that to his advantage. In the course of his rambles, he came into the Crown-Inn, in Baconsfield, where he heard great singing, dancing, and playing upon the hautboy and violin. He instantly enquired into the reason of it, and found that there was a wake or fair kept there that day; at which were present most of the young men and maids for several miles about. This, he thought, was a promising place; and therefore he set up his horse for that evening, went into the kitchen, and called for a pint of wine. Here he met with an old rich farmer, who had just received an hundred pounds, and ty'd it up in a bag, putting it into his coat pocket. Du Vall was very attentive to all that past, and by this means he heard the farmer tell an acquaintance what money he had about him, which our sharper immediately put down for his own, more especially did he depend upon it, when the countryman asked leave to go into the room where the music was, to see and hear the diversions. It was his next business to ask the same favour, which he as easily obtain'd, and very innocently to all appearance, entered to see the country-dancing, making an apology to the company, when he came in, and telling them, that he hoped it would be no offence. They replying as courteously, that he might stay there and welcome.

His business now was more to watch the old farmer's bag of money, than to mind the diversions of the young people; and, after considering sometime for a way to excuse his designs in the most dexterous manner: he observed a chimney with a large funnel, which he thought would favour his project. Having contrived

T. Bowles Sculp.

Du Vall *Robbing Squire* Roper, *Master of ẏ Buck Hounds to King* Charles II.
in Windsor Foreſt.

the whole affair, he went out and communicated it to the hostler, who, being a downright hostler, consented for a reward of two guineas, to assist him. He was to dress up a great mastiff dog in a cow-hide, which he had in the stable, placing the horns directly on his forehead, and then by the help of a ladder and a rope to let him down the chimney. All this he performed, while the company were merry in the chamber. Du Vall being returned from the yard, the dog howling as he descended, came down the chimney, and pushing among them in this frightful manner, they were all put into a hurry and confusion: the music was silenced, the table overthrown, and the drink spilt; the people all the while screaming, and crowding down stairs as fast as they were able, every one crowding to be foremost, as they supposed the Devil would unavoidable take the hindmost. Their heels flew up, the women's coats flew over their heads, and the mens noses, some of them, in their breeches. The pipe and the fiddle were trod to pieces, and some of the company let go behind, and sent forth a very unsavoury odour. While they were in this condition the supposed Devil made his way over them all, and got into the stable, where the hostler instantly uncased him; so that when the company came to examine the matter, as they could hear no more of him, they concluded was vanished into the air.

Now was the time for Du Vall to take care of the farmer's hundred pounds, which he very easily did by diving into his pocket. As soon as he had got the money, he took horse, and spared neither whip nor spur, 'till he came to London, where he thought himself safe. As soon as things were a little in order, again at the inn, there was a dismal outcry for the money: all the suspicious persons were searched, and the house was examined from top to bottom to no purpose. What could they suppose after this, but that the Devil had taken it away? It past in this manner, and was looked upon as a judgement inflicted by permission of Providence on the farmer for his covetousness; the farmer being, in reality, a miserable wretch, who made it his business to get money by all the methods he could, whether lawful or otherwise.

One time Du Vall met with Esquire Roper, Master of the Buck-Hounds to King Charles II as he was hunting in Windsor-Forest. As their rencounter happened in a thicket, Du Vall took the advantage of the place, and commanded him to stand and deliver his money, or else he would shoot him. Mr Roper, to save his life, gave our adventurer a purse full of guineas, containing at least fifty, and Du Vall afterwards bound him neck and heels, fastened his horse by him, and rode away a cross the country.

The hunting, to be sure, was over for that time, but it was a pretty while before the huntsman could find his master. When the 'squire was unbound, he made all the haste he could to Windsor, and as he entered the town, was met by Sir Stephen Fox, who asking him whether or no he had had any sport, Mr Roper replied in a great passion, 'Yes, Sir, I have had sport enough from a son of a whore, who made me pay damn'd dear for it. He bound me neck and heels, contrary to my desire, and then took fifty guineas from me, to pay him for his labour, which I had much rather he had omitted.'

But the proclamation, which we spoke of at the beginning of this life, and the large reward that was promised for taking him, made Du Vall think it unsafe to stay any longer in England; whereupon he retired into France. At Paris he lived very highly, boasting prodigiously of the success of his arms and amours, and affirming proudly, that he never encountered with any one person of either sex, whom he did not overcome. He had not been long here, before he relapsed into his old disease, want of money, which obliged him to have recourse to his wits again. He had an uncommon talent at contrivance, particularly at suiting his stratagems to the temper of the person they were designed to ensnare, as the following instance will prove.

A learned Jesuit, who was Confessor to the French King, was as much noted for his avarice, as he was for his politicks; by which latter he had rendered himself very eminent. His thirst of money was insatiable; and though he was exceeding rich his desires seemed to increase with his wealth. It came immediately into Du Vall's head, that the only way to squeeze a little money out of him, was to amuse him with hopes of getting a great deal, which he did in the following manner.

He put himself into a scholar's garb, to facilitate his admittance into the miser's company, and then waited very diligently for a proper time to make his address, which he met with in a few days: seeing him alone in the piazza of the Fauxbourg, he went up to him very confidently, and said: 'May it please your Reverence, I am a poor scholar, who have been several years travelling over strange countries, to learn experience in the sciences, purely to serve my native country, to whose advantage I am determined to apply my knowledge, if I may be favoured with the patronage of a man so eminent as yourself.'—'And what may this knowledge of yours be?' replied the Father very much pleased: 'If you will communicate any thing to me that may be benificial to France, I assure you no proper encouragement shall be wanting on my side.'—Du Vall, upon this growing yet bolder, proceeded: 'Sir, I have spent most of my time in the study of alchimy, or the transmutation of metals, and have profited so much at Rome and Venice, from great men learned in that science, that I can change several base metals into gold, by the help of a philosophical powder, which I can prepare very speedily.'

The Father Confessor appeared to brighten with joy at this relation: 'Friend,' says he, 'such a thing as this will be serviceable indeed to the whole state, and peculiarly grateful to the King, who, as his affairs go at present, stands in some need of such a curious invention. But you must let me see some experiment of your skill, before I credit what you say so far as to communicate it to his Majesty, who will sufficiently reward you, if what you promise be demonstrated.' Upon this, he conducted Du Vall home to his house, and furnished him with money to build a laboratory, and purchase such other materials as he told him were requisite, in order to proceed in this invaluable operation, charging him to keep the secret from every living soul, 'till he thought proper, which Du Vall promised to perform.

The utensils being fixed, and every thing in a readiness, the Jesuit came to behold the wonderful operation. Du Vall took several metals and minerals of the basest sort, and put them into a crucible, his Reverence viewing every one as he put them in. Our learned alchymist had prepared a hollow stick, into which he had convey'd several sprigs of pure gold, as black-lead is in a pencil: with this stick he stirred the preparation as it melted, which with its heat melted the gold in the stick at the same time; so that it sunk imperceptibly into the vessel. When the excessive fire had consumed in a great measure all the lead, tin, brass, and powder, which he had put in for a shew, the gold remained pure to the quantity of an ounce and an half. This the Jesuit caused to be essayed, and finding it what it really was, all fine gold, he was immediately so devoted to Du Vall, and blinded with the prospect of future advantage, that he believed every thing our impostor could say, still furnishing him with whatever he demanded in hopes to be at last made master of this extraordinary secret, the whole fame, as well as profit of which, he did not question would redound to him, as Du Vall was but an obscure person.

Thus were our alchymist and Jesuit, according to the old saying, as great as two pickpockets; which proverbial sentence, if we examine it a little closely, hits both their characters. Du Vall was a professed robber, and what is any court-favourite, but a picker of the common people's pockets? So that it was only two sharpers endeavouring to out-sharp one another. The Confessor was as open as Du Vall could wish. He shewed him all his treasure, and among it, several rich jewels, which he had received as presents from the King, hoping, by these obliga-tions to make him discover his art the sooner. In a word, he grew by degrees, so importunate and urgent, that Du Vall began to apprehend a too close enquiry, if he denied the request any longer; and therefore he appointed a day when every thing was to be communicated. In the mean time he took an opportunity to steal into the chamber, where all the riches were deposited, and where his Reverence generally slept after dinner, and finding him at that time very fast, with his mouth wide open, he gagged and bound him, then took his keys, and unhoarded as much of his wealth, as he could conveniently carry out unsuspected; and so bid farewel to both him and France.

Du Vall had several other ways of getting money, besides these which I have mentioned, particularly by gaming, at which he was so expert, that few men in his age were able to play with him; no man living could slip a card more dexterously than he, nor better understood all the advantages that could be taken of an adversary, yet, to appearance, no man play'd fairer. He would frequently carry off ten, twenty, thirty, or sometimes an hundred pounds at a sitting, and had the pleasure commonly to hear it all attributed to his good fortune; so that few were discovered by their losses with him from playing with him a second, third, or fourth time.

He was moreover a mighty man for laying wagers, and no less successful in this particular than any of the former. He made it a great part of his study to learn all the intricate questions, deceitful propositions, and paradoxical assertions, that are made use of in conversation. Add to this, the smattering he had attained in all the sciences, particularly the mathematicks, by means of which, he frequently won considerable sums on the situation of a place, the length of a stick, and a hundred such little things, which a man may practice without being liable to any suspicion, or casting any blemish upon his character, as an honest man, or even a gentleman, which Du Vall affected to appear.

177

But what he was most of all celebrated for, was his conquests among the ladies, which were almost incredible to those who had not been acquainted with intriegue. He was a handsome man, and had abundance of that sort of wit, which is most apt to take with the fair-sex. Every agreeable woman he saw, he certainly died for, so that he was ten thousand times a martyr to love: 'Those eyes of yours, Madam, have undone me'—'I am captivated with that pretty good natur'd smile'—'O that I could by any means in the world recommend myself to your Ladyship's notice'—'What a poor silly loving fool am I!'—These, and a million of such expressions, full of flames, darts, racks, tortures, death, eyes bubbies, waste, cheeks, &c. were much more familiar to him than his prayers, and he had the same fortune in the field of love, as Marlborough had in that of war, (*viz.*) Never to lay siege, but he took the place.

Our hero had once a mind to try the utmost of his influence over the fair-sex; and to that end, he bought a good sizeable pocket-book, and set out upon a progress. It were in vain to pretend to give the reader a catalogue of those that fell victims to his address. Maids, widows, and wives; the rich, the poor, the noble, the vulgar, all, all submitted to the powerful Du Vall: in a word his pocket-book was filled, and his strength almost spent in less than six months.

While he was on his journey, he met with a young gentleman of wit and humour, to whom he communicated the occasion of his travelling. The gentleman being also a very agreeable person, and having been lately crossed in love, he soon consented to try his fortune with him. They came together to an inn, where was a beautiful demure girl, an only daughter. It was soon agreed to see what they could do with the damsel, of whose virginity he had no room to doubt. They soon found an opportunity of speaking to her alone, when they promised her a ring which they then shewed her, if she would come and lie with them every night, while they tarried at her father's house. The wench made no scruple of the matter, after a few words of form. But now the great point to be debated was who should have her maidenhead. The gentleman claimed it as a thing due to his dignity, and Du Vall as positively insisted upon it, that in such cases there was no respect of persons to be observed. At last they both consented to draw cuts for the imaginary treasure and the longest share fell to Du Vall.

At night our young innocence came and slipped in between them, when Du Vall, immediately, as he thought, took possession of what was his right, and he was entirely satisfied with what he discover'd. There is no reason to say what further pass'd that night; it was sufficient that Du Vall was very merry with his companion in the morning, who repined as much at his ill fortune.

There was a young lad, apprentice to her father, who had some months before been blessed in reality (if there be any reality in such blessings) with what Du Vall had now gotten in imagination, and had every night since came to the girl's bed. He was surpriz'd when he found his mate had left him, and as soon as he had opportunity, he demanded the reason of her slight. The poor wench freely confess'd the whole affair, promising, that if he would stay till the gentlemen were gone, he should have part of what they gave her, and the entire possession of her person for the future. 'I stay,' said the young man, 'I'll assure you Madam; no indeed, I will have a merry touch this night, or, by heaven, I will never speak to you again. Don't the gentleman sleep sound?' 'Yes, when they are asleep,' said she, 'but that is not often, for they teize me between them almost all the night long. However, I will give a gentle tap on the bed's tester when they are both fast, and then do you come, without saying a word.' At proper time the sign was given, the boy enter'd, and crept up between the two gentlemen directly in the right place. The bed shook, the travellers wak'd, and each thought his companion was in the saddle, till they both fell asleep again, being weary with waiting. And the young man went away without being detected.

In the morning the companions were ready to quarrel, each being angry at the other's unreasonable greediness. 'Sure,' says the gentleman, 'you had eaten something more than ordinary yesterday.' 'I wish,' quoth Du Vall, 'you have no occasion of something to strengthen your back to day, for I am sure you laboured hard enough.' At last it was agreed that the girl should decide between them, who confess'd all. They laugh'd at one another, gave the ring, and departed. Shortly afterwards, the young virgin was married, and lost her maidenhead for good and all, with many an artful struggle.

At another place on the road our two adventurers perform'd another prank of almost the same nature. They were benighted, and called at a house not an usual place of entertainment. The good man told them he was willing to serve them as much as he could, but he had no more than one chamber, with two large beds, and a truckle-bed, in it. 'If you please,' says he, 'to accept of one of the beds, as you look like honest gentlemen, you shall be very welcome. I and my wife will lay in the other, and my daughter in the truckle bed.' Any proposal at such a time, without doubt, was acceptable.

The daughter was about sixteen years of age, young, plump, and handsome, enough to make any man's mouth water. Du Vall took care to ogle her pretty sufficiently in the evening without the old people's notice, so that she understood his meaning, and let him perceive as much. About eleven they went to bed, and the good landlord and landlady as soon as our assignators could wish. When he heard them snore, Du Vall slipp'd out of his own bed into the wench's, where we leave them for the present.

There was an infant in a cradle by the good people's bed-side, and the young gentleman who was left alone, having some occasion to go down, ran against the wooden machine. As he could not otherwise pass, he took and lifted it into the middle of the room, did what he wanted, and went to bed again. It was not long afterwards before the landlady had a motion of the same nature, and it came into her head at the same time to feel for the cradle. She groped about so long in the dark, that she lost the bed-side, and walked round about till she happened to fall on the other bed, where the gentleman was alone. She felt of his head, and finding there was but one man, concluded it must be her husband, in which confidence she went to bed.

Our gallant quickly discovered her mistake, and, by his vigour, she soon perceived the same; however, she was not so ill-natur'd as to leave him immediately. We must go no farther in our relation, because we know not how many ladies may read it. In a word, the old man being still fast asleep, every one in the room was entirely satisfied, and, getting all into their proper places before morning, their satisfaction continued.

These two stories may serve for specimens of our adventurer's gallantry; all we shall add on that head, is, that Du Vall has often protested, that, after he was deceived by the inn keeper's daughter, he could never fancy he met with a maid above fourteen.

There's no certain account how long Du Vall followed his vicious courses in England before he was detected, after his coming from France, before he fell into the hand of justice. All we know, is, that he was taken drunk at the Hole in the Wall in Chandois Street, committed to Newgate, arraign'd, convicted, condemn'd, and (on Friday the 21st day of January 1669–70) executed at Tyburn, in the 27th year of his age.

Abundance of ladies, and those not of the meanest degree, visited him in prison, and interceded for his pardon: not a few accompanied him to the gallows, under their vizards, with swoln eyes, and blubber'd cheeks. After he had hanged a convenient time, he was cut down, and, by persons well dress'd, convey'd into a mourning coach. In this he was carried to the Tangier tavern at St Giles's, where he laid in state all night. The room was hung with black cloth, the herse cover'd with scutcheons, eight wax tapers were burning, and as many tall gentlemen attended with long cloaks. All was in profound silence, and the ceremony had lasted much longer, had not one of the judges sent to interrupt the pageantry.

As they were undressing him, in order to his lying in state, one of his friends put his hand into his pocket, and found therein the following paper, which as appears by the contents, he intended as a legacy to the ladies. It was written in a very fair hand.

> I should be very ungrateful to you, fair English Ladies, should I not acknowledge the Obligations you have laid me under. I could not have hoped that a Person of my Birth, Nation, Education, and Condition, could have had Charms enough to captivate you all; though the contrary has appeared, by your firm Attachment to my Interest, which you have not abandoned even in my last Distress. You have visited me in Prison, and even accompanied me to an ignominious Death.
>
> From the Experience of your former Loves, I am confident that many among you would be glad to receive me to your Arms, even from the Gallows.
>
> How mightily, and how generously have you rewarded my former Services? Shall I ever forget the universal Consternation that appeared upon your Faces when I was taken; your chargeable Visits to me in Newgate; your Shrieks and Swoonings when I was condemned, and your

zealous Intercession and Importunity for my Pardon? You could not have erected fairer Pillars of Honour and Respect to me, had I been a Hercules, able to get fifty of you with Child in one Night.

It has been the Misfortune of several English Gentlemen to die at this Place, in the Time of the late Usurpation, upon the most honourable Occasion that ever presented itself; yet none of these, as I could ever learn, received so many Marks of your Esteem as my self. How much the greater, therefore, is my Obligation?

It does not, however, grieve me, that your Intercession for me proved ineffectual; for now I shall die with a healthful Body, and, I hope, a prepared Mind; my Confessor has shewn me the Evil of my Ways, and wrought in me a true Repentance: Whereas, had you prevailed for my Life, I must in Gratitude have devoted it to your Service, which would certainly have made it very short; for had you been found, I should have died of a Consumption; if otherwise, of a Pox.

182 He was buried with many flambeauxs, amid a numerous train of mourners (most of them ladies) in Covent-Garden: a white marble stone was laid over him with his arms, and the following epitaph engraven on it.

> Here lies Du Vall, Reader, if Male thou art,
> Look to thy Purse; if Female, to thy Heart.
> Much Havock hath he made of both; for all
> Men he made stand, and Women he made fall.

> The second Conqueror of the Norman Race,
> Knights to his Arms did yields, and Ladies to his Face.
> Old Tyburn's Glory, England's bravest Thief,
> Du Vall the Ladies Joy! Du Vall the Ladies Grief.

A PINDARICK ODE.

To the Happy Memory of the most Renown'd
DUVALL.

By the Author of HUDIBRAS.

I.

'Tis true, to complement the Dead,

Is as impertinent and vain,

As 'twas of old to call 'em back again.

Or, like the Tartars, give 'em Wives,

With Settlements for After-Lives.

For all that can be done or said,

Though ne'er so noble, great, and good,

By them is neither heard nor understood.

All our fine Slights, and Tricks of Arts,

First to create, and then adore Desert;

And those Romances which we frame,

To raise ourselves not them a Name.

In vain are stuft with ranting Flatteries,

And such as, if they knew, they would despise:

For as those Times, the golden Age they call,

In which there was no Gold at all;

So we plant Glory and Renown,

Where it was ne'er deserv'd, nor known.

But to worse Purpose many Times,

To varnish o'er nefarious Crimes,

And cheat the World that never seems to mind,

How good or bad Men dye, but what they leave
    behind.

II.

And yet the brave Du Vall, whose Name,
Can never be worn out by Fame;
That liv'd and dy'd to leave behind
A great Example to Mankind:
That fell a publick Sacrifice,
From Ruin to prevent those few
Who, tho' born false, may be made true;
And teach the World to be more just and wise,
Ought not, like vuglar Ashes, rest
Unmention'd in the silent Chest,
Not for his own, but publick Interest.
He, like a pious Man, some Years before
Th' Arrival of this fatal Hour,
Made ev'ry Day he had to live,
To his last Minute a Preparative.
Taught the wild Arabs on the Road
To act in a more genteel Mode,
Take Prizes more obligingly than those
Who never had been bred Filous,
And how to hang in a more graceful Fashion,
Than e'er was known before to the dull English
    Nation.

III.

In France, the Staple of new Modes,
Where Garbs and Courts are current Goods,
That serves the ruder northern Nations
With Methods of Address and Treat,
Prescribes new Garnitures and Fashions,
And how to drink, and how to eat,
No out-of-Fashion Wine or Meat.
To understand Crevats and Plumes,

And the most modish from the old Perfumes.
To know the Age and Pedigrees,
Of Points of Flanders and Venice,
Cast their Nativity, and to Day
Foretel how long they'll hold, and when decay,
'T affect the purest Negligences,
In Gestures, Gaits, and Miens,
And speak by Repartee Routines,
Out of the most authentick of Romances:
And to demonstrate with substantial Reason,
What Ribbands all the Year are in or out of Season.

IV.

To this great Academy of Mankind,
He ow'd his Birth and Education,
Where all are so ingeniously inclin'd,
They understand by Imitation;
Are taught, improve before they are aware,
As if they suck'd their Breeding from the Air,
That naturally does dispense
To all a deep and solid Confidence.
A Virtue of that precious Use,
That he whom bounteous Heav'n endues,
But with a mod'rate Shew of it.
Can want no Worth, Abilities, nor Wit.
In all the deep Hermetick Arts,
(For so of late the Learned call
All Tricks, if strange and mystical)
He had improv'd his nat'ral Parts,
And with his magick Rod could sound,
Where hidden Treasure might be found
He, like a Lord o'th' Mannor, seiz'd upon
Whatever happen'd in his Way,
As lawful Waif and Stray,
And after, by the Custom, kept it as his own.

V.

From these first Rudiments he grew
To nobler Feats, and try'd his Force
Upon whole Troops of Foot and Horse;
Whom he as bravely did subdue:
Declar'd all Caravans that go
Upon the King's High-Way, his Foe,
Made many desperate Attacks,
Upon itinerant Brigades
Of all Professions, Ranks, and Trades;
On Carriers Loads, and Pedlars Packs,
Made them lay down their Arms and yield,
And, to the smallest Piece, restore
All that by cheating they had got before.
And after plunder'd all the Baggage of the Field;
In ev'ry bold Affair of War
He had the chief Command, and led them on:
For no Man is judged fit to have the Care
Of other's Lives, until he 'as made it known,
How much he does despise, and scorn his own.

VI.

Whole Provinces 'twixt Sun and Sun,
Have by his conqu'ring Sword been won;
And mighty Sums of Money laid
For Ransom upon ev'ry Man,
And Hostages deliver'd 'till 'twas paid.
Th' Excise, and Chimny-Publican,
The Jew-forestaller and Inhanser,
To him for their Crimes did answer.
He vanquish'd the most Fierce, and fell
Of all his Foes, the Constable,

That oft had beat his Quarters up,
And routed him, and all his Troop.
He took the dreadful Lawyers Fees,
That in his own allow'd High-way,
Does Feats of Arms as great as his,
And when th' encounter in it, wins the Day;
Safe in his Garrison, the Court,
Where meaner Criminals are sentenc'd for it,
To the stern Foe he oft gave Quarter,
But as the Scotchman did to Tartar,
That he in Time to come
Might in Return from his receive his Doom.

VII.

He would have starv'd this mighty Town,
And brought his haughty Spirit down;
Have cut it off from all Relief,
And, like a wise and valiant Chief,
Made many a fierce Assault,
Upon all Amunition-Carts,
And those that bring up Cheese and Malt,
Or Bacon from remoter Parts.
No Convoy, e'er so strong, with Food
Durst venture on the desp'rate Road;
He made th' undaunted Waggoner obey,
And the fierce Higler Contribution pay;
The savage Butcher, and stout Drover
Durst not to him their feeble Troops discover:
And if he had but kept the Field,
In Time he'd made the City yield.
For great Towns, like the Crocodiles, are found
I' th' Belly aptest to receive a mortal Wound.

VIII.

But when the fatal Hour arriv'd,
In which his Stars began to frown,
And had in close Cabal contriv'd
To pull him from his Height of Glory down,
When he by num'rous Foes oppress'd,
Was in th' enchanted Dungeon cast,
Secur'd with might Guards,
Lest he by Force or Stratagem,
Might prove too cunning for their Chains and them,
And break thro' all their Locks and Bolts, and Wards,
He'd both his Legs by Charms committed
To one another's Charge,
That neither might be set at large,
And all their Fury and Revenge out-witted.
As Jewels of high Value are
Kept under Locks with greater Charge.
Than those of meaner Rates;
So he was in Stone Walls, and ponderous Chains, and
    Iron Grates.

IX.

Thither came Ladies from all Parts,
To offer up close Pris'ners, Hearts,
Which he receiv'd as Tribute due,
And made 'em yield up Love and Honour too,
But in more brave Heroicks,
Than e'er were practis'd yet in Plays:
For those two spiteful Foes who never meet,
But full of hot Contest and Piques,
About Punctilio's and meer Trick,
Did all their Quarrels to his Doom submit,

And far more generous and free,
With only looking on him did agree,
Both fully satisfy'd; the one
With the fresh Lawrels he had won,
And all the brave renowned Feats
He had perform'd in Arms;
The other with his Person and his Charms:
For just as Larks are catch'd in Nets,
By gazing on a Piece of Glass;
So while the Ladies view his brighter Eyes,
And smoother polish'd Face,
Their gentle Hearts, alas! were taken by Surprize.

X.

Never did bold Knight to relieve
Distressed Dames such dreadful Feats achieve,
As feeble Damsels for his Sake
Would have been proud to undertake,
And bravely ambitious to redeem
The World's Loss and their own,
Strove who should have the Honour to lay down
And change a Life with him:
But finding all their Hopes in vain,
To move his fix'd determin'd Fate,
They Life itself began to hate,
And all the World beside disdain:
Made loud Appeals and Moans
To less hard-hearted Grates and Stones,
Came swell'd with Sighs, and drown'd in Tears,
To yield themselves his Fellow-Sufferers:
And follow him like Prisoners of War,
Chain'd to the lofty Wheels of his triumphant Car.

THE LIFE OF
WILLIAM NEVISON

As arts and sciences of use and morality admit of improvement, so likewise those of villainy grow up with them, the Devil being as industrious to improve his followers in the schools of vice, as our best instructors are in those of virtue, which will be illustrated in the following memoirs of the life of William Nevison, who was born at Pomfret in Yorkshire, about the Year 1639, of well-reputed, honest, and reasonably-estated parents, who bred him up at school, where he made some progress as to his learning, and in the spring of his youth promised a better harvest, than the summer of his life produced; for, to say truth, he was very forward and hopeful, 'till he arrived at thirteen or fourteen years of age, when he began to be the ring-leader of all his young companions to rudeness and debauchery.

So early as this he also took to thieving, and stole a silver spoon from his father: for which being severely punished at school, the punishment was the subject of the next night's meditation, which issued into a resolution of revenge on his master, whatever fate he met with in the execution thereof; to which end, having hit on a project for his purpose, and lying in his father's chamber, he gets softly up before such time as the day appeared, and hearing that his father slept, he puts his hand into his pocket, where he found the key of his closet, which unperceived he drew thence, and down he creeps to the said closet, where he supplies himself with what cash he could readily find, which amounted to about ten pounds, and with this, knowing that his said master had a horse he had particular delight for, that then grazed behind his house, he gets a bridle and saddle from his father's stable, and an hour before morning, arrays and mounts the said horse onward for London, to which he arrived within four days; when the evening coming upon him, he cut the throat of the horse, within a mile or two of the town, for fear he should prove a means of his discovery, if he should have carried it to an inn.

When he came to London, he changed his garb and name, and being a lusty well-looking lad, had put himself into the service of a brewer, where for two or three years he lived, not at all changed in mind, though opportunity was not, during that time, ripe to put his ill intentions in practice, tho' he watched all seasons to advance himself, by having several times attempted to rob his master, which at last he thus effected. Taking the advantage one night of the clerk's drunkenness, who was his master's cashier, he got up by stealth after him into the compting-house, where the said clerk falling asleep, he rifled the same of all such cash as he could conveniently come at, which amounted to near two hundred pounds, and fled to Holland, where running away with a burgher's daughter, that had robbed her father of a great deal of money and jewels, he was apprehended, had the booty taken from him, and clapt in gaol; and, had he not broke out, he had certainly made his exit beyond sea. Having thus made his escape, he got, after divers difficulties, into Flanders, and listed himself amongst the English voluntiers, who were under the command of the Duke of York, who about the same time was made Lieutenant-General of the Spanish forces, under Don John of Austria, that were then designed to raise the siege of Dunkirk, which was besieged by the English and French armies, and behaved himself very well, while he was in a military employment; but not greatly liking it, and having got some money whilst he was in the service, he came over to England, and bought himself a horse and arms, and resolving for the road, and perhaps a pleasant life, at the hazard of his neck, rather than toil out a long remainder of unhappy days in want and poverty, which he was always averse to: being thus supplied every day, one booty or other enriched his stores, which he would never admit a sharer in, chusing to manage his designs alone, rather than trust his life into the hand of others, who by favour or misfortune might be drawn in to accuse him.

191

One day Nevison, who went otherwise by the name of Johnson, travelling on the road, and scouring about in search of prize, he met two countrymen, who, coming up toward him, informed him, that it was very dangerous travelling forward, for that the way was set, and they had been robbed by three highwaymen, about half a mile off; and if he had any charge of money about him, it were his safest course to turn back. Nevison, asking them what they had lost, they told him 40 pounds; whereupon he replied, 'Turn back with me, and shew me the way they took, and my life to a farthing, I'll make them return you your money again'; they rid along with him till they had sight of the highwaymen; when Nevison ordering the countrymen to stay behind them at some distance, he rid up and spoke to the foremost of them, saying, 'Sir, by your garb and the colour of your horse, you should be one of those I looked after, and if so, my business is to tell you, that you borrowed of two friends of mine 40 pounds, which they desired me to demand of you, and which before we part you must restore.' 'How!' quoth the highwayman, '40 Pounds! Damn you, Sir, what is the fellow mad?' 'So mad,' replied Nevison, 'as that your life shall answer me, if you do not give me better satisfaction': with that he draws his pistol, and suddenly claps it to his breast, who finding then, that Nevison had also his rein, and that he could not get his sword or pistols, he yielded, telling him, his life was at his mercy: 'No,' says Nevison, ''tis not that I seek for, but the money you robbed these two men of, who are riding up to me, which you must refund.' The thief was forced to consent, and readily to deliver such part thereof, as he had, saying his companions had the rest; so that Nevison having made him dismount, and taking away his pistols, which he gave to the country-man, ordered them to secure him, and hold his own, whilst he took the thief's horse, and pursued the other two, who he soon overtook; for they thinking him their companion, stopt as soon as they saw him; so that he came up to them in the midst of a common. 'How now, Jack,' says one of them, 'what made you engage with yon fellow?' 'No gentlemen,' replies Nevison, 'you are mistaken in your man: Thomas, by the token of your horse and arms, he hath sent me to you for the ransom of his life, which comes to no less then the prize of the day, which, if you presently surrender, you may go about your business, if not, I must have a little dispute with you at sword and pistol.' At which, one of them let fly at him, but missing his aim, received Nevison's bullet into his right shoulder; and being thereby disabled, Nevison, about to discharge at the other, he call'd for quarter, and came to a parly, which, in short, was made up, with Nevison's promise to send their friend, and their delivering him all the ready money they had, which amounted to 150 pounds, and silver. With this, Nevison rides back to the two countrymen, and releases their prisoner, giving him their whole forty pounds, with a caution, for the future to look better after it, and not like cowards, as they were, to surrender the same on such easy terms again.

In all his pranks he was very favourable to the female sex, who generally gave him the character of a civil obliging robber; he was charitable also to the poor, as relieving them out of their spoils, which he took from them that could better spare it; and being a true Royalist, he never attempted any thing against that party. One time Nevison meeting with an old sequestrator on the road, he stop'd the coach, and demanded some of that money which he had thievishly extorted from poor widows and orphans, and ought to be returned: at which words the old man in a fit of terror, and especially so, when a pistol was clap'd to his breast, begun to expostulate for his life; offering whatsoever he had about him for his ransom, which he readily delivered to the value of 60 broad-pieces of gold. But this not serving the turn, Nevison told him that he must come thence, and go with him about some other affairs he had to concert with him, and beg leave of three young gentlewomen that were also passengers in the coach with him, that they would spare one of the coach-horses for one hour or two, which should certainly be returned that night for the next days journey. So Nevison left them, and took his prize with him on the postillion, which he loos'd from his coach, and carried him from them in a great fright, thinking he was now near his end, the gentlewomen pursued their journey; about two hours after they were got to their inn, in comes the old sequestrator on the postillion's horse before mentioned, and gave a lamentable relation how he had been used, and forced to sign a bill under his hand, of 500 pounds for his redemption, payable by a scrivner in London on sight, which he doubted not but would be received before he could prevent the same, and indeed he did not doubt amiss, for Nevison made the best of his way all night, and the next day by noon received the money, to the no small vexation of him that owned it.

About the year 1661, having one day met a considerable prize, to the value of 450 pounds, from a rich country grazier, with this he was resolved to set down quietly, and go back to Pomfret, where he was most joyfully received by his father, who never hearing of him in his absence of seven or eight years, thought he had been really dead. He lived very honestly with his father till he died, and then returned to his old courses again, committing such robberies, and rendered his name the terror of the road; insomuch, that no carrier or drover that pass'd the same, but was either forced to compound for their safety by a constant rent, which he usually received from them at such and such houses, where he appointed them to leave it, or they were sure to be rifled for the failure thereof.

Committing some robberies in Leicestershire, he was there taken, and committed to Leicester gaol, where he was so narrowly watch'd, and strongly ironed, that he could scarce stir; yet, by a cunning stratagem, he procured his enlargement before the assizes came. For one day, feigning himself extremely ill, he sent for two or three trusty friends, one of which was a physician, who gave out that he was sick of a pestilential fever; and that, unless he had the benefit of some open air, in some chamber, he would certainly infect the whole gaol, and die of the said distemper. Hereupon, the gaoler takes off his fetters, and removes him into another room, to lie by himself; in the mean time, a nurse was provided him, and his physician came twice or thrice a day to visit him, who gave out there was no hopes of his life, and that his distemper was extremely contagious: on which report, the gaoler's wife would not let her husband, nor any of the servants, go nearer than the door; which gave Nevison's confederates a full liberty to practise their intent, which they did thus: a painter was one day brought in, who made all over his breast blue spots, resembling those that are the forerunners of death in the disease commonly called the plague; as likewise, several marks on his hands, face, and body, which are usually on such that so die: all which being done, the physician prepared a dose whereby his spirits were confined for the space of an hour or two, and then immediately gave out that he was dead. Hereupon, his friends demand his body, bringing a coffin to carry him away in. The gaoler, as customary, orders a jury; the nurse having formally laid him out to examine the cause of his death, who fearing the contagion he was said to die of, staid not long to consider thereon; but having view'd him, seeing the spots and marks of death about him, his eyes set, and his jaws close muffled, they brought in their verdict that he died of the plague; and thereupon he was put in the coffin, and carried off.

Being thus discharged, he falls to his trade again, and meeting several of his old tenants the carriers, who had used to pay him his rents, as aforesaid, told them they must advance the same, for that his last imprisonment had cost him a great sum of money, which he expected to be reimburs'd among them. They being strangely surprized at sight of Mr Nevison, after the reports of his death, brooked about that his ghost walked, and took upon him the employment it was wont when living, which was the more confirmed by the gaoler at Leicester, who had brought in his verdict of the jury on oath, who had examined the body, and had found it dead, as abovemention'd; whereby he had been discharged by the court, as to the warrant of his commitment. But afterwards, when the same came to be known, and the cheat detected, the said gaoler was ordered to fetch him in, at his peril. Whereupon great search was made for him in all places, and a reward of twenty pounds set upon his head for any person that should apprehend him.

Nevison, after this, was determined to visit London; and the company he happen'd to fall into upon the road, was a crew of canting beggars, pilgrims of the earth, the offspring of Cain, vagabonds and wanderers over the whole world, fit companions for such who made a trade of idleness and roguery, and these were at this time fit companions for him, who, seeing the merry life they led, resolved to make one of their company; whereupon, after he had a little more ingratiated himself amongst them, and taken two or three cups more of rum-booz, he imparted his inventions to one of the chief of them, telling him, he was an apprentice, who had a curst master, whose cruelties had caused him to run away from him; and that whatever fortune might betide him, yet should not the most necessitous condition he could be plunged into ever make him to return to him again: and therefore if he might be admitted into their society, he should faithfully observe and perform what rules and orders were imposed upon him. The chief beggar very much applauded him for his resolution, telling him, that to be a beggar was to be a brave man, since it was then in fashion. 'Do not we,' said he, 'come into the world like arrant beggars, without a rag upon us? And do not we all go out of the world like beggars, without a rag upon us? And do not we all go out of the world like beggars, without any thing, saving only an old sheet over us? Shall we then be ashamed to walk up and down in the world like beggars, with old blankets pinn'd about us? No, no; that would be a shame to us, indeed: have we not the whole kingdom to walk, at our pleasure? Are we afraid of the approach of quarter-day? Do we walk in fear of bailiffs, serjeants, and catch-poles?

Who ever knew an arrant beggar arrested for debt? Is not our meat dress'd in every man's kitchen? Does not every man's cellar afford us beer? And the best men's purses keep a penny for us to spend.'

Having by these words, as he thought, fully fixed him in love with begging, he then acquainted the company with Nevison's desires, who were all of them very joyful thereat, being as glad to add one to their society, as a Turk is to gain a proselite to Mahomet; the first question they asked him was, If he had any loure in his bung: he stared on them, not knowing what they meant; till, at last, one told him it was money in his purse. He told them he had but eighteen pence, which he freely gave them. This, by a general vote, was condemned to be spent in bouze for his initiation. Then they commanded him to kneel down, which being done, one of the chief of them took a gage of bouze, which is a quart of drink, and poured the same on my head, saying, 'I do by virtue of this sovereign liquor, instal thee in the roage, and make thee a free denizon of our ragged regiment. So that henceforth it shall be lawful for thee to cant, and to carry a doxy or mort along with thee, only observing these rules: first, that thou art not to wander up and down all countries, but to keep to that quarter that is alloted to thee: and, secondly, thou art to give way to any of us that have born all the offices of the wallet before; and upon holding up a finger, to avoid any town or country village, where thou seest we are foraging for victuals for our army that march along with us. Observing these two rules, we take thee into our protection, and adopt thee a brother of our numerous society.'

Having ended his oration, Nevison rose up, and was congratulated by all the company's hanging about him like so many dogs about a bear, and leaping and shouting like so many madmen, making such a confused noise with their gabling, that the melody of a dozen of oyster-wives, the scolding at ten conduits, and the gossiping of fifteen bakehouses, were not comparable unto it. At length he that installed him, cried out for silence, bidding the French and English pox to light on their throats for making such a yelping. Then fixing their eyes upon Nevison, he read a lecture to him out of the Devil's horn-book, as followeth:

'Now,' saith he, 'thou art entered into our fraternity, thou must not scruple to act any villainies, which thou shalt be able to perform, whether it be to nip a bung, bite the Peter Cloy, the Lurries Crash, either a Bleating Cheat, Cackling Cheat, Grunting Chat, Quacking Cheat, Tib-oth-buttery, Margery Prater, or to cloy a

Mish from the Crackman's; that is, to cut a purse, steal a cloak-bag, or portman-teau, convey all manner of things, whether a chicken, sucking-pig, duck, goose, hen, or steal a shirt from the hedge; for he that will be a Quier Cove, a profest rogue, must observe this rule, set down by an antient patrico in these words:

> Wilt thou a begging go.
> O per se-o, O per se-o.
> Then must thou God forsake,
> And to the Devil thee betake.
> O per se-o, &c.

'And because thou art yet but a novice in begging, and understandest not the mysteries of the canting language, to principle thee the better, thou shalt have a doxy to be thy companion, by whom thou mayst receive fit instructions for thy purpose.' And thereupon he singled him out a girl, which tickled his fancy very much, that he had gotten a young wanton to daily withal, but this was not all, he must presently be married to her, after the fashion of their patrico, who amongst beggars, is their priest; which was done after this manner.

They got a hen, and having cut off the head of it, laid the dead body on the ground, placing him on the one side, and his doxy on the other; this being done, the patrico standing by, with a loud voice, bid us live together till death did us part; then one of the company went into the yard, and fetched a dry cow-turd which was broken over his doxy's head in imitation of a bride-cake; and so shaking hands and kissing each other, the ceremony of the wedding was over, and for joy of the marriage, they were are all as drunk as beggars; but then to hear the gabling noise they made would have made any one burst himself with laughing. Some were jabbering in the canting language, others in their own; some did nothing but weep, and protest love to their morts, others swore swords and daggers to cut the throats of their doxies, if they found them tripping; one would drink a health to the bride till he slaver'd again; some were for singing bawdy songs, others were divising oaths for Justice of Peace, headboroughs and constables. At last night approaching, and all their money being spent, they betook to a barn not far off, where they couched a hogshead in the darkman's, and went to sleep.

197

Nevison having met with this odd piece of diversion in his journey, slipt out of the barn, when all were asleep, took horse and posted directly away. But coming to London, and finding his name too much noised about to induce him to stay there, he returned into the country, and fell to his own pranks again. Several who had been robbed by him, happened to meet him, and could not help thinking but his ghost walk'd, considering the report of his pestilential death in Lincoln gaol. In short, his crimes became so notorious, that a reward was offered for any that would apprehend him. This made many way-lay him, especially two brothers, named Fletchers, one of whom Nevison shooting dead, he got off; from whence going into a little village about thirteen miles from York, he was taken by Capt. Hardcasle, and sent to York gaol, where in a week's time he was tried, condemned, and executed, aged forty-five.

THE LIFE OF THE
GOLDEN FARMER

T he Golden Farmer was so called from his occupation, and paying people, if it was any considerable sum, always in gold; but his real name was William Davis, born at Wrexham in Denbighshire, in North-Wales; from whence he removed, in his younger years, to Sudbury in Glocestershire, where he married the daughter of a wealthy inn keeper, by whom he had eighteen children, and followed the farmer's business to the day of his death, to shroud his robbing on the highway, which irregular practice he had followed for forty-two years, without any suspicion among his neighbours.

He generally robbed alone, and one day meeting three or four stage-coaches going to Salisbury, he stopped one of them who was full of gentlewomen, one of which was a Quaker: all of them satisfied the Golden Farmer's desire, excepting this Perciscan, with whom he had a long argument to no purpose; for upon her solemn vow and affirmation, she told him, she had no money, nor any thing valuable about her; whereupon, fearing he should lose the booty of the other coaches, he told her, he would go and see what they had to afford him, and he would wait on her again; so having robbed the other three coaches, he returned according to his word, and the Quaker persisting still in her old tone of having nothing for him, it put the Golden Farmer into a rage, and taking hold of her shoulder, shaking her as a mastiff does a bull, he cried, 'You canting bitch, if you dally with me at this rate, you'll certainly provoke my spirit to be damnable rude with you: you see these good women here were so tender hearted, as to be charitable to me, and you, you whining whore, are so covetous as to lose your life for the sake of Mammon. —Come, come, you hollow-hearted bitch, unpin your purse-string quickly, or else I shall send you out of the land of the living.' Now the poor Quaker being frighted out of her wits at the bullying expressions of the wicked one, she gave him a purse of guineas, a gold watch, and a diamond-ring, and parted then as good friends, as if they had never fallen out at all.

Another time this desperado meeting with the Dutchess of Albermarle in her coach, as riding over Salisbury-Plain, was put to his trumps before he could assault her Grace, by reason he had a long engagement with a postillion, coachman, and two footmen, before he could proceed in his robbery; but having wounded them all, by the discharging several pistols, he then approached to his prey, whom he found more refractory than his female Quaker had been, which made him very saucy, and more eager for fear of any passengers coming by in the mean while; but still her Grace denied parting with any thing; whereupon by main violence he pulled three diamond rings off her fingers, and snatched a rich gold watch from her side, crying to her, at the same time, because he saw her face painted, 'You bitch incarnate, you had rather read over your face in the glass every moment, and blot out pale to put in red, than give an honest man, as I am, a small matter to support him on his lawful occasions on the road'; and then rode away as fast as he could without searching her Grace for any money, because he perceived another person of quality's coach, making towards them, with a good retinue of servants belonging to it.

Not long after this exploit, the Golden Farmer meeting with Sir Thomas Day, a Justice of Peace living at Bristol, on the road betwixt Gloucester and Worcester, they fell into discourse together, and as riding along, he told Sir Thomas, whom he knew, though the other did not know him, how he had like to have been robbed but a little before by a couple of highwaymen; but as good luck would have it, his horse having better heels than theirs, he got clear of them, or else, if they had robbed him of his money, which was about forty pounds, they had certainly undone him for ever. 'Truly,' quoth Sir Thomas Day, 'that had been very hard; but nevertheless, as you had been robbed between sun and sun, the county, upon suing it, must have been obliged to have made your loss good again'; but not long after this chatting together, coming to a convenient place, the Golden Farmer shooting Sir Thomas's man's horse under him, and obliging him to retire some distance from it, that he might not make use of the pistols that were in his holsters, he presented a pistol to Sir Thomas's breast, and demanded his money of him. Quoth Sir Thomas, 'I thought Sir, that you had been an honest man.' The Golden Farmer replied, 'You see your Worship's mistaken, and had you had any guts in your brains, you might have perceived by my face, that my countenance was the very picture of mere necessity; therefore deliver presently; for I am in haste.' Then Sir Thomas Day, giving the Golden Farmer what money he had, which was about sixty pounds in gold and silver, he humbly thanked his Worship, and told him, 'that what he had parted with was not lost, because he was robbed betwixt sun and sun, therefore the county,' as he told him, 'must pay it again.'

One Mr Hart, a young gentleman of Enfield, who had a good estate, but not over-burden'd with wit; and therefore, could sooner change a piece of gold, than a piece of sense, riding one day over Finchley-Common, where the Golden Farmer had been hunting about four or five hours for a prey, he rides up to him, and giving the gentleman a slap with the flat of his drawn hanger o'er his shoulders: quoth he, 'A plague on you how slow you are to make a man wait on you all this morning: come deliver what you have, and be poxt to you, and go to hell for orders.' The gentleman who was wont to find a more agreeable entertainment betwixt his mistress and his snuff-box, being surprised at the rustical sort of greeting, he began to make several sorts of excuses, and say, he had no money about him; but his antagonist, not believing him, he made bold to search his pockets himself, and finding in them above an hundred guineas, besides a gold watch, he gave him two or three slaps over the shoulder again, with his hanger; and at the same time bid him not give his mind to lying any more, when an honest gentleman desired a small boon of him.

Another time this notorious robber had paid his landlord above forty pounds for rent, who going home with it, the goodly tennant disguising himself, met the old grave gentleman, and bidding him stand: quoth he, 'Come, Mr Gravity from head to foot; but from neither head nor foot to the heart, deliver what you have in a trice.' The old man, fetching a deep sigh, to the hazard of losing several buttons of his waistcoat, said that he had not above two shillings about him;

therefore he thought he was more of a gentleman, than to take a small matter from a poor man. Quoth the Golden Farmer, 'I have not the faith to believe you; for you seem by your mien and habit to be a man of better circumstance than you pretend; therefore open your budget, or else I shall fall foul about your house.'—'Dear Sir,' replied his landlord, 'you can't be so barbarous to an old man: what! have you no religion, pity, or compassion in you? Have you no conscience? nor have you no respect for your own body and soul, which must be certainly in a miserable condition, if you follow unlawful courses.'—'Damn you' (said the Tennant to him) 'don't talk of age and barbarity to me; for I shew neither pity nor compassion to any. Damn you, what talk of conscience to me! I have no more of that dull commodity than you have; nor do I allow my soul and body to be governed by religion, but interest; therefore, deliver what you have, before this pistol makes you repent your obstinacy'; so delivering his money to the Golden Farmer, he received it without giving the landlord any receipt for it, as his landlord had him.

Not long after committing this robbery, overtaking an old grasier at Putney-Heath, in a very ordinary attire, but yet very rich, he takes half a score guineas out of his pocket, and giving them to the old man, he said, 'There was three or four persons behind them, who looked very suspicious; therefore he desired the favour of him to put that gold into his pocket; for in case they were highwaymen, his indifferent apparel would make them believe he had no such charge about him.' The old grasier looking upon his intentions to be honest, quoth he, 'I have fifty guineas tied up in the fore lappet of my shirt, and I'll put it to that for security'; so riding along both of them cheek by jole, for above half a mile, and the coast being clear, the Golden Farmer said to the old man, 'I believe there's no body will take the pains of robbing you or me to day; therefore, I think I had as good take the trouble of robbing you myself; so instead of deli-vering your purse, pray give me the lappet of your shirt.' The old grasier was horridly startled at these words, and began to beseech him not to be so cruel in robbing a poor old man.—'Pr'ythee,' quoth the Golden Farmer, 'don't tell me of cruelty; for who can be more cruel than men of your age, whose pride it is to teach their servants their duties, with as much cruelty as some people teach their dogs to fetch and carry?' So being obliged to cut off the lappet of the old man's shirt himself, for he would not, he rode away to seek out another booty.

202

Another time, this bold robber lying at an inn in Uxbridge, he happened into company with one 'Squire Broughton, a barrister of the Middle-Temple, which he understanding, pretended to him that he was going up to London, to advise with a lawyer about some business; wherefore, he should be much obliged to him, if he could recommend him to a good one. Counsellor Broughton, thinking he might be a good client, he bespoke him for himself. Then the Golden Farmer telling his business was about several of his neighbour's cattle, breaking into his grounds, and doing a great deal of mischief, the barrister told him, 'that was very actionable, as being Damage Fesant.' 'Damage Fesant,' says the Golden Farmer, 'what's that, pray Sir?' He told him, 'that it was an action brought against persons when their cattle broke through hedges, or other fences, into other people's grounds, and did them damage.' Next morning, as they both were riding toward London, says the Golden Farmer to the barrister, 'If I may be so bold as to ask you, Sir, what is that you call trover and conversion?' He told him it signified in our common law, an action which a man has against another, that having found any of his goods, refuses to deliver them upon demand, and perhaps converts them to his own use also. The Golden Farmer being now at a place convenient for his purpose, 'Very well, Sir,' says he, 'and so, if I should find any money about you, and convert it to my use, why then that is only actionable I find.'—'That's a robbery,' said the barrister, which requires no less satisfaction than a man's life.'—'A robbery!' replied the Golden Farmer, 'why then I must e'en commit one for once and not use it; therefore deliver your money, or else behold this pistol shall prevent you from ever reading Cook upon Littleton any more.' The barrister, strangely surpris'd at his client's rough behaviour, asked him, 'if he thought there was neither Heaven nor Hell, that he could be guilty of such wicked actions'. Quoth the Golden Farmer, 'Why, you son of a whore, thy impudence is very great to talk of Heaven or Hell to me, when you think there's no way to Heaven, but through Westminster-Hall. Come, come, down with your rino this minute; for I have other guess customers to mind, than to wait on your arse all day.' The barrister being very loath to part with his money, he was still insisting on the injustice of the action, saying, 'it was against law and conscience to robb any man'. However the Golden Farmer, heeding not his pleading, he swore, 'he was not to be guided by law and conscience any more than any of his profession, whose law is always furnished with a commission to arraign their

203

The Golden FARMER and the TINKER

consciences; but upon judgment given, they usually had the knack of setting it at large'. So putting a pistol to the barrister's breast, he quickly delivered his money, amounting to about thirty guineas, and eleven broad pieces of gold, besides some silver, and a gold-watch.

One time overtaking a tinker on Black-Heath, whom he knew to have seven or eight pounds about him, quoth he, 'Well overtaken, brother tinker, methinks you seem very devout; for your life is a continual pilgrimage, and in humility you go almost bare-foot, thereby making necessity a virtue.'—'Ay Master,' replied the tinker, 'needs must, when the Devil drives, and had you no more than I, you might go without boots and shoes too.'—'That might be,' quoth the Golden Farmer. 'And I suppose you march all over England with your bag and baggage?'—'Yes,' said the tinker, 'I go a great deal of ground, but not so much as you ride.'—'Well,' quoth the Golden Farmer, 'go where you will, it is my opinion, your conversation is unreproveable, because thou art ever mending.'—'I wish,' replied the tinker, 'that I could say as much by you.'—'Why you dog of Egypt,' quoth the other, 'you don't think that I am like you, in observing the statutes; and therefore had rather steal than beg in spite of whips or imprisonment.' Said the tinker again, 'I'll have you to know I take a great deal of pains for a livelihood.'—'Yes,' replied the Golden Farmer, 'I know thou art such a strong enemy to idleness, that mending one hole, you make three, rather than want work.'—'That's as you say,' quoth the tinker; 'however, Sir, I wish you and I were farther asunder; for i'faith I don't like your company.'—'Nor I yours,' said the other; 'for though thou art entertained in every place, yet you enter no farther than the door to avoid suspicion.'—'Indeed,' replied the tinker, 'I have a great suspicion of you.'—'Have you so,' replied the Golden Farmer, why then it shall not be without a cause: come open your wallet forthwith, and deliver that parcel of money that's in it.' Here their dialogue being on a conclusion, the tinker pray'd heartily, that he would not rob him; for if he did, he must be forced to beg his way home, from whence he was above an hundred miles. 'Damn you,' quoth the Golden Farmer, 'I don't care, if you beg your way two hundred miles; for if a tinker escape Tyburn and Banbury, it is fate to die a beggar': so taking money and wallet too from the tinker, he left him to his old custom of conversing still in open fields and low cottages.

After this encounter with the tinker, our adventurer had but a few pranks to play upon the stage of human life, his name being now spread all around the

205

country, so that hue-and-cries were pretty numerous after him: in short, there was no possibility to make his escape, every one turning his enemy now at the last extremity; when, if love of man had influenced them, they should have befriended him. He was aprehended, and carried to gaol, where, during his confinement, he behaved with the same alacrity, as he had spent the merry moment of his foregoing life; neither the thought of the place, nor the apprehensions of death in the least terrifying him. After three weeks imprisonment, he was tried and condemn'd, and the gallows became the just punishment of all the miscarriages and villianies he had been guilty of during his vicious scene of life.

THE LIFE OF
JACK BIRD

This notorious malefactor was born at Stainford in Lincolnshire, of very honest parents, by whom, after he had been at school to learn reading, writing, and accounts, he was put apprentice to a baker at Godmanchester, near Huntington. He had not served three years before he run away from his master, came to London, and listed in the foot-guards. While he was in the army, he was at the siege of Maestricht, under the command of the Duke of Monmouth, who was general of the English forces in the Low Countries.

Here he was reduced to such necessities as are common to men who engage themselves to kill one another for a groat or five-pence a-day. This occasioned him to run away from his colours, and fly to Amsterdam, where he stole a piece of silk off a stall; for which fact he was apprehended, and dragged before a magistrate. The effect of this was a commitment to the Rasp-House, where he was put to hard labour, such as rasping log-wood and other drudgeries, for a twelve-month.

As Jack had never been used to work, he fainted under the sentence, though to little purpose; for his task-masters imputing it to a stubborn laziness, inflicted a severer punishment upon him: the manner of which was as follows: he was chained down to the bottom of a dry cistern by one foot; immediately upon which, several cocks were set a running into it, and he was obliged to pump for his life. The cistern was much deeper than he was high; so that if the water had prevailed, he must inevitably have been drowned without relief or pity. Jack was very sensible of his danger, which occasioned him to labour with all his might for an hour, which was as long as the sentence was to continue.

Having overcome his difficulty, he ply'd his business very well the remaining part of the year, when being released, he returned into England, with a resolution to try his fortune on the highway. Near St Edmundsbury he stole a horse, and he had before provided half a dozen good pistols, and a sword. Success attended him in his three or four first robberies; but an unlucky adventure soon brought about a turn in his affairs.

In the road between Gravesend and Chatham, he met with one Mr Joseph Pinnis, a pilot of Dover, who had lost both his hands in an engagement. He had been at London to receive ten or twelve pounds for carrying a Dutch ship up the river. When Bird accosted him with the salutation common to gentlemen of his profession; 'You see, Sir,' quoth Pinnis, 'that I have never a hand; so that I am not able to take my money out of my pocket myself. Be so kind, therefore, as to take the trouble of searching me.' Jack soon consented to this very reasonable request; but while he was very busy in examining the contents of the pilot's purse, the boisterous old tar suddenly clapp'd his arms about his neck, and spurring his own horse, pulled our adventurer from his; then falling directly upon him, and being a very strong man, he kept him under, and maul'd him with his stumps, which were plated. In the midst of the scuffle some passengers came by, and enquired the occasion of it. Mr Pinnis replied with telling them the particulars, and desiring them to supply his place, and give the villain a little more of the same, adding, 'that he was almost out of breath with what he had done already'. When the company understood what was the reason of the pilot's labouring so hard upon the bones of our ruffian, they apprehended him, and carried him before a Justice, who committed him to Maidstone Gaol, where he continued till the assizes, and then was condemned to be hang'd.

This time Jack had the good fortune to receive mercy, and afterwards to obtain his liberty. The remembrance of his being so heartily thumped by a man without hands, stuck so much in his stomach that he had almost a mind to grow honest; and indeed he continued pretty orderly, till he was again reduced to necessitous circumstances, for want of employment. He had no trade that he was master of, nor learning enough to secure him a maintenance in a genteel way; so that when he found himself in the utmost streights, he could see no other method of supporting himself, than what he had formerly followed.

The first that he met with, after he had resolved to set out in pursuit of new enterprizes, was a Welsh drover, about a mile beyond Acton. The fellow being almost as stout as Mr Pinnis, would not obey the usual precept, but was going to lay about him with a good quarter staff, which he had in his hands. Jack, when he saw Taffy's courage, leapt nimble out of the way of his staff, and told him, 'that he had been taken once by a son of a whore without hands; and for that trick,' says he, 'I shall not venture my carcass within reach of one that has hands; for fear of something worse.' While he was speaking, he pulled out a pistol, and instantly shot him through the head. Rifling his pockets, and finding but eighteen-pence, said ironically, 'This is a prize worth killing a man for at any time.' He then rode away about his business as little concern'd as if he had done no mischief at all.

Another time Jack Bird met with Poor Robin the almanack writer, on the road going to Waltham-Abbey. Poor and rich were all the same to him, when they came in his way; so the honest astrologer was greeted with the salutation of 'stand and deliver'. It was the first time that Robin had been attacked on the highway; and as he received no intimation of this from the stars, he stood and star'd, as if he had been planet struck. Bird told him he was in earnest, and Robin reply'd with a complaint of his poverty. 'That,' says Jack, 'is a common thread-bare excuse, and will not save your bacon.'—'But,' quoth the star-gazer, 'my name is Poor Robin: I am the author of those almanacks that come out yearly in my name, and I have canoniz'd a great many gentlemen of your profession. Look in my calendar for Guzman, Jonas Allen, Hind, Du Val, Dun, Cambray-Bess, Moll Cutpurse, and others: let this be my protection.' All was in vain; our inexorable free-booter ransack'd his pockets of fifteen shillings, took a new hat from his head, and then told him, 'that now he had given him cause to cannonize him too'. Which Robin promised to do the first year after he had suffered martyrdom at Tyburn, and so they parted.

Being again encouraged by a series of successful adventures, and having remounted himself on a very good horse, he was resolved to venture on higher exploits. An opportunity for putting this resolution into practice, soon fell in his

209

way, by his meeting the mad Earl of P—, and his chaplain, who was little better than himself, in a coach, with no more attendants than the coachman, and one footman. 'Stand and deliver' was the word. His Lordship told him, that he did not trouble himself about losing the small matter he had about him: 'But then,' says he, 'I hope you will fight for it.' Jack, upon this, pulled out a brace of pistols, and let off a volley of imprecations. 'Don't put yourself into a passion, friend,' says his Honour, 'but lay down your pistols, and I will box you fairly for all the money I have, against nothing.' 'That's an honourable challenge, my Lord,' quoth Jack, 'provided none of your servants be near us.' The earl immediately order'd them to keep at a distance.

The chaplain, like Withrington in the old Ballad of Chevy-Chace, could not bear to see an earl fight on foot, while he stood looking on; so he desired the honour of espousing the cause of his Lordship: to which both parties readily agreeing, off went the divinity in a minute, and to blows and bloody-noses they came.

Tho' Jack had once the ill-fortune to be stumped out of his liberty by a sturdy old sailor, he was nevertheless too hard for his Reverence in less than a quarter of an hour. He beat him in such a manner that he could not see, and had but just breath enough to cry, 'I'll fight no more.' About two minutes after this victory (which he took for a breathing time) Jack told his Lordship, 'that now, if he pleased, he would take a turn with him'.—'By no means,' quoth the earl, 'for if you beat my chaplain, you will beat me; he and I having tried our manhood before.' So giving our hero twenty guineas, his Honour rode off in a whole skin.

While Jack resided in town, he married a young woman, who had been servant to a dyer near Exeter Exchange in the Strand. This girl, while she was in place, us'd to set up a-nights for her master; and, in short, to use him so very civily, that it was the occasion of her destruction. A particular account of this affair will not be disagreable, nor entirely foreign to our design.

The dyer's wife, having entertain'd a jealousy from some observations she had made, as well as from her husband's backwardness in the performance of family duty, she was resolved to examine into the bottom of the affair. Accordingly, she one night commanded the maid to go to bed, and undertook to sit up for her husband herself. Betwixt twelve and one he came home, and madam open'd the door in the dark, without speaking a word. The good man was silent as his supposed maid, and very orderly laid her on a counter, exerted his manhood, and gave her half-a-crown, according to custom. Madam immediately slipp'd away to bed, and her dear spouse follow'd her, as soon as he had fasten'd up the street-door, without the least suspicion of what had passed.

The next morning Mr — was amaz'd to see his servant packing up her cloaths, as soon as he was out of bed. The surprize encreased when he observed the surly behaviour of his wife, saw her pay the girl her wages, and bid her be gone forth with. The young woman, without doubt, was as much confused as her master, being altogether as ignorant of the cause; she durst not speak one word for herself, such a hurry was her mistress in. At last Mr — took the courage to speak. 'Pray, my dear, what's the meaning of all this? What has the poor wench done to be thus turn'd out of doors at an hour's warning? I never found her dishonest; if you have, let her know what you accuse her with. Perhaps she may do better another time; or, if you are bent upon discharging her, don't give people room to say you have us'd her unhandsomely.' The devil a word could be get more than, 'She was a saucy baggage, and go she should.' Accordingly, when her things were all ready, she came into the parlour to bid her master and mistress good-bye. Just as she was going out of doors, 'Hold! Hold! Betty,' says the mistress, 'here's half a crown that I earn'd for you last night upon the counter; take that along with you.' The dyer, upon this, apprehended how matters went, and was willing afterwards to make his submission, that he might come to terms with his dear offended wife, who continually teiz'd him with the half-crown and the counter.

The Athenian Society, who made themselves sufficiently famous about this time by their monthly productions, took a great deal of pains in the case above, before they could resolve whether or no the dyer had committed adultery with his own wife. They concluded at last, that tho' the act of copulation was with him own spouse, yet he was chargeable with the crime of adultery, as his design was on another person, whom he could not lawfully touch. This enquiry gave considerable diversion to the town, and made the poor dyer a general subject of ridicule.

But though Bird was married, he did not confine himself to any one woman; for we are told that he was continually in company with whores and bawds: one night in particular, having a woman with him, he knock'd down a man, between

Dutchy-Lane, and the Great-Savoy-Gate in the Strand, and having robb'd him, made off safely; but the woman was apprehended, and sent to Newgate. Jack went to her, in hopes to make up the affair with the prosecutor, and was thereupon taken, on suspicion, and confin'd with her.

At his trial he confessed the fact, and took it wholly upon himself; so that the woman was acquitted, and he condemn'd to suffer death; which sentence was inflicted on him at Tyburn, on Wednesday the 12th of March, 1690, he being forty-two years of age. After execution his body was convey'd to Surgeon's Hall, and there anatomiz'd.

He spoke but very little at the gallows, what he did say consisted chiefly to invectives against lewd women, and advice to young men not to be seduc'd, by their conversation, from the rules of virtue and morality.

THE LIFE OF
CAPTAIN
DUDLEY

Richard Dudley, commonly called Capt. Dudley, was born in Leicestershire, at a place called Swepston. His father was a gentlemen of a good estate, but had not the fortune to keep it, he living in such a manner, that his expences by much exceeded his income; so that he was oblig'd to mortgage and sell the greatest part to satisfy his creditors, and having about threescore pounds a-year left, came up to London, with his family, hoping by the obscurity of the living, to contain himself within the bounds of the small remainder he had left; but we shall leave the father, and give an account of the son, who is the unhappy occasion of our present writing.

Richard Dudley, the son, had a good education bestow'd upon him at St Paul's School, he seeming of a very promising genius, but when a vicious inclination is rivetted in the nature of any person, no care of his education, no rules of religion or morality are sufficient to controul him, as plainly appears by too fragrant an instance in the life of this unfortunate person; for when but nine years old, he discover'd his tendency to thieving, by robbing one of his sisters closets of thirty shillings, and marching off with it: but being some days after found out, and brought home again, he was sent back to school; but not liking that sort of confinement, he robb'd his father's house of a considerable sum of money, and so ran away again; yet his father had the luck to discover him, and took him with a couple of lewd women, a little way out of town.

After this, his father despairing of his doing any good at home, procured him the King's Letter to be a reformade on board a man of war, in which station, he went up the streights, and behaved himself gallantly in several actions. Amongst the rest, this was one, being, on shore at Cadiz, in order to refresh himself, and walking quietly along, he was abused and attack'd by a Spaniard; but he not only defended himself, but run the don quite through, left him dead on the spot, and got safe on ship-board: upon his arrival in England, he quitted the ship, pretending he did so on account of a younger, reformade being preferr'd before him, on the death of a lieutenant; but whether that was his motive, or not, this is certain, that he associated himself with a notorious gang of thieves, ready for any mischief, and assisted them in breaking open and robbing the house of Admiral Carter in the country, and getting off undetected, came to London, and from that time commenced a professed thief. The first remarkable robbery he was concerned in, was, that of a lady's house at Black-heath, from whence he and his accomplices stole a very considerable quantity of plate, which they brought to town, and sold to a refiner; but for this robbery he was apprehended not long after, and when he was in Newgate he sent for the refiner, and complain'd how hard a thing it was to find an honest man, and a fair dealer. 'For you cursed rogue' (says he) 'among the plate you bought, there was a cup with a cover, which you modestly told us was but silver gilt, and bought it at the same price with the rest; but it plainly appeared by the advertisement in the *Gazette*, that it was a gold cup and cover; but I see you are a rogue; and that there's no trusting any body.' For this robbery he was tried at Maidstone, convicted, and condemn'd; but his youth, and the interest of his friends, first procur'd him a reprieve, and then a pardon; which, for about two years, had such an effect upon him, that he lived pretty soberly for that time; so that his father bought him a commission in the army, in which station he behaved very well, and had the good fortune to marry a young lady of a good family, with whom he had an estate of seven-score pounds a-year; upon which, and his commission, they for some time lived comfortably; but the captain loving company too much, and having contracted a large acquaintance, engaged himself for some money, which one of his companions owed, who was afterwards arrested for the debt, in which arrest a bailiff was killed, and the captain (being then present) was suspected to have done it, he always declaring his detestation and abhorrence of that sort of men, and often wishing to kill some of them, his character and opinion of them being as follows.

A serjeant is a rogue that would undo one of the twelve companies for a crown; the counter gate is his proper kennel, and the miseries of poor men the offal on which he feeds. He does not carry his captives directly to Hell (the counter) but first torments them in a purgatory hard by, where you must pay two Shillings a night for a lowsy bed, and spend as much in liquoring his chops, as would pay half the debt. This he calls his civility. If you seem to fear other actions coming against you, he will pretend to pity you, and agrees for a daub in the fist to keep the matter private, till you make an end of it; but goes directly to find out some other creditors, bids them strike whilst the iron is hot; and thus when the poor prisoner has satisfied the first debt, and thinks to regain his liberty, he is charged a-fresh. Thus he picks your pocket by degrees, and when he finds that is empty, he delivers you over to the turnkey, where the Lord have mercy on your soul; for to be sure, they will have little enough on your body.

A common bailiff exceeds a serjeant as much as an Irish mastiff does a spaniel in fierceness. He is a raven that pecks not out mens eyes, as others do, but all his spite is at their shoulders. These land pyrates cruise up and down Holbourn, as thick as Algier and Sallee men in the Mediterranean, and carry those they take to a worse slavery. In the country they are called bums, being of the very scum and dregs of the people, rascalls who have generally escaped the gallows once or twice, and yet must at last come to it; for a rope is certainly their destiny. It is deplorable to think how they abuse poor people, for there is hardly a writ in five, against those they arrest; they are setters by day, thieves in the night, bailiffs all the week, and informers on Sundays, and yet never thrive: for as they live rogues, they die beggars.

A marshal's man is yet a more insufferable grievance, a false die of the same bale, but not the same gut; for it runs somewhat higher, and does more mischief. He is a perfect blood-hound, that haunts upon the smallest scent, and worries all to death he lays hold on. The circle this devil is confin'd in, is twelve miles over, and in that circuit he commonly undoes above twelve hundred people a year. He plies among poor people, and upon every petty quarrel, scoulding-bout, or chandler's score, he sets them to law; as soon as he has arrested, one persuades him to snap the other, and then they are both forced to lie at his mercy, till they pawn their beds to raise what money he pleases to demand; and that he may fleece them the more commodiously, he keeps a tipling-house, where he imprisons them, by his own authority, and his wife over-reckons a groat in a shilling; and tho' you know it, you must not speak, because it is his kindness to keep you there, and not carry you to the lake of perdition, on the other side the water. There is nothing more frequent than to see here a chimney-sweeper prosecuting a broom-man for breaking his head at cudgels, and an oyster-wench suing a kitchen staff-woman, for calling her draggle-tail. What a deplorable thing it is that a family shall be ruin'd, and a poor man buried alive, for such an inconsiderable matter!

As for the yeomen, followers, and setting vermin, they are such contemptible rascals, they are not worth thinking on: we may call them the hooks that hang under water, and their master the floats above, which pop down as soon as ever the bait is swallowed. Necessity makes them valiant, for they will greedily take a cut with a sword, and suck more silver out of the wound than a surgeon; so that they commonly die with their guts ripped up, or else the Devil by a sudden stale sends a habeas cum anima for them.

As to the villains about White-Chapel, St Katherine's, the click, and the rest of the Devil's houses, I shan't trouble myself about, but I must have a word or two with the gaoler, for he is a creature mistaken in the making, for he should be a tyger, but the shape being thought too terrible it is covered, and he wears the visage of a man, yet retains his fierceness; his conscience, and his shackles, he hangs up together, and they are made very near of the same metal, having that one is harder than the other, and hath one property above iron, that it never melts; he distills money out of poor mens tears, and grows fat by their curses; his ears are stop'd to the cries of others, and God's to his, by all likelihood, for lay the life of a man in one scale, and his fees in the other, he would cast away the first to get the second, and in brief is one that can look for no mercy (if he desires justice to be done him) for he shews none.

But to return to the captain, he absented himself from his house, lurking about in bye-places; and by that idle way of living, he got acquainted with a gang of highwaymen, by whose easiness of living, and extravagant expences, he was easily persuaded to be one of their gang, for few persuasions were needful to one who had got the upper hand of virtue, who was more inclined to live upon the ruins of his countrymen, than by his own industry; having been more used to fight than work. He was not long about learning his trade, but in a little time became master of it; for there was scarce a notable robbery committed, in which he had not a hand, and finding it easy and profitable, he drew in his brother (whose name was Will Dudley) to be one of their gang; he had not long gone on in his new trade, before he was apprehended in the country, for robbing a gentleman of a watch, a sword, a whip, and nine shillings in money; but the evidence not being very clear, he escaped once more.

No sooner had he obtained his liberty, but he fell again to his old trade, but did not confine himself to any particular part, but robbed on the highway, broke houses, or pick'd pockets, or any thing else that procured him any money; in which several ways he for a time went on with impunity, but was at length detected for breaking and robbing Sir John Friend's house, and for that fact he received sentence of death, but his friends again got him a reprieve on condition of transportation, pursuant to which, he with several other convicts, were put on board a ship, in order for Barbadoes: but they were hardly got as far as the Isle of Whight, before he had drawn in the rest of the rogues to a conspiracy, in order to escape, and having concerted their measures, accordingly the ships company being under hatches, they went off with the long-boat.

Being now on shore, he left his comrades, and travelled by himself through woods and by-ways, and being now in a very mean habit, when he had no opportunity to steal, he begged, till he came to Hounslow-Heath, where he attacked a country farmer, robbed and unhorsed him, and mounting himself, set forward to seek for more prey, and before he got off the heath, another opportunity offered, for he met with a man in a genteel habit, and with a better horse than that which he took from the farmer. He soon gave him the word of command to stand, and leading him into a bye-place, made him exchange horse and cloaths with him, telling the man that he ought never to accuse him with robbing him, 'for' says he, 'you know the old proverb, exchange is no robbery', so wishing him well, he made the best of his way for London, where he immediately resorted to his old haunts, to find out his companions, which was very easy for him to do, and they all submitted to his conduct, and dubbed him with the title of captain. Thus got at the head of a hardened gang, no part of the country was secure from his rapine, nor any house strong enough to keep him out, so that he became notorious every where.

To avoid the continual searches made for him, and to divert enquiries, he paid a visit to the north, and being out one day in search of booty, he met with a Dutch colonel very well armed, but not couragious enough to fight for his money; so that the captain made bold with both horse and arms, and took his laced coat into the bargain. Thus mounted and equipped, he committed abundance of robberies, but shifting the colonels accoutrements, he used only his horse upon which he robbed a great many people, particularly a gentleman near Epsom, who being a man of courage, would not deliver, but exchanged a pistol with him: however, the captain got the better, and wounded the gentleman in the leg; upon which he rode up to him, lent him his assistance, and conducted him to the next village, to get some help, and then left him, having first taken his money. As for the Buckinghamshire laceman, the captain and his gang robbed them for a pastime, and only called it an airing for their horses. No stage of other coach, when they had intelligence of any passenger, could escape their search, and so diligent were they in pursuit of their villany, that scarce a day passed in which they did not commit some robbery or other.

Thus did he and his confederates riot in the spoils of others, and remained undiscovered for several months, till at length robbing the Southampton coach they were pursued, and several of them taken, yet he escaped not taken warning. At this he joyned himself with some house-breakers, and with them committed many burglaries and robberies, and in particular, he with three of his accomplices, got into an old woman's house, in Spittle-Fields, they gagg'd her, tied her in her chair; rifled her house, and carried off a considerable sum of money, which the old woman had been many years hoarding up. She hearing the money chink, and going to be taken from her, struggled in the chair, and fell down upon her face, with the gagg in her mouth, and the chair upon her, by which means she was stifled; but they got safe off, and passed undiscovered, till the old woman came to be buried, when one of them (who was her grand child, and privy to the robbery) going to be fitted with gloves, was observed to change his countenance often, and tremble very much; several persons seeing the disorder he was in, began to suspect him, and charged him with the fact, he confessed the whole affair, and two of them being found guilty on his evidence, of the murder and robbery, were hang'd in chains. Yet the captain all this while passed unapprehended, though his name was publickly mentioned as an accessary to the fact: but being at length taken up for divers highways robberies, (of which by his dextrous management he was acquitted) he was called to his trial for that, also when the evidence swore they saw him lurking about, go into and come out of the house of the murdered woman; and several strong circumstances appeared to prove him guilty; but he upon whose evidence the two former were convicted, was not to be found; and this gave Dudley an opportunity to make such a sham defence, as would have deceived the most penetrating judge and jury on earth. He himself thought it so great a master-piece, that he often boasted of it in prison, and from his account I shall acquaint the reader with it.

The first witness that appeared on his behalf, was a young gentleman, who deposed that he and another gentleman, going through Somerset-House yard on the day set forth in the indictment, to be that on which the robbery and murder was committed; he accidently met the captain who had been his schoolfellow, and was surprized to see him, having heard that he had been transported for some crime, which he was very sorry for. That the captain told him he was indeed ordered for transportation, and expressed a very great concern, that he should ever be guilty of a crime to deserve such punishment; but that his relations being not so kind as he expected, he was put on board a ship, with some more unfortunate persons, as a common convict, and made his escape, and depended on his friends good-will, to put him in a condition to transport himself, resolving so to do the very first opportunity. The same witness further deposed, that finding him so very sorry for his offence, he desired him to accompany him and his friend to Chelsea; intending to make use of that time, in exhorting him to lead his life more regular for the future. That the prisoner accepting the offer, they took boat at Somerset Stairs, and went to the Swan at Chelsea, where they staid till seven at night, and then walk'd to a publick house on the bank-side, supped on a dish of fowls and bacon, and stayed there till almost eleven; when they took boat again for Somerset Stairs, walked into the Strand, and there parted. The witness being asked why he should take such particular notice of the day of the month; answered, 'that the next day he heard a paper cried about the streets, concerning the murder and robbery of the old woman, that buying it, he found the captain's name mentioned as an accessary in the fact, and upon that made a memmorandum in his pocket-book, (which he produced in court) and afterwards went to his friend, who was with him at Chelsea, and to the waterman who carried them, desiring them likewise to take notice of the day, for that Dudley being a person of but an indifferent character, some other rogue might make use of his name, and he be hanged for a fact he was innocent of.'

The next witness, was the other friend, who said, 'that he saw him, and the prisoner talk together in Somerset House yard, but did not know what they said; that they went to Chelsea, and there the former witness was very earnest with the captain (who then understood his name to be, having never seen him before) to reform some ill practices he had been too much addicted to; that the next day the former witness came and desired him to take particular notice of the day and person who went with them to Chelsea, which he accordingly did, and was very positive that the prisoner at the bar, was the man that they supped with at the Red-Lyon, at the bank-side, that they afterwards came back to Somerset-House Stairs, and in the Strand parted with the prisoner about eleven at night.'

The waterman corroborated their evidence, and affirmed, that he carried the two gentlemen aforesaid to Chelsea, and a third person with them; and being asked if the prisoner was that third person, he said his eyes were very bad, and went up close to the bar to look him in the face, and, turning about said, 'Yes, my Lord, this is the gentleman.' He also deposed that he waited on them at Chelsea, and carried them from thence to the bank-side; where he received four shillings and sixpence for his fare, upon condition he would carry them back again, which he did; and landed them about eleven at night. That the next day his master (the first witness) came and bid him take notice of the day of the month, which he did, and chalked it down at home.

The next who was called, was the pretended landlord of the house, where they supped, 'who swore that on such a day of the month, three gentlemen came to his house about seven at night, (of which the prisoner was one) and ordered a couple of fowls and bacon to be got ready with all speed, which was done; they supped, and between ten and eleven at night, they took boat, and ordered the waterman to carry them to Somerset Stairs': being asked how he came to take such notice of the day, he readily answered; 'When these gentlemen came on shore, I was starting of beer, and they ordered me to give the waterman four shillings and sixpence, I paid him, and told him he must stay till the gentlemen went, and my Lord, I find by my book now in my hand, that it was on that day my beer was started.'

The last witness who appeared, was a man who lived in Burleigh-Street in the Strand, who said, 'the captain was his lodger, and came home at eleven of the clock on the night before mentioned; that he knew it to be the same night, because Dudley not being very well, did not stir out of doors the next day, and paid him his rent for his lodging, for which he gave him a receipt, by the date of which he knew the time'; and the prisoner producing a receipt, the fellow swore it to be the same. Such a set of profligate witnesses as these, were enough to screen an offender from justice for a time; and they had such an influence over both judge and jury, so much, that the captain was easily acquitted.

His liberty regain'd, he hastened to his old companions, with whom he committed many notorious robberies, especially one on a nobleman, on Hounslow Heath, from whom they took fifteen hundred pounds. After a desperate skirmish with the servants, three of whom they wounded, and killed two of their horses; from thence they proceeded on the West Country road, and near Hartley-row in Hamshire, robbed a parson, whom they commanded to preach a sermon in praise of thieving, swearing his destruction, if he refused to do it.

The parson was forced to comply: however, to make him some amends, the sermon being ended, they gave him his money again that they took from him, and four shillings to drink, for his sermon.

After they had this their diversion, for we cannot call it a robbery, they made the best of their way for London, and for some time left infesting the highways. During which time the captain's brother, employ'd himself in shewing his dexterity about town, some of which we believe will prove diverting to the reader. The first of his tricks, was, he dressed himself like a countryman, with a pair of dirty boots, and a whip in his hand, and going into Bartholomew-Fair, met with no prize worth speaking of: but as he was going out, he met with a countryman, and said to him, 'Honest friend have a care of your pockets, you are going into a cursed place, where are none but whores, rogues, and pick-pockets; I am almost ruined by them, and I am glad they have not picked the teeth out of my head, let one take ever so much care of one's pockets, they'll be sure of your money; I am sure the Devil helps them.' 'I defie all the devils in Hell', says the countryman, 'to rob me of any thing I value, I have a broad-piece that I'll secure', so clapping it into his mouth, he went confidently into the fair; Will desired no more than to know if he had any money, and where it lay, he gives a sign to a hopeful boy of his, and telling him out some six pences and groats, told him what he should do; the boy immediately runs, and falls down just before the countryman, and scattering the money, starts up and roars like a Bedlamite, crying he was undone, he must run away from his apprenticeship, his master was a furious fellow, he would certainly kill him. The countryman with other people gathered about, helping the boy to take up the money, says one of them 'Have you found all', 'Yes, all the silver' says the boy, 'but what does that signifie, there is a broad-piece of gold, that I was carrying to my master for a token, sent from the country, and I like a fool must come thro' this unlucky place to lose it; I shall be killed, what will become of me.' Will coming up, tells some of the by-standers who were pitying the boy, he observed that country fellow there to stoop, and put something into his mouth: whereupon, they flew upon him, and one of them wresting open his chops, made him spit out the gold, and some blood along with it; endeavouring to speak for himself, they kick'd him, punch'd him, and tossed him about, and some calling to privy or pump, he was glad to call for mercy, and thought himself well off when he got out of their clutches. The boy in the mean time slipt into the crowd, and went to Will with the gold, to the appointed place of rendezvous.

Will and his boy changing cloaths, and going into the crowd heard some talking of the country fellow, how he had got into a house, and had sent for some respon-sible people that knew him, and his master, a knight of a vast estate in the North, who was come to town upon great business with some merchant. Will knew the gentleman and his estate very well, and by what he heard expecting to see him at the Exchange, went immediately thither, and picked his pocket of a great many guineas, except one, which he left for the gentleman's dinner, or other charges, till he should receive a recruit. The knight going to the tavern laugh'd heartily when his tenant came and told him how he had been serv'd at the fair: but calling for the reckoning, and telling the company he was robbed too, 'twas comical to see how the countryman laughed. 'Shud, Sir, says he, let us make our escape from this roguish place, 'slidking, Sir, they'll steal our small guts to make fiddle-strings of them.'

The gentleman lined his pockets again, and went out the next day to the Change, and notwithstanding all the care he took, he was robbed again; but Will being not an ordinary rogue and having something of a generous principle, would not take all, but left him some. The knight admired how it was possible for the wit of man to rob one that had been so forwarned as he was; at last looking hastily about, he perceived Will standing by him, and recollecting he had seen him near him several times before, he had a strong suspicion he was the man, and coming up to him, took hold of his buttons, and told him, he had good ground to think he was the man that had robbed him several times, but being a gentleman of a great estate, his loss did not trouble him; and if he would be so generous, as to tell him by what means he had so serv'd him, he would not only forgive him, but treat him well at the tavern, and help him to a better way of living, if he pleased; 'and this,' says he, 'I promise upon my honour.' 'Sir,' says Will, 'your word of honour is sufficient: I know the greatness of your estate: I am the man. I'll wait on your Worship to the tavern, and there shew you some of my art, more freely than I would do to my fellow rogues.' As they went towards the tavern, the gentleman told him, he resolved to make a frolick of it; and, to that end, he would send for some gentlemen of his acquaintance, and would take care he should come to no harm by any discovery he should make to them. 'I know you're a gentleman,' says Will; 'and men of honour scorn to keep base company: call as many as you please. I'll take their word, and I know I am safe.'

When the gentry came, Will told them many things to their admiration and satisfaction, and when he pulled out the piece of gold, and told them how he had served Roger, the gentleman's tenant, Roger was immediately sent for to make up the frolick: when he came it 'twas good sport to see how he scraped to the ground. His master smiling asked of whom he learn'd to make such a handsome leg: 'But what would you say,' says the knight, 'if you saw your gold again.'—'Oh,' says he, 'I would I could; but if my mouth can't keep it, where should I put it?' ''Shud I'd rather see the rogue; I'd make a jelly of his bones.'— 'There he is,' says the knight, 'and there's your broad-piece.'—As Roger began to heave and bulk, his master commanded him to take his gold, and sit down by him. Roger seeing which way things went, drank to Will. One of the gentlemen pulling out a curious watch, another said, he wondered how it was possible for them to pick a watch out of a fob; and that it was certainly carelesness. 'No,' says Will, 'if the gentleman will take a turn or two in Moorfields, I'll wager a guinea, I'll have the watch before he returns, let him take what care he pleases, and I shan't stir out of this room.'—'Done,' says the gentleman. However, every gentleman in the room laying down a guinea, Roger laid down his broad-piece, and went his half. The gentleman went out with his watch; and, as he walk'd was very careful not to suffer man, woman, or child, to come within arm's length of him; thinking the Devil was in't, if any body could rob him at a distance. When it was almost time he should return, a boy came softly behind him; and when he came pretty near, he ran past him, yet not so near as to give the gentleman suspicion: as he pass'd him, he looks over his shoulder, and tells the gentleman his back was cover'd with lice, which he perceiving, loath'd the sight, fretting, and wondering where he had been that day. 'Good boy,' says he, 'take them off, and I'll give you a shilling.' The boy does so, and picking the lice off his back, and the watch out of his fob, he received his reward, and run. The gentleman returns to the tavern, wondering all the way how he could have come by such vermin, yet carefully avoiding any that came near him all the way.

224

When he return'd, Will ask'd him, what a-clock it was by his watch? Which thinking to pull out, he was amaz'd to find it gone. Will pulls it out, and ask'd the gentleman, if that was it? The gentleman stood as dumb as a fish, turning up the whites of his eyes. Roger laugh'd so loud and outragiously, that after the gentleman had born him company a good while, the knight was forced to command him silence; for he would have laughed all night. The gentleman, full of amazement, said, certainly he must have had the assistance of the Devil. 'Of a boy,' says Will: 'Did not a boy pick you clean?'—'There's the Devil,' says the gentleman; 'and he threw them on too, I suppose?' 'Ay, thro' a quill,' says the other.

The whole company was mightily pleased with the ingenuity of the trick, especially Roger, who could not forget how the gentleman looked, when he came in, and missed his watch, and was now and then bursting out into a laughter. Says Will, 'Alas, gentlemen, this trick is not worth the talking of, it is such a thing as we send our boys about: there's a nobleman goes now by the window, with a very rich coat on, I'll wager, as before, I'll steal it off his back before all his followers, and bring it hither on my own.' The gentlemen stak'd each their guinea, and Will and Roger cover'd 'em. 'Now,' says Will, 'I'm to shew you a master-piece of my art. I must not send a boy about it, but crave leave to go myself; neither can I set a time for my return, but I hope to do it sooner than you imagine.' So out he runs, and dogging the nobleman from street to street, at last follow'd him into a tavern. The nobleman was conducted up stairs. Will goes to the bar-keeper, and desires her to lend him an apron; 'for the nobleman, my master, wherever he comes, will be served by none but myself: he is a very good customer, and expects the best of wine. I must go down into the cellar, and taste it for him': whereupon they let him have the apron, and he went into the cellar, and soon found out the best of every sort. He ran so nimbly up and down stairs, and was so quick at his work, none of the servants kept pace with him. The company looked upon him to be a servant of the house, and were mightily pleased with his quickness and diligence, and the goodness of the wine, and every thing he brought them. Will promised him that should have attended the room, large vails, and he was very well satisfy'd to receive money for doing nothing. Will never came in the room, but he passed some merry jest, which pleased them wonderfully, and when they spoke to him, his answers were so smart, that when he went for more wine, they said one to another, 'This is a merry witty fellow, such a one as he, is fit to make a house; he deserves double wages.' When Will had sufficiently amused the company, and saw his project ripe for execution, he was resolved to trifle no longer: wherefore, when he returned into the room with some wine, and as he passed by my lord, he laid hold on the opportunity, and with his incision knife, which he used in pocket-picking, he nicely, and with admirable dexterity, made a slit in the seam of my lord's coat, and runs down stairs for more liquor. When he returned with a bottle in one hand, and the other full of glasses, before he came near my lord, Will starts, saying, 'What cobling fellows are they that made this coat? Could they not sew a coat to hold one day? This cabbage-monger deserved the pillory before for filching; but now grudging to allow another stitch, has committed a *scandalum magnatum*, and caused my Lord to go in a rent coat the first day of wearing perhaps.' Some of the company rising, and seeing the great slash, told my lord, the taylor had affronted him. Says my lord, 'I gave the fellows sufficient vails, and both they and their master shall hear it.'—'My Lord,' says Will, ''tis only the end of a thread has slipt: such things will happen sometimes; the coat may be faithfully sewed in other places; it's not a farthing the worse. There's a curious fine-drawer of my acquaintance lives in the next lane; be pleas'd to let me carry it to him, he will make it as good as at first. I'll carry it secretly under my master's cloak, and return

225

with it before you want more wine.' The nobleman borrows a great coat of one of the company, and lets him have the coat. Will comes down to the vintner, tells him what had happened to his lord's coat; and, to prevent its being seen in the street, desires him to let him have a cloak, and he would return immediately. The vintner shewed him where the cloak was, which Will put on, and claps the vinter's beaver on his head, which hung on the next pin. Thus he troops off with them, and coming to the tavern, where the gentlemen were, he went into a room, and having put on the nobleman's coat, the cloak, and beaver, he came into the room where they sat, saluting them very civily. Says one of them, 'What, instead of a coat, you come with a cloak,' 'and great need for it; for,' says he 'there's a deal of knavery under it.' So opening the cloak, they were all amazd to see the rich embroider'd coat, besides the cloak and beaver, which he told them, he had got into the bargain. But when he told them how he had performed the exploit, they all laugh'd heartily, and Roger with his base made up the consort.

My lord and his company waited so long, that they were quite out of patience, the people of the house likewise wondring they sat so long without calling, ordered the fellow that should have waited on that room, to go up stairs and force a trade. The fellow comes in, and says, 'Call here, call here, gentlemen?' 'Yes,' says one of them, 'where is your fellow-servant that waited on us?' 'My fellow-servant,' says the other, 'he said, he was my Lord's servant, and that my Lord would be attended by none but himself, and I should have good vails notwithstanding.' Says my lord, 'How can that be, I have but one gentleman here of my own retinue, the rest are with my lady; he that served us, came in with an apron, and is a servant of the house, call up our landlord.' The vintner coming up, a gentleman of the company asked him if he kept sharpers in the house to affront gentlemen, and rob them. 'Nay,' says the vintner, who was a very passionate man, 'do you bring sharpers along with you to affront me, and rob my house? I'm sure I have lost a fine new cloak, and beaver; and for ought I know, though you look like gentlemen, you may be sharpers yourselves; and of you I expect to be paid for my losses and reckoning to boot.' Immediately one of them drew upon him; but the vintner ran down stairs, and called all the house together, bidding them get what they could, and not to suffer one to come down stairs, and snatching his sword in a fury, ran up stairs again, the servants arming themselves with spits, fire-forks, and such weapons as they could find, followed him. The uproar was very great, and my lord coming out first, to force his way down, made a pass at the landlord, but was put by with a fire-shovel, which was in one of the drawer's hands, narrowly escaping being thrust in the guts with a long spit, which Margery, the cook wench, pushed at him; so that my lord seeing the door so well guarded with stout fellows, and sturdy wenches, retired into the room, and told his company, he had almost died by the hands of a wench with a spit in her hand. They seeing it neither safe nor honourable to sally out, shut the door; and standing on the defensive part, began to consult what to do.

Mean while, the gentlemen foreseeing a quarrel betwixt my lord and the vintner, immediately dispatched their own landlord to tell them, they had caught the rogue that had abused them, and had him in safe custody, praying my lord to know, if they should wait on him.

The landlord runs in all haste, and coming to the house, found it in an uproar. The servants knowing him, let him go up stairs, where he no sooner came, but he told his brother vintner, that they were all in a mistake; that the rogue was catched, and in his house; whereupon, calling my lord, inform'd him of the whole business. Immediately a cessation of arms was proclaim'd, the swords sheath'd, the spits, fire-forks, and fire-shovels disbanded, and an end happily made of a terrible war. The nobleman and his company drinking friends with the vintner, promised to be a friend to his house for the future; but resolved to go along with their peace maker to the tavern where Will was to mend the frolick. The vintner being well pleased with the conceit, went along with them: when they were come to the place, after passing the usual compliments, they sat down, and Will deliver'd the coat, cloak, and beaver. As for what he told them, and the other tricks he then shewed them, not having room here to relate, we must now beg leave to pass on to his brother, the captain.

The captain had committed so many and great robberies, with his companions and his brother Will (for the small tricks he above committed were only his pastime, when absent from the road) that a proclamation was issued out against them, with a reward for the taking them, dead or alive, which made people more inquisitive after them, and not long after Captain Dudley, and some others were apprehended.

The manner of their being seiz'd was as follows: the captain, with five others, having committed a robbery, and being closely pursued by the country, were forced to ride hard for their safety, and having got to Westminster-Ferry, they endeavour'd to pass; but the wherrymen declared, they would not go any more that night; upon which two rid away, and the other four gave their horses to a waterman to lead to an inn, which was not far off, being all of a foam with their hard riding, which made the waterman mistrust they were highwaymen, and had been pursued; that day two of them, after their horses were set up, took oars to Lambeth. The waterman imparting his suspicion to several people, the constable got news of it, and he made it his business to find them out: getting a good guard, he went to the inn, and enquired what kind of persons they were, secured the horses, and made search after the men.

Being in the yard, he observed a person to walk up and down, as if he was sent for a spy; he demanded what he wanted? The other ask'd him, if such a one lived there? He told him, 'No'; then he enquired for another name, which was the name of the man of the house. The constable told him, he would go to the house with him, which he did; and knocking at the door, inquired for a person, whom the maid denied, and suddenly shut the door upon him, which gave the constable a greater mistrust; upon which he asked the man, who he wanted? and told him he suspected him to be one of those who had committed the robbery that day, or that he belong'd to some of them (the constable being all this while at a distance from his guard, and without his staff) and drawing the fellow nearer to his assistants, he boldly seiz'd him, and threatened to carry him before a magistrate. The fellow being amazed at this unexpected surprize, presently confessed he was sent by those who had made their escapes, to see what became of their horses, and whether any enquiry or pursuit was after them, and told the constable two of them were in the house he knocked at, and the other two at an inn in Lambeth. Upon this the constable takes his guard with him, goes to the house, and knocks at the door, which was not open'd, till he threaten'd to break it open: he was no sooner enter'd, but he discovered Dudley going down a pair of stairs into the cellar: he follow'd him; but not so fast, but Dudley had time to get into a further cellar, and bolt himself in; but it was soon forced open, where they found Dudley with his sword in one hand, and a pistol in the other, threatning the death of the first man that touch'd him; but seeing so many men arm'd, and finding it in vain to resist, he surrender'd his arms up, and was taken prisoner. The constable left a good guard over him for his security, and went to Lambeth, and took the other two, who in the morning being carried before a Justice was by him committed to Newgate.

At the next sessions, Captain Dudley had his trial, and was found guilty on no less than five indictments for the highway, and received sentence to be hanged accordingly, with his brother, and two of his accomplices.

After he had received sentence, and was brought back to Newgate, be began to have a sense of his near approaching end, and demean'd himself very well at chapel. He confessed he was a great offender, that he justly deserved death; but yet was very unfit to die, which troubled him much; for he desired longer time to make his peace with God. An acquaintance, who came to visit him, asked him if the nearness of his death (he being in perfect health, and to die the next day) did not startle him? He reply'd 'Yes; I have now but twenty four hours to live,' and shaking his head, desired of the Lord to forgive him; and to those who were with him, he said, 'Pray for me.' A gentleman who came to see him, gave him some tobacco, and would have given him more, which he refused, telling him, 'He thanked him for what he had got already, that being sufficient for him, during the short space he had to live.'

He did not seem to be much cast down, but endeavour'd to appear as chearful as possible. He confessed he had robbed many men, but never committed any murder, and when strongly charged with killing the serjeant as above, he utterly denied it to the last, but own'd he promoted the doing of it. He was carried from Newgate with six prisoners more: his brother was very sick, and lay all along in the cart; but the captain look'd pretty chearful all the way. Being come to the place of execution he confessed he had been a notorious offender; and that he justly deserved death, desiring the prayers of all good Christians; and after the usual duties performed by the ordinary, they were all turned off together. After hanging the usual time, they were cut down, and his body, with his brother's, put into separate coffins, to be carried to a disconsolate father, who at the sight of them, was so much overwhelm'd with grief, that he fell down upon the dead bodies, and never spoke more, but was buried at the same time, and in the same grave, with his two unfortunate sons. It must needs be a sad, shocking, and most affecting spectacle to see so many persons going to an ignominious death by the impiety of their lives; to behold such a sight, one would think, might awaken all who saw it, to fly from such wicked practices to leave off their vitious company, and debauched conversation, and seriously imploring mercy and forgiveness for past iniquities, strenuously endeavour to redeem their time for the future.

THE LIFE OF
OLD MOB

There is a beauty in all the works of nature, which we are unable to define, tho' all the world is convinced of its existence: so in every action and station of life, there is a grace to be attain'd which will make a man pleasing to all about him, and serene in his own mind. This also as well as the former, every one will own, and at the same time fancy he can reach, though almost all mankind find themselves mistaken.

As every virtue has its foil, or a sort of counterfeit vice, which very nearly resembles it, so near as often to impose upon the very possessor; in like manner the beauty, grace, or decorum, which we have mentioned, often occasions that we pursue a wrong scent: we are convinced that there really is such a thing, and while we are inquiring what it is, our own favourite passions present us with something which we mistake for it, and which we ever after make the object of our pursuit.

Thus a man of a healthy, robust constitution, who has at the same time an impetuous and violent temper, such a one thinks of nothing so much as of being esteem'd the bravest man of his neighbourhood, and is never so well pleased as when he sees others agree to his opinion, for fear of incurring his displeasure. Manly exercises are his whole delight, and he can scarce bear to hear the name of a man given to one of less strength and fire than himself. Others on the contrary, delight only in the exercises of reason, and amusements of the mind: these frequently look upon the former, as a sort of creatures in human shape, who differ from the irrational world in nothing but figure and speech. These are the two extremes of mankind, and make, perhaps, the most discernable difference; but there is a like contrast subsisting throughout the whole species.

Not to carry the reader too far into this abstracted manner of reasoning, it will be obvious to every one who compares these reflections with the character of some villains of the first magnitude; that these unhappy wretches, from a wrong turn of thought, have even placed the beauty we have been speaking of, in vice itself, and conceive a sort of excellence in being more vile and profligate than other men; otherwise it is hardly probable, that they could commit so many irregularities with a strong gust, and an appearance of satisfaction.

What we are still more to wonder at, is, that other people should delight to hear the actions of these men rehearsed, and be even pleased with a highwayman, who robs like a gentleman. It seems as if it was, in reality, something great to excel upon any account whatsoever. But let us consider whether such a pleasure as this be consistent with a virtuous inclination. Lives of wicked men are doubtless both lawful and useful, for the same end as sea-marks, and no other; that we may avoid the road in which they perished: ought not therefore the greatest villain to raise in us the greatest abhorrence.

After these general thoughts, we shall give the reader a sketch of the life and adventures of Thomas Sympson, commonly called Old-Mobb, who was perhaps, as notorious a robber as almost any one of the last age, for the space of five and forty years together; during which time it was reported he never acted in any company, except now and then a little with the Golden Farmer.

This man was born at Ramsey in Hampshire, which continued to be the place of his habitation, when he resided any where under his right name, till the day of his apprehending; and he had a wife and five children, besides grand-children, living there at the time of his shameful death.

We have no particular account of his education and private life, from whence we may conclude, there was nothing remarkable in either. His adventures on the road we shall relate in the order which we have received them, which is the only method we can follow.

Riding one time between Honiton and Exeter, he met with Sir Bartholomew Shower, whom he immediately called to an account for the money he had about him. Sir Bartholomew gave him all he had without any words, which proved to be but a very little: Old Mobb looked upon his prize, and finding it infinitely short of his expectations, he readily told him, that there was not enough to answer his present demands, which were very large, and very pressing; 'And therefore, Sir,' says he, 'as you are my banker, in general, you must instantly draw a bill upon some body at Exeter for one hundred and fifty pounds, and remain in the next field as security for the payment, till I have received it.' The knight would fain have made some evasion, and protested that there was no body in Exeter who would pay such a sum at a moment's warning; but Old Mobb so terrified him with holding a pistol to his breast, that his Worship at last consented, and drew upon a rich goldsmith.

As soon as Old Mobb had got the note, he made Sir Bartholomew dismount, and walk far enough from the road to be out of every bodies hearing, then bound him hand and foot, and left him under a hedge, while he rode to Exeter, and receiv'd the money, which was paid without any scruple, the goldsmith knowing the hand-writing perfectly well. When he return'd, he found the poor knight where he left him. 'Sir,' says he, 'I am come with a habeas corpus to remove you out of your present captivity'; which he accordingly did by untying him, and sending him about his business: but Sir Bartholomew was obliged to walk home, which was full three miles; for our adventurer had cut the girths and bridle of his horse, and turn'd him astray, ever since he went to Exeter with the note.

Old Mobb had one time some high words with a woman in his neighbourhood, when among other hard names he called her whore: every one knows what a tender thing the honour of a woman is, and how ready poor English husbands are to vindicate their wives virtue. Whether or no the saddle fitted at this time, or whatever else was the occasion, we can't say, but a prosecution in the spiritual court was set a foot against Old Mobb, and the good man was so zealous in defence of his beloved rib, that he put our highwayman to a pretty deal of expence; for a spiritual process generally hurts the temporal estate, as much at least as a suit at common law. To the honour of our holy religion be it spoken.

Soon after this trouble was over, Old Mobb met the proctor, who had managed against him, and drawn not a little money out of his pocket. He quickly knew his dear ghostly friend; but being very much disguis'd, was not at all apprehensive of being known, which pleased him extremely. 'Sir,' quoth he, 'stand and deliver this moment, or I shall have no more mercy on you than the Devil; or, if you please, you yourself would have on an excommunicated person.' The proctor made some resistance, but was soon obliged to surrender, and pull out a fine embroider'd purse, with fifteen guineas in it. He was a-going to take out the guineas, and deliver them; but Old Mobb liking the purse, assured him, he must have that also. The proctor told him, it was given him by a particular friend, and that he had promised to keep it as long as he lived; for which reason he begged of him to leave that. 'Suppose now,' says Old Mobb, 'that you had a process against me, and were come to me for your fees; if I had no money, nor any thing of value, but what was given me by a friend, would you take it for payment, if I told you that I had promised to keep it as long as I lived?—No, Sir, stay there; I love people should do as they would be done unto. What business had you to promise a thing that you were not sure of performing? Am I to be accountable for your vows?' 'Twas in vain for the poor proctor to use any more words, for he plainly saw that if he offer'd to separate the purse and money, his own body and soul would be in danger of separation; and notwithstanding his spirituality, his inward man did not much care at this time to leave its earthly tabernacle; so e'en gave both together.

Mr John Gadbury, the astrologer, was another that fell into the hands of Old Mobb, who notwithstanding his familiarity with the stars, was not wise enough to foresee his own misfortune, which has been a common case with men of his profession. This rencounter was on the road between Winchester and London. Poor Gadbury trembled, and turned as white as a clout, when Old Mobb told him what he wanted, professing that he had no more money about him, than just enough to bear his expences to London; but our highwayman was not at all moved with compassion at what he said: 'Are not you a lying son of a whore,' quoth he, 'to pretend you want money, when you hold twelve large houses of the planets by lease parole, which you let out again to the Stationer's Company at so much *per ann*. You must not sham poverty upon me, Sir, who know as good things as yourself, and who have a pistol that may prove as fatal as Sirius in the dog days, if you stand trifling with me.' Mr Gadbury was at this time, indeed, more apprehensive of Old Mobb's pistol, than of any star in the firmament; for he was sensible the influence of it, if discharged, would be much more violent

233

and sudden; so that he looked like one out of his senses. He was now even afraid to deliver his money, least he should suffer for telling a lye: however, as he saw there was no remedy, he pulled out a bag, in which was about nine pounds in gold and silver, which he gave with a few grumbling expressions. Old Mobb told him, he should take no exceptions at what he said; for it was but just, that the loser should have leave to speak; so setting spurs to his horse, he left the star-gazer to curse the disastrous constellations.

One day Old Mobb overtook the stage-coach going for Bath, with only one gentlewoman in it: when he had commanded the coachman to stop, and was come to the door to raise contribution after his usual manner, the passenger made a great many excuses, and wept very plentifully, in order to move him to pity; she told him she was a poor widow, who had lately lost her husband, and therefore she hoped, he would have some compassion on her: 'And is your losing your husband then,' says he, 'an argument that I must lose my booty? I know your sex too well, Madam, to suffer myself to be prevail'd on by a woman's tears. Those crocodile drops are always at your command; and no doubt but that dear cuckold of yours, whom you have lately buried, has frequently been perswaded out of his reason by their interposition in your domestick debates. Weeping is so customary to you, that every body would be disappointed, if a woman was to bury her husband, and not weep for him; but you would be more disappointed, if no body was to take notice of your crying; for according to the old proverb, the end of an husband is a widow's tears; and the end of those tears is another husband.'

The poor gentlewoman upon this ran out into an extravagant detail of her deceased husband's virtues, solemnly protesting, that she would never be married again to the best man that wore a head, for she should not expect a blessing to attend her afterwards; with a thousand other things of the same kind. Old Mobb, at last, interrupted her, and told her he would repeat a pleasant story in verse, which he had learn'd by heart, so, first looking round him to see that the coast was clear on every side, be began as follows:

> A Widow Prude had often swore
> No Bracelet should approach her more;
> Had often prov'd that second Marriage
> Was ten Times worse than Maid's Miscarriage,

234

And always told them of their Sin,
When Widows would be Wives agen:
Women who'd thus themselves abuse,
Should die, she thought, like honest Jews:
Let her alone to throw the Stones;
If 'twere but Law, she'd make no Bones.
   Thus long she led a Life demure;
But not with Character secure:
For People said (what won't Folks say?)
That she with Edward went astray:
(This Edward was her Servant Man)
The Rumour thro' the Parish ran,
She heard, she wept, she called up Ned,
Wip'd her Eyes dry, sigh'd, sobb'd, and said:

Alas! what sland'rous Times are these!
What shall we come to by Degrees!
This wicked World! I quite abhor it!
The Lord give me a better for it!
On me this Scandal do they fix?
On me? who, God knows, hate such Tricks!
Have Mercy, Heav'n, upon Mankind!
And grant us all a better Mind!
My Husband—Ah that dearest Man!
Forget his Love I never can;
He took such Care of my good Name,
And put all sland'rous Tongues to Shame.—
But, ah! he'd dead—Here Grief amain,
Came bubling up, and stop'd the Strain.

Ned was no Fool; he saw his Cue,
And how to use good Fortune knew:
Old Opportunity at Hand,
He seiz'd the Lock, and bid him stand;

Urg'd of what Use a Husband was
To vindicate a Woman's Cause,
Exclaim'd against the sland'rous Age;
And swore he could his Soul engage,
That Madam was so free from Fault,
She ne'er so much as sinn'd in Thought;
Vowing he'd lose each Drop of Blood,
To make that just Assertion good.

This Logic, which well pleas'd the Dame,
At the same Time eludes her Shame:
A Husband, for a Husband's Sake,
Was what she'd ne'er consent to take.
Yet, as the Age was so censorious,
And Ned's Proposals were so glorious,
She thought 'twas best to take upon her,
A second Guardian of her Honour.

'This,' says Old Mobb, 'is an exact picture of womankind, and as such I committed it to memory; you are very much obliged to me for the recital, which has taken me up more time than I usually spend in taking a purse; let us now pass from the dead to the living, for it is these that I live by: I am in a pretty good humour, and so will not deal rudely by you. Be so kind therefore, as to search your self, and use me as honestly as you are able; you know I can examine afterwards, if I am not satisfied with what you give me.' The gentlewoman found he was resolute, and so thought it the best way to keep him in temper, which she did by pulling out forty guineas in a silk purse, and presented them to him. 'Tis fifty to one but Old Mobb got more by repeating the verses above, than the poor poet that wrote them, ever made of his copy. Such is the fate of the sons of Apollo.

Scarce was Old Mobb parted from this gentlewoman, before he saw the appearance of another prize at some distance. Who should it be, but the famous Lincoln's-Inn Fields mountebank, Cornelius a Tilburgh, who was going to set up a stage at Wells. Our adventurer knew him very well, as indeed, did almost every one at that time, which occasioned his demanding his money in a little rougher language than usual. The poor quack-salver was willing to preserve what he had; and to that end, used a great many fruitless expostulations, pretending that he had expended all the money he had brought out with him, and was himself in necessity. But Old Mobb soon gave him to understand, that he would not be put off with fine words; and that he had more wit than to believe a mountebank whose profession is lying. 'You get your money,' says he, 'as easily as I do, and 'tis only fulfilling an old proverb, if you give me all you have: lightly come, lightly go. Next market-day, Doctor, will make up all, if you have any luck. 'Twill excite people to buy your packets, if as an instance of your great desire to serve them, you tell them what you suffer'd upon your journey, which nevertheless, could not hinder your coming to exercise your bowels of compassion among them, and restore such as are in a languishing condition.'

The empirick could scarce forbear laughing to hear Old Mobb hold forth so excellently well, and lay open the craft of his occupation with so much dexterity. He was notwithstanding, very unwilling to part with his money, and began to read a lecture of morality to our desperado, upon the unlawfulness of his actions, telling him, that what he did might frequently be the ruin of poor families, and oblige them afterwards to follow irregular courses, in order to make up what they had lost: 'And then,' says he, 'you are answerable for the sins of such people.' 'This is the Devil correcting sin with a witness,' quoth Old Mobb. 'Can I ruin more people than you, dear Mr Theophrastus Bombastus? You are a scrupulous, conscientious son of a whore, indeed, to tell me of ruining people. I only take their money away from them; but you frequently take away their lives; and what makes it the worse, you do it safely, under a pretence of restoring them to health; whereas I should be hanged for killing a man, or even robbing him, if I were taken. You have put out more eyes than the small-pox, made more deaf than the cataracts of Nile, in a word, destroy'd more than the pestilence. 'Tis in vain to trifle with me, Doctor, unless you have a remedy against the force of gun-powder and lead. If you have any such excellent specifick, make use of it instantly, or else deliver your money.'

Our itinerant quack still continuing his delays, Old Mobb made bold to take a portmanteau from his horse, and put it upon his own, riding off with it, till he came to a convenient place for opening it. Upon examining the inside, he found five and twenty pounds in money, and a large golden medal, which King Charles II

237

had given him for poysoning himself in his Majesty's Presence; besides all his instruments, and implements of quackery.

Another time Old Mobb met with the Dutchess of Portsmouth, on the road between New-Market and London, attended with a very small retinue. He made bold to stop the coach, and ask her Grace for what she had about her; but madam, who had been long used to command a monarch, did not understand the meaning of being spoken to in this manner by a common man. Whereupon she briskly demanded, if he knew who she was? 'Yes, Madam,' replied Old Mobb, 'I know you to be the greatest whore in the kingdom; and that you are maintain'd at the publick charge.—I know that all the courtiers depend on your smiles, and that even the K— himself is your slave. But what of all that? A gentleman collector is a greater man upon the road, and much more absolute than his Majesty is at court. You may now say, Madam, that a single highwayman, has exercised his authority, where Charles II of England has often begged a favour, and thought himself happy to obtain it, at the expence of his treasure, as well as his breath.'

Her Grace continued to look upon him with a superiour, lofty air, and told him, he was a very insolent fellow; that she would give him nothing, and that he should severely suffer for this affront: adding, that he might touch her if he durst.—'Madam,' says Old Mobb, 'that haughty French spirit will do you no good here. I am an English freebooter; and insist upon it as my native privilege to seize all foreign commodities. Your money indeed is English, and the prodigious sums that have been lavished on you will be a lasting proof of English folly. Nevertheless, all you have is confiscated to me by being bestowed on such a worthless B—h. I am king here, Madam, and I have a whore to keep on the publick contributions, as well as King Charles: 'Tis for this that I collect of all that pass, and you shall have no Favour from me.'—As soon as he had spoke, he fell on board her in a very boistrous manner, so that her Grace began to cry out for quarters, telling him, she would deliver all she had. She was as good as her word; for she surrendered two hundred pounds in money, which was in the seat of the coach, besides a very rich necklace, which her royal cully had lately given her, a gold watch, and two diamond rings.

Being once at Abingdon, on a market-day, when there is always a great quantity of corn bought and sold, Old Mobb, happened to fall into company with a person at the Crown-Inn, whom he knew to be a great ingrosser of corn; and that he had just bought as much of that commodity as came to fifty pounds. Having a pretty deal of money in his pocket at this time, it came into his head, how to cheat the monopolizer out of his bargain. To this end, he put on the appearance of a man of business, pretended that he was come from London to buy, and desired to see this purchase of the countryman's.

As soon as he saw it, he seem'd to like it mightily, and demanded the price of the owner, who asked him but a small advance above what he had just given for it. Old Mobb presently paid down the money, and sent the goods away, where he was sure of having it disposed of again at prime cost.

This was all that there was to be done that day; for the ingrosser did not go out of town till the next morning. Old Mobb against that time, took care to be well informed of the way he was to take, and was at his heels before he got two miles out of town. He soon found an opportunity to clap a pistol to his breast, and tell him that he must have the money again, which he had lent him yesterday, and whatsoever else he had about him. The countryman was sufficiently surpriz'd to see himself addressed to by his late companion in such a manner as this, and asked him, with trembling, if it was justice, in him to take away both goods and money too. 'Hast thou the impudence to talk of justice,' says Old Mobb? 'Can any man in the world act more unjustly than an ingrosser of corn, who buys up the produce of his country, robs the poor of their bread, and pretends a scarcity in times of plenty, only to increase his own substance, and leave behind him abundance of ill-gotten wealth? You are for inclosing all the land in the kingdom, and call our fore-fathers fools, because they sold corn for twelve-pence a bushel. No picture pleases you so well as that of Pharoah's lean kine, who eat up the fat ones, this you hang up in your parlours, recommend to your neighbours, and pray secretly to see the interpretation of it frequently fulfilled. Such vermin as you are unfit to live upon the earth; for you dread what all the world besides esteem a blessing; and dare not wish well to your country lest her prosperity should disappoint your hopes, and oblige you to bring out your hoarded stock, and sell it for less than it cost you. Talk no more of justice, Sir, but deliver your money, or I shall do the world so much justice as to send you out of it.' Hereupon the countryman delivered a bag with all Old Mobb's money in it, and about as much more, which occasion'd our adventurer to ride away with a great deal of satisfaction.

LIFE OF OLD MOB, THE HIGHWAYMAN.

OLD MOB ROBBING JUDGE JEFFERIES.

240   Not long after the committing of this robbery, Old Mobb met with Sir George Jefferies, at that time Lord Chief Justice of the King's-Bench, as he was going to his country seat. My Lord Chief Justice upon the road, was no more than another man; for he first disabled two servants that attended him, by shooting one through the arm, and the other through the thigh, and then stopped the coach, and demanded his Lordship's money. Jefferies had before this made himself sufficiently famous, by his Western Assizes, and other very severe proceedings, so that he imagined his name carried terror enough in it, to intimidate any man; but he was mistaken in Old Mobb, who had courage to speak his mind without any respect to persons, and when his Lordship told him his name, only said, 'He was glad he could be revenged on him in any manner for putting him in bodily fear at Hartford Assizes a few months before. According to law, my Lord,' says he, 'I might charge a constable with you, and bind you over to the quarterly sessions, for threatning to take away my life: however, if you please, as I don't love to be spiteful, I will make up the matter with you for what money you have in the coach, which, I think, is as easy as you can desire, and easier than you deserve.'

      Jefferies expostulated with him, upon the great hazard he ran, both of soul and body, by following such wicked courses, telling him, that he must expect

justice to follow his crimes, if he believed there was any such thing as a providence that govern'd the world. 'I don't doubt,' says Old Mobb, 'but that when
justice has overtaken us both, I shall stand at least, as good a chance as your
Lordship; who have already writ your name in indelible charactars of blood,
by putting to death so many hundred innocent men, for only standing up in
defence of our common liberties, that you might secure the favour of your
prince. 'Tis enough for you to preach morality upon the bench, where no body
dares to contradict you; but your lessons can have no effect upon me at this time;
for I know you too well not to see that they are only calculated to preserve
money.'—This speech of Old Mobb, was followed with fifty oaths and imprecations against the poor judge, which threaten'd him with nothing but immediate
death, if he did not deliver his money. Jefferies saw his authority would now
stand him in no stead; so he gave what money he had, which amounted to about
fifty-six guineas.

We took notice at the beginning of this 'Life of Old Mobb', that he sometimes was engaged with the Golden Farmer, the reader may therefore justly
expect an account of some of their actions in concert, two stories, the most
remarkable and diverting that we have seen concerning them, now follow.

241

Having both of them a pretty deal of ready cash, and being willing to retire a
little while from the highway, where they had lately made a great noise, and were
now very much sought after, they came to London, in order to make use of their
wits, of which they had both as great shares as they of strength and courage.
Here their first work was to observe the humours and manners of the citizens,
which neither of them was well acquainted with before, that they might know
the better how to proceed, and impose upon them in their own way.

Every one knows that London is all hurry and noise; every man there is a
man of business, and those who make good appearances never want credit, all
people there live by mutual dependance upon one another, and he who has dealt
for two or three hundred pounds, and made good his payments, may afterwards
be trusted for five. Our adventurers soon perceived all this, and what advantages
many designing men made of the general confidence, that people reposed in
each other, they saw that no body could teach them how to cheat a citizen, so
well as a citizen himself, and thereupon be concluded, that the best way they
could take, was, to both turn tradesmen.

Each of them now, takes a large handsome house, hires two or three servants, and sets up for a great dealer. The Golden Farmer's habitation was in Thames-Street, where he passed for cornchandler, which occupation he had the most knowledge in of any. Old Mobb took up his residence somewhere near the Tower, and call'd himself a Holland trader, he having been abroad when a boy, and knowing pretty well what commodities were exported to that country, of the language of which he had also a small smattering. They went for near relations, of the name of Bryan, and said they were north-country men.

They now employ all their time in enquiring after goods in their several ways, buying whatever comes to their hands, and either paying ready money themselves, or drawing upon each other, for one, two, or three days; at which time payment was always punctually made. This constant tide of money was kept up by their continually selling privately what they bought (sometimes, perhaps, not a little to loss) to such persons as are glad to make use of their cash in this manner; and always wink at things, which they can't comprehend, while they find their interest in it. As they deal in very different ways, the chapmen of the one, had no knowledge of those of the other; so that though every one of them had been sent at one time or another, by his respective customer, to receive money of his kinsman, none of them had any notion, that the correspondence was mutual, and consequently no suspicion of a fraud at the bottom.

Thus they continued till they both found their characters thoroughly established: perhaps in this time, they might each of them lose a hundred or two of pounds, but they very well knew that this loss would get them as many thousands. When they saw that all who dealt with them were ready to send in what goods they required, and not in the least care about their money, they thought their project ripe for execution, accordingly a day was appointed for that purpose.

They now order all their customers to bring them in goods on such a day, as much, at least in quantity, as they had ever before received at one time of the respective sorts; confining them all to particular hours for the delivery of what they brought, that they might not interfere with one another, and so suspect that some unfair design was on foot. At the same time they inform'd those who usually bought every thing off their hands, that they should have such and such quantities of so many sorts to dispose of, naming the next day to that when they were to receive them; that they would sell them cheap, because they were obliged to make up a large sum of ready money; that therefore they desired them to be punctual, and bring only cash for what they design'd to buy. The whole scheme succeeded as well as they could wish; on one side there was no suspicion; and on the other, if there was any, it was not the interest of the parties to discover what they thought, because every one of them promised himself some advantage.

The goods were all delivered according to order, at the day and hour appointed, and notes were mutually drawn by the kinsman in Thames-Street upon him by the Tower; and by the kinsman by the Tower, upon him in Thames-Street, for the several sums, to be paid at three days after date. Never were men better satisfied than these poor dupes, not one of them doubting but he should have all his money the moment he went for it, as usual. They went home, and slept soundly that night, and the two nights succeeding.

Next day came the buyers, and entirely cleared both houses, paying down ready money for all they carried off. These too were as well pleased as the rest, and with much better reason. They imagined indeed, that their chapmen were going to break, but what was that to them? No matter how the poor men were to live for the future, so long as they could have good bargains at present.

There was now time enough before the day of payment, for our two merchants to take care of themselves, and the money they had raised, which they did very effectually.

When they came to computation they found, that by this one bold stroke, they had got clear into their pockets, about sixteen hundred and thirty pounds: a pretty considerable sum for three months, which was the longest time they were in trade.

When the creditors came to receive their money, they were surpriz'd at both places to see the doors fast, and the windows shut, till they were informed by the neighbours, that the birds were flown the day before; and that all their furniture was either carried off in the night, or seiz'd for rent. How the men now looked upon one another! Every one began to suspect that the rest who were attending came about the same business as himself; and indeed when they came to examine the matter, they found themselves not mistaken. Those who were earliest in Thames-Street, and had heard the melancholy news, went forthwith to the Tower to complain that Mr Cousin was gone; and those at the Tower set out for Thames-Street. Now was the whole plot unravell'd, when they saw both were

243

departed quietly, and had learned of each other how they had been mutually imposed upon by the pretended relations, when they told their several cases.

One such trick as this, is enough for a man's whole life, and as much as he can safely play in the same kingdom. Our two Bryans now, therefore, resum'd their old names and habits, taking to the highway again for some time, till fresh danger of being apprehended, put them once more to their shifts. There was not less art in what they now did, than in what we have just related, only they acted in a lower sphere, not daring to aspire so high as to be merchants, after they had brought so much scandal upon the name.

Men whose thoughts are all turn'd upon money, have no regard to the manner in which they get what they desire; nor need they, provided they come off with impunity; for all people honour the rich, without enquiring how they came to be so.

There were two wealthy brothers of the name of Seals, Philip and Charles, both jewellers: Philip lived in London, and Charles resided at Bristol; where they were both born, in a house which his father left him. The Golden Farmer and Old Mobb knew every circumstance of the family, from which these men were descended, and were moreover particularly instructed in the private history of our brothers. This made our desperados fix on them for their next prize, now they were again reduced to extremity. The brothers were sickly consumptive men, which inclined these arch villains to undertake and perform what will be as diverting in the relation, as it was unparrallell'd in itself, and worthy of the men who acted in it.

Having contriv'd and order'd the whole affair, the first step they took towards executing it, was writing, and copying the following letter, making only the alteration of the place and name, as they saw necessary.

March 26. 1686.

Dear Brother,

This comes to bring you the sorrowful News, that you have lost the best of Brothers, and I the kindest of Husbands, at a Time when we were in Hopes of his growing better, as the Spring advanced, and continuing with us at least one Summer longer: He died this Morning, about Eleven of the clock, after he had kept his Bed only three Days.

I send so hastily to you, that you may be here before we prepare for the Funeral, which was the Desire of my dear Husband, who informed me, that he had made you joint Executor with me. The Will is in my Hands, and I shall defer opening it till you arrive here. I am too full of Grief to add any more, the Messenger, who is a very honest Man, and a Neighbour of mine, shall inform you of such Particulars as are needful from

Your Sorrowful Sister

———— Seals.

P. S. I employ'd a Friend to write for me, which I desire you to excuse; for I was not able to do it myself, nor indeed to dictate any more.

These letters being sealed, and properly directed, our two adventurers dressed themselves according to the characters they were to bear, and parted from each other; one of them riding towards London, and the other towards Bristol, having so ordered it before-hand, that they might both come to the end of their journey at the same time.

They arrived, they delivered their credentials, and were kindly received: 'tis not to our purpose to declare how many tears were shed upon opening the letters, and how many eulogias each of the living brothers bestow'd upon him whom he supposed to be dead. Much less shall we pretend to describe the secret joy which they both concealed under a sorrowful countenance; but which naturally arose in their breasts, when they understood that an addition would now accrue to their fortunes by the death of a brother. It is true, they both loved one another; but of all love, self-love is the strongest.

The evening at each place was spent in talking over several particulars of the family. Subjects that at such a time as this always come in the way: our messengers were both very expert, and each brother was convinced, that the man whom his sister had sent, had been long conversant in the family, by the exact account which he gave of things. They moreover, added of their own heads a great deal of stuff concerning the manner of the respective Mr Seal's death, and what he said in his last moments, which at this time, was doubtless very moving.

In a word, the best bed in both houses was made ready for our two sharpers, who were to depart the next morning, and tell the sisters-in-law that their brothers would come two days after, which was as soon as their mourning could be made, and other things prepared for the journey.

It may be proper to observe, that Old Mobb went to Bristol, and the Golden Farmer to London. The first of these found means in the evening to secure jewels, to the value of two hundred pounds, which was all the booty he had any opportunity to make: but the Golden Farmer having well observed the position of Mr Philip Seal's shop, arose in the night, came silently down stairs, and took to a much greater value; among other things a diamond necklace, which was just made for a lady of the first quality, but not to be delivered 'till some days after, three very large diamond rings, and five small ones.

In the morning both our adventurers set out, one from Bristol, and the other from London. They met at a place before appointed, and congratulated one another upon their success.

But we must leave them together, and return to the brothers, who were both getting ready for their journey.

Such was the hurry and confusion which our messengers had put the two families in, that no body in either of them took any notice of the shops, so that nothing of the robberies was discovered time enough to prevent the masters setting out, and let them see that they were imposed on. The shops were well furnished out, and what was carried off, took up but little room; wherefore 'twas not surprizing, that such a thing should be overlooked, at a time when no business was thought of, but the preparations for travelling, and appearing decently at the funeral.

The merriest part of the whole story was our two brothers setting out the same morning, and coming the same evening to Newberry, where they took up their lodging also at the same inn. He from London came in first, and being fatigued went to bed before the other arrived. The Bristol man about two hours after, passed through his brother's room, and a companion with him, whom he had engaged to attend him, and reposed themselves where but a thin partition was between the two chambers. Philip, the Londoner, was asleep when his brother went by him, but the discourse between Charles, and his friend, surpriz'd him; he could not tell what they talk'd off; but was certain one of the tongues was his brothers, whom he was going to see buried.

By and by Charles had occasion to go to the necessary house; upon which he rises, and attempts to go through Philip's chamber again, who by the moon-light was still more convinced that he had not been deceived in the voice: upon this he screamed out, and Charles was now as much surpriz'd as his brother; so that he ran back to bed half dead with fear.

In a word, they both continued sweating, and frightning themselves till morning, when they arose and dressed themselves in their mourning apparel. Below stairs for some time they shunn'd one another till they were taken notice off by the people of the house, who with some difficulty brought them together, after they had heard both their stories. They now saw themselves imposed on, but could not imagine the reason of it, till after spending two days together at the inn, they both returned, and found themselves robbed. Now was the plot unravell'd.

Old Mobb, was at last apprehended in Tuthill-Street, Westminster, committed to Newgate, and tried at the Old-Bailey on thirty-six indictments; of thirty-two of which he was found guilty.

On Friday the 30th of May, 1690, he was executed at Tyburn, without making any speech or confession; but continuing to act with his usual intrepidity.

Thus does the divine vengeance pursue the workers of iniquity, and very seldom suffers them to depart out of this life, without exposing them to shame and iniquity. This, one would think, would be sufficient to convince the greatest libertine of the government of a just providence; and make him tremble at his own thoughts and actions. It is also very shocking to reflect upon the departure of such a man out of the world, in such an insensible manner as Old Mobb made his exit, since at best death is a launching forth into a state of uncertainty.

I Nichols delin.   Toms sculp

Whitney Robbing an old Userer tyeing his hands behind him with his face to ẙ horses taile

THE LIFE OF
WHITNEY

This notorious malefactor was born at Stevenage in Hertfordshire, where he was put apprentice to a butcher, as soon as he was fit for servitude. He serv'd his time, as far as we have heard, very faithfully; but was not long his own master before he took to the irregular courses that brought destruction upon him, and branded his name with infamy.

He was pleasantly disappointed, as he would himself frequently confess afterwards, in the first piece of knavery that ever he contrived. Going with another butcher to Romford in Essex, in order to buy calves, they met with one which they had a particular fancy to; but the owner demanded what they thought an extravagant price for it, so that they could not strike a bargain: however, as the man kept a publick house, our companions agreed to go in and drink with him. They were very much vex'd in their minds, to think that they could not have their wish, and were contriving how to be revenged of their landlord; when Whitney suddenly whispered these words to his comrade, 'What business have we to give so much money out of our pockets, for what we may by and by get for nothing? We know where the calf is, and what should hinder our taking him, when we have an opportunity?' The other came directly into his measure, and so they sat boozing till night.

In the evening there came a fellow into the town with a great she bear, which he carried about for a show, and was his fortune to put up at the house where our two butchers were drinking in an inner room; for it being just at the town's end, there was no place so convenient besides. The man of the house was some time before he could conclude where to put the bear, at last he resolved to move the calf into another out-house, and tie Madam Bruin up in his place, which was done accordingly, without the knowledge of Whitney, and his friend, who continued drinking till they were told, it was time to go to bed.

Upon this warning they paid their reckoning, and went out, staying in the fields near the town, 'till they imagined the time favour'd their design. The night was very dark, and they came to the stall without making any noise or disturbance. Whitney was to go in and fetch out their prey, while the other watched without. When he was entered, he groped about for the calf till he got hold of the bear, which lying after the sluggish manner peculiar to these creatures, he began to tickle it to make it rise. At last being awaked, the poor beast, being muzzled and blind, rose up on her hind legs, not knowing but it was her master going to show her. Whitney still continued feeling about, wondering at the length of the calf's hair, and that he should stand in such a posture, till the bear caught hold of him, and hugg'd him fast between her fore feet.

In this posture he remain'd, unable to move, and afraid to cry out, till the other butcher, wondering at his long stay, put his head in at the door, and said, with a low voice, 'What a pox, will you be all the night stealing a calf?' 'A calf,' quoth Whitney, 'I believe it's the Devil, that I am going to steal; for he hugs me as closely as he does the witch in the statue.' 'Let it be the Devil,' says t'other, 'bring him out, however, that we may see what he is like, which is something that I should be very glad to know.' Whitney was too much surprized to be pleased with the jesting of his companion, so that he replied with some choller: 'Come and fetch him yourself; for may I be pox'd, if I half like him.' Hereupon t'other enter'd, and after a little examination, found, how they were bit. By his assistance Whitney got loose, and they both swore, they would never attempt to steal calves any more for this trick.

Whitney, after this, took the George-Inn at Cheshunt in Hertfordshire, where he entertain'd all sorts of bad company; but not thriving in this way, he was in a little time obliged to shut up his doors; and entirely give over the occupation.

He now came up to London, the common sanctuary of such men, where he lived very irregularly, and at last, when necessitous circumstances came on him apace, wholly gave himself up to villainy.

It was still some time before he took to the highway, following only the common tricks practised by the sharpers of the town, in which he was the more successful as he always went dressed like a gentleman; it being easier to impose upon mankind with a good suit of cloaths, than any other way whatsoever. But the world is governed by appearances, and always will be, unless Providence should ever see fit to make the characters of virtue and vice more visible. A poor man, tho' endow'd with ever so honest, and generous a soul, is avoided by every body; so that he can hardly in his life find an opportunity to discover himself, and let a mistaken world see what he possesses: while the greatest villain that ever was born, may be caressed by all companies, if he has but credit enough to get good apparel, and impudence to thrust himself forwards.

One morning, Whitney stood on Ludgate-Hill, at a mercer's door, waiting for a friend whom he expected to come by, when two misses of the town well habited came along. These ladies took our gentleman for the master of the shop, and supposing him by his looks to be an amorous young batchelor; one of them, in order to begin a little conversation, asked him, if he had any fine silks of the newest fashion, Whitney readily replied, 'that he had none by him at present, but in a day or two's time, he should have choice. Several weavers being to bring him in pieces made from the cast patterns that were going. Then ladies,' says he, 'I shall be glad to supply you with what you want; and there is no man in England will use you better. Only please to leave your names, and where you live, that I may do myself the honour to wait on you.' Here our madams were put to it for an answer; but looking a little on one another, she that spoke first told him, 'that being newly come to town, they did not remember the name of the street where they lodged; but it was not far off, and if he pleased to go with them, they would show him their habitation, such as it was'.

Whitney, to be sure consented, and to make the affair appear with a better face, he stepp'd into the shop as if he went to give orders to the apprentice, to whom he only put some impertinent questions, and came out again unsuspected. Away trudge the ladies and their 'squire, who when they told him they were come to the door, very civilly offered to take his leave of them. 'Nay, Sir,' says one

251

of them, 'but you shall walk in, and take a glass of wine with us, since you have been so good as to give yourself all this trouble?' Whitney thanked them, and with abundance of complisance, accepted the favour.

Hitherto both parties were deceived. Whitney really took them for gentle-women of fortune, and came home with them only to learn something that might forward him to make a prey of them, and they as confidently believed him to be the mercer, who own'd the shop at which they picked him up. Their designs were to get his money out of his pocket, and if they could, a suit or two of cloaths into the bargain. What confirm'd them in this opinion was, the notice he took of several gentlemen as he passed along the street, by pulling off his hat to them; and their returning the same compliment. Whitney did it for this very purpose, and it is natural and common for men of fashion to re-salute those who salute them, whether they know them or no, because a man may be known by one whom he can't remember on a sudden to have ever seen before.

The ladies introduced their supposed cully into an appartment splendidly furni-shed, where a table was instantly spread with a fine cold collation. This being over, the maid and one of the mistresses withdrew, leaving the other to manage Whitney. She immediately fell into amorous discourse, and soon proceeded to greater free-doms, telling him, he was bashful, and offering to teach him a soft love-lesson. Whitney now began to understand his company, yet, as he hoped to get a little love by the bargain, he was willing to keep on the mask, and professed himself her slave, devoted to her service, and willing to fulfil her pleasure, promising withal after a great many mutual endearments, to give her as much silk as would make a suit of cloaths. This was all she required of him before she granted him the last favour, and upon this single promise, she suffer'd him to play over the jeu d'amour as often as he pleased, entertaining him, after all, with two or three more bottles free-cost.

Whitney was so well pleased with his reception at this place, that he was resolved, if possible, to have a little more of the same sport; and to that end went to a mercer, and told him, that such a lady had sent him to desire that he would let one of his men carry two or three pieces of the richest silk in his shop, for her to choose a gown and peticoat. The mercer knew the person of quality whom he named, she having been his customer before, and without mistrusting any thing, sent a youth, who was but newly come 'prentice, telling him the prices in Whitney's hearing. Our adventurer led the lad through as many by-streets as he could, in order to carry him out of his knowledge, till observing a house in Suffolk-Street, which had a thorough-fair into Hedge-Lane, he desired the young man to stay at the door, while he carried in the silks to show them to the lady, who lodged there. The youth obey'd very readily, and Whitney went into the house, and asked the people for somebody whom they did not know; upon their telling him no such person lived in that neighbourhood, he desired leave to go through, which was granted.

Now, good night Mr Mercer, you may wait till you are weary, and go back lighter by all your load. In a word, Whitney went to his mistresses, and distributed the prize between them. After which he revelled on all manner of excess for several days, till he was glad to retire of himself.

He was resolved, however, that no body but himself should enjoy the fruit of his industry, since he could not have the profit of his cheat, it would be a piece of honesty in him, he thought, to restore the mercer's goods again. To this end he writes a letter where the women lived, and the shop-keeper getting a warrant, and a constable, went and found the silks in their custody. To be sure they were enough frighten'd to see themselves apprehended for what they thought had been given them by the right owner; but all their excuses were in vain, they were hurried before a magistrate, who committed them to Tuthil-Fields, Bridewell, where they were taught the discipline of the place, by that celebrated lictor, Mr Redding, and their backs were covered with stripes of the cat-and nine-tails, instead of the eleemosynary silks, which they thought themselves so sure of.

When Whitney was grown a confirmed highwayman, he one day met a gentleman on Bagshot-Heath, whom he commanded to stand and deliver. To which the gentleman replied, 'Sir, 'tis well you spoke first; for I was just going to say the same thing to you.' —'Why, are you a gentleman thief then,' quoth Whitney?—'Yes,' said the stranger, 'but I have had very bad success to day; for I have been riding up and down all this morning, without meeting with any prize.' Whitney, upon this, wished him better luck, and took his leave, really supposing him to be what he pretended.

At night it was the fortune of Whitney, and this impostor to put up at the same inn, when our gentleman told some other travellers by what a stratagem he had escaped being robb'd on the road: Whitney had so alter'd his habit and speech, that the gentleman did not know him again; so that he heard all the story without being taken any notice of. Among other things he heard him tell one of

253

the company softly, that he had sav'd an hundred pounds by his contrivance. The person to whom he whisper'd this, was going the same way the next morning, and said, he had also a considerable sum about him, and if he pleased, should be glad to travel with him for security. It was agreed between them, and Whitney at the same time resolved to make one with them.

When morning came, our fellow-travellers set out, and Whitney about a quarter of an hour after them. All the discourse of the gentlemen was about cheating the highwaymen, if they should meet with any, and all Whitney's thoughts were upon being revenged for the abuse which was put on him the day before.

At a convenient place he got before them, and bid them stand. The gentleman whom he met before, not knowing him, he having disguised himself after another manner, briskly cried out, 'We were going to say the same to you, Sir.'—'Were you so?' quoth Whitney, 'And are you of my profession then?'—'Yes,' said they both. 'If you are,' reply'd Whitney, 'I suppose you remember the old proverb, Two of a trade can never agree, so that you must not expect any favour on that score. But to be plain, gentlemen, the trick will do no longer. I know you very well, and

must have your hundred pounds, Sir; and your considerable sum, Sir,' turning to the other, 'let it be what it will, or I shall make bold to send a brace of bullets through each of your heads. You, Mr Highwayman, should have kept your secret a little longer, and not have boasted so soon of having out-witted a thief. There is now nothing for you to do but deliver, or die.'—These terrible words put them both into a sad consternation: they were both to lose their money, but more loth to lose their lives; so of two evils, they chose the least; the tell-tale coxcomb disbursing his hundred pounds, and the other a somewhat larger sum, professing that they would be careful for the future not to count without their host.

Another time Whitney met with one Mr Hull, an old userer in the Strand, as he was riding a-cross Hounslow-Heath. He could hardly have chosen a wretch more in love with money, and consequently who would have been more unwilling to have parted with it.

When the dreadful words were spoken, he trembled like a paralitic; and fell to expostulating the case in the most moving expressions he was master of, professing that he was a very poor man, had a large family of children, and should be utterly ruined, if he was so hard hearted as to take his money from him. He added, moreover, a great deal concerning the illegality of such an action, and how very dangerous it was to engage in such evil courses. Whitney, who knew him, cried out in a great passion: 'Sirrah, do you pretend to preach morality to an honester man than yourself? Is it not much more generous to take a man's money from him bravely, than to grind him to death with eight or ten per cent. under colour of serving him? You make a prey of all mankind, and necessity in an honest man, often is the means of his falling into your clutches, who are certain quite to undo him. I am a man of more honour than to shew any regard to one whom I esteem an enemy to the whole human species. This once, Sir, I shall oblige you to lend me what you have without bond, and consequently without interest; so make no words.'—Old Hull, hereupon, pulled out about eighteen pound, which he gave with a pretty deal of grumbling; telling him withal, that he should see him one time or another, ride up Holbourn-Hill backwards.

Whitney was going about his business, till he heard these words, when he returned, and pulled the old gentleman off his horse, putting him on again with his face towards the horse's tail, and tying his legs. 'Now,' says he, 'you old rogue, let me see what a figure a man makes when he rides backwards, and let me have the pleasure, at least, of beholding you first in that posture.' So giving the horse three or four good licks with his whip, he set him a running so fast, that he never stop'd till he came to Hounslow town, where the people loosed our gentleman, after they had made themselves a little merry with the sight.

Whitney, like a great many others of the same profession, affected always to appear generous and noble: there is one instance of this temper in him, which it may not be amiss to relate. Meeting one day with a gentleman on New-market-Heath, whose name was Long, and having robb'd him of an hundred pounds in silver, which was in his portmanteau, tied up in a great bag: the gentleman told him, that he had a great way to go, and as he was unknown upon the road, should meet with many difficulties, if he did not restore as much as would bear his expences. Whitney upon this open'd the mouth of the bag, and holding it to Mr Long, 'Here,' says he, 'take what you have occasion for.' Mr Long put in his hand, and took out as much as he could hold: to which Whitney made no opposition, but only said with a smile, 'I thought you would have had more conscience, Sir.'

Doubtless it must make some of our readers merry, when they observe how often the heroes of these sheets are introduced as talking of conscience, virtue, honour, generosity, &c. And it must be confessed, that they have reason for their

255

mirth. This may, however, prove the real beauty of these perfections of human nature, 'that even those who have least of them, discover a sort of secret value for them, and would affect to possess what they are of all men the farthest from'.

Our dexterous butcher came once to Doncaster in Yorkshire, where he put up at the Red-Lyon-Inn, and made a very great figure, having a pretty round sum in his possession. While he resided here, he was informed that the landlord of the house was reputed rich; but that he was withal so covetous, as that he would do nothing to help a poor relation or neighbour in distress; and so very sharp in his business, that it was next to impossible for any one living to impose on him in the least particular. Nothing could be so pleasing to such a man as Whitney, as out-witting one who was esteemed able to out-wit all the world, wherefore he was resolved to attempt this master-stroke of invention, as he supposed it must be, if he succeeded.

He now gives it out, that he had a good estate, that he travelled about the country merely for his pleasure, and had his money remitted to him as the rents came in, still continuing for some time to pay for every thing he had, till suppo-sing his host sufficiently satisfy'd that he was really what he pretended, he one day took an opportunity to tell him that his money ran short, and he should be obliged to him for credit, till he could have returns. 'O dear, Sir,' says my landlord, 'you need not give yourself the least uneasiness about such an affair as this. Every thing that I have is at your service, and I shall think myself honoured, if you please to make use of me as a friend.' Whitney returned the compliment with abundance of thanks and other expressions of esteem, eating and drinking from day to day at the good man's table, his horse also, all the while, being fed plentifully with the best of corn and hay. And the better to colour the matter, and to prove that he really came out of curiosity to see the country, there was seldom a day passed, but he rode out to some of the neighbouring villages, sometimes getting Mr Inn-Keeper; sometimes other gentlemen in the town, to bear him company, they being all proud of the honour.

It happened, that while he remain'd there, there was a fair, according to annual custom. Upon the fair day in the morning a small box, carefully sealed, and very weighty, came directed to him. He open'd it, took out a letter, and read, lock'd it up, and gave it to his landlady, desiring her to keep it in her custody for the present, because it would be safer than in his own hands; and ordering the landlord, at the same time to write out his bill, that he might pay him next morning. As soon as he had done thus, he went out, as though to see the fair.

In the afternoon he comes home again in a great hurry, and desires his horse may be dressed and saddled, he having a mind to shew him in the fair, and, if he could, to exchange him for one which he had seen, and which he thought was the finest that ever he fix'd his eyes on. 'I will have him,' says he, 'if possible, whether the owner will buy mine or no, and though he cost me forty guineas': he then asked for his landlady to help him to his box, but was told she was gone to the fair; whereupon he fell a swearing like a madman, that he supposed she had locked up what he gave her, and taken the keys with her, 'If she has,' quoth he, 'I had rather have given ten guineas; for I have no money at all, but what is in your possession.' Enquiry was made, and it was found to be as he said, which put him into a still greater passion, though it was what he wished for, and even expected, the whole comedy having been invented for the sake of this single scene.

The landlord quickly had notice of our gentleman's anger, and the occasion of it; upon which he comes to him, and begs of him to be easy, offering to lend him the sum he wanted, till his wife came home. Whitney seemed to resent it highly, that he must be obliged to borrow money when he had so much of his own; however, as there was no other way, he condescended, with abundance of reluctance, to accept the proposal, adding, that he desired an account of all he was indebted as soon as possible, for it was not his custom to run hand over head.

Having received forty guineas, the sum he pretended to want, he mounts his horse, and rides towards the fair; but instead of dealing there, for another horse, he spurred his own thro' the crowd, as fast as he could conveniently, and made the best of his way towards London. At night the people of the inn sat up very late for his coming home, nor did they suspect any thing the first, or even the second night, when they saw nothing of him, he having been out before a day or two together in his progress round the country, which they concluded was now the case. But at the end of two or three days, the landlord was a little uneasy; and after he had waited a week to no purpose, it came into his head to break open the box, in order to examine it. With this view he goes to the magistrate of the place, procures his warrant for so doing, and a constable, with other proper witnesses to be present. We need not tell the reader he was cheated, for every one will naturally conclude so, nor need we say, he was ready to hang himself, when he found only sand and stones covered over, his character may give an idea of his temper at this time: but Whitney did not care for his landlord's passion, so long as he got off safe, with the money.

This was, however, the last of his adventures in the country, for not long after his arrival in town, he was apprehended in White-Friars, upon the information of one Mother Cosens, who kept a bawdy-house in Milford Lane, over-against St Clement's Church. The magistrate who took the information, committed him to Newgate, where he remained till the next sessions at the Old-Bailey.

After his conviction, Sir S—l L—e, Knt. Recorder of London, made an excellent speech before he passed Sentence of Death, to him, and the other malefactors, setting forth the nature of their several offences in very strong expressions, and addressing himself to Whitney in particular, who he exhorted to a sincere repentance, as it was impossible for him to hope for any reprieve, after such a course of villainies. Vindicating the justice of the law, and urging the certainty of a providence, which pursues such as him, and at last takes vengeance on them for their crimes.

On Wednesday, the 19th of December, 1694 Whitney was carried to the place of execution, which was at Porter's Block, near Smithfield. When he came there, and saw no hopes of any favour, he addressed these few words to the people:

> I Have been a very great Offender, both against God, and my Country, by transgressing all Laws both Human and Divine. I believe there is not one here present but has often heard my Name, before my Confinement, and seen a large Catalogue of my Crimes, which has been made publick since. Why should I then pretend to vindicate a Life stain'd with so many enormous Deeds?
>
> The Sentence past on me is just, and I can see the Footsteeps of a Providence, which I had before profanely laugh'd at, in my Apprehending and Conviction. I hope the Sense which I have of these Things, has enabled me to make my Peace with Heaven, the only Thing that is now of any Concern to me. Join in your Prayers with me, my dear Countrymen, that God would not forsake me in my last Moments.

Having spoke thus, and afterwards spent a few moments in private devotion, he was turned off, being about 34 years of age.

THE LIFE OF
CAPT. URATZ

HIGHWAYMAN, AND MURDERER
OF THOMAS THYNN, ESQ;
IN THE PALL-MALL

Christopher Uratz, the youngest son of a very good gentleman, and born in Pomerania, a country adjoyning to Poland, having but a very small patrimony left him, he was incited, thro' the slenderness of his fortune, to betake himself to the highway; and being a man of a great courage, and undaunted spirit, he ventured on such attempts by himself, which would not be undertook by half a dozen men; for once John Sobieski, King of Poland, who, with the Duke of Lorrain, raised the siege of Vienna, going disguised out of the Christian camp, in company only with three officers, to observe the motion of the Turks, he intercepted his coming back, and robbed him and his attendants of as many diamonds, which he sold to a Jew at Vienna, for above 8000 ducatoons, besides taking from them a considerable quantity of gold. He had also committed some robberies in Hungary; but having somewhat of a more generous soul, than always to get his bread by that diminutive way of living, he was contrary to all others of that profession, not extravagant whilst he maintained himself by those fearing words, 'stand and deliver'; therefore having saved a good purse by him, he bought a captain's commission in a regiment in the Emperor of Germany's service.

Whilst he was in this post, he became acquainted with Count Coningsmark, and came over with him into England; where the said count being baulked in his amours with a certain lady by Thomas Thynn, Esq; his ill success therein he so highly resented, that nothing could pacify his resentment, but the death of his rival. Captain Uratz being made privy to his disgust, he procured two other assassins, namely, John Stern, a lieutenant, and George Borosky alias Boratzi, who, about a quarter after eight a night, on Sunday the 12th of February, 1681, meeting Esquire Thynn riding in his coach up to St James's-Street, from the Countess of Northumberland's Boroski, a Polander, shot him with a blunderbuss, which mortify'd him after such a barbarous manner, that Mr Hobbs, an eminent chyrurgeon, found in his body four bullets, which had torn his guts, wounded his liver, and stomach, and gall, broke one of his ribs, and wounded the great bone below, of which wounds he dyed.

These murderers being taken the next day, and carry'd before Justice Bridgman, he committed them to Newgate; from whence being brought to the Old Bailey on Tuesday the 28th of February following, they were try'd before the Lord Chief Justice Pemberton; and being cast for their lives, the recorder pass'd Sentence of Death on them.

Whilst Captain Uratz was under condemnation, Dr Anthony Horneck, and Dr Gilbert Burnet, the late Bishop of Salisbury, went to visit him; the first of which divines thus writes.

> That putting the Criminal in Mind of the All-seeing Eye above, who knew his Crimes, tho' he did conceal them from Man, he was pleas'd to tell me, That he had far other Apprehensions of God, than I had; and was confident God would consider a Gentleman, and deal with him suitably to the Condition and Profession he had Plac'd him in; and would not take it ill, if a Soldier, who liv'd by his Sword, reveng'd the Affronts offer'd to him by another. I reply'd, That there was but one Way to eternal Happiness; and that God, in his Laws has made no Exception for any Sorts or Degrees of Men; and consequently Revenge in a Gentleman, was a Sin God would not pardon without true Repentance, any more than he

would forgive it in a Peasant. He asking me hereupon, What Repentance was? I told him, it was so to hate the Sin we had done, that for the future no Argument should prevail with us to commit it again. To which he said, That if he were to live, he should not forbear to give any one as good as he brings; with some other Expressions, which I am loth to repeat; for they made me so melancholick, that I was forced to leave him. Yet I bid him consider what he had said, as he Lov'd his own Soul. The last Time I visited him, was on the 8th of March, whom, when I had saluted, I told him I hop'd he had taken his dangerous Condition into Consideration, and wrought himself into a greater Sense of his Sins, than I could observe in him when I was last with him. He said, he knew not what I meant by this Address. I then explained my self, gave him to understand, that I spake it with Relation to the late great Sin he had been engag'd in; and that I hop'd his approaching Death had made him more penitent, than I had found him t'other Day. To which he reply'd, That he was sensible he was a great Sinner, and had committed divers Enormities in his Life-time, of which he truly repented, and was confident that God had pardon'd him; but he could not well understand the Humour of our English Divines, who press'd him to make particular Declarations of Things they had a Mind he should say, tho' never so false, or contrary to Truth; and at this, he said, he wondered the more, because in our Church we were not for auricular Confession. I let him run on; and then I told him, that he was much mistaken in the Divines of the Church of England, who neither us'd to reveal private Confession, nor oblige Offenders in such Cases, to confess Things contrary to Truth; that this was both against their Practice and their Principles: The Confession, I said, he was so often exhorted to, was no private, but a public Confession; for as his Crime had been publick Confession; for as his Crime had been publick, so his Repentance and Confession ought to be publick too; and farthermore, I told him, that Christ's Blood was actually applied to none but the true Penitent, and that true Repentance must discover it self in Meekness, Humility, Tender-heartedness, Compassion, Righteousness, making ingenious Confessions, and, so far as we are able, Satisfaction too, else, notwithstanding the Treasure of Christ's Blood, Men might drop into Hell. Upon this, he replied, that he fear'd no Hell. I answer'd, possibly he might believe none; or, if he did, it might be a very easy one of his own making. He said he was not such a Fool as to believe that Souls could fry in material Fire, or be roasted as Meat on a great Hearth, or in a Kitchin, pointing to the Chimney. His Belief was, that the Punishment of the Damn'd consisted in a Deprivation of the gracious and beatifick Presence of God; upon which Deprivation, there arose a Terror and Anguish in their Souls, because they had miss'd of so great a Happiness. He added, that possibly I might think him an Atheist; but he was so far from those Thoughts, that he could scarce believe there was any Man so sottish in the World, as not to believe the Being of a God, gracious, and just, and generous to his Creatures; nor could any Man, that was not either mad or drunk, believe Things came fortuitously, or that this World was govern'd by Chance. I said that this Truth I approv'd of, and was glad to see him so well settled in the Reasonableness of that Principle; and as for material Fire in the other World, I would not quarrel with him for denying it, but rather hold with him, that the Fire and Brimstone spoken of in Scripture, were but Emblems of those inward Terrors which would gnaw and tear the Consciences of impenitent Sinners; but still this was a greater Punishment than material Fire: And this Punishment he had Reason to fear, if he could not make it out to me, or other Men, that his Repentance was sincere. I was at first in some Doubt whether I would publish the Captain's Answers to my Queries and Expostulations, because some of them favour of Prophaneness; yet, considering that the Evangelist hath thought fit to acquaint the World with the ill Language of the one, as well as with the penitent Expressions of the other Malefactor, I was willing to follow that great Example, hoping that those loose Discourses of the Man may serve as Sea-marks to warn Passengers from running upon those Sands. That which I chiefly observ'd in him, was, that Honour and Bravery was the Idol he ador'd, a Piece of preposterous Devotion, which he maintain'd to the last, as if he thought it would merit Praise, not to decede from what he had once said, though it was with the Loss of God's Favour, and the Shipwreck of a good Conscience. He consider'd God as some generous, yet partial Prince, who would regard Men's Blood,

Descent, and Quality, more than their Errors, and give vast Grains of Allowance to their Breeding and Education; and possibly the stout Behaviour of some of the ancient Roman Bravo's, (for he had read History) might roll in his Mind, and tempt him to write Copies after those Originals; or, to think that it was great to do ill, and to defend it to the last. Whether after my last Conference with him he relented, I know not: Those that saw him go to his Execution, observ'd that he look'd undaunted, and with a Countenance so steady, that it seem'd to speak his Scorn, not only of all the Spectators that look'd upon him, but of Death it self. But I judge not of the Thoughts of dying Men, those the Searcher of all Hearts knows best, to whom Men stand or fall.

Dr Gilbert Burnet writes thus of Captain Uratz:

It is certain, that never Man died with more Resolution, and less Signs of Fear, or the least Disorder. His Carriage in the Cart, both as he was led along, and at the Place of Execution, was astonishing; he was not only undaunted, but look'd chearful, and smil'd often. When the Rope was put about his Neck, he did not change Colour, nor tremble; his Legs were firm under him. He look'd often about on those that stood in Balconies and Windows, and seem'd to fix his Eyes on some Persons. Three or four Times he smil'd. He would not cover his Face as the rest did, but continu'd in that State, often looking up to Heaven, with a Chearfulness in his Countenance, and a little Motion of his Hands. I saw him several Times in the Prison; he still stood to the Confession he made to the Council, till the last Day of his Life. He often said to me, he would never say any Thing but what he had said at first. When I was with him on Sunday before his Death, he still denied all that the Lieutenant and Polonian had said, and spake severely of them, cheifly of the Lieutenant, as if he had confess'd those Things, which he then call'd Lies, in Hopes of saving his own Life by it, or in Spite to him, that he might not be pardon'd; and all I could say, could not change his Mind in that. I told him, it was in vain for him to dream of a Pardon; for I assur'd him, if any kept him up with the Hopes of it, they deceiv'd him. He had two

Opinions that were, as I thought, hurtful to him; the one was, That it was enough if he confess'd his Sin to God, and that he was not bound to make any other Confession; and he thought that it was a Piece of Popery to press him to confess. He had another odd Opinion, also, of the next State: He thought the Damn'd were only excluded from the Presence of God, and endur'd no other Misery but that of seeing others happier than themselves; and was unwilling to let me enter into much Discourse with him for undeceiving him. He said it was his own Affair, and he desir'd to be left to himself. But he spake with great Assurance of God's Mercy to him. I left him, when I saw that nothing I could say had any good Effect on him, and resolv'd to have gone no more to him; but when I understood by a German Minister that attended him, and by the Message which I heard deliver'd in his Name to the Lieutenant and the Polander, the Night before his Execution, that he was in another Temper than when I saw him last, I went to him. He receiv'd me more kindly than formerly; most of his Discourse was concerning his going to the Place of Execution, desiring it might be in a Coach, and not in a Cart; and when I pray'd him to think of that which concern'd him more, he spake with great Assurance, that it was already done; that he knew God had forgiven him: And when I wish'd him to see that he might not deceive himself, and that his Hope might not be ill grounded, he said it was not Hope, but Certainty; for he was sure God was reconcil'd to him, through Christ. When I spake to him of confessing his Sin, he said he had written it, and it would be publish'd to all Europe; but he did not say a Word concerning it to me: So I left him, and saw him no more till I met him at the Place of Execution. When he saw me, he smil'd on me; and whereas I had sometimes warn'd him of the Danger of affecting to be a Counterfeit Bravo, (Faux brave) he said to me, before I spake to him, 'That I should see it was not false Bravery, but that he was fearless to the last.' I wish'd him to consider well upon what he grounded his Confidence: He said he was sure he was now to be receiv'd into Heaven; and that his Sins were forgiven him. I ask'd him if he had any Thing to say to the People. He said No. After he had whisper'd a short Word to a Gentleman, he was willing the Rope should be ty'd to the Gibbet. He call'd for the German

Minister; but the Crowd was such, that it was not possible for him to come near. So he desir'd me to pray with him in French; but I told him I could not venture to pray in that Language; but, since he understood English, I would pray in English. I observ'd he had some Touches in his Mind, when I offer'd up that Petition, that for the Sake of the Blood of Christ, the innocent Blood shed in that Place might be forgiven; and that the Cry of the one for Mercy, might prevail over the Cry of the other for Justice. At these Words, he look'd up to Heaven with the greatest Sense that I had at any Time observ'd in him. After I pray'd, he said nothing, but that he was now going to be happy with God; so I left him. He continu'd in his undaunted Manner, looking up often to Heaven, and sometimes round about him, to the Spectators. After he and his two Fellow-Sufferers had stood about a quarter of an Hour under the Gibbet, they were ask'd when they would give the Signal for their being turn'd off. He answer'd, that they were ready, and that the Cart might be driven away when it pleas'd the Sheriff to order it. So, a little While after, it was driven away. And thus they all ended their Lives.

265

As for Lieutenant Stern, the illegitimate son of a baron of Sweden, afterwards made a count, and Borosky the Polander, they were very penitent from first to last, being with Captain Uratz, aged 38, executed in the Pall-Mall on Friday the 10th of March 1681–2; but Borosky was afterwards hung up in chains, a little beyond Mile-End, by the command of King Charles the Second.

THE LIFE OF
MOL CUTPURSE

Mary Frith, otherwise call'd Mol Cutpurse, from her original profession of cutting purses, was born in Barbican in Aldersgate-street, in the year 1589. Her father was a shoe-maker; and though no remarkable thing happened at her nativity, such as the flattering soothsayers pretend in eclipses, and other the like motions above, or tides, and whales, and great fires, adjusted and timed to the genitures of crown'd heads, yet, for a she-politician, she was not much inferior to Pope Joan; for in her time, she was superior in the mystery of diving in purses and pockets, and was very well read and skill'd too in the affairs of the placket among the great ones.

Both the parents (as having no other child living) were very tender of this daughter; but especially the mother; according to the tenderness of that sex, which is naturally more indulgent than the male; most affectionate she was to her in her infancy, most careful of her in her youth, manifested especially in her education, which was the more strictly and diligently attended, by reason of her boisterous and masculine spirit, which then shewed itself, and soon after became predominant, she was above all breeding and instruction. She was a very tomrig or hoyden, and delighted only in boys-play and pastime, not minding or companying with the girls; many a bang and blow this hoyting procured her, but she was not so to be tam'd, or taken off from her rude inclinations; she could not endure that sedentary life of sewing or stitching; a sampler was as grievous to her as a winding-sheet; and on her needle, bodkin, and thimble, she could not think quietly, wishing them changed into sword and dagger for a bout at cudgels. Her head-geer and handkerchief (or what the fashion of those times was for girls to be dress'd in) were alike tedious to her, she wearing them as handsomely as a dog would a doublet; and so cleanly, that the sooty pot-hooks were above the comparison. This perplex'd her friends, who had only this proverb favourable to their hope, 'That an unlucky girl may make a good woman'; but they liv'd not to the length of that expectation, dying in her minority, and leaving her to the swing and sway of her own unruly temper and disposition.

She would fight with boys, and courageously beat them; run, jump, leap, or hop with any of her contrary sex, or recreate herself with any other play whatso-ever. She had an uncle, brother to her father, who was a minister, and of him she stood in some awe, but not so much, as to restrain her in these courses; so that seeing he could not effectually remedy that inveterating evil in her manners, he trappanned her on board a merchant-ship lying at Gravesend, and bound for New-England, whither he designed to have sent her; but having learned to swim, she one night jump'd over-board, and swimm'd to shore, and after that escape would never go near her uncle again. Farthermore, it is to be observed, that Mercury was in conjunction with, or rather in the House of Venus, at the time of her nativity; the former of which planets is of a thievish, cheating, deceitful influence; and the other hath dominion over all whores, bawds, and pimps; and, joyn'd with Mercury, over all trepanners and hectors: she hath a more general influence than all the other six planets put together; for no place nor person is exempted from her, invading alike both sacred and prophane; nunneries and monasteries, as well as the common places of prostitution; Cheapside and Cornhill, as well as Bloomsbury or Covent-Garden. Under these benevolent and kind stars, she grew up to some maturity; she was now a lusty and sturdy wench, and fit to put out to service, having not a competency of her own, left her by her friends to maintain her without working; but as she was a great libertine, she liv'd too much in common, to be enclos'd in the limits of a private domestick life. A quarter-staff was fitter for her than a distaff; she would go to the ale house when she had made shift to get a little stock, spend her penny, come into any one's company, and club till she had none left; and then she was fit for any enterprize. Moreover, she had a natural abhorrence to tending of children, to whom she ever had an averseness in her mind, equal to the sterility and barrenness in her womb, never (to our best information) being made a mother.

She generally went dress'd in man's apparel; which puts me in mind how Hercules, Nero, and Sardanapalus are laugh'd at and exploded, for their effeminacy and degenerated dissoluteness in their extravagant debauchery; the first is pour-trated with a distaff in his hand; the other recorded to be marry'd as a wife, and all the conjugal and matrimonial rites perform'd at the solemnity of the marriage; and the other lacks the luxury of a pen, as loose as his female riots, to describe them. These were all monsters of men, and have no parellels either in old or modern histories, till such time as Mol Cutpurse approach'd their examples; for her heroick impudence hath quite outdone every romance; never woman before being like her. No doubt but Mol's converse with herself, informed her of her defects, and that she was not made for the pleasure or delight of man; and therefore, since she could not be honoured with him, she would be honoured by him, in that garb and manner of rayment which he wore. This she took to from her first entrance into a competency of age, and to her dying day she would not leave it off.

Though she was so ugly in any dress, as never to be woo'd nor sollicited by any man, yet she never had the green-sickness, that epidemical disease of maidens, after they have once pass'd their puberty; she never eat lime, coles, oatmeal, tobacco-pipes, cinders, or such like trash; no sighs, dejected looks, or melancholly clouded her vigorous spirits, or repress'd her jovialty; she was troubled with none of those longings which poor maidens are subject to: she had the power and strength to command her own pleasure of any person who had reasonable ability of body; and therefore she needed not whine for it, as she was able to beat a fellow to a compliance, without the unnecessary trouble of entreaties.

Now Mol thinking what course of life she should betake herself to, she got acquainted with some fortune-tellers of the town, from whom learning some smatch and relish of that cheat, by their insignificant schemes, and calculating of figures, she got a tolerably good livelihood; but her income being not equivalent to her expences, she enter'd herself into the society of divers, otherwise call'd file-clyers, cut-purses, or pick-pockets; which people are a kind of land pyrates, trading altogether in other men's bottoms, for no other merchandise than bullion and ready coin, and they keep most of the great fairs and marts in the world. In this unlawful way she got a vast deal of money; but having been very often in Old Bridewell, the compters, and Newgate, for her irregular practices, and burnt in the hand four times, she left off this petty sort of theft, and went on the highway, committing many great robberies, but all of 'em on the Round-heads, or rebels, that fomented the Civil War against King Charles the First; against which villains she had as great an antipathy, as an unhappy man, that, for counterfeiting a half-crown in those rebellious times, was executed at Tyburn, where he said, 'that he was adjudg'd to die but for counterfeiting a half-crown; but those that usurp'd the whole Crown, and stole away its revenue, and had counterfeited its seal, were above justice, and escap'd unpunish'd'.

A long time had Moll Cutpurse robb'd on the road; but, at last, robbing General Fairfax of 250 jacobus's on Hounslow Heath, shooting him thro' the arm for opposing her, and killing two horses on which a couple of his servants rid, a close pursuit was made after her by some Parliamentarian officers, quartering in the town of Hounslow, to whom Fairfax had told his misfortune. Her horse fail'd her at Turnham-Green, where they apprehended her, and carried her to Newgate. After this, she was condemn'd, but procur'd her pardon, by giving her adversary 2000 *l*. Now Moll being frighten'd by this disaster, she left off going on the highway any more, and took a house, within two doors of the Globe tavern in Fleetstreet, over-against the conduit, almost facing Shoe-Lane and Salisbury-Court, where she dispens'd justice among the wrangling tankard-bearers, by often exchanging their burden of water for a burden of beer, as far the lighter carriage, though not so portable.

In her time tobacco being grown a great mode, she was mightily taken with the pastime of smoaking, because of its singularity, and that no woman ever smoak'd before her, though a great many of her sex, since, have follow'd her example.

Moll being quite scar'd from thieving herself, she turn'd fence, that is to say, a buyer of stolen goods; by which occupation she got a great deal of money. In her house she set up a kind of brokery, or a distinct factory for jewels, rings, and watches, which had been pinch'd or stolen any manner of way, at never so great distance, from any person. It might properly enough be call'd the insurance-office for such merchandise; for the losers were sure, upon composition, to recover their

269

goods again, and the pyrates were sure to have a good ransom, and she so much in the gross for brokage, without any more danger; the hue-and-cry being always directed to her for the discovery of the goods, not the takers.

Once, a gentleman that had lost his watch, by the busy fingers of a pickpocket, came very anxiously to Moll, enquiring if she could help him to it again. She demanded of him the marks and signs thereof, with the time when, and where he lost it, or by what crowd, or other accident. He replied, 'that coming through Shoe-Lane, there was a quarrel betwixt two men; one of which, as he afterwards heard, was a grasier, whom they had set in Smithfield, having seen him receive the sum of 200 *l.* or thereabouts, in gold. There was one Bat Rud, as he was since inform'd, who, observing the man hold his hand in his pocket where his gold was, just in the middle of a lane whitherto they dogg'd him, overthrew a barrel trimming at an alehouse door, while one behind the grasier push'd him over, who, withal, threw down Bat, who was ready for the fall. Betwixt these two presently arose a quarrel; the pickpocket demanding satisfaction, while his comrades interposing, after two or three blows in favour of the countryman, who had drawn his hands out of his pocket to defend himself, soon drew out his treasure; and while he was looking on the scuffle, some of them had lent him a hand too, and finger'd out his watch'. Moll smil'd at the adventure, and told him, 'he should hear farther of it within a day or two, at the farthest'. When the gentleman came again, she understood by his discourse that he would not lose it for twice its value, because it was given him by a particular friend; so she squeez'd 20 guineas out of him before he could obtain his watch.

Moll was always accounted by her neighbours to be an hermaphrodite, but at her death was found otherwise. She had not liv'd long in Fleetstreet, before she became acquainted with a new sort of thieves, call'd heavers, whose employment was stealing shop-books from drapers and mercers, or other rich traders; which bringing to her, she, for some considerable profit for her self, got them a *quantum meruit* for restoring them again to the losers. While she thus reign'd free from the danger of the common-law, an apparator, set on by an adversary of hers, cited her to appear in the court of Arches, where was an accusation exhibited against her for wearing indecent and manly apparel. She was advis'd by her proctor to demur the jurisdiction of the court, as for a crime, if such, not cognizable there: but he did it to spin out the cause, and get her money; for, in the end, she was there sentenc'd to stand and do penance in a white sheet at St Paul's Cross, during morning sermon on a Sunday. They might as soon have sham'd a black dog as Moll, with any kind of such punishment; for a halfpenny she would have travell'd through all the market-towns in England with her penitential habit, and been as proud of it as that citizen who rode to his friends in the country in his livery-gown and hood. Besides, many of the spectators had little cause to sport themselves then at the sight; for some of her emissaries, without any regard to the sacredness of the place, spoil'd a good many cloaths, by cutting part of their cloaks and gowns, and sending them home as naked behind as Æsop's crow, when every bird took its own feather from her.

However, this penance did not reclaim her, for she still went in men's apparel, very decently dress'd; nor were the ornaments of her house less curious and pleasing in pictures, than in the delight of looking-glasses; so that she could see her sweet self all over in any part of her rooms. This gave occasion to folks to say, that she us'd magical glasses, wherein she could shew the querists, who resorted to her for information, them that stole their goods; as likewise to others, curious to know the shapes and features of their husbands that should be, the very true and perfect idea of them; as is very credibly reported of your African sorcerers. We have a tradition of it in the story of Jane Shore's husband, who, by one of the like glasses, saw the unchaste embraces of his wife and Edward IV.

One night late, Moll going home almost drunk from the Devil tavern, she tumbled over a great black sow, that was rousting in a dunghill near the kennel; but getting up again, in a sad dirty pickle, she drove her to her house, where finding her full of pigs, she made her a drench to hasten her farrowing, and the next morning she brought her eleven curious pigs, which Moll and her companions made fat and eat; and then she turn'd the sow out of doors, who presently repair'd to her old master, a bumpkin at Islington, who with wonder receiv'd her again. Having given her some grains, he turn'd her out of his gates, watching what course she would take, and intending to have satisfaction for his pigs wheresoever he should find her to have laid them. The sow, naturally mindful of her squeaking brood, went directly to Moll's door, and there kept a lamentable noise to be admitted: this was evidence enough for the fellow, that there his sow had laid her belly; when knocking, and having entrance, he tells Moll a tale of a sow and her litter. She replied, he was mad: he swore, he knew his sow's meaning by her grunting, and that he would give her sawce to her pigs. 'Goodman Coxcomb,' quoth Moll, 'come in, and see if this house looks like a hog-stye'; when, going into all her rooms, and seeing how neat and clean they were kept, he was convinc'd that the litter was not laid there, and went home cursing his sow for misinforming him.

To get money, Moll would not stick out to bawd for either men or women; insomuch, that her house became a double temple for Priapus and Venus, frequented by votaries of both sorts. Those who were generous to her labour, their desires were favourably accommodated with expedition; whilst she linger'd with others, laying before them the difficult but certain attainment of their wishes, which serv'd as a spur to the dulness of their purses. For the Lady Pecunia and she kept the same pace, but still in the end she did the feat. Moll having a great antipathy against the Rump Parliament, she lit on a fellow very dextrous for imitating people's hands; with him she communicated her thoughts, and they concurr'd to forge and counterfeit their commissioners and treasurers hands to the respective receivers and collectors, to pay the sums of money they had in their hands, without delay, to such as he in his counterfeited orders appointed: so that, wheresoever he had intelligence of any great sum in the country, they were sure to forestal the market. This cheat lasted for half a year, till it was found out at Guild-Hall, and such a politick course taken, to avoid cozenage, that no warrants would pass among themselves. But when the government was seiz'd and usurp'd by that arch-traytor, Oliver Cromwell, they began this trade a-fresh, it being very easy to imitate his single sign manual, as that ambitious usurper would have it stil'd; by which means, her man also drew good sums of money out of the customs and excise, nay, out of the Exchequer itself, till Oliver was forc'd to use a private mark, to make his credit authentick among his own villains.

After 74 years of age, Moll being grown crazy in her body, and discontented in mind, she yielded to the next distemper that approach'd her, which was the dropsy; a disease which had such strange and terrible symptoms, that she thought she was possess'd, and that the Devil was got within her doublet. Her belly, from a wither'd, dry'd, wrinckled piece of skin, was grown to the titest, roundest globe of flesh, that ever any beauteous young lady strutted with. However, there was no blood that was generative in her womb, but only that destructive of the grape, which by her excesses was now turn'd into water; so that the tympanied skin thereof sounded like a conduit-door. If we anatomize her any farther, we must say her legs represented a couple of mill-posts, and her head was so wrapp'd with cloaths, that she look'd like Mother Shipton.

It may well be expected, that, considering what a deal of money she got by her wicked practices, she might make a will; but yet, of 5000 *l.* which she had once by her in gold, she had not above 100 *l.* left her latterly, which she thought too little to give to the charitable uses of building hospitals and alms-houses. The money that might have been design'd that way, as it came from the Devil, so it return'd to the Devil again, in the Rump's Exchequer and Treasury at Haberdashers and Goldsmiths-Hall. Yet, to preserve something of her memory, and not leave it to the courtesy of an executor, she anticipated her funeral expences; for it being the fashion of those times to give rings, to the undoing of the confectioners, who liv'd altogether by the dead and the new-born, she distributed some that she had by her among her chief companions and friends.

These rings (like princes jewels) were notable ones, and had their particular names likewise; as the Bartholomew, the Ludgate, the Exchange, and so forth; deriving their appellations from the places whence they were stolen: they needed no admonition of a death's head, nor the motto *memento mori*; for they were the wages and monuments of their thieving masters and mistresses, who were interr'd at Tyburn; and she hop'd her friends would wear them, both for her sake and theirs. In short, she made no will at all, because she had had it so long before to no better purpose; and that if she had had her desert, she should have had an executioner instead of an executor.

Out of the 100 pounds which she had by her, she dispos'd of 30 pounds to her three maids which she kept, and charg'd them to occupy it the best way they could; for that, and some of her arts in which they had had time to be expert, would be beyond the advantage of their spinning and reeling, and would be able to keep them in repair, and promote them to weavers, shoe-makers and taylors. The rest of her personal estate, in money, moveables, and household-goods, she bequeath'd to her kinsman Frith, a master of a ship, dwelling at Reddriff, whom she advis'd not to make any ventures therewith, but stay at home and be drunk, rather than go to sea, and be drown'd with them.

And now, the time of her dissolution drawing near, she desir'd to be bury'd with her breech upwards, that she might be as preposterous in her death as she

273

had been all along in her infamous life. When she was dead, she was interr'd in St Bridget's church-yard, having a fair marble-stone put over her grave; on which was cut the following epitaph, compos'd by the ingenious Mr Milton, but destroy'd in the great conflagration of London.

> Here lies, under this same Marble,
> Dust, for Time's last Sieve to garble;
> Dust, to perplex a Sadducee,
> Whether it rise a He or She,
> Or two in one, a single Pair,
> Nature's Sport, and now her Care.
> For how she'll cloath it at last Day,
> Unless she sighs it all away;
> Or where she'll place it, none can tell:
> Some middle Place 'twixt Heav'n and Hell —
> And well 'tis Purgatory's found,
> Else she must hide her under Ground.
> These Reliques do deserve the Doom,
> Of that Cheat Mahomet's fine Tomb;
> For no Communion she had,
> Nor sorted with the Good or Bad;
> That when the World shall be calcin'd,
> And the mix'd Mass of human Kind
> Shall sep'rate by that melting Fire,
> She'll stand alone, and none come nigh her.
> Reader, here she lies till then,
> When, truly, you'll see her again.

THE LIFE OF
TOM JONES

Tom Jones was born at Newcastle upon Tine, in the county of Northumberland; where his father, being a clothier, brought him up to the same trade. He follow'd this calling till he was two and twenty years of age, though not without discovering his vicious inclinations many years before, by running in debt, and taking to all manner of irregular courses. At last, being reduc'd to extremity, he resolv'd at once to apply himself to the highway, as the only way left to retrieve his fortune. A very odd way indeed! but what is too often embrac'd by reduc'd extravagants.

To make a beginning, he robb'd his father of 80 *l.* and a good horse; upon which he rode cross the country with all speed, for fear of being pursu'd. The Devil, he knew, was sometimes apt to leave his children in the lurch; and therefore he thought it safer to trust to the legs of his horse, than to his good fortune. This, and the conscious dread of justice, which is always ready to terrify young villains, occasion'd his galloping 40 miles before he stopp'd; all which way, he was afraid of every one he saw, and every noise he heard.

After this, riding into Staffordshire, and meeting a stage-coach, with several passengers in it, he commanded the coachman to stop, and the people within to deliver. Some of the gentlemen were resolute, and refus'd to comply with his demand; upon which he fir'd several pistols, taking care to do no hurt; and still preserving three or four, well loaded, for his defence, if he should have occasion of them. The fright which the gunpowder put a couple of ladies into, who were in the coach, obliged the gentlemen to surrender, before there was any mischief done; and Tom rode off with a considerable booty.

There is a pleasant story related, as the consequence of this adventure, which we believe it will not be amiss to rehearse. A monkey, belonging to one of the passengers, being ty'd behind the coach, was so frighten'd at Jones's firing, that, with skipping about, he broke his chain, and ran about the fields so that the owner could not catch him again. At night, a country fellow coming over a stile, Pug leap'd out of the hedge upon his back, and there hung very fast. The poor man, having never seen a monkey before, imagin'd the Devil had laid hold of him, in which opinion he ran home, and thunder'd at the door like a mad man. His wife look'd out at window, and ask'd him what he had got. He told her, the Devil; begging she would go to the parson, and require his assistance. 'Nay,' quoth she, 'you shall not bring the Devil in here. If you belong to him, I don't: so pray be content to go without company.' Poor Hob was oblig'd to wait at his door, till a man, a little wiser than his neighbours, came by, and, with a few apples and pears, dispossess'd the unfortunate wretch, who was very willing to let our exorcist keep the Devil for his own use, as a reward for this signal piece of service: and he, upon hearing the monkey cry'd, carry'd him to the owner, and receiv'd a reward.

An Attorney of Clifford's-Inn, whose name was Story, having been drinking at a friend's house in the country till he was entirely drunk, as he was riding along the road towards town, he was necessitated to alight and tie his horse to a tree, while he went under a hedge to untruss a point. It was Tom Jones's fortune to come by in the interim; whereupon he also dismounted, with the same pretence. As soon as Story had done, Jones commanded him to deliver his money; but he, being in the condition just mention'd, took no notice of what was said: whereupon our highwayman caught him by the collar, and began to shake him. 'Have a care what you do,' says the attorney, 'for I am brim full, and shall run over if you move me ever so little.' 'Brim full of what?' quoth Jones. 'Of liquors,' reply'd the other. 'But 'tis your money I want, Sir; are you brim full of that? If you are, run over as fast as you please.' Story was so sick he could speak no more; but, before Jones was aware, giving a great belch, he discharg'd a large quantity of his friend's punch into the face of our adventurer, which almost blinded him, and set him to swearing like a mad man. At last, having clear'd his phyz with a handkerchief, he put his hand into the attorney's pockets, and oblig'd them to discharge six pounds odd money; which shining vomit a little pacify'd him, and made him forgive the affront, and suffer our drunken man. who was by this time a little soberer, to remount, and ride off.

Tom was by this time so grounded in vice, that nothing less powerful than the gallows was able to convert him from his wicked courses. This is, indeed, commonly the last teacher which such wretches have; and he never fails to make them as honest as any of their neighbours, and as quiet as any of the descendants of Adam, who have been departed in peace some thousands of years. The sooner he does his duty, it is generally the better.

But this is another digression from our history, to which we now return. Not long after the committing of the above recited robbery, Tom Jones met with one Samuel P—s upon the road, a Quaker, who formerly kept a button shop, between the two gates of the Savoy in the Strand, to whom he put the usual demand. Mr Primitive, having reduced himself to very low circumstances, as 'tis said, by whoring, gaming, and drinking, he was now riding down into the country to his friends, in order to avoid an arrest: as he was therefore in much greater apprehension of a bailiff than of a highwayman, and as he did not understand what Tom said, till he had got fast hold of him by the throat, he very formally cried out, 'At whose suit dost thou detain me?' Jones, who was not acquainted with our friends condition, smartly reply'd, 'I detain thee on my own suit, and my demand is for all thy substance.' The Quaker now perceived how the case stood; nevertheless, being a dry queer sort of a man, he was resolved to carry on the jest, whereupon he added, 'Indeed friend, I don't know thee, nor can I tell how to imagine that ever thee and I have had any dealings together,'—'You shall find then,' says Jones, 'that we must deal together now.' So clapping a pistol to his breast, he was going to explain himself, when friend Samuel cry'd out; 'Pray neighbour use no violence! for if thou carriest me to gaol, I shall be utterly undone. I have at least 14 guineas about me, and if that will satisfy thee, thou art welcome to take them: here they are; and give me leave to assure thee, that I have frequently stopp'd the mouth of a bailiff with a much less sum, and made him affirm to my creditors, that he could not find me.' Jones was pleas'd to receive the money, upon any account whatsoever; yet, being willing to convince the Quaker of his mistake, (tho' indeed the Quaker, as we have observ'd, was not mistaken, but only willing to carry on the affair in the strain it begun with) he said to him; 'Friend, I am not such a rogue as thou takest me to be: I am no bailiff, but an honest generous highwayman.' 'I shall not trouble myself,' the friend reply'd, 'about the distinction of names; if a man takes my money from me by force, it concerns me but little what he calls himself, or what his pretence may be for so doing.' After this they rode about their several affairs, the Quaker homewards, and Tom in quest of more prey.

Being once like to be apprehended, as he was robbing a coach on Hounslow heath, Jones was put into a terrible pannic; this being the first time he had been in danger since he took to his present calling. This surprize had such an effect upon him, as even to make him think of reformation, and form fine ideas in his mind, of honour and honesty. But he soon diverted these childish melancholick thoughts, as he afterwards called them, by living profusely, keeping lewd company, staying out all night, and other such like practices, to which he had long accustomed himself. Besides, his course of life soon brought him again to extremity, the usual inlet to villainy, when it is occasioned by our own neglect. So that all his resolutions, or rather all the flourishes of his imagination, vanish'd when necessity appeared, and he return'd to his natural disposition, like a dog to his vomit, becoming as audacious as ever.

It was after this, that he met the late Lord Wharton and his Lady on the road, stopp'd their coach, and demanded their money, tho' they had three men on horseback to attend them. His Lordship at first made some hesitation, and ask'd him if he understood what he was about? 'Do you know me, Sir,' says he, 'that you dare be so bold as to stop me on the road?' 'Not I,' reply'd Jones very readily, 'I neither know nor care who you are, tho', before you spoke, I took you for a brewer, because you carry your cooler by your side: now, indeed, I am apt to imagine you are some great man, because you speak so big; but be as great as you will, Sir, I must have you to know, that there is no man upon this road so great as myself; therefore pray be quick in answering my demands, for delays may prove dangerous.' His Honour now saw our gentleman was resolute, so he and his Lady e'en delivered up what they had about them, without more words.

The whole prize consisted of two hundred pounds in money, three diamond rings, and two gold watches: all this being secured, Jones commanded his Lordship to bid his servants ride on to some distance before, threatning him with death if he refused; which being done, and the servants obeying, he had a fair opportunity of riding off, without being pursued.

Tom received intelligence one day, that a certain gentleman was on the road, with two hundred pounds in his coach. This, to be sure, was a sufficient invitation for him. He got upon a hill to wait for his customers coming, who spy'd him at a distance without apprehending any thing. But a steward of the gentleman's, observing the behaviour of our chapman at a distance, he told his master, that he believed the man on the hill was a highwayman. 'If you please Sir,' quoth he, 'to trust me with your money, I'll ride by him, which I may do unsuspected, for he certainly waits for you.' The gentleman was pleas'd at his servant's care, and lik'd his proposal very well: so giving him the bag, he rode on as fast as he could, and pass'd by Jones, without being examin'd, getting out of sight before the coach came up.

In short, the coach was stopp'd, and the money demanded, when our gentleman gave him about ten guineas, assuring him that he had no more. Jones boldly nam'd the sum he wanted, and swore 'twas in the coach, the traveller as often asserting that he was mistaken. At last, the real state of the case came into our adventurer's head; whereupon, without taking his leave of the gentleman, he set spurs to his horse, and rode after the steward full speed, who was by this time got at least a mile and a half from the place. Jones was well mounted, and it was five miles from the next town, so that he came in sight of the steward before he could get into any inn; but the steward saw him, mended his pace, and sav'd the money. This disappointment vex'd poor Tom to the heart, but there was no remedy. As to the gentleman, he gave his servant a handsome gratuity for what he had done, as he deserved.

After many adventures, most of them of a piece with the foregoing, Tom was apprehended in Cornwal, for robbing a farmer's wife, and afterwards ravishing her. For this fact he was try'd, and condemn'd, the assizes following, and about ten days afterwards, executed at Launceston, on Saturday the 25th of April, 1702, being thirty two years of age.

At the gallows he gave a pretty large account of his robberies, to some gentlemen who desired it, behaving with more modesty and decency than such

279

wretches commonly do. Before he was turn'd off, he delivered a pretty deal of good advice to the young men present, in very pathetic words: exhorting them to be industrious in their several callings, and careful not to entangle themselves with debts, contracted by their own extravagances: desiring them to follow the dictates of their reason, and have a due regard for every man's property; and enforcing all his admonitions, with putting his hearers in mind of a providence, which governs the world, and will certainly call every man to an account for his actions.

THE LIFE OF

JOHN

COTTINGTON

ALIAS MUL–SACK

The father of John Cottington, or Mul-sack, as he was oftener called, was a haberdasher of small wares in Cheapside, and one time reputed to be pretty wealthy; but having a large expensive family, and being himself very fond of what is commonly called good company, he so far wasted his substance, as to die very poor, even so poor as to be bury'd by the parish. This was an unhappy thing for his children, who were no less than nineteen in number, fifteen of which were daughters, and John was the youngest of them all of either sex, which exposed him perhaps to more misfortunes than those who had some reason to govern themselves by, at the time when they became orphans.

At about eight years of age he was put out apprentice, to a trade no less honourable than chimney-sweeping. He was bound for a great many years, as he was so young at the time of going to his master; but he took care not to make his servitude longer than ordinary, for instead of adding six or seven years, he cut off two from the usual term, and ran away in the fifth year of his apprenticeship;

apprehending that as he was got into his teens he was as good a man as his master, and being confident that he had learned enough of his trade for him to live upon.

He had not been long gone from his master, before he perceived business coming on him even as fast as he could wish, and he made all the advantage possible of his good fortune; not in the usual sneaking manner, by hoarding up all he got; but by behaving himself like a gentleman, swearing at every one that offended him, and assuming to himself almost as much state as the old chimney-sweeper below; who we may be certain is haughty, because to say any 'One is as proud as Lucifer' is become a proverb. Not was it only in Cottington's carriage that you might observe the effects of his good fortune; for he lived in the best manner possible; no liquor but sack, forsooth, would go down with him, and that too must always be mull'd, to make it the more pleasant. It was from this that he got his name of Mul-Sack, by which he was commonly called, and by which we shall chuse to distinguish him in the following account of his exploits.

One evening Mul-Sack was drinking at the Devil tavern in Fleet-street, when he observed what he thought was a beautiful woman; and being naturally pretty amorous, and at the time in particular warm with his favourite liquor, he made his addresses to her. Madam appeared to be none of the coyest, for she received him very freely, only nothing but matrimony would go down with her, which did not thoroughly please him: 'Yet why,' (thought he at last) 'should I be against it? I can keep myself and a wife very well, and I never saw a woman whom I could like better than this, therefore, hang it, I'll e'en take her, for better for worse.' Upon this, he immediately gave her his hand, and there were no more words to the bargain, but away they tramp'd to the Fleet together; where divinity link'd their hands, pronounc'd 'em man and wife, and pray'd heartily for their welfare; in particular, that they might be successful in their honest and lawful endeavours for the procreation of children, which, as the holy office of the Church informs us, is the principal end of matrimony.

But how was our jolly bridegroom deceived at night, when he found himself espoused to an hermaphrodite, and that the lady he had marry'd was no other than a person well known by the name of Anniseed Robin? The redundancy of nature was soon discovered, and the bride confess'd *her* fault, or if you please *his* fault, with abundance of seeming contrition, while poor Mul-Sack had nothing more to do in bed than to go to sleep as usual.

This disappointment in matrimony had a great effect upon our gentleman's manners; for whereas he was never before known to be guilty of any worse crime than spending his money, sitting up late, and keeping jovial company, he now run into all sorts of extravagancies: in particular, he got acquainted with five noted Amazons in Drury-lane, who were called the Women-shavers, and whose actions were then much talk'd of about town; till being apprehended for a riot, and one or two of them severely punished, the rest fled to Barbadoes. Mul-Sack was once present when these furies got a poor woman among them, whom one of them suspected of having been great with her husband. As a punishment for this they stripp'd her as naked as she was born, beat her with rods in a terrible manner, and then shav'd off all the hair about her whole body: after that they sous'd her in a tub of soap suds over head and ears, and in fine almost kill'd her, in spite of all her tears, cries, and protestations of innocency.

After the law, the greatest enemy that people of this character have in the world, had deprived Mul-Sack of these worthy companions, he resolv'd to pursue his amours elsewhere, and to that purpose appeared when out of his business in a very smart, and genteel manner; being withal a graceful person, and having a very extraordinary flow of words for a man of his calling. With these accomplishments, he found means to insinuate himself into the good liking of a merchant's wife in Mark-lane, who had before this none of the best of characters. This lady had originally been very handsome, but by a long course of amours, her beauty was a little the worse for wearing when Mul-Sack became acquainted with her. However, what she wanted in person she made up in purse; for our smut made a shift to squeeze out of her about 120 *l.* before she fell sick and dy'd, which happened not a great while afterwards.

Captain Smith has told a long story of this lady's sickness, death-bed repentance, and confession to her husband in her last moments, the substance of which is, that she desired her good man to call up all her children, to the number of twelve, one of which she told him she believed might be his, because she did not remember that any other man had enter'd upon the premises time enough to have had any share in it: 'but for the rest, my Dear,' (said she with a deep sigh) 'I am afraid you are just as much their father, as the kings of England have been kings of France for some hundreds of years past; that is, you know very well, in name only.' Here she nam'd whom she believ'd to be the father of every one, tho' she could not be very positive in either; because always more than one man had been dabbling about the proper time. She concluded all with telling him, that as they were all taken in his net, she hoped he would not expose himself and her after her death, but put up his horns without words, and contentedly act the part of a father. We have not heard how far the husband comply'd with his dying wife's request, but there is good reason to think it caused a grumbling in his gizzard.

Mul-Sack had lately been so plentifully supply'd with money, that, when his kind benefactress departed this life, and changed this vain world, as we ought in Christian charity to believe, for a better, he could not think of applying himself to business anew, and relapsing again to his sooty occupation. We may observe, that there is a sort of vanity inherent in us all, that makes us try any shift, rather than go backwards in the world. This temper is doubtless the original of knavery in a great measure. Citizens that have been reputed rich will hold up their heads to the last, and think it much more honourable to pay six pence in the pound after a statute of bankruptcy, provided they can be trusted again, than honestly lay down their trades while they can pay twenty shillings, and seek a meaner way of livelihood. So a courtier that has attain'd to be first minister of state, generally prefers bringing his neck to the block, before attending at the levee of his successor, after having quitted his post with universal applause. 'Tis just the same in inferior life, a man that has once commenc'd villain, seldom, as we said before, cares to go backwards, till he is drawn backwards up Holborn Hill, or some other place for the same purpose.

After this short digression then, we are to tell you, that Mul-Sack now turn'd pickpocket, a calling that generally serves for an introduction to the gentlemen who make the heroes of this history. As a tryal of his dexterity, the first thing he did was to take a very valuable gold watch, set with diamonds, from a lady of chief quality in those times of usurpation. One Mr Jacomb, a man very much followed by the precisians, preached at that time a weekly lecture at Ludgate church, and the gentlewoman we are speaking of was one of his admirers and constant attendants. Mul-Sack had taken notice for some time how the pretty bauble hung dangling at her side by a gold chain. One of the companions he had engaged on this occasion found means to take out the pin of one of the coach-wheels, so that the wheel fell, and the coach caused an obstruction just under the gate. The end of this was to make a crowd, and oblige madam to alight before she came to the church door; all which was effected, and Mul-Sack stood ready, dress'd in what was then the height of the mode, to offer the lady his arm into the church. He presented himself very impudently, the favour was kindly accepted, and by the way he found means to cut the gold chain in two, and secure the watch as they passed through the crowd. The loss was not perceived till Mr Jacomb concluded, when the devout gentlewoman was going to see how long the spiritual meal had lasted: but alas! all the consolation she had received vanish'd after her darling watch.

It is reported that there never was in England a more dexterous gang of pickpockets than in the time of this Mul-Sack. We might here introduce by the way of episode, (as the criticks phrase it) abundance of their surprising, performances; but because we would avoid prolixity, only remark in general, that they would lay wagers of taking any gentleman's watch, tho' warned of it but a minute before, and perform it by jostling them, asking a question, pretending some urgent business, giving them a letter, and a thousand other methods of diverting their attention, and leaving the prize unguarded long enough for them to accomplish their pleasure: nor was there any one of these fellows, who understood his business better than our hero, Mul-Sack, so that it would be almost incredible to relate all the tricks of that kind he play'd about the city, and the numerous stratagems he had recourse to.

We are inform'd, that, before Mul-Sack left off this trade, he was once so impudent as to attempt the pocket of Cromwel himself, and the danger he then run of being detected, was the occasion of his leaving this secret sort of knavery, and taking to the highway, in company with one Tom Cheney.

These two fellows had the courage and confidence to set upon Colonel Hewson, a great man in those times, and one who had been advanced from a cobler to the dignity he then enjoy'd, merely because his conscience was according to the measure of that time; that is very large, or if you please very small, which expressions the witty author of Hudibrass tells us, signify the same thing. The colonel's regiment was then marching to Hounslow, and he not so far before it, but some of the troopers saw the action of our bravoes. No body can doubt but they were soon pursu'd; yet by the help of a good horse, Mul-Sack got clear off; but Cheney's beast failing him, he was obliged to stand in his own defence,

285

I. Nicholls delin.

I. Atkins Sculp.

Iohn Cottington alias Mul-Sack, Robbing y̆ Oxford Waggon
Wherein he found four Thousand Pounds in Money.

which he did very stoutly, till he was overpower'd by numbers, desperately wounded, taken prisoner, and carry'd to Newgate. Sessions began at the Old Bailey within a few days after, and Cheney being brought to the bar, begg'd to have his tryal put off on account of his wounds: but the favour could not be obtain'd; for they caused a chair to be brought for him to sit in, obliged him to plead, and passed sentence of death upon him. What he had urged as a motive for putting off his tryal, was made the means to hasten his execution; for, tho' 'twas two o'clock in the afternoon when he was condemn'd, he was carry'd in a cart that very day to Tyburn, and there executed, lest he should have evaded the sentence of the law, by dying in Newgate.

The next companion Mul-Sack enter'd into articles with was one Mr Horne, a very bold man, and a pewterer by trade, tho' he had been formerly a captain in Colonel Downe's regiment of foot. Their engagement was to act in concert, offensively and defensively, like generous highwaymen: but neither did this partnership subsist long; for the first considerable action they ventur'd on was fatal to the poor captain, he being taken in the pursuit, while Mul-Sack had still the good fortune to escape. The captain's fate was the same as Cheney's; saving that he continued in good health till the hour of his execution, when he behaved with so much bravery and gallantry, that his death drew tears from a great part of the spectators, particularly from that sex, who know the value of a brave man so well, as always to be griev'd when such a one dies, especially at Tyburn.

His companions having such ill success, Mul-Sack was resolv'd to try his fortune alone, and he several times practis'd his calling upon committee men, sequestrators, Members of Parliament, &c. who were then almost the only men in the nation worth robbing; they having plunder'd every body else, and gotten the wealth of England into their own hands. In all these adventures he was as fortunate as he could wish, which prompted him forwards to attempt still greater things. Being inform'd that four thousand pound was coming from London, to pay the regiments quarter'd at Oxford and Gloucester, he resolv'd to venture his life for so considerable a sum, tho' two or three men well arm'd were appointed for a convoy. Just at the close of day, when the waggon was past Wheatley, and at the foot of a hill he started from an ambuscade, presented his pistol, and bid the carrier stand. He had certainly now gone to pot, if the guard had not thought it impossible he should atttempt such an action without company; but the apprehension of more behind the hedge made these sturdy fellows ride for their lives, and leave our adventurer to secure the booty; which he spent with as much mirth as he had obtain'd it with danger.

There were also two or three passengers in this waggon, who were frighted terribly; but Mul-Sack generously told them he had no design upon what they had. 'This' (says he) 'that I have taken, is as much mine as theirs who own it; being all extorted from the publick by the rapacious Members of our Commonwealth, to enrich themselves, maintain their janizaries, and keep honest people in subjection; the most effectual way to do which, is to keep them very poor.'

It is said, that Mul-Sack got more money than any highwayman of his time, though no man was less suspected than he by his acquaintance in town. When out of his calling he appeared like a merchant, talk'd always about business, and was seen on 'Change very often, being the methods he us'd to conceal his trade; for nothing betrays a man so soon as endeavouring to hide himself.

One time having notice that the Receiver General at Reading was to send up six thousand pound to London by an ammunition waggon, he immediately contrived to save that trouble, and bring it up to town himself on his own horse. An accomplice was necessary in this undertaking, and he soon found one, by whose assistance he scal'd the Receiver's house the night before the money was to be carted. The window they got in at was next to the garden, where they left the ladder standing, and came off at the present very well, having bound all the family to prevent any alarm whereby they might be discover'd.

But an affair of this kind, as might very well be expected, made a great noise, and Mul-Sack was apprehended in town, by some who had seen him in Reading the evening the fact was committed. Upon this he was sent down to Reading, and try'd at the next assizes for Berkshire, before Judge Jermyn, who did all he could to hang him. Nevertheless, by his cunning, he found means either to baffle the evidence, or to corrupt the jury by his money, so far, that he was acquitted; the proofs against him being only circumstantial.

Not long after this narrow escape, our offender growing in wickedness, added murder to his former crimes: the person on whom it was committed was one John Bridges, with whose wife he had before contracted a familiarity. On this account he fled beyond sea, and got himself introduc'd at the court of King Charles the Second, who was then in exile.

He got so much intelligence here, that he ventur'd home again, upon a presumption of obtaining his pardon from Oliver Cromwell, as a reward for what he could discover of affairs amongst the King's friends. Accordingly he apply'd himself to the usurper, confess'd his crime, and made very large promises, upon the performance of which Cromwell assur'd him of his life: but, whether he could not be as good as his word, or whether the Protector thought such an abandon'd wretch utterly unfit to live, so it was, that he was apprehend'd, condemn'd, and executed in Smithfield Rounds, in April, 1685, being 45 years of age.

289

THE LIFE OF
PATRICK FLEMMING

Patrick Flemming was a native of Ireland, and born at Athlone, which is remarkably situated in the counties of East and West Meath, as well as in the provinces of Leinster and Connaught. His parents rented a potato-garden of about 15 s. per annum, upon the produce of which, and the increase of their geese, hens, pigs, &c. they wholly depended for the subsistence of themselves and nine children. They, and their whole family of swine, poultry, and progeny, all took up their lodging at night not only under the same roof, but in the same room; according to the practice of abundance of their country-people, who build only for necessity, without any idea of what we call beauty and order. One may guess from the circumstances of the father, that the son had small share of liberal education, tho' he had the most claim to it of any one of the children, as he was the eldest: but what he wanted in acquirements was made up with impudence, a quality which in most ignorant people happily fills up their void of knowledge.

When he was about thirteen years of age the Countess of Kildare took him into her service, in the capacity of footboy; and finding him so utterly destitute of learning, she was so indulgent as to put him to school: but instead of being grateful to her Ladyship in improving his time to the best advantage, he was entirely negligent, and discover'd no inclination to his book. His Lady admonish'd him frequently, but to no purpose; for he grew not only careless but insolent, till at last, being found incorrigible, he was discharged from the family.

It was not long, however, before he was so fortunate as to get to be a dome-stick of the Earl of Antrim's; but here his behaviour was worse than before. He was a scandal to the whole family; for the little wit he had was altogether turned on mischief: his Lord bore it a pretty while, notwithstanding the repeated complaints of his fellow servants, and took no notice so long as he could avoid it; but at last this nobleman also was obliged to turn him out of doors; and this was the occasion. The Earl of Antrim was a Roman Catholick, and kept a priest in the house, as his chaplain and confessor, to whom every one of the servants was requir'd to pay great respect. Patrick on account of his disorderliness was often reprov'd by this gentleman, and he receiv'd it very well till one day he happen'd to find the holy Father asleep in some private part of the house, in a very indecent posture: whereupon he went and got all the family to that place, and shew'd them what he had discover'd as a revenge upon the parson, who at that instant awak'd. With respect to the servants this had the desir'd effect, and expos'd the priest to ridicule: but the Earl, when he heard it, took the part of his chaplain, believ'd the story a slander, and immediately gave Flemming a discharge, as desir'd. Patrick found means, however, before he entirely left the neighbourhood, to rob his Lordship of money and plate to the value of about two hundred pounds, with which he fled to Athenrea in the province of Connaught.

He hid himself here in a little hut that he found for ten or twelve days, till he imagin'd the hue and cry after him might be over, and then made the best of his way to Dublin; where he soon enter'd into a gang of house-breakers, and during the space of six years was concern'd in more robberies than had ever before been committed in that city in the memory of man.

While he continued in Dublin, he was twice in danger of being hang'd for his offences, which were so great as to make him the publick subject of conversation all over the city. He now perceiv'd he began to be too well known to stay there any longer in safety, and so he retir'd into the country, and turn'd highwayman. The chief place of his haunt was about the Bog of Alan, where he attack'd almost all that pass'd that way, of whatever quality; telling them, 'that he was absolute lord of that road, and had a right to demand contribution of all that travell'd it, and to punish those with death who refused to comply; therefore, if they had any regard for their lives, he advised them to deliver what they had peaceably, and not put him to the trouble of exerting his prerogative'. By these means he became more dreaded in the countries where he robb'd than any thief of his time: for he not only threaten'd those with death who disputed with him, but actually murder'd several, and us'd many others with abundance of barbarity.

'Tis reported, that in a few days he robb'd one hundred and twenty five men and women upon the mountain of Barnsmoor; near which is a wood which they call Colorckedie, where he had assembled a numerous gang, out of which not a few at several times were taken and executed. Persons of quality he usually address'd in their own style, and told them he was as well bred as they, and therefore they must subscribe towards maintaining him according to his rank and dignity.

Among the principal persons whom he stopp'd and robb'd were the Archbishop of Armagh, and the Bishop of Rapho, both in one coach; the Archbishop of Tuam; and the Lady Baltimore, with her young son, a child of four years old; whom he took from her, and obliged her to send him a ransom within twenty four hours, or else he told her, he would cut the young puppy's throat and make a pye of him. From the Archbishop of Tuam he got a thousand pounds. After this he fled into Munster, and continu'd the same trade there, till he was apprehended for robbing a nobleman of two hundred and fifty pound, for which fact he was carry'd to Cork, and committed to prison.

But even now they were far from having him so safe as they imagin'd; for the county-jayl was not strong enough to hold him. He was no sooner confin'd than his eyes were about him, and his head plotting an escape: at last he found means to get up a chimney, and by removing some few obstacles, to get out at the top, and so avoid hanging for that offence.

He follow'd his villanies for some years after his breaking out of prison, during which time he murder'd five men, two women, and a boy of fourteen years old. Besides which he mangled and wounded a great many others; in particular Sir Donagh O Brian, whose nose, lips, and ears he cut off, for making some small resistance while he robb'd him. At last he was apprehended by the landlord of a house where he used to drink, near Mancoth. The landlord sent advice to the sheriff of the county when he would be there with several of his associates, and the sheriff, according to the instruction, came one evening with a strong guard, and beset the house. Patrick and his company would have defended themselves; but the landlord had taken care to wet all their fire-arms, and prevent their going off; by which means they became useless, and our desperado with fourteen more were taken, carry'd to Dublin, and there executed on Wednesday the twenty fourth of April, in the year 1650. After which Patrick Flemming was hang'd in chains on the high road a little without the city.

THE LIVES OF
EDWARD AND JOAN BRACEY

These two criminals flourish'd from the year 1680 to 1684, during which time they committed a great number of robberies and frauds. Their natural inclinations to such a manner of living first brought them together, and kept up the union between them till they were separated by justice, though we cannot learn that they were even marry'd, Joan only assuming the name of her companion, as is common in such cases, the better to colour their living together, and impose on the world.

Edward Bracey had been a highwayman before he fell into company with his pretended wife, who was the daughter of a wealthy farmer in Northamptonshire, named John Phillips. The beginning of their acquaintance was Bracey's making love to her, in hopes to get a large sum of money out of the old man for a marriage-portion, and then to have left both wife and father-in-law: but he was very agreeably deceiv'd; for Joan was as good as he: she suffer'd her self to be first debauched by him, and then consented to rob her father, and go along with him on the pad; all which she accordingly accomplish'd. They now passed for husband and wife wheresoever they went, frequently robb'd together on the highway, and as often united in picking of pockets and shop-lifting at all the country fairs and markets round about.

'Twas next to impossible that they should continue this course of life long together, without coming into trouble: one or t'other of them was often in danger of the gallows, but they had both the good fortune to escape till they had got a large quantity of money. The dread of justice more than a desire to live honestly now prevail'd upon them to quit their vocation, and take to some creditable business, in which they might spend the remainder of their days in quiet, and live comfortably upon what they had acquir'd by their industry. In order to this, they took an inn in the suburbs of Bristol, where they met with success; having a large trade in particular for wine; which was occasion'd by the beauty of our landlady. 'Tis no uncommon thing for a husband to get money by his having a handsome wife; especially if they have both art enough to manage an intrigue; which was the present case. All the gay young fellows of the place came to drink with Madam Bracey, purely for the sake of having an opportunity to discover their love: she gave them all encouragement so long as they could spend a great deal of money, and then took care not only to turn them out of doors, but to expose them sufficiently.

It may not be amiss to give an instance of this her manner of using her suitors. One Mr Day, an eminent citizen of Bristol, was among the number of her humble servants. He made her a great many fine proposals, and she receiv'd 'em all with abundance of complaisance, consenting at last that he should make use of the first opportunity that offer'd to take a night's lodging with her. In a little time Mr Day was inform'd that his landlord Bracey was to be abroad such a night, and that nothing could happen more favourably to his wishes. He went at the time appointed with all the ardor of a lover, and was receiv'd by a maid-servant, who told him her mistress was gone to bed, and waited impatiently for him; but desiring him however to pull off his clothes, and leave them in another room, where he might be conceal'd, and have time to dress himself again, in case any surprise should happen. The innocent Mr Day thanked her for the contrivance, and hugg'd himself in the thought of the mistress's sincere affection, because the maid was so careful for his safety.

Mrs Abigail led him to the room appointed, put out the candle on account of mere modesty, and staid at the door while Mr Day undress'd himself; which he did in two minutes. Now the best of the comedy was to be play'd; our tractable maid conducted the gallant to a door, which she told him open'd into her mistress's chamber, bid him enter softly, and immediately turn'd the key upon him. Here Mr Day wander'd about to find the bed, and pronounc'd the name of Mrs Bracey as loud as he dar'd, that she might give him directions; but no Mrs Bracey answer'd. He was sufficiently amaz'd at the odness of the scene, but was yet more surpriz'd when he tumbled down a pair of stairs against the back door of the house. The contrivance was now plain; he saw that mistress and maid were agreed not only to baulk his passion, but to strip him of his clothes also. It was in vain to call, and make protestations; he receiv'd no other answer, than that the back-door was only bolted, and he might open if he pleas'd, and go about his business.

This door open'd into a narrow dirty lane, down which the common sewer ran; and there was no going out at it, unless you got into a coach, or upon a horse, directly off the steps, which was the only use made of it, and that not often especially in the winter-time, as it was at present. Mr Day knew all these inconveniences; but the terrible pinching cold, and the shame of being discover'd, if he staid till broad day-light, made him go out, wade through the mud, and make the best of his way home, where he was heartily laugh'd at by those friends to whom he told the story; which were only such as he could not conceal it from, and even upon these he laid the severest injunctions imaginable never to divulge a word of it. They kept the secret from every body else, but diverted themselves privately with poor Mr Day all his life afterwards.

Every one whom our honest inn-keepers impos'd on were not however so easy as Mr Day; so that in less than a twelvemonth's time their house became so scandalous that they were obliged to leave it; and then they had nothing to do but to take to their old courses again, being by this time pretty well got over the apprehensions they were under of a halter. At their first setting out again, they play'd such a trick as was hardly ever match'd, which was the woman's contrivance as well as the former. We shall relate this also in as few words as we can conveniently.

A young gentleman, who had spent his fortune, had us'd their house all the time they had been at Bristol, and got a pretty deal into their debt. They knew he was heir to an estate of about an hundred pounds a year, which was kept from him only by the life of an old distemper'd uncle, and they had a mighty itching to get this reversion into their hands. In order to this Joan threaten'd him grievously with a prison for what he ow'd them, till she perceiv'd he was heartily frighten'd, and would do any thing to keep his liberty: she knew besides that he was viciously inclin'd, and only wanted a little introduction to be made any thing of that they could wish. Upon this she told him what she and her husband were going upon, and prevail'd with him to join them. In a day or two after, she inform'd him that a rich tradesman was coming to Bristol with a large quantity of money, and that he must accompany her husband to-morrow to take it from him. Accordingly Bracey and the young man set out, stopp'd a person on the road, and took from him above an hundred pounds, with which they return'd home together. The man that was robb'd had been sent out with the money in his pocket for that very purpose.

As soon as the fact was over, and they had got their dupe safe, Madam told him plainly, that he must make over the reversion of his estate to them, or her husband should immediately swear the robbery upon him, and get him hang'd for it. The terror he was under, and the promise of liberty upon complying, made him do all they desir'd. After which they still kept him in their house till they had sold it again, obliging him to assure the purchaser, that he had receiv'd a valuable consideration of Mr Bracey; which was readily enough believ'd, because every body knew the young gentleman's extravagancy. They got fourteen hundred pounds by this bargain, with which they immediately made off, leaving the unfortunate spark to lament his folly. The name of this young man was Rumbald.

Joan after this usually dress'd herself in men's apparel, and she and her fellow adventurer committed a great many robberies together on the highway. At last, however, fortune put an end to their progress in iniquity; for as they were robbing a person of quality's coach together in Nottinghamshire, Madam was apprehended, and carry'd to Nottingham-jayl. At the next assizes she was condemn'd by the name of Joan Bracey, and in April, 1685, she was executed, aged twenty nine years.

Her pretended husband got off at the time when she was taken, and conceal'd himself for some time after by skulking about the country. One day being at a publick inn he was seen by some body whom he had robb'd, who immediately got assistance, and came to take him, being at the stair-foot with armed men before Bracey knew any thing of the matter. It happen'd that in the room where he was one of the drawers had left his cap and apron, which Bracey in a moment snatch'd up, and put on, running down stairs ready to break his neck, and crying out as he run, 'Coming, gentlemen, coming'; as if he was waiting upon company above. This stratagem preserv'd his life a little longer; for the gentleman, who came to secure him, not apprehending any thing, let him pass as a drawer, though he had taken so much notice of his face before; so that he got his horse out of the stable and rode off, while they were searching the house after him. Two or three of his companions, who were with him in the inn, and knew nothing of the occasion of his running down so, were apprehended and brought to justice.

This escape however did him but little service; for about three or four days after, stopping at a little house to drink, and leaving his white mare, on which he usually robb'd, at the door, another gentleman who had suffer'd by him came by, alarmed the neighbourhood upon his knowledge of the beast, and beset the house, before he had the least notice. As soon as he heard a noise of men at the door, he ran out, and attempted to mount; but two or three pieces were instantly discharged at him, one of them killing his mare, and another taking off several of his fingers. He then endeavoured to leap over some pales, and get off by the backside of the house, when another discharge was made at him from a fowling-piece, which lodg'd several great goose-shot in his guts, and wounded him so that he dropp'd down on the place, and dy'd in three days afterwards.

We should have mention'd before, that Bracey's pretended wife was handsomely bury'd by her friends, and that a reputed witch told him about the time of her execution, that he should not survive her many days, which happen'd to be verify'd. This, at least, is what was reported in the country, and those who give any credit to the stories of witches, may believe as much of it as they please: those who laugh at these things can't blame us for relating what we have been informed of.

THE LIFE OF
WILLIAM BEW

We have little more to say of this fellow, than that he was the brother of Captain Bew, the notorious highwayman, who was kill'd some years ago at Knightsbridge, by one Figg, and some thief-takers; and that he was himself as great an offender in that way as his said brother for most of his time; only his reign was shorter than that of some others, he being apprehended at Brainford before he had pursued the course many years, brought from thence to Newgate, and at the next execution tuck'd up at Tyburn. This fatal day to him was Wednesday the seventeenth of April, in the year 1689.

It cannot be expected that we should give a particular detail of all the actions of every one whom we introduce into this collection; nor is it at all material; since the reader cannot but think as well as we, that the most remarkable particulars have been transmitted to us, and consequently, that those things which are passed over in silence, would, if they had been recorded, have afforded him but very little pleasure. Captain Smith indeed, in his 'Lives', has generally found something to relate of every one he mentions, but then most of his stories are such barefac'd inventions, that we are confident those who have ever seen his books will pardon us for omitting them. It will not be long before we shall come down to more certainty, and then a more particular account of every malefactor's crimes may be procured; and we may be depended upon for taking care on our parts, that every thing shall be related with the utmost exactness. That this 'Life' of Bew may not, however, appear more barren than any other, we shall insert in it two short stories, which he used, as we are inform'd, to tell himself in his life-time.

The first of them is, that being at Bristol, he took a lodging in the house of one Mr Stone, who kept the Dolphin-Inn in Dolphin-lane. This landlord of his had never any child, and was reputed to be a very covetous fellow. Bew lay in the next room to him, and heard his wife tell him one night, that she believed she was with child. The old gentleman upon this began to be terribly uneasy, and reckon'd up all the charges that a bantling would bring upon him, not forgetting the extraordinary expences of a lying-in. He then consider'd whether a boy or a girl would cost him most, and concluded, upon the whole, that a son was likely to be soonest got off his hands, and put into a capacity to maintain himself. Hereupon he told his spouse very abruptly, 'that he must have her bring him a boy'. Madam reply'd, 'that it was not in the power of her, or of any woman living to be deliver'd of which sex she pleased'. To this the old man answer'd with a severe snub, 'that it was in vain for her to talk, for a boy he must have, if he had any child at all; and that if nature sent a girl into the world, he would metamorphose it into the sex he liked; for he would put only boy's clothes upon it, and oblige her never to let any body into the secret, at least till she was able to shift for herself'. This dialogue, doubtless, was pleasant enough to Bew, who did not stay to see the event of his landlady's great belly. But making himself merry was not the only advantage he found in this apartment; for he overheard the miserable old wretch tell his wife, every night, whither he was to go the next day, and upon what business. By this means he got intelligence of his being to go one day a pretty way out of town, to receive one hundred and thirty pounds, and he took care to lighten him of his burden before he came home again, and rode off with it into another part of the kingdom; 'it being worth while,' as he often merrily used to say, 'to change his quarters for such a lump as this.'

The other story is of an adventure of Bew's with a young lady, whom he overtook on the road, with her footman behind her. He made bold to keep them company a pretty way, talking all along of the lady's extraordinary beauty, and carrying his compliments to her to an unreasonable height. Madam was not at all displeased with what he said; for she look'd upon herself to be every bit as handsome as he made her: however, she seem'd to contradict all he told her, and professed with a mighty formal air, 'that she had none of the perfections he mentioned, and was therefore highly obliged to him for his good opinion of a woman who deserv'd it so little'. They went on in this manner; Bew still protesting, that she was the most agreeable lady he ever saw, and she declaring, that he was the most complaisant gentleman she ever met with: this was the discourse till they came to a convenient place; when Bew took an opportunity to knock the footman off his horse; and then addressing himself to the lady, 'Madam,' says he, 'I have been a great while disputing with you about the beauty of your person; but you insist so strongly on my being mistaken, that I cannot in good manners contradict you any longer: however, I am not satisfy'd yet, that you have nothing handsome about you, and therefore I must beg leave to examine your pocket, and see what charms are contain'd there.' Having deliver'd his speech, he made no more ceremony, but thrust his hand into her pocket, and pull'd out a purse with fifty guineas in it. 'These are the charms I mean,' says he; and away he rode, leaving her to meditate a little upon the nature of flattery, which commonly picks the pocket of the person 'tis most busy about.

These two relations, and what we have said at the beginning concerning the time of his execution, are all the particulars we know of William Bew.

THE LIFE OF
PATRICK
O-BRYAN

The parents of Patrick O-Bryan were very poor; they liv'd at Loughrea, a market-town in the county of Galway and province of Connaught in Ireland. Patrick came over into England in the reign of King Charles the Second, and listed himself into his Majesty's Coldstream Regiment of Guards, so called from their being first raised at a place in Scotland which bears that name. How good a soldier he made is little to our purpose; only we may observe, that 'twas not possible he should be more expert in the use of his arms than he was in the practice of all manner of vices. The small allowance of a private centinel was far too little for him; and he was not like a great many poor men, who make the same complaint, yet sit down honestly to live on it, and only endeavour to make up the scantiness of their salary by their good husbandry. No; Patrick's maxims were widely different from those; he was resolv'd to have money if there were any in the land, and not to starve in the midst of plenty, from a foolish principle of justice and honour. The first thing he did was to run in debt at all the publick houses and shops that would trust him; and when his credit would maintain him no longer, he had recourse to borrowing of all he knew, being pretty well furnish'd with the common defence of his countrymen, a front that would brazen out any thing, and even laugh at the persons whom he had imposed on, to their very faces. By such means as these he subsisted for some time.

At last, when he found fraud would no longer support him, he went out upon the foot-pad. Dr Clewer, the parson of Croydon, was one of those whom he stopp'd. This man had in his youth been try'd at the Old-Baily, and burnt in the hand, for stealing a silver cup. Patrick knew him very well, and greeted him upon their lucky meeting; telling him, 'that he could not refuse lending a little assistance to one of his old profession'. The doctor assured him, 'that he had not made a word, if he had had any money about him; but he had not so much as a single farthing'. 'Then,' says Patrick, 'I must have your gown, Sir.' 'If you can win it,' quoth the doctor, 'so you shall, but let me have the chance of a game at cards.' To this O-Bryan consented, and the Reverend Gentleman pull'd out a pack of the Devil's books; with which they fairly play'd at All-Fours, to decide, who should have the black robe. Patrick had the fortune to win, and the other went home very contentedly, as he had lost his divinity in such an equitable manner. Indeed, according to the idea which this story seems to give of the doctor, our highwayman might become a canonical habit as well as he, and be no more a scandal to the sacred cloth.

There was in Patrick's time a famous posture-master in Pall-Mall; his name was Clark. Our adventurer met him one day on Primrose-Hill; and saluted him with 'stand and deliver'. But he was mightily disappointed; for the nimble harlequin jump'd over his head, and, instead of reviving his heart with a few guineas, made it sink into his breeches for fear; he imagining the Devil was come to be merry with him before his time, for no human creature, he thought, could do the like. This belief was a little mortification to him at first; but he soon saw the truth of the story in the publick prints, where Mr Clark's friends took care to put it, and then our teague's qualm of conscience was changed into a vow of revenge, if ever he met with his tumblership again; which however he never did.

Another time Patrick O-Bryan was got behind a hedge in the way to Hackney, late in the evening, in order to wait for a booty. He had not been here long before he heard a very merry dialogue between one of the sons of Apollo, and an old bawd, whom he had employ'd to get him into the company of a young lady at a boarding-school just by. The conversation ended so much to our poet's satisfaction, that he pronounc'd the following lines in a kind of rapture.

> Oh! thou art wondrous in thy Art! thy Head
> Was form'd for mighty Things; like those who rule
> The Fates of Empires: But our kinder Stars
> Have sent thee to direct the Realms of Love.

Just as his transport was over, out stepp'd O-Bryan, and presented a pistol to the head that conceiv'd those fine imaginations. It must be allow'd, that such a surprize as this was enough to make the poor bard a little cooler; but lest it should not cool him enough, O-Bryan order'd him to strip himself to the skin; which he did with abundance of reluctance; for the fine embroidered sute of clothes he had on was only hired as an additional charm to his verses, that he might the more effectually win the young lady's heart. Madam the Procuress was also dress'd in her richest brocade, that her visit might be perform'd with the better grace: she suffer'd the same fate, and was reduc'd to the condition of our first parents before the fall; Patrick telling them both, 'that as he perceived neither of them had any religion before, 'twas proper they should begin to have some; and therefore out of charity to their souls he had converted them to Adamitism'. We may suppose they did not very well like their new religion: but Patrick was a downright pope; if they had not hearkened to his arguments he would have made use of his arms, and fairly have sent them out of the world, because they would not be implicitly obedient to their superiors in it. This they both consider'd, and so thought in their best way to receive his *ipse dixit*.

O-Bryan at last intirely deserted from his regiment, and got a horse, on which he robb'd on the highway a long time. One day in particular he met Nell Gwyn in her coach on the road to Winchester, and address'd himself to her in the following manner. 'Madam, I am a gentleman, and, as you may see, a very able one: I have done a great many signal services to the fair sex, and have in return been all my life long maintain'd by them. Now, as I know you are a charitable W—e, and have a great value for men of my abilities, I make bold to ask you for a little money, though I never have had the honour of serving you in particular. However, if an opportunity should ever fall in my way, you may depend upon it

I will exert myself to the uttermost; for I scorn to be ungrateful.' Nell seem'd very well pleas'd with what he had said, and made him a present of ten guineas: however, whether she wish'd for the opportunity he spoke of, or no, cannot be determin'd, because she did not explain herself; but if a person may guess from her general character, she never was afraid of a man in her life.

While Patrick robb'd on the highway, he perverted several young men to the same bad course of life. One Claudius Wilt in particular was hang'd at Worcester for a robbery committed in his company, though 'twas the first he was ever concern'd in. Several others came to the same end through his seducements; and he himself was at last executed at Gloucester, for a fact committed within two miles of that city. When he had hung the usual time, his body was cut down and deliver'd to his acquaintance, that they might bury him as they pleased: but being carry'd home to one of their houses, some body imagin'd they perceiv'd life in him; whereupon an able surgeon was privately procured to bleed him, who by that and other means which he used brought him again to his senses. The thing was kept an entire secret from the world, and 'twas hoped by his friends that he would spend the remainder of his forfeited life, which he had so surprizingly retriev'd, to a much better purpose than he had employ'd the former part of it.

These friends offer'd to contribute in any manner he should desire towards his living privately and honestly: he promis'd them very fairly, and for some time kept within due bounds, while the sense of what he had escap'd remain'd fresh in his mind; but the time was not long before, in spite of all the admonitions and assistances he receiv'd, he return'd again to his villainies like a dog to his vomit; leaving his kind benefactors, stealing a fresh horse, and taking once more to the highway, where he grew as audacious as ever.

It was not above a year after his former execution, before he met with the gentleman again who had convicted him before, and attack'd him in the same manner. The poor gentleman was not so much surprized at being stopp'd on the road as he was at seeing the person who did it, being certain 'twas the very man whom he had seen executed. This consternation was so great, that he could not help discovering it; by saying, 'How comes this to pass? I thought you had been hanged a twelvemonth ago.' 'So I was,' says Patrick, 'and therefore you ought to

305

imagine that what you see now is only my ghost: however, lest you should be so uncivil as to hang my ghost too, I think it my best way to secure you.' Upon this he discharg'd a pistol thro' the gentleman's head; and, not content with that, dismounting his horse, he drew out a sharp hanger from his side, and cut the dead carcass into several pieces.

This piece of barbarity was followed by another, which was rather more horrible yet. Patrick with four more as bad as himself, having intelligence that Lancelot Wilmot, Esq., of Wiltshire, had a great deal of money and plate in his house, which stood in a lonely place, at about a mile and a half from Truebridge; they beset it one night, and got in. When they were entered, they ty'd and gagg'd the 3 servants, and then proceeded to the old gentleman's room, where he was in bed with his lady. They served both these in the same manner, and then went in the daughter's chamber. This young lady they severally forced after one another to their brutal pleasure, and when they had done, most inhumanly stabb'd her, because she endeavoured to get from their arms. They next acted the same tragedy on the father and mother, which they told them, 'was because they did not breed up their daughter to better manners'. Then they rifled the house of every thing valuable which they could find in it, that was fit to be carried off, to the value in all of 2500 *l*. After which they set the building on fire, and left it to consume with the unhappy servants that was in it.

Patrick continued above two years after this before he was apprehended, and possibly might never have been suspected of this fact, if one of his bloody accomplices had not been hang'd for another crime at Bedford. This wretch at the gallows confessed all the particulars, and discovered the persons concerned with him; a little while after which, O-Bryan was seized at his lodging in Little Suffolk-Street, near the Hay-Market, and committed to Newgate; from whence before the next assizes he was convey'd to Salisbury, where he own'd the fact himself, and all the other particulars of his wicked actions that have been here related. He was now a second time executed, and great care was taken to do it effectually. There was not, indeed, much danger of his recovering any more, because his body was immediately hung in chains, near the place where the barbarous deed was perpetrated. He was in the 31st year of his age at the time of his execution, which was on Tuesday the 30th of April, in the Year 1689.

THE LIFE OF
JACK COLLET

ALIAS COLE

This unfortunate person was the son of a grocer in the borough of Southwark, where he was born, and from whence at fifteen years of age he was put out apprentice to an upholsterer in Cheapside. He did not serve above four years of his time before he ran away from his master, and took to the highway. We have not an account of abundance of his robberies, tho' 'tis said he committed a great many; but there is this remarkable particular recorded of him, that he frequently robb'd in the habit of a bishop, with four or five of his companions at his heels in the quality of servants, who were ready to assist him on occasion. Some, who love to make themselves merry with the Reverend and the Right Reverend the Clergy, would be apt to insinuate, that 'tis no very uncommon thing to see a thief in the habit of a clergyman. For our parts, we are so far from making any such prophane observation, that we think the sacred order give daily proofs, that England has but very few wolves in sheep's clothing. Give us leave to add however, concerning our adventurer, that he generally got much larger booties on the road than most of our lay highwaymen.

Collet had once the ill fortune to lose his canonical habit at dice, so that he was forced to take a turn or two on the road to supply his present necessities, in unsanctify'd garments: but it was not long before he met with a good opportunity of taking orders again, and becoming as holy as ever. Riding from London down into Surrey, a little on this side Farnham, he met with Dr Mew, Bishop of Winchester, and commanded his coachman to stop. The Bishop was not at all surpriz'd at being ask'd for his money, because when he saw his coach stopp'd he expected that would follow: but when Collet told him he must have his robes too, his Lordship thought him a madman. There was no resisting however; the old doctor was obliged to strip into his waistcoat, besides giving him about fifty guineas; which Collet told him he had now a right to demand, by having the sacerdotal habit in his possession: 'For that, you know, Doctor,' quoth he, 'is a proof of my indelible character, and the property I have in the revenues of the Church; and as good a proof, I believe, as many others can shew, who have just as much learning and honesty as I have, and yet are acknowledg'd to be good clergymen, and some of the receivers general of Heaven.'

Collet follow'd this trade till he was about thirty two years of age, and, as if he had been determin'd to live by the Church, he was at last apprehended for sacrilege and burglary, in breaking open the vestry of Great St Bartholomew's in London, in company with one Christopher Ashley, alias Brown, and stealing from thence the pulpit-cloth, and all the communion-plate. For this fact he receiv'd sentence of death, and was executed at Tyburn, on Friday the fifth of July, in the year 1691. This Brown and Collet had before robb'd St Saviour's church in Southwark in conjunction.

At the same time and place were executed, 1. Robert Trumbal, once a soldier in the Lord Lisbon's Regiment in Ireland, for felony and burglary. 2. Robert Anderton, for robbing a gentleman in Stepney Fields, of a silver watch, a diamond ring, a silver-hilted sword, and four guineas. 3. Jane Williams, for privately stealing thirty pounds worth of gold and silver lace from a lace-woman in the Strand; and 4. John Gwyn, a writing master, who once kept a school in Bedford Bury; for stealing a piece of silk, value nine pounds, from one Mr Rigby, a mercer, at the Sign of the Seven Stars, in the Little Piazza, Covent-Garden.

THE LIFE OF
TOM AUSTIN

Never was a a more barbarous villain than this of whom we are now to give some account, nor is it possible there ever should be. 'Tis true, another may commit more barbarities in number than he did, but they cannot be more horrible in their kind; and God knows to what a number they would have increased, if he had not been so soon detected as he was. But to proceed to the narrative:

Thomas Austin was born at Columpton in Devonshire, of very honest parents, who at their death left him a farm of their own, worth about eighty pounds per annum, which is a pretty estate in that country; and as his land was without incumbrances, and he had a good character at that time, he soon got a wife with a suitable fortune, she having no less than eight hundred pounds to her portion. But this increase of his riches, and the thought of having so much ready money by him, made him neglect the improvement of his living, and take to an idle extravagant course; by means of which in less than four years time he had consumed all that his wife brought him, and mortgaged his own estate.

Being now reduced to pinching circumstances, and not knowing which way to turn himself for a livelihood, the Devil so far got the upper hand of him, as to excite him to the commission of all manner of unlawful actions for the support of himself and his family. Several frauds he was detected in, which his neighbours were so good as to forgive, out of respect to his family, and to what he had once been. At last he was so desperate as to venture on the highway, where assaulting Sir Zachary Wilmot, on the road between Wellington and Taunton Dean, that unfortunate gentleman was murder'd by him, for making some attempts to save his money.

The booty he got from Sir Zachary was forty six guineas, and a silver-hilted sword, with which he got home undiscover'd and unsuspected. This did not however last him long, for he follow'd his old riotous course. When 'twas all spent he pretended a visit to an uncle of his, who lived at about the distance of a mile from his own habitation, and it was one of the bloodiest visits that ever was made.

When he came to the house he found no body at home but his aunt and five small children, who informed him that his uncle was gone out on business, and would not be at home till evening, desiring him to stay a little and keep them company. He seemingly consented to stay; but had not sate many minutes before he snatch'd up a hatchet that was at hand, and cleaved the scull of his aunt in two; after which he cut the throats of all the children, and laid the dead bodies in a heap all weltring in their gore. Then he went up stairs and robb'd the house of sixty pounds.

He made all the haste he could home to his wife, who perceiving some drops of blood on his clothes, ask'd him how they came there? 'You bitch,' says he, 'I'll soon shew you the manner of it!' pulling at the same time the bloody razor which he had before used out of his pocket, and cutting her throat from ear to ear. When he had gone thus far, to complete the tragedy, he ripp'd out the bowels of his own two children, the eldest of whom was not three years of age.

Scarcely had he finish'd all his butcheries, before his uncle, whom he had been to visit, came accidentally to pay him the same compliment in his way home; when entering the house, and beholding the horrid spectacle, he was even thunder-struck with the sight, though as yet he little thought the same tragedy had been acted on all his family too, as he soon after fatally found. What he saw however was enough to point out the offender, whom he immediately laid hold of, and carry'd him before a magistrate, who sent him to Exeter jail.

In the month of August, 1694, this inhuman wretch suffer'd the punishment provided by the law, which appears much too mild for such a black unnatural monster! But the laws of England aggravate nothing, and are content with barely taking away the lives of the very worst of criminals.

Austin's behaviour both in prison and at the gallows was very sullen and dogged, yet he would now and then say something that discover'd he was very far from having a just sense of his crimes. An instance of this was while the halter was about his neck, when he was ask'd by the minister who attended him, what he had to say before he dy'd; 'Only,' says he, 'there's a woman yonder with some curds and whey, and I wish I could have a pennyworth of them before I am hang'd, because I don't know when I shall see any again.' This extravagant request was not granted, and so he was turned off without offering to give a reason for his committing the murder for which he suffer'd; nor indeed can it be thought he had any other reason than his own inhuman temper.

311

THE LIFE OF
CAPTAIN
EVAN EVANS

The title of Captain, was only assumed by this noted criminal, who was born in South-Wales, and his father, who kept an inn at Brecknock, the chief town in Brecknockshire, having given him good education, put him apprentice to an attorney at law; but his vicious inclinations, together with the opportunity he had of corresponding with some gentlemen of the road, (as such rogues affected call themselves) who frequented his father's house, he soon came to act in the same wicked courses they follow'd, and in a little time became the most noted highwayman in these parts, having made prodigious booties of the Welsh grasiers and others.

The Captain once happening to be under a guard, who were conducting him to Shrewsbury gaol, with his legs ty'd under the belly of the horse, one of his attendants had got an excellent fowling-piece, which was then loaded, and the prisoner espying a pheasant pearching upon a tree, with a deep sigh express'd the dexterity he had used formerly in killing such game; so humbly requesting the gun, that he might shoot at so fine a mark, the ignorant fellow readily complied with his request. But no sooner had the Captain got the piece into his hands, but he charged upon his guard, and swore a whole volley of oaths, that he would fire upon them if they stirred one step farther. Then retreating from them on his little poney to a convenient distance, he commanded one of them that was best mounted, to come near him and alight; which being done, and the bridle of the horse hung on a hedge, the poor fellow was obliged to throw him his pistols, and then was admitted to approach nearer the Captain, who, presenting one of them at his head, obliged him to lose his legs, and retire to his companions: this being also done, he soon left his little scrub, mounted the fine gelding, and rode off.

The Captain then coming to London, the country being too hot to hold him, up on his handsome behaviour and carriage, which was somewhat extraordinary, as likewise his person, he got to be clerk to Sir Edmund Andrews, then Governor of Guernsey, and continued there in that capacity for three or four years; but money not coming in fast enough in that honest employment, to support his wicked inclinations, he soon left that service, return'd to London, and took a lodging at the Three Neats Tongues in Nicholas-Lane, where he passed for a Guernsey-merchant, or captain of a ship, and took his younger brother, William Evans, as a servant to wait on him, giving him a livery, under the colour of which he committed several notorious robberies on the highways about London.

One of his boldest and most daring robberies, was committed on 'Squire Harvey of Essex, between Mile-End and Bow, in the day-time, from whom he took a diamond ring, and money, to a considerable value, as he was riding home in his coach from the cathedral church of St Paul's, the late Queen Anne having that day honoured the City with her Royal Presence.

Sometime after that, meeting not far from Hampstead, with one Gambol a writing-master, living in Exeter-Street, behind Exeter-Exchange, in the Strand, walking with his wife, he made bold to command them to deliver what money they had, which they very obstinately refusing, the Captain violently took what money he found in their pockets, which was about thirty or forty shillings, and for their presumption of not being obedient to the doctrine of non-resistance, obliged them upon pain of death, to strip themselves stark naked, and then tying them close belly to belly, with their clothes by them, (for he did not take them away) bound them to a tree, and rode off. But before he left them, he had chalk'd in great letters just over their heads on the body of the tree, that Gambol and his wife were Adamites; which is a sort of sect which teaches their proselytes both men and women, to pray in their meetings, and perform other divine

313

services, stark naked; which posture they call the state of innocency, and the places they assemble in, Paradise.

Another time, Captain Evans and his brother, with two other persons, attacked a Member of Parliament on Bagshot-Heath, who was travelling in a coach and six horses, with three other gentlemen in it, and no less than four gentlemen on horseback well arm'd, besides three footmen, a coachman, and postillion. This honourable person and the rest had a jealousy they were highwaymen coming to approach them, and with their arms, as two blunderbusses, a carbine, and pistols loaded, stood upon the defensive part, which occasion'd, a field fight for above the space of a quarter of an hour, several charges and discharges being made between them, but to no other hurt done but the horse shot dead on which the Captain's brother William, alias his footman, rode on.

The Captain and the rest of his accomplices being still desperate, the parliament man drew his sword, and Evans his, and ventur'd to engage in a single combat to save farther blood-shed; but in this fairly trying their skill, Evans disarming the other, generously return'd him his sword again, accepting only of a good horse to carry his brother off, and what money they pleas'd to collect among them; for which genteel piece of behaviour, that honourable person afterwards endeavoured to save his life.

Not long after this exploit, Captain Evans meeting by Kilburn Warren, one Wargent a bricklayer, who for his vast bulk might be term'd a coloss, his vast bigness at first, put our highwayman into a surprize, till approaching him nearer, he commanded him to stand; when narrowly searching his head, and viewing his back part, he found by his having no horns and tail, that he was no ox, as he first supposed him to be at some distance, he ventured to search his breeches next, in which he found a silver watch, and seventeen or eighteen shillings in money, which converting to his own use, he rode off in quest of another prey.

One remarkable robbery he committed with his brother, was this: as he was travelling Portsmouth Road in Surrey, meeting a parcel of headboroughs or constables conducting about 30 poor fellows they had prest to Portsmouth Garrison, Captain Evans asked the reason of their being led so as captives ty'd with cords. The officers told him they were for the service, and that they had ten shillings for each man they had so imprest. He highly commended them for performing their duty, and rode off: but coming up with them again in a more convenient place, he and his brother attacked them with so much fury, that setting all the prisoners at liberty, they robbed all the headboroughs of every penny they had, and then binding them hand and foot in a field, they made the best of their way off.

Another time Captain Evans meeting on Finchly Common, one Cornish an informer, and common affidavitman, he saluted him with the unwelcome words 'stand and deliver', or otherwise he would shoot him thro' the head. Poor Cornish stood trembling like an aspin leaf, and heartily begged and prayed that he would save his life, tho' he took all he had from him; but if he did rob him, he was certainly ruined and undone. Quoth Evans, 'What a plague are you a Spaniard, that you carry all your riches about you?' 'No, Sir,' (reply'd Cornish) 'I am a poor honest man, as all my neighbours in St Sepulchre's parish know, belonging to the chamberlain.' Said Evans then, 'What inn do you live at? Perhaps you may do me a piece of service, by informing me of wealthy passengers lying at your house; and if so, I shall generously reward you.' Quoth Cornish, '(Sir) I belong to no chamberlains of inns, but to the Chamberlain of London, to whom I give an information of persons setting up in the City, that are not freemen, of apprentices not taking up their freedom when out of their times, and other matters which come under the cognizance of that officer.' Said Evans, 'D—n you and the Chamberlain of London too, I thought all this while you had belonged to some inn, and so might have given me intelligence in my way of business, but as I find the contrary, I have no more time to lose with you: deliver, or you are a dead man!' So searching Cornish's pockets, in which he found but five pence in brass money, he was so confounded mad, that he flung them over the heath, and then severely caning him, in the midst of twenty G— d—n me's and more, he mounts his horse again, and rode off to seek a better booty.

Amongst the many robberies which he committed, we shall now proceed to that which prov'd most fatal to him. He having intelligence of the Chester coach's coming with passengers to London, sent his brother William the night before to lie at Barnet, and to be in Baldock Lane at a certain time next morning. But the poor lad happening to light on a Scotch cheesemonger, who was travelling to Edinburgh, and he pretending to be going some part of the way on his master's occasions, they must needs lie together, and proceed on their journey next day.

When they were got into Baldock Lane, a pistol, to the great surprize of the Scotchman, was fired over Will's head by the Captain, that being the signal proposed; they then soon commanded the Scotchman to lie by, and in sight robbed all the coaches. Then in thunderclaps of oaths, the Captain riding up to the Scotchman, he robb'd him of seven guineas, and two watches; but by Will's intercession, who had lain with him all night, return'd him his best watch, and three guineas to bear his charges into his own country; for which generous action the same Scotchman hang'd them both at the assizes held at Hartford, in 1708, the Captain aged 29 years, and his brother Will 23. Several persons of quality, and others of no small distinction, whom they robbed, would not appear against them, but rather endeavoured to save their forfeited lives.

THE LIFE OF
STEPHEN BUNCE

This unfortunate malefactor took to all manner of disorderliness and theft, even in his very childhood; for playing very often with one of his neighbour's children, whose father was a charcoal-man, he would privately fill his pocket with that commodity, and vend it for codlings, to an old apple-woman that kept a little bulk, or stall, in Newtners-Lane; but, at length, being weary of this petty thieving, he wanted once to have so many codlings before-hand, and allow for them in the next bargain; tho' he design'd to merchandize no more with her. The old woman mistrusting his intent, would not give him credit. Stephen was very angry to himself that she should scruple his honesty, and resolved to be even with her. To this intent, one cold frosty morning, bringing her a good parcel of charcoal, whose hollowness in the middle he had fill'd with gun-powder, and sealed it up with black wax, he had for it what the old woman thought fit to give him in her ware. She presently thrust an heap of it under her kettle which was boiling, and being hard bitter weather, she sat hovering over it with her coats almost up to her navel. At length the gunpowder concealed in the charcoal taking fire, up bounced the kettle, out flew the codlings and water about her ears, whilst in the midst of fire and smoak, the old woman cry'd out, fire and murder in a hideous manner, which brought a great mob about her presently, to assist her in her great distress. However, it was the goodness of her kind stars, to let her come off in this imminent danger, with the damage only of scalding her a little, and burning a large hole thro' her smock, and the trouble of picking up her codlings again.

After Stephen Bunce was grown to years of discretion, he soon undertook great exploits: for instance, being one day very genteely dress'd, and going into a coffee-house, where an old gentleman had then a silver tobacco box, which opened in two separate parts, lying on the table where this sharper sate, after turning the news papers over and over, whilst he was drinking a dish of tea, he paid for the same, and went privately away with the lid of the box, and had his cypher presently engraved thereon; then returning back to the coffee-house, and very courteously pulling off his hat, quoth he, 'Gentlemen, have not I left the bottom of my tobacco box behind me?' So rumbling among the news papers, he there found it, crying, as he clapp'd the lid on, 'Oh, here it is!' At this, the owner thereof claim'd it for his; but Stephen impudently shewing his cypher on it, he challeng'd it as his property, and kept it, which put all the company in the coffee room into a great consternation, about what should become of the other gentleman's box.

Another time, Stephen Bunce being benighted near Bramyard and Herefordshire, and much straiten'd for want of money, a thought came into his head to make up to the parson's house, where knocking at the door, he desired the maid to tell her master a stranger fain would have the honour of speaking with him; the parson coming out, and enquiring his business, he being a good tongue pad, told him, he was a poor student lately come from Oxford, in order to go home to his friends, and being belated, he most humbly begged the favour that he would give him entertainment under his roof, but for one night. The parson being taken with his modest carriage and behaviour, withal believing what he said to be true, he kindly received him, and courteously entertained him at supper with him and his family; which being over, the maid was ordered to shew him his bed chamber.

When he was bidding them all good night, Stephen most humbly requested of the parson, that he might give him a sermon in the morning, which was Sunday, and the parson very thankfully accepted of his proffer. So the morning being come, the Levite equipp'd his young student in his gown and cassock; and, because it was about a mile to the church, lent him his horse too, whilst he, his wife, and children, would go the foot path over the fields. When Sir Reverend came to church, one was bowing, another scraping, to the parson of the parish, wondering to see him without his canonical habit, on a day when he should perform his sacred function. But he soon alleviated their admiration, by telling his parishoners, that a young gentleman of the University of Oxford, would be there presently, that would preach to them an excellent sermon. Now prayers were said, and the last psalm sung, but none of the gentleman came; so staying till dinner time, the congregation was forc'd to go home without a sermon, as well as their parson without his gown and horse, which Stephen to be sure had ordained for another use than to ride to church to preach in.

Another time this pickled blade being upon his patrole in Essex, as he was on one side of the hedge he espy'd at some distance, a gentleman very well mounted on a good gelding; so getting into the road, he lay all along on the ground with his ear close to it, till the gentleman came up; who asking him the reason of that posture, Stephen held up his hand to him, which was as much as to bid the gentleman be silent; but the gentleman being of a hasty temper, quoth he, 'What a pox are you a listening to?' Hereupon, Stephen sitting on his breech, he said, 'Oh, dear! Sir, I have often heard great talk of the fairies, but I could never have the faith to believe there were any such things in nature, till now, in this very place, I hear such a ravishing and melodious harmony of all sorts of musick, that it is enough to charm me to sit here, if possible, to all eternity.'

This story made the gentleman presently alight to hear this ravishing musick too; so giving Stephen his gelding to hold, and laying his ear to the ground, quoth he, 'I can hear nothing.' Mr Bunce bid him turn t'other ear, which he did, and then his face being from him, Stephen presently mounted his gelding, and galloped away with all speed, till he came within sight of Rumford. Then alighting he let the gelding loose, supposing that if the owner us'd any inn in that town, he would make to it, as accordingly he did, and Stephen at his heels. The hostler, who was at the door, cry'd out, 'Master, Master, here's Mr Bartlet's horse come without him.' By this stratagem, Stephen having got the owner's name, quoth he to the inn-keeper, 'Mr Bartlet being engaged with some gentlemen in play at Ingerstone, he pray'd him to send him 15 guineas, and to keep his gelding in pledge thereof till he came himself, which would be in the evening.' 'Ay, Ay,' (reply'd the innkeeper) '100 guineas, if he wanted them.' So giving Stephen

15 guineas, he made the best of his way to London, when in about four or five hours, the gentleman came puffing and blowing in his great jack boots to the inn, and the inn-keeper stepping up to him, said, 'Oh, dear! Sir, what need you have sent your gelding, and so put yourself to the trouble of coming this sultry weather on foot, for the small matter of fifteen guineas, when you might have commanded ten times as much without a pledge?' Quoth the gentleman, 'Hath the fellow then brought my gelding hither? A son of a whore! He was pretty honest in that; but I find the rogue hath made me pay fifteen guineas for hearing his d—n'd fairies musick.'

Stephen Bunce was a great visiter of billiard-tables, and cock-pits, as leaving no place unsearched wherein there might be any thing worthy of a bait. Tho' he had ever so fair an opportunity of reclaiming, yet was he so profligate in all roguish transactions, that he abhorr'd any thing which looked virtuously. Once turning foot-pad, he set upon a butcher betwixt Paddington and London, who being also a lusty stout fellow, he would not part with that he had without some blows. To cudgelling one another therefore they went; but tho' the butcher play'd his part very well, yet after a very hard battle, wherein they were both sadly battered and bruised, he was forced to cry 'Peccavi'. Then the victor, searching him all over, from head to foot, and finding but a groat in his pocket, quoth he, 'Is this all you have?' The butcher reply'd, 'Yes, and too much to lose.' Said Bunce then, 'Oh! d—n you for a son of a whore, if you'd fight at this rate but for a groat, what a plague would you have done if you'd had more money?' So they both parted.

But this small sum not sufficing for one night's extravagancy, as Stephen was coming home by one Mr Sandford's shop, a goldsmith, in Russel-street, Covent-Garden, he saw the old man telling a great parcel of money on the compter, and presently stept to an oil shop for a farthingworth of salt; then coming back to the goldsmith's house, and flinging it all in his eyes, it caused such a terrible smarting, that he did nothing but stamp and rub his peepers, whilst Mr Bunce swept about fifty pounds into his hat, and went off with it.

It is a true saying, 'that what is got over the Devil's back, is always spent under his belly'; for Stephen going that same night to a bawdy-house in Colson's-Court in Drury Lane, he lit into a strumpet's company, call'd for her great bulk, which was like a colossus, the Royal Sovereign, who pick'd his pocket of twenty pounds, and vanish'd away with it in the twinkling of an eye. This disaster made him fret, fume, and storm, like a mad man, and vent more oaths and curses, than any losing gamester at the groom-porter's. But all his exclamations being to no purpose, he began to vent his passion next with a general raillery against all the female sex; swearing that there was not a woman on Earth but what was a crocodile at ten, a whore at fifteen, a devil at forty, and a witch at threescore.

Spending the remainder of his money in a day or two vexation, necessity (which is always the best whetstone to sharpen the edge of man's invention) compell'd him to contrive ways and means for a fresh supply; then going to one of his comrades, whom the sight of line, rope, or halter, could not daunt with the fear of coming home short at last, they went one night, when the shop was just shut up, to one Mr Knowles, a wollen-draper, in King-Street, Westminster, where, whilst Stephen was bargaining for three quarters of a yard of cloth, to make him, as he said, a pair of breeches, his companion had the opportunity of taking the feather, as thieves call it, or key, out of a pin in the window. Then going away, but without buying any thing, and the man not thinking any otherwise than that his shop was fast shut, as having secured all before, they came in the dead of the night, which was very dark by reason the moon did not shine, and taking the pin out which had no key, they had an easy access into the shop, from whence they took away as much cloth as came to above eighty pounds.

When Stephen Bunce was but a lad about 14 or 15 years of age, he was a tapster at the Nag's-Head alehouse, in Tuttle Street, Westminster, where he had not been above a month before he convey'd a silver tankard privately to one of his thieving companions, which held two quarts. At night, when his master came to lock up his plate, the tankard was missing, which put all the house into disorder; Mr Nick and Froth swore like an emperor, the mistress scolded as bad as any fish-woman at Billingsgate, and the servants had all a grumbling in the gizzard, but whom to blame none could tell. However, after some small inquisition about it, it was generally concluded, that some of the guests had taken it away; whereupon it was agreed by a general consent, that the next morning the maid and Stephen Bunce should go to John Partridge, the astrologer and translator of shoes, in Salisbury-Street in the Strand, who was cry'd up for his dexterity in that art, and thought to be little inferior to Friar Bacon. For tho' he could not make a brazen head of speak, yet he had such a brazen face of his own as could outface the D—l himself for lying.

Accordingly going to this astrologer's house, and popping a shilling into his hand, he very formally set himself down in a chair, laid half a sheet of white paper before him, and then taking a pen in his hand, he made thereon several triangles about a square, which he call'd the 12 houses, and said, Jupiter being Lord of the Ascendant, signifies good luck for the gaining your tankard again, did not Mars interpose with an evil aspect towards Mercury. Now, Venus being on the fiery trigon, denotes the party that had it, lives either east or west; and Saturn being retrogado, and in the cusp of Taurus, it must needs be, that it is hid under ground either north or south.

Then he asked if there was not a red hair'd man at the house that day? They told him, 'No'. 'Nor a black hair'd man neither?' said he. They still answered, 'No'. 'Nor was there not a brown hair'd man there, with grey cloaths, not very tall, nor very low?' They told him, 'Yes'. Then he asked whether they knew him or not? They answered, 'No'. 'The Sun' (saith he) 'being ill posited in the 11th House, and Mercury in trine with Virgo, it was without all doubt a brown hair'd man that had the tankard.' Then Stephen asked, whether it might not be a woman, as well as a man? This put the conjurer something to his trumps; but when the maid said that could not be, for there was never a strange woman in the house all that day, he grew bold, and said 'No', too; 'for Venus being weak in reception with Gemini, and the Moon in her detriment, both feminine planets, it plainly tells that it was a man, and one betwixt 40 and 50 years of age'. 'Upon my life,' said the maid, 'I saw the party then that had it; he was a curl'd pated fellow, with a sad coloured sute, and about that age; he drank in the Rose; but if ever I see the rogue again, I'll teach him to steal tankards, with a murrain to him.' Stephen could not but laugh in his sleeve at the maid's confidence; so taking their leave of the astrologer, they went homewards, with a deal of news to tell their master; but by the way Stephen dropt the maid, to go and take share of his booty, and never went any more to his place.

We should not have rehearsed so much of this astrological cant, but to expose both the professors of that pretended science, and those who consult them; neither of whom can ever be sufficiently ridicul'd. But to proceed:

This notorious fellow being once, by an order of court at the Sessions-House in the Old-Bailey, sent for a soldier into Spain, while he was there, in an enemy's country, he was so much upon the duty of fasting, that the civil war which the

322

wind made in his empty stomach, oblig'd him very often to look out sharp for some employment for his teeth. So one day Stephen, and a comrade he had got, being as hungry as two tarpaulins kept upon short allowance, but altogether moneyless, they went loitering up and down the market in Barcelona, to see what fortune might offer in relief of their bellies, which had been mere strangers to any sustenance for above forty eight hours. At length they espy'd a country man going out of town on an ass: they follow'd him at some distance, and about half a mile from the town, there being a very high hill, the country man alighted, and led the ass up leisurely by a loose bridle. Hereupon Stephen Bunce going with his comrade softly after them, he dexterously slipt the bridle off the ass's head, and puts it on his own; then the other going off with the booty, Stephen crawls upon all fours, 'till he ascended on the top of the hill; when the country-man turning about to mount again, he was almost frighten'd out of his wits, to see a man bridled instead of an ass. Stephen perceiving his great consternation, quoth he, 'Dear Master, don't be troubled at this strange alternation which you see in your beast, for indeed was no ass, as you suppos'd it, but a man, real flesh and blood, as you may be; but you must know, that it being my misfortune to commit a sin against the Virgin Mary once, she resented it so heinously, that she transform'd me into the likeness of an ass for seven years; and now the time being expired, I assume my proper shape again, and am at my own disposal. However, Sir, I return you many thanks for your goodness towards me; for since I have been in your custody, you put me to no more labour than what I, you, or any other ass, might be able to bear.'

The country man was astonish'd at the story; but nevertheless was glad that his ass which was could not charge him with any ill usage. So parting, Stephen went to his comrade, who had already chang'd the ass again into money, to put their teeth in use once more, for fear they should forget the way of eating; whilst the poor country man was oblig'd to return to town again to buy him another ass to carry him home. When he came into the ass market he espied his old ass again; whereupon stepping up hastily to him, and whispering in his ear, he said, 'Oh! pox on you, you have committed another sin against the Virgin Mary, I find; but I shall take care how I buy you again.'

He was lawfully married at Plymouth to a victualler's daughter, who had so much education bestow'd upon her, as to read, sew, and mark on a sampler; after

323

which she was kept at home to sit in the bar, and keep the scores; which post pleas'd the young woman very well, because there was great variety of guests us'd the house, especially merry drunken sailors, who, when they had liberty to come ashore, would lustily booze it, and sing and dance all weathers. But Stephen, within a very little while after he was enter'd into the state of matrimony, catching the gunner of the *Swiftsure* man of war boarding his wife, he quickly shew'd his spouse a light pair of heels, and came up to London; where growing debauch'd to the highest degree, he was very seldom out of the powdering tub: nevertheless, the impairing of his health after this profligate way did not alienate his inclination from keeping company with such cattle, who ruin both body and soul; and for the maintenance of lewd women, he cared not what hazards he underwent, as he confess'd when under sentence of death. At last, as common whores were his ruin, he would, but it was then too late, exclaim aganist 'em, and say, a strumpet was the highway to the Devil; and he that look'd upon her with desire, began his voyage to inevitable destruction; he that stay'd to talk with her mended his pace; and he who enjoy'd her was at his journey's end.

He had been an old offender, and was such a debauch'd fellow in his conversation, that he could invent no other method of gracing his discourse, and making it taking, but by a complaisant reherasal of his own, and other mens uncleannesses; in fine, he could not find an hour's talk, without being beholden for it to a common whore; but his wickedness made its exit at Tyburn, in 1707, with Jack Hall and Dick Low.

THE LIFE OF
JACK OVET

T his notorious malefactor, John Ovet, a shoemaker by trade, was born at Nottingham, where his abode was for four or five years, after he had serv'd his apprenticeship. But being always of a daring, audacious disposition, his unruly temper induced him to keep very lewd and quarrelsome company, and depending on his manhood, it inspir'd him with an inclination of laying aside his mechanical employment, to translate himself into a gentleman, by maintaining that quality on the highway.

Immediately equipping himself, as a highwayman ought, with a good horse, hanger, and pistols, he rid towards London; and on the road had the good success of robbing a gentleman of twenty pounds; who being one of great courage, told Ovet, that if he had not come upon him unawares, and surpriz'd him at a disadvantage, he should have given him some trouble before he would have parted with his money. Quoth Ovet, 'Sir, I have ventur'd my life once already, in committing this robbery; however, if you have the vanity to think yourself a better man than me, I'll venture once more, for here's your money again, let it be betwixt us, and whoever of us is the best man let him win it and wear it.' The gentleman very willingly accepted the proposal, and making use of their swords on foot, Jack Ovet had the fortune to kill his antagonist on the spot.

THE ADVENTURES OF JACK OVET, A HIGHWAYMAN.

COMBAT BETWEEN OVET AND A GENTLEMAN, FOR HIS PURSE.

326

Not long after he kill'd another man in a quarrel at Leicester; but flying from justice, he still cheated the hangman of his due, and without any dread pursued his unlawful courses to the highest pitch of villany. One day in particular meeting the pack-horses of one Mr Rogers, who goes from Leominster in Herefordshire to London, and being in great want of money, he turn'd one of them out of the main road into a narrow lane, where cutting open the pack, he found therein about 280 guineas in gold, besides three dozen of silver-hafted knives and forks, and spoons, which he carry'd off. The other pack-horses were gone above two miles before Mr Rogers miss'd this; and then making a strict search after it, he found it ty'd to a tree, and the pack thrown off his back, and rifled of what was most valuable; but not knowing who had done this great injury, he was forc'd to make the loss good to the owner of the plate and money.

Another time Jack Ovet being drinking at the Star inn in the Strand, he overheard a soap-boiler contriving with a carrier how he should send an hundred pounds to a friend in the country. At length, it was concluded upon, to put the money into a barrel of soap; which project was mightily approved off by the carrier, who answer'd, 'If any rogues should rob my waggon (which they never did but once) the Devil must be in them if they look for any money in the soap barrel.' Accordingly the money and soap was brought to the inn, and next morning the carrier going out of town, Jack Ovet was with him in the afternoon, and commanding him to stop, or otherwise he would shoot him and his horses too, he was oblig'd to obey the word of command. Then quoth the honest highwayman, 'I must make bold to borrow a little money out of your waggon, therefore if you have any direct me to it, that I may not lose any time, which you know is always precious.' The carrier told him he had nothing but cumbersome goods in his waggon, as he knew of; however, if he would not believe him, he might search every box and bundle there if he pleased.

Ovet soon got into the waggon, and threw all the boxes and bundles about, till at last he came to the soap barrel, which feeling somewhat heavy, quoth he to the carrier. 'What a pox do you do with this nasty commodity in your waggon? I'll fling it away.' So throwing it on the ground the hoops bursted, out flew the head, and the soap spreading abroad, the bag appear'd: then jumping out of the waggon, and taking it up, says he again, 'Is not he that sells this soap a cheating son of a whore, to put this bag of lead into it, to make the barrel weigh heavy? If I knew where he lived I'd go and tell him his own; however, that he may not succeed in his roguery, I'll take it, and sell it at the next house I come to, for it will wet ones whistle to the tune of two or three shillings.'

He was going to ride away, when the carrier cry'd after him, 'Hold, hold, Sir, that is not lead that's in the bag, it is an hundred pounds, for which (if you take it away) I must be accountable.' 'No, no,' (reply'd Jack Ovet) 'this can't be money, but if it is, tell the owner that I'll be answerable for it if he'll come to me.' 'Where, Sir,' (said the Carrier) 'may one find you?' 'Why, truly,' (reply'd Jack) 'that's a question soon ask'd, but not so soon to be answered; the best directions I can give is, 'tis like you may find me in a jail before night, and then, perhaps, you may have again what I have took from you, and forty pounds to boot.'

Another time Jack Ovet meeting with the Worcester stage-coach on the road, in which were several young gentlewomen, he robb'd them all; but one of them being a very handsome person, he entertain'd such a passion for her exquisite charms, that when he took her money from her, he said, 'Madam, cast not your eyes down, neither cover your face with those modest blushes, your charms have softened my temper, and I am no more the man I was; what I have took from you (through meer necessity at present) is only borrow'd; for as no object on earth ever had such an effect on me as you, assure yourself that if you please to tell me where I may direct to you, I'll upon honour make good your loss to the very utmost.' The young gentlewoman told him where he might send to her; and then parting, it was not above a week after that before Jack sent the following letter to the aforesaid gentlewoman, who had gain'd such an absolute conquest over his soul, that his mind ran now as much upon love as robbing.

MADAM,

These few Lines are to acquaint you, that tho' I lately had the Cruelty to rob you of Twenty Guineas, yet you committed a greater Robbery at the same time, in robbing me of my Heart; on which you may behold yourself enthroned, and all my Faculties paying their Homage to your unparalell'd Beauty. Therefore be pleased to propose but the Method how I may win your Belief, and were the Way to it as deep as from hence to the Centre, I will search it out: For, by all my Hopes, by all those Rites that crown a happy Union, by the Rosy Tincture of your Cheeks, and by your all subduing Eyes, I prize you above all the World. Oh! then, my fair Venus, can you be afraid of Love? His Brow is smooth, and his Face beset with Banks full of Delight; about his Neck hangs a Chain of golden Smiles. Let us taste the Pleasures which Cupid commands, and for that unmerited Favour I shall become another Man to make you happy. So requesting the small Boon of a favourable Answer to be sent me to Mr Walker's, who keeps an Alehouse at the Sign of the Bell in Thornbury in Glocestershire, give me leave to subscribe myself your most humble Servant to command for ever,

JOHN BURTON.

The Gentlewoman's Answer.

SIR,

Yours I received with as great Dissatisfaction as when you robbed me, and admire at your Impudence of offering me yourself for a Husband, when

I am sensible 'twould not be long 'ere you made me a hempen Widow. Perhaps some foolish Girl or another may be so bewitch'd, as to go in White to beg the Favour of marrying you under the Gallows; but indeed I should neither venture there, nor in a Church, to marry one of your Profession, whose Vows are treacherous, and whose Smiles, Words, and Actions, like small Rivulets, thro' a thousand Turnings of loose Passions, at last arrived to the dead Sea of Sin. Should you therefore dissolve your Eyes into Tears, was every Accent a Sigh in your Speech, had you all the Spells, and Magick Charms of Love, I should seal up my Ears that I might not hear your Dissimulation. You have already broke your Word, in not sending what you villainously took from me; but not valuing that, let me tell you, for fear you should have too great a Conceit of yourself, that you are the first, to my Remembrance, whom I ever hated; and sealing my Hatred with the Hopes of quickly reading your dying Speech, in case you die in London, I presume to sucscribe myself Yours never to command,

D.C.

This was the end of Jack Ovet's warm amour, and he was soon after as unsuccessful in his villany, as he was here in love; for committing a robbery in Leicestershire, where his comrade was killed in the attempt, he was closely pursued by the country, apprehended, and sent to jail. At last the assizes being held at Leicester, he was condemned. Whilst he was under sentence of death, he seem'd to have no remorse at all for his wickedness, nor in the least to repent of the blood of two persons, which he had shed; so being brought to the gallows, on Wednesday the fifth of May 1708, he was justly hang'd in the thirty second year of his age.

THE LIFE OF
DICK HUGHES

This great villain, Richard Hughes, was the son of a very good yeoman, living at Bettus in Denbighshire, in North Wales, where he was born, and followed husbandry, but would now and then be pilfering in his very minority, as he found opportunity. When he first came up to London, in his way, money being short, his necessity compell'd him to steal a pair of tongs at Pershore in Worcestershire, for which he was sent to Worcester gaol; and at the assizes held there, the matter of fact being plainly proved against him, and the judge asking the poor Welshman what he had to say in his defence, he said, 'Why, could her Lord Shudge, hur has nothing to say for hurself, but that hur found dem.' 'Found them!' quoth his Lordship again, 'Where did you find them?' Taffy reply'd, 'Why truly, hur found dem in the chimney corner.' Whereupon the judge telling him, that the tongs could not be lost there, because that was the proper place they should be in, and finding the fellow to be simple, he directed the jury to bring him in guilty only of petty larceny; and accordingly giving in their verdict Guilty to the value of ten pence, he came off with crying carrots and turnips; a term which rogues use for whipping at the cart's arse.

After this introduction to farther villany, Dick Hughes coming up to London, he soon became acquainted with the most celebrated villains in this famous metropolis; especially with one Thomas Lawson, alias Browning, a tripe man, who was hang'd at Tyburn on Tuesday the 27th of May, 1712, for felony and burglary, in robbing the house of one Mr Hunt, at Hackney. In a very short time he became noted for his several robberies; but at last breaking open a victualling house at Lambeth, and taking from thence only the value of three shillings, because he could find no more, he was try'd and condemned for that fact, at the assizes held at Kingston upon Thames; but was then repriev'd and afterwards pleaded his pardon at the same place. Now being again at liberty, instead of becoming a new man, he became rather worse than before, in breaking open and robbing several houses at Tottenham Cross, Harrow on the Hill, a gentle-woman's house at Hackney, a gentleman's at Hammersmith, a minister's near Kingston upon Thames, a tobacconist's house in Red Cross Street, and a house on Hounslow Heath.

This fellow was very intimate with one Jack Waldron, who being a young man, but an old rogue, 'twill be very material to take notice, that he was condemned to be hang'd when he was scarce in the teens, for picking a gentle-man's pocket; but receiving mercy, in respect to his tender age, he travelled to Ireland; where, at Dublin, he went upon the glaze, which is robbing goldsmiths shew-glasses on their stalls by cutting them, as an opportunity offers, with a glazier's diamond; or else waiting for a coach coming by, and breaking them with the hand, which sometimes is not heard, thro' the noise which is made by the rattling of the said coach.

This trade Waldron followed in that country, till he was pretty well noted and punish'd there; then coming to London again, such was his unaccountable impu-dence and insolence, that he would in a manner rob people before their faces; and had done more damage to the goldsmiths, than any six rogues that went upon the like villany. But after having been about 18 times in Newgate, besides New Prison, and all the Bridewells in town, often whipt at the cart's arse, burnt in the hand, and once in the face, he became very well known, whenever he came to the Sessions-House in the Old Bailey, as an old offender. Whereupon, the Right Worshipful Sir Peter King, then Recorder of London, was pleas'd to tell him, 'That if ever he came there but for an egg, he would hang him for the shell.' But this notorious villain yet taking no warning, and coming before Sir Peter again, his Worship was as good as his word; for tho' the fact which he last committed was but simple felony, yet he cast him for his life, which he justly forfeited at Tyburn in 1711, aged but nineteen years.

Now to Dick Hughes again. When he first came to London, he lit on a sad mischance, for happening one night into a lumber house, not far from Billingsgate, he had not been long there, before one Joe Haynes, the commedian, and a broken officer, came raking thither too, without a farthing in either of their pockets. Joe Haynes having sav'd a great deal of dust, which he got off an old rotten post, and wrapt it up nicely in a clean sheet of paper, as soon as he and his comrade were sat down at a table, with a tankard of beer before them, he pull'd out the dust of the rotten post, and was sealing it up in several pieces of paper; which occasioned some folks that were drinking there, to enquire what it was that he was so choicely making up. Joe Haynes told them it was an incomparable powder, which was the only thing in the universal world, for a burnt hand, a scalded leg, or any accident whatever that should befal a man by fire; nay, farthermore, it would prevent also any hurt that might happen by that raging element: 'for proof whereof,' says he, 'make a kettle of water presently scalding hot, and my friend here, by rubbing a little of my powder on his leg, shall put it into the said water, and receive no damage.'

The people were very eager to try the experiment, and a kettle of water was immediately made scalding hot. Then Joe Haynes rubbing some of his powder on the stocking of his friend's right leg, which was artificially made of wood, for his natural one he had lost three years before in Flanders, he put it into the scalding water, and bringing it out unhurt, it put the spectators into such an admiration of its virtue, that they bought it all as fast as they could, at twelve pence a paper; so that Joe Haynes and his friend, who had no money before, had now above 30 shillings to pay what they had call'd for, and something in their pockets beside.

Dick Hughes being one of the fools that was taken in thus, the next day he was in some company, where bragging what an excellent powder he had for a burn or a scald, he would lay a wager with them of ten shillings, that he would put his leg into a kettle of scalding water, and not hurt it. Whereupon, his companions thinking it a thing impossible, they laid what he propos'd; and a kettle of water was forthwith put on the fire, whilst Dick went into another room, (because they should not see how he prepared his leg for the fiery trial) to rub some of the powder on his stocking, as Joe Haynes had on his friend's. Then coming out, and putting his leg all at once into the scalding water, he roar'd out in a most prodigious manner, and could not pull it out again till he was help'd. Thus he did not only lose his ten shillings, but had like to have lost his leg too; for he was above nine months in St Bartholomew's hospital, before he went abroad again.

No sooner was this villain roving about once more, but he got into Old Bridewell, by Fleet Ditch. But obtaining his liberty after one court day, he still continued in his villany, and attempted once to go on the foot-pad. In which enterprize, the first person whom he attacked in this kind, was that very honest coney-wool comber, William Fuller; taking from him about fourteen shillings, in the road betwixt Camberwell and Southwark, for all he might have insisted on a sort of privilege from being robb'd, by telling Dick Hughes, 'that tho' he was no thief, yet he was a great cheat; and since he first pretended to discover the pedigree of that son of a whore the Prince of Wales, he had ruined more people by tongue-padding, than ever all the thieves in London had done damage by any bad practices whatever'.

Another time, he met on the road betwixt Clapham and Vaux-Hall, with D—n the broken bookseller; and taking from him three half crowns, and stripping him stark naked beside, he ty'd his hands behind him, and his head betwixt his legs, to contrive, in that musing posture, what seditious libel might be most edifying to a Republican Party.

But burglaries being the master-piece of Dick Hughes's villany, he went chiefly on them; till at last breaking open and robbing the house of one Mr George Clark, at Twittenham, he was apprehended for this fact and committed to Newgate; where he led a most profligate sort of life, till he was condemned; and then his fatal circumstances wrought so little on his bad manners, that he was often heard to say, 'that if he could have but a whore before he died, he should die with great satisfaction'. But this wicked behaviour may very well be imputed to his great ignorance in matters of religion, he being not able so much as to read.

Whilst he lay under condemnation, his wife, to whom he had been married in the Fleet-Prison, constantly visited him at chapel. She was a very honest woman, and had such an extraordinary kindness for her husband, under his great afflictions, that when he went to be hang'd at Tyburn, on Friday the 24th of June,

1709, she met him at St Giles's pound, where the cart stopping, she stept up to him, and whispering in his ear, she said, 'My Dear, who must find the rope that's to hang you, we or the sheriff?' Her husband reply'd, 'The sheriff, Honey; for who's obliged to find him tools to do his work?' 'Ah!' reply'd his wife, 'I wish I had known so much before, it would have saved me two-pence, for I have been and bought one already'. 'Well, well,' said Dick again, 'perhaps it mayn't be lost, for it may serve a second husband.' 'Yes,' quoth his wife, 'if I have any luck in good husbands, so it may.' Then the cart driving on to Hyde-Park Corner, this notorious villain ended his days there, in the 30th of his age; and was after anatomiz'd at Surgeons-Hall, in London,

THE LIFE OF
ANDREW BAYNES

This Andrew Baynes was from his infancy of a vicious inclination, and tho' he had the natural sense to know he was in an error, yet was he resolved his heart should be still the same. When he first display'd his vanity, he began with defrauding and cheating all he had to deal with, especially by taking great houses, and then getting upholsters to furnish 'em, which when he had done, he would run away with their goods by night. Thus would he also trick brasiers, pewterers, limners, cabinet-makers, and other tradesmen; as particularly once by taking a house in Red-Lyon Square, from whence he carried above four hundred pounds worth of goods into the mint; but was took out from thence by virtue of a posse comitatus, and sent to gaol.

Another time being in great want of money, (for what such rogues get by villany, is always spent in luxury and excess), he went to a Justice of the Peace at Norwich, before whom he swore (tho' he had not lost a farthing) that he was robb'd of one hundred and fifty pounds, within five miles of that city, betwixt sun and sun; and brought three or four as great knaves as himself, to depose he had, to their knowledge, so much money when he left such a place; then suing the county, he recovered his pretended loss.

T. La Vergne Inv.   M. Vryuche Sculp.

Andrew Baynes a Foot Pad

Afterwards his profligate course of life tempting him to greater villanies, he turned house-breaker with one Tom Bets, who was a notorious offender in this kind. This Bets being cast once for a felony at the Sessions-House in the Old Bailey, he was, by an order of court, sent into the foot service in Flanders; after which he suffered a great deal of hardship: for, being first commanded into Germany, he was there taken prisoner by the French, and carried to Lewk. After a long starving confinement, he made his escape, and went to Fern in Sweden, where being listed into that king's service to go into Poland, he ran away. Then coming into Holland, he entered himself on board a Dutch man of war, that was to convoy a fleet from Moscovy; where going ashore, he stole one of the czar's bears in the night, and returning to Holland again, shew'd it, after his discharge from five months service, about Amsterdam; and getting money thereby, he came over to England; where he was hanged at Tyburn, on Wednesday the 15th of May, 1706, for robbing the house of the Lord Georges in Covent-Garden.

But his untimely end working no good effects in his comrade Andrew Baynes, he still followed the faculty of house-breaking, till he was condemned for it in 1709, and had the good fortune to be repriev'd; yet not making good use of that mercy, a little after his liberty was obtain'd, he robb'd the Earl of Westmorland's house, taking from thence several good medals, his Lordship's Parliament robes, damask curtains, cloaths, linnen, and other goods, to the value of five hundred pounds; for which being apprehended upon the information of one Daniel Waters, (a shoemaker concerned with him in the same fact, and hanged in August, 1713, at Maidstone in Kent) he was committed to the Marshalsea prison, in Southwark; from whence being removed by a writ of habeas corpus to Newgate, he was condemned again; but saved his life once more, by a restitution of most part of the goods which he had stolen from that peer.

Having obtain'd his enlargement a second time, and being so unsuccessful in house-breaking, he resolved to try his fortune in turning foot-pad; so he and his comrades (who likewise followed this exercise, which is the high road to Hell) meeting with one Mr Archer, a taylor, living in Blackmore-Street by Clare-Market, coming one evening from Highgate, they set upon him; but he having some knowledge of Andrew Baynes, who was indebted to him for making a coat, when once in Newgate, quoth he, 'Mr Baynes, don't you know me?' 'Yes,'

337

reply'd Baynes, 'I know you well enough, and therefore am resolved to send you home like a gentleman, for you shall have no money in your pockets.'

Searching him, they found about eight shillings in his breeches, and a silver watch; which taking from him, quoth Baynes, who had a good bull-dog with him, 'By G——d I fancy it is pretty sport to see a live taylor baited; therefore I'll bait this fellow to try the experiment.' So stripping him stark naked, they bound him to a tree; then setting the dog at him, he flew like a dragon on the taylor, who cried and roar'd like a bull indeed, and had had a mischief done him, if Baynes's companions had not been more merciful, in timely taking off the dog, which had grievously bit him in several parts of the body: but for this civility, they kept his cloaths, as looking upon him to be a sort of an alchymist, who could soon extract another sute out of customers apparel.

Another time Andrew Baynes, and his associates, meeting, betwixt Hampstead and London, with one Mr Blanchard a shoe-maker, formerly living in the Strand, they commanded him, without much ceremony, to 'stand and deliver'; but not obeying the word of command, he begg'd 'em to use conscience, and not to ruin him and his family at once. Quoth Baynes, 'You son of a whore, don't talk of conscience to us, for we shall now stretch it as large as you do your leather.' So rifling his pockets, they found about sixty pounds, most in gold, received that evening of a customer; then, as they were tying his hands and feet, quoth Baynes again, 'Is this all the money you have?' The poor shoe-maker answer'd, 'Yes, indeed.' Mr Baynes cried, 'You son of a b——h, you ought to have every bone in your skin broke for bringing no more with you; for this small matter is no more in our pockets than a man in Paul's.' In the mean time the shoe-maker begg'd and pray'd, that if they would not give him all his money, they would give him but some; but Baynes said, 'How can you be so unconscionable, Crispin, as to ask for our charity out of this little sum? Pray hold your chattering; for was you to stand as hard with us, as for a piece of carrot, we would not give you a doit; so stay here till we come to unloose you, which may be about the Day of Judgment.'

Not long after this robbery, Andrew Baynes and his comrades meeting three women, who were Quakers, coming from a little way out of town, they set upon these holy sisters, and having first searched all their pockets, in which was not above two guineas, and twelve shillings in silver, they thought this a very small prey, without taking their cloaths too. So stripping them stark naked, quoth one of the lambs, as they were tying her to a tree, 'Ye Men of Belial! What is the meaning of all this violence, in taking away our garments?' Andrew Baynes reply'd, 'Nothing at all, beloved ones, but only to make your bodies as light as your souls; and on my word, if ye always keep in this manner, as ye came into the world, ye will never offend the statute made against the excess of apparel.'

Now Andrew's comrades, because they were tolerably handsome, were for untying them, saying, ''twas easy to get away, without any danger of their having us secured'. But Andrew Baynes, in a great passion reply'd, 'They shall not be unty'd; for tho' I'm of no religion myself, yet I mortally hate a Quaker, or any other Precisian, because he is a demure creature, only full of oral sanctity, and mental impiety. Though he will not swear, he'll lye confoundedly; nevertheless, his presumption is so sure of his salvation, that he will not change places in heaven with the Virgin Mary. He will not stick out from committing fornication or adultery, so it be done for the propagation of the godly; and can find in his heart to lye with any whore, but the Whore of Babylon. He thinks every organist is in the state of damnation, and had rather hear a ditty of his own making, than the best hymn a cherubim can sing. In fine, he had rather see Antichrist himself, than pictures in a church window; and prophanely thinks his discourse is so good, that he durst challenge the Almighty to talk with him extempore. Truly, this character I have heard discreet men give of this sort of cattle; and for this reason the spirit moves me to shew no favour here to these female hypocrites, who we'll leave in the dark, till their own light conducts them to a better place.' So his companions being satisfied with what he said, they left the three yeas and nays to hold forth by themselves.

Andrew Baynes being once impress'd by Dent, the informing constable, (who was killed in Covent-Garden, by one Tooly, a soldier) and sent to Flanders, he ran away from his colours into England, and being one day at a house in Chelsea, where Dent was also drinking, and knowing him again, he and another way-laid him at Bloody-Bridge; where setting on him, quoth Baynes, 'Thou insolent rascal! who hast sold many a man's blood at twenty shillings per head, I am sensible, you can use your long staff well enough, I'll see how you can exercise your short one.' So pulling out his generation-tool, they applied a blister plaister to it, bought for that purpose at an apothecary's in the abovesaid town, and tying his hands and feet, left him in that condition till morning, before any passengers came by to release him.

This malefactor, executed at Tyburn, in 1711, aged 26 years, was born in Essex, and served as a drawer last at the Blue Posts tavern, at the corner of Portugal-Street, by Lincolns-Inn back-gate. He was very undutiful to his ancient mother, who went a begging; and the woman he kept company with, was called Flum, from her formerly selling flummery; being the leavings of one George Purchas, a bailiff, condemned (but reprieved) for high treason, with one Dammary, a waterman, for the insurrection made by the rabble in London, when Dr Henry Sacheverell was tried by the Peers, upon several articles exhibited against him by the House of Commons.

THE LIFE OF
NICHOLAS WELLS

T his noted criminal, Nicholas Wells, was born at Pemsworth, in the county of Kent, but afterwards lived at East-Grinstead, with his grand-mother; and keeping a horse, travelled from thence to London, and bought and sold goods, by which he helped to keep two of his younger sisters. He was a butcher by trade, and married a woman in Barnaby Street, with whom he had one hundred and twenty pounds for a portion. Whilst this money lasted, which was not long, he lived constant with his wife; but having by extravagant courses quickly consumed it, they then lived like married quality, for they would see one another once a week perhaps, lie together once a month, and eat together once a year.

Being by his folly reduced to great necessities, and much in debt, he, for a livelihood, drove a woodmonger's cart in Southwark; and one day carrying three loads of faggots to a gentleman's house at Lambeth, as he was making water not far from the door, where the gentleman's wife stood, her extraordinary beauty had such an influence on his carnal mind, that he was over heard by the gentlewoman to say to himself these words: 'Was I to lie with that handsome creature, I vow and swear I'd give her my cart and horses.'

The gentlewoman, who was none of the chastest, calling him into her parlour, she wanted to know what 'twas he said, as he was making water, or otherwise, if

341

he would not tell her, she would call her footman to kick him well. Our new carman was somewhat bashful to declare what he had said; but fearing to be ill us'd in case he did not satisfy the gentlewoman's demands, he very bluntly told her the words above-mentioned. The lady now taking him at his word, she carried him to her bed-chamber, where obtaining the pleasure, for which he had forfeited his cart and horses, and finding no difference betwixt her and his wife in that sort of sport, he swore, 'they were all alike'.

In this tone he hankered about the street-door a great while, for home to his master he durst not go, without the cart and horses; but, at last, the gentle-woman's husband coming home to dinner, and hearing the fellow swear, 'they were all alike, by G—d'; quoth he, 'What are all alike?' 'The faggots,' replied the carman. Quoth the gentleman again, 'And what of that?' To which Nick thus answered, 'An't please you, Sir, I have brought home the three loads of faggots which you bought, and your lady being not satisfied, that the last faggots are so big as the first, she hath ordered her servants to lock up my cart and horses in your coach-yard, and says, that she will keep them.' 'O! fie, fie, Madam,' said the gentleman to his wife, 'you must not do so; the cart and horses are none of the poor man's, they're his master's, therefore you must speak to him, if he has not us'd you well.'

The gentlewoman then presently delivered the cart and horses, and privately gave the carman a guinea besides, for his handsome come off. But the next day Nick bringing some coals to the same house, he then left the gentlewoman his cart and horses for good and all; for finding an opportunity of slipping into a back parlour, where a scrutore was open, he took out of it, a rich gold watch, several diamond rings, and two hundred and fifty guineas, which he carried clear off, without going to his master any more.

Not long after this exploit, meeting with Handsome Fielding, riding on horse-back by himself over Putney-Heath, as he came by Nick, he knock'd him off his gelding, and seconding his blow with another, which stunn'd him worse than the first, he ty'd his hands and feet, and searched his pockets, wherein he found about twenty guineas, which made him break forth into this exclamation: 'O! Gold almighty, thou art good for the heart sick at night, sore eyes in the morning, and for the wind in the stomach at noon; indeed, thou art a never failing remedy for any distemper, at any time, in all cases, and for all constitutions.'

Whilst Nick was expostulating to himself on the excellent qualities of gold, Handsome Fielding recovering his senses, quoth he, 'Sirrah, dost know on whom thou hast committed this insolence?' 'Not I,' (replied Nick) 'nor I don't care, for 'tis better you cry than I starve.' Quoth the robb'd person again, 'I'm General Fielding, who'll make you dearly suffer for this, if ever you come into my clutches.' 'Art thou' (replied Nick then) 'Beau Fielding? Why truly I've heard of thy fame and shame long enough ago; I think thou art one of those amorous coxcombs who never go without verses, in praise of a mistress, and write elegies on the great misfortune of losing your buttons. Thou art one of the whining puppies, that waste day and night with her that you admire for a whore, taking up her glove, and robbing her a handkerchief, which you'll pretend to keep for her sake. In fine, let me tell you, thou art translated out of a man into a whimsy.' So leaving Beau Fielding to shift for himself, he made the best of his way to Rosemary-Lane; where his landlord and landlady were transported at the sight of his booty, for he treated them, as in duty bound, plentifully; and there was never a servant in the house of iniquity but fared the better for his villany.

Altho' Nick Wells was a fellow that ventured his neck in these dangerous enterprizes, yet he was not master of any true courage, for he was much of the nature of those who are always challenging people that will not fight, and cuffing such as all the town has kick'd; upon many occasions it has appeared that he was as cautious of dealing with a man that is truly rough, as an honest man would have been of dealing with him. He was very bloody-minded, where he had the advantage of a man, as may be perceived by an enterprize which he once undertook for one Elizabeth Harman, alias Bess Toogood.

This woman being condemned for picking the pocket of one Samuel Winfield, a lock smith, living near St George's church in Southwark, such was her implaceable malice before she was hanged, that she said she could not die satisfied, unless she had the blood of her prosecutor. Proposing her wicked inclinations to Nick Wells, quoth he, 'Bess, not that I matter a murder or two committing, but I don't love to work without hire; what am I to have, first? and who am I to dispatch? But I care not who it is, if you content me.' Then this wicked wretch acquainting him where her adversary liv'd, and giving him three guineas to murder him, he took his last farewell of her in the chapel of Newgate, and that same day going to Mr Winfield's house, with pretence of bespeaking a lock, that he might have a fight of the man he was to kill, in the evening he watch'd his going out, and coming home, which was about twelve at night, and coming behind him as he was knocking at his own door, he ran him thro' the back with a tuck, of which wound he presently died on the spot: but the murderer was never known till he confess'd this barbarous crime at the gallows.

Whilst he followed these ill courses he was much addicted to all manner of lasciviousness, and seldom saw his wife, whom he greatly slighted; for he was often want to say, 'he was not curst with the plague of constancy'. Nay, how little regard he had for his wife, may plainly be seen by the following contract, drawn betwixt him and William Maw.

> We the Subscribers, William Maw of London, Joyner, and Nicholas Wells of Pemsworth, in the Country of Kent, Butcher, being each of us burdened with an useless Moveable, the former with a Jack-Daw, and the latter with a Wife, declare, That we have thought fit, for the Convenience of one another, out of our own pure and free Will, to make a Barter and Truck of the Jack-Daw for the Wife; yielding up the one to the other, all Right and Title that we have to the said Wife and Jack-Daw, and quitting for ever all Claim to them, without any Manner of Complaint or Demand hereafter to the Premises so trucked. To which Bargain and Agreement, in token of hearty Consent and Satisfaction, we have hereunto set our Hands and Seals. Dated at Deptford, the 10th Day of May, 1710.

> William Maw.
Nicholas Wells.

Accordingly, the wife went with the buyer, and her husband, without repenting his bargain; pursu'd his vicious practices still. But at length being apprehended for robbing one James Wilmot, a butcher, near Epsom, of thirty guineas, some silver, and a silver watch, he was committed to the Marshalsea prison in Southwark. For this fact he was hanged in the twenty eighth year of his age, at Kingston upon Thames, on Saturday the 28th of March, 1712. Mr Noble an attorney being also executed there at the same time, for the barbarous murder of one John Sayer, Esq.

THE LIFE OF
WILLIAM HOLLOWAY

T

he criminal of whom we are now to speak, was born at Newcastle-under-Line, in Staffordshire, and was bred up to husbandry; but not liking his occupation, he came up to London, where falling into such company as had rather be the Devil's soldiers, than fight under the banners of honesty, he soon became such an enemy to virtue, that no sort of theft miss'd his inclination, to support himself in the extravagancies of a most licentious course of life.

First he went upon petty matters of thieving, in which he was very successful; for one day going to a knight's house in Bloomsbury-Square, with an apron before him just like a scowrer, he had the impudence to go up stairs and take three or four footmens liveries; but just coming out with them on his arms, the coachman stopping at the door with his coach, he stopp'd Holloway, and ask'd him, 'whither he was going with those coats, and wastecoats?' Quoth Holloway, 'The Parliament being to sit within this week, and your master being willing his mens liveries should look somewhat fresh and decent, the steward has ordered me to scower them against then.' 'Here, here, then,' said the coachman, 'take my cloak too, and scower it well.' So stepping on his coach-box, he took his cloak off the seat, and gave it Holloway, who never took the pains to bring it back again: but the poor coachman was sadly jeer'd about it, for whereever the boys met him, who knew of the trick, they would cry to him, 'Here, here, take my cloak too.'

Another time there being a great stop of coaches in Fleet-Street, Mr Holloway stepping up to a gentleman's coach, and pretending to have some earnest business with him, whilst Holloway was talking to the gentleman as he lean'd over the door of the coach to him, one of his comrades took out a rich coach seat, and got clear off with it in the dark; and whilst the gentleman turn'd his head out of the other door to look after it, Holloway snatch'd off the other seat, and in the crowd went away with that. The gentleman being in a great surprize to see how suddenly he had lost both his seats, he call'd out to his coachman, saying, 'Tom, hast thou got the horses there?' Quoth Tom, 'Yes, Sir. Ay,' 'but (said the gentleman) are you sure you have them?' 'Why yes, Sir,' reply'd the coachman, 'I'm sure I have them; for their reins are now in my hand.' 'Well,' (quoth the gentleman) see and keep them there, for I have lost the seats out of the coach; and by heavens, if you've not a special care, you'll lose my horses too.'

346

Not long after this exploit, Mr Emes, who kept the punch house in Hemlock-Court, having been one day recreating himself in his calash, Will observing it to come a soft pace in the road betwixt Turnham-Green and Hammersmith, he perceived the driver thereof, who had been drinking very hard where he had been, to be fast asleep. Hereupon Will stopp'd the horse, which was but one, and softly stepping up, rifled Mr Emes's pockets, unfelt of him, of a watch and two guineas, and so sneaked off from him, supposing that was all the booty he could get at that time, unless he stripped him of his cloaths too, which he could not well carry off without some suspicion, in that place. However, the road being clear of passengers, and finding Mr Emes still in a profound sleep, he ty'd his legs together, and, that he might have the pleasure to see what would be the issue of it, he pull'd the pins out of the axle-tree of the wheels, and set the horse a going, which he had not done above an hundred paces, but the wheels flew off, and down came the booby-hutch.

Mr Emes now waked in a great consternation, whilst Will lay peeping behind a hedge, and could perceive his surprize. But the horse's rein being cut, and he not able to unloose his legs, for want of a knife to cut the cord, the horse never stopp'd nor staid, till, in that manner, he had drawn the calash through thick and thin into Hammersmith; from whence sending for the wheels, and having them put on again, he slept no more till he got quite home.

Now Holloway having cast all honesty and goodness quite out of doors, he was resolved to prosecute his villany to the highest degree; so from committing small matters of theft, he was resolved to turn highwayman, and being accoutred for this purpose, with a good horse, hanger, and pistols, he set out for such enterprizes.

The first action he went upon, was upon the road betwixt Faringdon and Abingdon, in Berkshire; where meeting with a country farmer, and asking him the time of the day, he told him it was about twelve o'clock. 'Why then' (quoth Holloway,) 'it may be about high time to ask one favour of you.' 'What's that?' (said the farmer) 'Why truly,' (reply'd Holloway) 'understanding that you received ten pounds at the inn from whence you now came, (for I was drinking in the next room when it was paid you) necessity obliges me to borrow it, and if you are not willing to lend it me by fair means, I shall take it by foul means.' The farmer being a man of some courage, presently drew his hanger in his own defence; but that being no security against pistols, which could kill at a distance, Holloway shot his horse under him; so dismounting his antagonist, and riding up to him with another pistol ready cock'd, and presenting it to the farmer's breast, he lent him his money without taking a note of his hand for it.

Another time Holloway meeting with a gentleman on the road, who had like to have been robb'd but a little before, he told the said Holloway, that there were some highwaymen before, wherefore he advis'd him, if he had any charge about him, to turn back. Quoth Holloway, 'I have no great charge about me, Sir, however, I'll take your advice for fear of the worst.' So as they were riding along, said Will again, 'Perhaps we may meet with more rogues of the gang by the way, for this is an ugly robbing road, therefore I'll secure that little I have, which is but three guineas, by putting it in my mouth.' Now the gentleman thinking him not of that profession, quoth he, 'And in case we should be set upon, I have secur'd my gold in the rowls of my stockings, which is no small quantity, for I received rent this day of some of my tenants'. They had not gone above half a mile farther, before they came into a very bye place, where he bidding the gentleman stand and deliver, he was in a great surprize; however, there was no remedy for preventing the loss of his gold, which was about eighty guineas; and for fear he should have more of the same metal in his boots too, he ript them from top to bottom; but finding none there, he left the gentleman cursing and swearing, for discovering where he he had laid up his hoard.

Will for a long time had been very successful in many robberies on the highway, but at length his devil failing him, he was apprehended for one committed on Hounslow-Heath, sent to Newgate, and condemned for the same; but had the good fortune to receive mercy. Now having a reprieve, and being impatient till he pleaded to Her Majesty's Pardon, he broke out of Newgate; after which having the impudence, when he was drunk, to go to the Sessions-House in the Old-Bailey, while the judges were sitting upon a commission of Oyer and Terminer, some of the turnkeys of Newgate offered to apprehend him for breaking out of gaol, which causing a scuffle betwixt him and them, he mortally shot Richard Spurling, a turnkey, thro' the body, in the face of the whole court, of which wound he died within eleven minutes. For this he was secured, with one Mrs Housden, who was try'd with him for the said murder, and condemned as an accessary to it; and to make their punishment more exemplary, he and the woman were not only hanged at the end of Gilt-Spur-Street in sight of Newgate, in September, 1712, but afterwards Holloway was also hanged in chains at a place call'd by his own name, on one side of Islington.

At the place of execution, he own'd he never had any antipathy against the person deceas'd, and did not know what he did, as being in drink. Thus we may evidently see the fatal consequences of drunkenness; which odious vice is now become so fashionable, that we may, too often, behold sots contending for victory over a pot, and talking the measure of their bravery by the strength of their brains, or capacity of their bellies. Taverns and alehouses are the common academics of sin, where drunkards make themselves expert in all those arts whereby they gratify Satan, and as it were, in so many open bravadoes, challenge the Almighty into the field, and dare him to do the worst he can.

Doubtless Satan hath but too much power over these men when they are most sober, they need not give him the advantage of finding them so often drunk; except in a bravado they desire to shew the world how boldly they dare defy Heaven, and how much they scorn to owe their ruin to any but themselves. Nay, it seems very evident, that even these bachanalians make this sottish pastime their beloved recreation, and only account him fit for their company, that can take off his cups handsomely, and is versed in all the methods and maxims of this hellish art. Indeed, they have made it a kind of science, and have given it so many rules and laws of late, that he that will now be expert in it, had need to serve out an apprenticeship, to learn all the circumstances and terms, tho' he ever so perfect in the substance before.

349

THE LIFE OF
AVERY

This malefactor, Avery by name, was born in Oxfordshire, and by his parents was put out an apprentice to a bricklayer, in London, where, after he was out of his time, which he served very faithfully and honestly, he married; and then following his trade for himself, he seemed to be so industrious at his business, that his neighbours had no suspicion in the least of his robbing on the highway; which unlawful practice he had followed for some years, to the great comfort of himself and all his family; who saw him work so hard till at last it killed him, much against his will.

One time Avery going out to look for a prize on the road, he got one by the byc, and to make sure of what he had (for you must know it is a maxim in politicks, that it is a harder matter to keep a kingdom than to conquer one) he rid all bye roads till he came into a field where several country fellows were standing at a gate. Now was he in a quandary what to do. Thinks he, 'should I ride back again in any precipitation, it will give them some mistrust, therefore I will put on a good face, and ride up to the men'. But the gate being lock'd he could not get out. However one of the men who had the key of it, wanting a young colt which he had in the field, he told Avery that if he would catch that colt, he would open the gate for him. Avery rid up and down the field after the colt, and had a long chace before he could catch him; then bringing him up to the owner, he let him out.

Now being in the road together, quoth he to the man that own'd the colt, 'What must I have for catching the colt for you?' 'Have?' (reply'd the countryman) 'O dear! Sir, what can you expect for such a matter? Why, I think that was a kindness to let you through the gate, or else you must have rid a great way about.' Avery swore most horribly he would be paid for his trouble. The countryman seeing him in a great passion, he promised him a pot or two of ale, if he would accept it. But this would not satisfy Avery; for pulling out his pistols, he swore he would not take all that pains for nothing about his damn'd colt, therefore, if they did not all deliver presently, he would shoot them every man. The poor country fellows being in a great consternation, and almost frighted out of their wits, at the sight of his murdering implements, they all pull'd out their leather purses, and gave him what they had; after which he rode away in great triumph for robbing half a dozen men by himself. And without doubt he had made his brags thereof to some of his intimate cronies; for when he was going to be hang'd, one of them meeting him in the cart, as he was riding up Holborn, thus call'd out to him: 'So ho! Friend Avery, what, are you going to catch another colt?' But Mr Avery had then so much business on his hands, that he could not make him any answer.

Another time Mr Avery roving up and down the road, to seek whom he might devour, he met with a good honest tradesman betwixt Kingston upon Thames and Guilford in Surry, with whom holding some chat, as they rode together, Avery asked him what trade he might follow when at home. Said he, 'I'm a fishmonger, pray what occupation may you be of?' Avery reply'd, 'Why I am a limb of St Peter too.' 'What' (quoth the fishmonger) 'are you a fisherman?' 'Ay,' (said Avery) I'm something towards it, for every finger I have is a fishhook.' Quoth the fishmonger, 'Indeed, I don't apprehend your meaning, Sir.' Then Avery pulling out his pistols, 'Now,' says he, 'my meaning may soon be apprehended; for there's not a finger on either of my hands, but what will catch gold or silver without any bait at all.' So taking twenty pounds from him, and cutting the girts and bridle of his horse, he rode as fast as he could for London.

Money growing short again with Mr Avery, he was forced to seek his fortune as usual, on the road; and meeting with an exciseman on Finchly-Common, whom he knew very well, though he was not known by him, by reason he was

351

very much disguised, with a mask on his face, Avery followed him at some distance, and a fair opportunity favouring his design, he rode up the exciseman, demanding his money at once. The assaulted person being somewhat sullen and obstinate, he would not deliver any thing till Avery threatened to kill him if he made any farther refusal. The exciseman being daunted at his words, and almost frighted out of his wits, to hear what dreadful vollies of oaths came out of his mouth, he stopp'd it as fast as he could with a dozen pound, saying, 'Here take what I have; for if there is a devil, certainly thou art one.' 'It may be so,' (reply'd Avery) 'but yet as much a devil as I am, I see an exciseman is not such a good bait, as people say, to catch him.' 'No, he is not,' quoth the exciseman, 'the hangman is the only bait to catch such devils as you.' But Avery giving the looser leave to speak, he rode away for fear of being caught indeed.

And it was not long after that he was apprehended, and sent to Newgate with one Waterman, that was condemned likewise for assisting him in these exploits on the highway; but he was reprieved. Avery being to die without his comrade, he made what friends he could to save his life also, which he had often forfeited for his villany, besides sending several petitions to the Queen, and Mr Recorder, in hopes of obtaining mercy for his manifold crimes; but all being rejected, he was executed at Tyburn, on Saturday the 31st of January, 1712–13.

THE LIFE OF
DICK ADAMS

This unhappy person, Richard Adams, was born of very good and reputable parents in Gloucestershire, who bestow'd some small matter of education upon him, as reading, writing, and casting of accompts. Coming up to London, he got into the service of a great dutchess at St James's, in which he continued about two years, when for some misdemeanor quitting his place, he contrived to live by his wits.

Having a general key which opened the lodgings in St James's Palace, he went one day to a certain mercer's on Ludgate-Hill, and desired him to send, with all speed, a parcel of the richest brocades and sattins, and other silks, he had in his shop, for his dutchess to make choice of some on an extraordinary occasion. The mercer knowing him to have come often upon such a like errand before, he presently sent away several pieces by his man and a porter, and being come to St James's Dick Adams brought them up to a door of some of the royal lodgings, where he ordered them to wait, while he, seemingly, went to acquaint his dutchess of their being without. In some short time after, coming out again, quoth he, 'Let's see the pieces presently, for my dutchess is just now at leisure to look on them.' So the mercer's man giving him the whole bundle, he convey'd it away backwards, and went clear off thro' St James's Park. The mercer's man and the porter having waited two or three hours, and receiv'd no answer about their goods, they began to make a strict enquiry after them; and finding they were trick'd, were forced to go home much lighter than they went out.

About a month after, Dick Adams having been drinking somewhat hard in the City, and forgetting the prank he had play'd the mercer, he came by his house one afternoon, and he being accidentally standing at the door, and espying his chapman, he presently seiz'd him, saying 'Oh! Sir, have I caught you? you are a fine spark, indeed, to cheat me out of two hundred pounds worth of goods; but before I part with you, I believe I shall make you pay dearly for them.' Mr Adams was much surpris'd at his being so suddenly apprehended, and, without doubt, curs'd his fate to himself, for being so forgetful as to come into the very mouth of his adversary; but seeing the late Bishop of London at some distance riding along in his coach, and having a good presence of mind at the same time, quoth he to the mercer, 'I must acknowledge I have committed a crime, to which I was forced by mere necessity, but I see my uncle, the Bishop of London, is coming this way in his coach; therefore hoping you'll be so civil as not to raise any hubbub of the mob about me, whereby I shall be expos'd and utterly undone, I'll go speak to His Lordship about the matter, if you please to step with me, and I'll engage he shall make you satisfaction for the damage I've done you.'

The mercer liking his proposal, as thinking it far better than sending him to gaol, he stepped along with Mr Adams, who boldly calling out to the coachman to stop, he approached the side of the coach, and desired the favour of speaking a few words with the Bishop. His Lordship seeing him have the mien and habit of a gentleman, he was pleas'd to hear what he had to say; so leaning over his coach door, quoth Adams, 'Begging your Lordship's pardon for my presumption, I make bold to acquaint your Honour, that the gentleman standing behind me is an eminent mercer, keeping house just by here, and is a very upright godly man; but being a great reader in books of divinity, especially polemical pieces, he hath met therein with some intricate cases, which very much trouble him, and his conscience cannot be at rest, till his doubts and scruples are cleared about them; therefore I humbly requested your Lordship would vouchsafe him the honour of giving him some ease before he runs farther to despair.'

The Bishop being ready to serve any person in religious matters, ordered Adams to bring his friend to him to next day. But said Adams again, 'It will be more satisfactory to him, if Your Lordship would be pleas'd to speak yourself to the gentleman to wait upon you.' Whereupon his Lordship beckoning to the mercer, who stood some distance off, whilst they discours'd together, when he came up to the side of the coach, quoth the Bishop, 'The gentleman has informed me of all the matter about you, and if you please to give yourself the trouble of coming to my house at Fulham, I will satisfy you then in every point.' The mercer making twenty bows and cringes, was very well pleased with his security; and taking Adams to the tavern, gave him a very good treat.

Next morning Adams came again to the mercer, who was drawing out his bill to give to the Bishop, and pretending that his coming in haste to go along with him to his uncle, had made him forget to put money in his breeches, he desired the mercer to lend him a guinea, and put it down in his bill; which he did very willingly; and then taking water, away they went to Fulham; where acquainting the Bishop's gentleman, that according to his Lordship's order over night, they were come to wait upon him at the time appointed, the gentleman introduc'd them into the hall, and having regal'd them there with a bottle or two of wine and a neat's tongue, the mercer was admitted into his Lordship's presence, and in the mean time Mr Adams made the best of his way by water again. The mercer being before the Bishop, quoth his Lordship, 'I understand that you are, or at leastwise have been, much troubled, how do you find yourself now, Sir?' The mercer reply'd, 'My trouble is much abated since your Lordship was pleas'd to order me to wait on you.' So pulling out a pocket-book, he gave His Lordship the following bill.

355

Mr Adams's Bill, April the 20th 1711.

	l.	s.	d.
For a Piece of green flowered Brocade, containing 23 Yards, at 1 l. 9 s per yard.	33	07	00
For a Piece of white strip'd Damask, containing 20 Yards, at 14 s. per Yard.	18	04	00
For a Piece of Cloth of gold Tissue, containing 18 Yards, at 4 l. 15 s. per Yard.	85	10	00

	l.	*s.*	*d.*
For a Piece of black watered Tabby, containing 29 Yards, at 4 *s.* 8 *d.* per Yard	06	15	04
For a Piece of blue Sattin, containing 21 Yards, at 16 *s.* per Yard.	16	16	00
For a Piece of crimson Velvet, containing 17 yards, at 1 *l.* 18 *s.* per Yard .	32	06	00
For a Piece of yellow Silk, containing 25 Yards, at 8 *s.* per Yard.	10	00	00
May the 17th. Lent your Lordship's Nephew.	01	01	06
Sum total,	203	19	10

His Lordship staring upon this large bill, quoth he, 'What is the meaning of all this? The gentleman last night might very well say your conscience could not be at rest; and I wonder how it should when you bring a bill to me which I know nothing off.' Said the mercer then bowing and scraping, 'Your Lordship last night was pleas'd to say that you would satisfy me to day.' 'Yes,' reply'd his Lordship, 'and so I would as to what the gentleman told me; who said, that you being much troubled about some points of religion, you desired to be resolved therein; and in order thereto, I appointed you to come to me to day.' 'Truly,' (said the mercer again) 'Your Lordship's nephew told me otherwise, for he said you would pay me this bill off, which goods, upon my word, he had of me, and in a very clandestine manner, if I was to tell Your Lordship all; but only in respect to your honour, I would not disgrace your nephew.' Quoth His Lordship, 'My Nephew! He is none of my nephew; I never, to my knowledge, saw the gentleman in my life before.' Thus when they came to unriddle the matter on both sides, they could not forbear laughing, the Bishop at his nephew, and the mercer for lending a man that had once cheated him, a guinea to cheat him again.

After this Dick Adams got into the Life-Guards, but his extravagancy not permitting him to live on his pay, he went on the highway. One day he and some of his accomplices meeting with a gentleman on the road, they took from him a gold watch, and a purse, in which was one hundred and eight guineas. But Adams not contented with this booty, and seeing the gentleman whom they robbed had a very fine coat on, he rode a little way back again, and saying to him, 'Sir, you have a very good coat on, I must make bold to change with you', he stripped him of it, and put on his. As the gentleman was riding along after he was robbed, and hearing somewhat jingle in the pocket of the coat which Adams had put on him, he felt therein, and, to his great joy, found his watch and guineas again, which Adams in a hurry and confusion had forgot to put into the other coat pocket when he changed coats with the gentleman. But he and his comrades coming to an inn to snack their booty, when they found what a mistake had been made, there was swearing and staring, cursing and raving, damning and sinking, with one another, as if they would have sworn the house down, but above all, they were ready to knock Adams on the head for his forgetfulness. However, since it could not then be help'd, and Adams promising to be more careful in his business for the future, his negligence was pardon'd for that time.

Dick Adams going out the same day again with his comrades, they stopp'd the Canterbury stage-coach on the road betwixt Rochester and Sittingborn, in which were several gentlewomen; and for the mistake they made last, they were very severe and boisterous upon these passengers, one of which, saying to Dick, as he was searching her pockets, 'Have you no pity nor compassion on our sex? Certainly ye have neither Christianity, conscience, nor religion in you.' 'Right, Madam,' (reply'd Dick) 'we have not much Christianity nor conscience in us but for my part you shall presently find a little religion in me.' So falling next on some fine jewels hanging to her gold watch, and a fine pair of bobs in her ears, quoth Dick, 'Indeed, Madam, supposing you to be an Ægyptian, I must beg the favour of you, as being a Jew, to borrow your jewels and ear-rings, according as my fore-fathers were commanded by Moses.' Thus having rifled all the gentlewomen, to above the value of two hundred pounds in money and goods, they left them to proceed on their journey, with very sorrowful hearts for their sad mischance.

But at last Dick robbing a man by himself, between London and Brainford, the person robbed met with a neighbour on the road, who closely pursued this highwayman. He made a running fight of it, in shooting Tartar-like behind him; but they at last apprehended him, and carrying him before a magistrate, he was committed to Newgate. Tho' he was very wicked before his affliction fell upon him, yet whilst he lay under condemnation, he was very devout. He was executed at Tyburn, in March, 1713.

357

THE LIFE OF
NED BONNET

E dward Bonnet was born of very good and reputable parents, in the Isle of Ely in Cambridgeshire, who bestowing some small education upon him, as reading, writing, and casting accompts, about the fifteenth year of his age, he was put out an apprentice to a grocer, living at Potten in Bedfordshire, whom he served honestly. When he was out of his time, he married a neighbour's daughter, by whom he had two small children at the time of his death, and set up for himself in the country, being at one time worth above six hundred pounds. He was ruined by a fire, which burnt all his goods and house to the ground; and not being in a condition to retrieve his loss, he came up to London, to avoid the importunate duns of creditors, where lighting into a gang of highwaymen, he took to their courses, to raise himself, if possible, once more. Having been upon several exploits, wherein he was successful, the sweet profit of his enterprises made him so in love with robbing on the highway, that he devoted himself wholly to it, and committed (as 'tis reported) above three hundred robberies, particularly in Cambridgeshire, insomuch that he was as much dreaded by the people in that country, as ever that great Tory, Patrick Flemming, was by the wild Irish.

After he was grown a good proficient in the gainful art and mystery of robbing on the highway, he oftentimes attempted to rob by himself, for he was an excellent horseman, and kept the best of horses which would leap a hedge, ditch, or five-bar gate, with him on his back, and knew the road by day and night, in that country, as perfectly as if he was directed by a compass.

Upon this Beast one time he met a young Cantabrigian, who had more money than wit, recreating himself abroad in his calash, with a brisk jolly courtezan, belonging to bawdy Barnwell, a little village, within a mile of the University of Cambridge, well stuft with such sort of cattle, as will sell the foul disease to a gentleman at a very moderate price. He made up to these gallants, and commanding them to stand, he very civilly demanded their money; which they refusing, he took the sum of six pounds or thereabouts from 'em by violence; and because they gave him some trouble before they would part with what they had, he was resolved to put them to some shame.

To accomplish this, he presented a couple of pistols towards them, and swore they should suffer no less than present death, if they did not strip themselves stark naked; and they, to save their sweet lives, obey'd his commands. Then tying their hands behind them, he bound their legs one to the other, and slashing the horse, away he ran upon a full trot with these Adamites, home to his inn in Cambridge. But as soon as they came into the town, such a multitude of men, women, and children, were hallooing and hooting after them, that the like to be sure was scarcely seen after the Lady Goditha, when she rid naked thro' the city of Coventry. But their shame did not end here; for the young gentleman being call'd to an account by the vice-chancellor, for this scandal which he had brought on the collegians, by his publickly keeping company with lewd women, he was expell'd by the University; and the strumpet sent to the house of correction, to do farther pennance by way of mortification for the flesh.

Having performed this exploit, and removing his quarters on t'other side the country, he met with his taylor and son, who had lately arrested him for a sum of four or five pounds, which he ow'd Mr Stitch. Resolving now to be revenged on him, he requested him to deliver his purse; but the taylor not approving of his proposition, he us'd a great many words and ceremonies to divert Ned Bonnet from his project. Ned not being to be tongue padded, he, by force of arms, took thirty six pounds away from his former creditor, and rid off; which made the son say to his father, 'I wonder what these fellows can think of themselves? Surely they must go to Hell for committing these notorious actions.' 'G—d forbid,'

359

reply'd the taylor, 'for to have conversation of such rogues there, would be worse than all the rest.'

After this, Ned Bonnet meeting on the road between Cambridge and Ely, Mr Piggot the Anabaptist preacher in Little-Wild-Street, he commanded him to 'stand and delive'r; whereupon, this pious and much pains-taking propagator of the Gospel, being very loath to part with his Mammon to this D—l of a robber, as thinking it false herauldry to put metal to metal, he dropp'd a great many devout sayings to divert him from his intended purpose. This putting Ned Bonnet into a great passion, he said, 'Pray, Sir, keep your breath to cool your porridge, and don't talk of religious matters to me, for I'll have you to know, that, like all other true bred gentlemen, I believe nothing at all of religion; therefore deliver me your money, and bestow your laborious cant upon your female auditors, who'll never scold at their maids without cudgelling them with broken pieces of scripture, which flow very fluently upon them on all occasions.' So taking from him a good watch, worth eight pounds, and as many guineas, he ty'd his legs under his horse's belly, and left him to steer his course as well as he could.

Another time Ned and his associates meeting with a person of quality, attended by four servants, on the descending of a hill into a hollow way, the one side whereof was inclos'd with a craggy shattered rock, and the other with a large wood, rising considerably higher than the road, here they thought it very proper to assault the nobleman and his attendants, whom they commanded to stand and deliver what they had. At this the person of quality smil'd, (thinking, or at least dissembling that he thought so) that they were only in jest, and told them, 'he believed they were gentleman only upon a frolick; therefore, if they would accompany him to the next town, they should be entertained with the best the place would afford.' To this Ned and his comrades reply'd surlily, 'they must convince him by stronger arguments if he persisted not to deliver his money, which *nolens volens* they were resolved to have'. So having made ready, they bore up to seize his horse's bridle. Upon this, perceiving they were in earnest, a sharp dispute began between them; but the nobleman's party being overpowered, they were forced to surrender themselves prisoners at discretion.

The robbers then taking from the nobleman a purse full of gold, a gold snuff-box, a gold watch, and a rich diamond ring, they carried him and his servants into the adjacent wood, where tying them hands and feet, they left them; but saying, 'that they would bring them more company presently'. Accordingly, they were as good as their word, for in less than two hours they made the nobleman and his four servants just a dozen persons, whom also binding, quoth Ned Bonnet, 'There are now twelve of you, all good men and true; so bidding you farewel, you may give in you verdict on us as you please when we are gone; tho' it will be none of the best, yet to give as little trouble as may be, we shall not stay now to challenge any of you: so once more farewel.'

Ned Bonnet and his comrades now going to their place of rendezvous, to make merry with what they had got, which was at a bye sort of an inn standing somewhat out of the high road between Stamford and Grantham, it happened at night to rain very hard, so that one Mr Randal a pewterer, living near Marygold-Alley in the Strand, before it was burn down, was oblig'd to put in there for shelter. Calling for a pot of drink, whereon was the inn-keeper's name, which was also Randal, the pewterer asked him, as being his name sake, to sit and bear him company.

They had not been long chattering before Ned, and one of his comrades, with a trull, came down stairs and placed themselves at the same table; and understanding, by the means aforesaid, what this stranger's name was, one of the rogues fixing his eyes more intent than ordinary upon him, in a deal of seeming joy, he leaped over the table, and embracing the pewterer, quoth he, 'Dear Mr Randal! who would have throught to have seen you here? 'Tis ten years, I think, since I had the happiness to be acquainted with you.'

Whilst the pewterer was recollecting whether he could call this spark to mind or not, for it came not into his memory, that he had ever seen him in his life, the highwayman again cry'd out, 'Alas! Mr Randal, I see now I am much altered, since you have forget me.' So being here arrived to a *ne plus ultra* how to go on, up starts Ned, and with as great seeming admiration, said to his companion, 'Is this, Harry, the honest gentleman in London, whom you so often us'd to praise for his great civility and liberality to all people? Surely then we are very happy in meeting thus accidentally with him.'

By this discourse they would almost have perswaded Mr Randal that they perfectly knew him; but being sensible of the contrary, he very seriously assured them, that he could not remember that he ever had seen any of them in his life. 'No!' said they, as struck with admiration, 'that's strange we should be altered so much within these few years.' Then Mr Randal began to ask the spark, who pretended to know him so well, some questions which he was certain he could not positively answer; but fearing they should then be put to a nonplus, they waved them, and strained compliments with Mr Randal to sup with them; which all his refusals could not avoid.

By that time they had supped, in came four more of Ned's comrades, who were invited also to sit down, and more provisions were called for, which were as quickly brought, and as quickly devour'd. When the fury of consuming half a dozen good fowls and other victuals was over, besides several flasks of wine, there was no less than three pounds odd money to pay. At this they star'd on each other, and held a profound silence, whilst Mr Randal was fumbling in his pocket. When they saw he only brought forth a moute, which was only as much as came to his share to pay, he that pretended to know him, started up, and protested he should be excus'd for old acquaintance sake: but the pewterer, not willing to be beholden, as indeed they never intended he should, to such companions, lest for this civility they should expect greater obligations from him, pressed them to accept his dividend of the reckoning, saying, 'if they thought requisite he would pay more'.

At last their trull taking the wink, said, 'Come, come, what needs all this ado? Let the gentleman, if he so pleases, present us with this small treat, and do you give him a larger at his taking his farewel in the morning.' Mr Randal not liking this proposal, it was started that he and Ned should throw dice to end the controversy; and fearing he was got into ill company, to avoid mischief, Randal acquiesced to throw a main for who should pay the whole shot, which was so managed that the lot fell upon Jonas. For putting the change upon him, the dice they threw with ran all fives and sixes on Ned's side, and but only fours and fives on the pewterer's side; which he perceiving, and going to detect them, their strumpet snatched them up, and by the art of hocus pocus, converted them into regular ones. By this means Randal, having the voice of the whole board against him, was deputed to pay the whole reckoning; tho' the dissembling villains vow'd and protested they had rather it had fell to any of them to have had the honour of treating him, with also making large promises what great things they would do the next morning, to make him amends.

Mr Randal dissembled his discontent at these shirking tricks as well as he could; and they perceiving he would not engage in gaming, but counterfeited drowsiness, and desired to be a bed, the company broke up, and he was shew'd to his lodging, which he baricado'd as well as he could, by putting old chairs, stools, and tables against the door. Going to bed and putting the candle out, he fell asleep; but was soon awaked by a capering up and down the room, and an outcry of murder and thieves.

Upon this surprising noise he leaped out of bed, and ran to the door, to see whether it was fast or not; and finding nothing removed (for the highwaymen came into his chamber by a trap-door which was behind the hangings) he wondered how the noise should be there in his apartment, unless it was enchanted. But as he was about to remove the barricado to run and raise the house, he was surrounded with a crew, who tying and gagging him, they took away all his cloaths, and left him to shift for himself as well as he could.

A little after, the inn-keeper, the better to colour his business, came thundering at the door, demanding what was the cause of this clamour at that time of night? But hearing no body answer, he jumbled open the door, and entered the room with a candle, bringing also his hostler and tapster along with him. Finding the gentleman in that condition, he soon unloos'd him, with a great deal of seeming sorrow for this disaster; for he had not only lost his cloaths, but also forty pounds which he had in gold in his breeches. In the mean while Ned Bonnet and one of his comrades came into Mr Randal's chamber, to enquire the meaning of this disturbance there, and when they were acquainted with his loss, they swore, in a seeming great rage, 'they would find out the rogues, if they went to a conjurer'. But the poor pewterer believed they need not consult the Devil to know who had robbed him, no more than they might have doubted going to him themselves when they died.

Mr Randal being thus cheated and robbed of all he had about him, he was obliged to borrow some old cloaths of the inn-keeper, and then with a heavy heart return early in the morning home again, as being not able to prosecute his intended journey, for want of money to defray his charges.

One time Ned Bonnet, in a rencounter on the road, met with the misfortune of having his horse shot under him; whereupon, he was obliged to follow his trade on foot, till he could get another. But it was not long before he took a good gelding out of the grounds of a man, who since kept the Red-Lyon-Inn in Hounslow; upon which, riding strait into Cambridgeshire, a gentleman one day overtook him on the road, who had just like to have been robbed. Hearing Ned Bonnet to be tuning something of a psalm, he, thereupon, took him to be a godly man, and desired his company to such a place, to which he said he was also going, (for a highwayman is never out of his way, tho' he is going, against his will, to the gallows.) But at length, Ned coming to a place convenient for his purpose, he obliged the gentleman to stand and deliver his money; which being above eighty guineas, he had the conscience to give him half a crown to bear his charges, till he had credit to recruit himself again. This gentleman ever after could not endure the tune of a psalm, and had as great an aversion against Sternhold, Hopkins, Tate, and Brady, as the Devil has to holy water.

The reader will observe by what precedes, that Ned Bonnet had always a sprightly imagination, and this was yet more apparent before the faculties of his mind were debauched by evil practices: we shall give one instance, which was omitted at the beginning, to prove the liveliness of his genius when he was but a child. Being sent by his father when he was no more than ten years old, with a present to the parson of the parish, he went and knocked manfully at the door. The gift was a spear-rib, the old man having just killed a hog, and it was wrapped up in a cloth, and put into a basket. A servant comes to the door, and demands of young Bonnet his business. 'I want to speak with your master' says he. Imediately the master was informed, and, he imagining what the affair was, comes to receive the dole of his pious parishioner, a thing that gentlemen of the cloth are as ready to do, as any men in the world. 'Well, my dear,' quoth he, 'what is your business?' 'Why only my father has sent you this,' says Ned, and gives him the basket, without moving his hat. 'O fie, fie, child,' says Levi, have you no manners? You should pull off your hat, and say, "Sir, my father gives his service to you, and desires you to accept this small token": come, go out again with the basket, and knock at the door, and I'll let you in, and see how prettily you can perform it.'

The parson waited within the door till he was weary, expecting Ned to knock; till at last, imagining the boy had mistook the case, he opens the door, and sees our gentleman at a distance, walking off with his present. 'So ho! So ho! Sirrah, where are you a going?' calls the parson with a loud voice. 'Home, Sir,' answered the boy as loudly. 'Nay, but you must come back, and do as I bade you first,' says the priest again. 'Thank you for that, Sir,' quoth Ned: 'I know better;

and if you teach me manners, I'll teach you wit.' So away he fairly went with the spear-rib, which his father, upon hearing the story, had wit enough to keep, and laugh at the parson into the bargain.

At length one Zachary Clare, whose father kept a baker's shop at Hackney, being apprehended for robbing on the highway, and committed to Cambridge gaol, to save his own bacon, he made himself an evidence against Ned Bonnet, who being secured at his lodging in Old-Street, was sent to Newgate, where remaining till the assizes held at Cambridge, before Mr Baron Lovel, he was carried down thither, and executed before the castle, on Saturday the 28th of March, 1713, to the general joy and satisfaction of all the people in that country; where a great number on horseback met him on the road, when he was going down, to conduct him safe to prison. Before he was turned off he shew'd himself very much troubled for the poor condition in which he left his wife and children, and owned that his shameful death was no more than what he deserved, in that he had been condemned for his life not above three years before, at Chelmsford in Essex, and was pardoned for the same; but not making good use of that royal mercy, which was extended towards him, the just judgment of GOD had now overtook him for all his wickedness.

365

THE LIFE OF
NED WICKS

This wretched person, Edward Wicks, was born of very good parents, who kept an inn at Coventry, and bestowed on him so much education in reading, writing, and casting accompts, as qualify'd him to be a clerk for extraordinary business. He was an exciseman about fourteen months; but not thinking that a post sufficient enough to cheat Her Majesty's subjects, he was resolved to impose upon them more, by taking all they had on the highway. Being well equipp'd for such enterprises, he travelled the roads to seek his fortune, and had the good luck to commit two robberies without any discovery: but a third time being apprehended for a robbery committed not far from Croydon in Surrey, he was sent to the Marshalsea in Southwark.

This prison is situated on such a cursed piece of land, that the son is ashamed to be his father's heir in't. It is an infected pest-house all the year long; and, 'Lord have mercy upon us', may well stand upon these doors; for debt here, as well as felony, is a most dangerous and catching pestilence. In this place is a lively representation of the Iron-Age, since nothing but jingling of keys, and rattling of shackles, bolts, and grates, are there to be heard; and it is the Trojan Horse, in whose womb were shut up all the mad Greeks that were men of action.

However, Wicks was not long under confinement, before he obtained his liberty, by his friends making up the business with his adversary, to whom sixty guineas were given, for taking from him but thirty shillings. Then running Jehu-like to his destruction as fast as he could, he kept company with one Joe Johnson, alias Sanders; with whom going once on the road, they met, between Hounslow and Colebrook, with a stage coach, having four gentlemen in it; who seeing them come pretty near the coach, and perceiving they had masks on, were apprehensive of their intention of robbing them; and upon that, to be beforehand with them, one of them shot Joe Johnson with a brass piece, or blunderbuss, and lodged seven or eight large shot in his body. Wicks now rode clear off, without any hurt, whilst his comrade was apprehended, and, on suspicion, sent to Newgate; where he was charged by one Mr Woolly, with robbing him of a silver watch, and some money, on the highway; for which he was hanged at Tyburn, on Wednesday the 17th of February, 1704–5, aged twenty two years.

But the untimely end of this fellow making no impression on Wicks's bad manners, he still pursues his wicked courses with a great deal of pleasure and satisfaction; and one day the Duke of Marlborough being at St Alhans, after he was in disgrace, Ned being then in the town, and ruminating on the old proverb, *Fallere fallentem non est fraus*, he thought it no injustice to finger a little of his Grace's money; but having too great a retinue with him when he left that place, our highwayman durst not venture to make an attack; whereupon, riding towards Cheshunt, in the same county, he put into a bye sort of a house a little out of the road, in which, finding only a poor old woman, bitterly weeping, and asking her the reason of shedding those tears, she told him, that she was a poor widow, and being somewhat indebted for rent to her landlord, she expected him every minute to come and seize what few goods she had, which would be her utter ruin.

Wicks bid the old woman rest contented, and he would make things easy; so he pulling off his rich lac'd cloaths, and putting on an old coat which his landlady lent him, and having also secur'd his horse in an old barn, presently after, the old miser of a landlord came and demanded his rent: hereupon, Ned rising out of the chimney corner, with a short pipe in his mouth, quoth he, 'I understand, Sir, that my sister here, poor woman! is behind-hand for rent, and that you design to seize her goods; but as she is a desolate widow, and hath not wherewithal to pay you at present, I hope you will take so much pity and compassion on her mean circumstances, as not to be too severe: pray let me persuade you to have a little forbearance.' The landlord reply'd, 'Don't tell me of forbearance, I'll not pity people to ruin myself; I'll have my money; I want my rent, and if I am not paid now, I'll seize her goods forthwith, and turn her out of my house.'

When Ned found that no intreaties nor persuasions would prevail with the old cuff to have patience with the poor woman a little longer, he said, 'Come, come, let's see a receipt in full, and I'll pay it.' Accordingly a receipt was given, and the rent paid. Then the landlord being upon going away, quoth Wicks, ''Tis drawing towards night, Sir, and there is great robbing abroad, therefore I would advise you to stay here till tomorrow, and take the day before you.' 'No, no,' reply'd the country fellow, 'I'll go home now; I shall reach seven miles yet, by that time it is dark.' 'Ah! Sir,' said Ned again, 'but let me persuade you to tarry here; for indeed there is great robbing abroad.' 'I don't care,' cry'd the landlord, 'what robbing there is abroad, I'll go home now; besides, I don't fear being robbed by any one man, let him be who he will.'

368

So taking his horse, away the old fellow rid, and Wicks after him, dressed then in his fine cloaths; and meeting him at a pond where he knew he must pass by, he did not only bid him stand and deliver, but presenting him also with a whole volley of first-rate oaths, he so frightened him out of his wits, that he delivered all the money he had lately received, and as much more to it.

Then Wicks riding back to the old woman again, and disguising himself as before, it was not long after 'ere the landlord came to the house again, and knocking at the door, quoth Wicks, 'Who's there.' The landlord said, 'It is I.' Reply'd Wicks, 'What I?' 'Why, it is *I*,' quoth the country fellow again. At these words, the old woman cried, 'O! 'tis my landlord.' So letting him in, he told his grievance with a great deal of sorrow; as how he was robbed by a rogue in a laced coat, who swore a thousand oaths at him, and had certainly killed him, if he had not given him all his money. 'Ay,' (quoth Wicks), 'I told you there was great robbing abroad, but you would not take my advice; now I hope you will stay here, Sir, till morning.' However, he did not; for having given an account of his misfortune, he made the best of his way homewards, having nothing more to lose.

A little after the performance of this exploit, Wicks being in London, and going one night along Drury-Lane, dressed much like a gentleman, who should make a sham stumble by him, but one Madam Toby, a noted jilt? whereupon, catching hold on her arm to save her from falling, she returned him many thanks, and for his civility, invited him to her lodging just by, in Princes-Street, where she would also make him a suitable return for his courtesy. Now Wicks, by his behaviour in not speaking, seemed to be dumb, but nevertheless, by the signs he made, he intimated that he accepted of Madam Toby's proffer; who thinking him to be really speechless, she said as they went along, 'Oh! dear, Sir! 'tis a thousand pities that such a handsome likely man as you are, should be dumb.'

As soon as he came to her lodgings, he made a sign for pen, ink, and paper, to be brought him; whereby signifying his desire of having a couple of bottles of clarret and a fowl for supper, he gave the maid a guinea to provide it. Whilst she was gone to get what was ordered, he, by writing his mind, desired to know of Madam Toby, who was every now and then crying, 'What a pity it is such a well-bred gentleman should be dumb', the price of a nights lodging, which was two guineas, as she signified by holding up two fingers.—So the bargain being made, after supper they went very lovingly to bed; but in the middle of the night, Ned Wicks arising, and taking a couple of pistols out of his pockets, which he presented to Madam Toby's breast, quoth he, 'You jilting b—h, I must have my two guineas again, and more to boot; therefore if you offer to make the least noise, these fatal instruments of death shall send your soul to the Devil.'

Our lady of iniquity was in a great surprize to hear her suppos'd cully use his tongue; but not daring to speak for her life, he did not only tie her hand and foot, but also took from her a very good watch, a gold locket, a gold bracelet, a silver cup, half a dozen silver spoons, a velvet hood, and velvet scarf, and then left her in a deep study how to get more. When Wicks was gone, she cry'd out, 'Murder and Thieves', with such an audible voice, that alarming all the house, the landlord, landlady, and maid, came running naked into Madam Toby's chamber; where finding her bound fast to her good behaviour, after they had set her loose, she told them of her irretrievable loss, and swore that she would never pick up dumb men again.

Another time Wicks meeting with the late Lord M— on the road betwixt Windsor and Colebrook, attended only with a groom and one footman, he commanded his Lordship to stand and deliver, for he was in great want of money, and money he would have before they parted. His Honour pretending to have a

369

great deal of courage, swore he should fight for it then. Wicks very readily accepted the proposal, and preparing his pistols for an engagement, his Lordship seeing his resolution, he began to hang an arse; which his antagonist perceiving, he began to swagger, saying, 'All the world knows me to be a man; and tho' your Lordship was concerned in the cowardly murdering of M—d the Player, and Captain C—t, yet I'm not to be frightened at that; therefore down with your gold, or else expect no quarter.'

His Lordship now meeting with his match, it put him into such a passionate fit of swearing, that Wicks, not willing to be outdone in any wickedness, said, 'My Lord, I perceive you swear perfectly well *ex tempore*: come, I'll give your Honour a fair chance for your money, and that is, he that swears best of us two, shall keep his own, and his that loseth.' His Lordship agreed to that bargain, and throws down a purse of fifty guineas, which Wicks matched with a like sum. After a quarter of an hour's swearing most prodigiously on both sides, it was left to my Lord's groom to decide the matter; who said, 'Why, indeed your Honour swears as well as ever I heard a person of quality in my life; but to give the strange gentleman his due, he has won the wager, if it was for a thousand pounds.' Whereupon, Wicks taking up the gold, he gave the groom a guinea, and rode about his business.

But not long after this, Wicks being apprehended in London, for a robbery done in Warwickshire, he was committed to Newgate; from whence attempting to break out, he was quickly removed to Warwick gaol; where being try'd the next July, he was condemned to be hang'd. His parents made great intercession for this their only child; but in vain; for he was executed on Saturday the 29th of August, 1713, aged twenty nine years.

THE LIFE OF
WILLIAM
GETTINGS

This malefactor was born in the parish of Wolhope, in Herefordshire, where he lived with his father, a grazier, till he was sixteen years of age, and then came up to London. He spent, after this, about 5 years in the service of several gentlemen, sometimes in the capacity of a butler, at other times as a footman. Had he continued honest, as he was at first, he might have done very well, for he was esteemed; but after these 5 years, he took to bad company, who soon debauch'd him, both in principles and practice.

When he first took to ill courses, he went by the name of William Smith, and sought his fortune originally by other ways of thieving than that of robbing on the highway; as house-breaking, shop-lifting, or the like.

Thus one evening going privately, dress'd like a porter, into the house of a Doctor of Physick, living in, or near Well-Close, by the Danes church in Ratcliff-High-Way, he there took down a rich bed, and pack'd it up: then bringing it out of the chamber, in order to carry it off, he fell headlong down stairs, insomuch that he had like to have broke his neck. The noise alarming the old doctor and his son, they came running out of the kitchen to see what was the matter; whereupon Gettings, who was puffing and blowing, as if he was quite tired and out of breath, perceiving them nearer than they should be, said to the Doctor, 'Is

371

not your name so and so?' 'Yes,' reply'd the doctor, 'and what then?' 'Why then, Sir,' quoth William Gettings, 'there's one Mr Hugh Hen and Penhenribus, has ordered me to bring these goods hither, which have almost broke my back, and for which he'll call about half an hour hence, and fetch them away to a new lodging which he has took somewhere hereabouts.' 'Mr Hugh Hen and Penhenribus,' reply'd the doctor again, 'pray who's he? for to the best of my knowledge, I don't know any such gentleman.' 'I can't tell for that,' said Gettings 'but indeed the gentleman knows you, and ordered me to leave the goods here.' 'I don't care,' quoth the doctor, 'how well he knows me, I tell you, I'll not take in people's goods, unless they were here themselves, therefore I say carry them away.' 'Nay, pray Sir,' said Gettings, 'let me leave the goods here, for I am quite weary already in bringing them hither.' 'I tell you,' reply'd the doctor, 'there shall none be left here, therefore take them away, or I'll throw them into the street else.' 'Well,' quoth Gettings, 'I'll take the goods away then, but I'm sure the gentleman will be very angry, because he ordered me to leave them here.' 'I don't care,' reply'd the doctor, 'for his anger, nor yours neither, I tell you I'll take no charge of other people's goods, unless they were here themselves to put them into my custody.' 'Very well, Sir,' quoth Gettings, 'but since I must carry them away, I beg the favour of you, and the gentleman there, to lift them on my back.' 'Ay, ay, with all my heart,' reply'd the doctor, 'come Son, and lend's a hand to lift them on the fellow's back.'

In a word, the goods being lifted on Gettings's shoulders, it was not long 'ere the doctor's wife came from market, and going into the room where the bed was taken down, she came running open-mouth'd at her husband, and said, 'Why truly this is a most strange thing, that I can never stir out of doors, but you must be making one whimsical alteration or other in the house.' 'What's the matter,' reply'd the doctor, 'with the woman? Are you beside yourself?' 'No,' said the wife, 'but truly you are, in thus altering things as you do almost every moment.' 'Certainly, my Dear,' reply'd the doctor, 'you must have been spending your market penny, or else you would not talk at this rate as you do of alterations, when none in the least have been made since you have been gone out.' Quoth the wife, 'I am not blind, I think; for I am sure the bed is took out of the room one pair of stairs backwards, and pray, Husband, where do you design to put it now?' At these words the husband and son going presently up stairs, they found the bed was stollen, which, to be sure, fretted them; but nevertheless, they durst not tell the old woman that they had a hand in the losing it, by helping the thief to carry it away and so they now made the best of a bad market, since all the fretting in the world would not bring it back again.

Tho' Gettings was so successful in robbing this house, yet his genius not agreeing with this sort of theft, he was resolved to try his fortune on the highway; and one day meeting with a noted evidence, that pretended to make a discovery of the world in the moon, by telling who was the Pretender's father and mother, trudging it on foot along the road betwixt Lewisham and Bromley in Kent, he commanded the sharper to stand and deliver; then taking from him two pence halfpenny, for which he stood as hard as a shoemaker would for a piece of carrot, but to no purpose, he said, 'The world was come indeed to a very sad pass, that one rogue must prey on another.'

Shortly after the robbing this incorrigible villain, Gettings robbed a man on the way to Chelsea, and took from him about twelve shillings, and a pair of silver buckles. Next he robbed a stage coach upon Hounslow-Heath, taking from the passengers a silver watch and some money. Next he robbed another stage coach, not far from Reading in Berkshire, and took from the passengers four guineas and some silver. And next he robbed Esq. Dashwood's coach a little beyond Putney, and took from him and his lady a gold watch, and three or four pieces of gold, with some money in silver.

But the most notable action he ever committed, was this which follows. Having been riding one day into the country for his pleasure, as he was returning home in the evening very well mounted, and dress'd much like a gentleman, just at Tooting, by Richmond, he perceived from a rising ground Sir James B— walking in his gardens, which were very fine indeed, and of a large extent. Then riding up to a gardener standing at a back-door, he enquired of him, whether a gentleman whom curiosity led to see those gardens, of which he had heard so much talk in their praise, might not have the liberty of taking a walk in them. The gardener knowing Sir James was free that any person appearing in good fashion might walk there, he gave Gettings admission into them.

Gettings alighting, he gave the gardener his horse to hold; and in the walks seeing Sir James B—, to whom he paid respects in a very submissive manner, withal hoping, that he would pardon his presumption of coming into his gardens,

373

when his Worship was therein recreating himself, the courteous knight assured him he was very welcome, and invited him to see his wilderness; where sitting down in an arbour, Gettings in their discourse was pleas'd to say, 'Your Worship has got a very fine diamond ring on your finger.' 'Yes,' reply'd Sir James, 'it ought to be a fine one, for it cost me a very fine price': 'Why then,' said Gettings again, 'it is the fitter to bestow on a friend; therefore if your Worship pleases, I must make bold to take it, and wear it for your sake.'

At these words Sir James began to startle at his impudence; but Gettings clapping a pistol to his breast, told him, he was a dead man if he made but the least noise or resistance. So taking it from him, quoth he again, 'I am sensible your Lordship does not go without a good watch too.' Converting this also to his own use, and some guineas out of his pocket, he then tied his hands and feet, and then came away with a booty worth ninety pounds; but bid Sir James be of good cheer, for he would send one presently to relieve him. And accordingly going to the gardener, who held his horse all this while, and giving him a shilling, quoth he, 'Honest Friend, Sir James wants to speak with you.' Then mounting, he rode presently off the ground, whilst the gardener made haste to his master, and was in a great surprize to see Sir James bound in that manner which Gettings had left him in; but immediately setting him loose, his Worship returned his servant many thanks, for sending a rogue to rob him in his own gardens.

He once went purposely from London into the country, to rob the house of a dear friend, and near relation of his, which he effectually and easily did, as being well acquainted with all the parts of that house, and the ways to go into it, taking away from thence a horse, some money, gold rings, and other things. And lastly, he robbed Esq. Harrison and his lady, riding in their calash towards Fulham, and took from them a purse with four guineas in it, and some money in silver. For this fact being apprehended by the Right Honourable the Lord Bolingbroke, one of whose servants he shot in taking him, he was committed to Newgate, and hanged in the twenty second year of his age, at Tyburn, on Friday the 25th day of September, 1713.

At the same time were also justly executed the following criminals, 1. George Hollinsby for house-breaking. 2. Thomas Turner for stealing a gelding. 3. John Joyner for breaking open the house of one Mr John Kelly. 4. Sarah Clifford, alias Atkins, for picking the pocket of a drover, whom she made so dead drunk, that he died in his drunkenness. 5. Jane Wells, alias Elizabeth Wells, alias White, alias Dyer, for shop-lifting. 6. John Heath, alias James How, for stealing a mare. This last person was about twenty two years of age, born at Thornwood in Essex, in which county his mother kept a turn-pike, or a gate, thro' which coaches, carts, waggons, and horses, pay toll for passing. He was married to, or at least kept company with, a pipe-maker's daughter living at Saffron-Hill. He was a most abominable swearer, and was justly condemned for stealing a horse or mare once before; but abusing the mercy of the Queen's Pardon, to which he, and other notorious malefactors, pleaded at the Old-Bailey, on the 12th day of August, 1713, he was deservedly hanged in less than seven weeks after the receiving of that royal indulgence, which too many have the benefit of, without making good use of it.

375

THE LIFE OF
ZACHARY CLARE

Zachary Clare was a baker's son, born at Hackney, and by his father bred up to his trade; but becoming acquainted with Ned Bonnet, who learned him the trade of robbing on the highway, they practised it together with good success for three or four years, in the counties of Hartford and Cambridge; and became such a terror to the people of the Isle of Ely, that they durst hardly stir out far from home, unless they were half a dozen, or half a score in a body together; but at length Clare being apprehended as robbing one day by himself, to save his own neck, he made himself an evidence against Ned Bonnet, who being apprehended, was committed to Newgate, from whence was convey'd to Cambridge, and there hanged as before related.

One would think that untimely end of his companion, would have reclaimed him, but instead of being reformed, he withdrew himself again from under his father's tuition, and took to his old courses, with a resolution of never leaving them off till he was hanged too. However, dreading a halter, he was resolved to rob by stratagem; and accordingly one afternoon riding over Bagshot Heath, he falls to blowing of a horn, just as if he had been a post, whereupon three or four gentlemen then on the road gave him the way, as is usual in such cases, and being not rightly acquainted with the place where they were, they made what haste they could after him for a guide, promising to give him somewhat for conducting them to such a town. Clare accepts of their civility, and being come upon the middle of the aforesaid heath, where was a lone house upon the side of the road, pretending to be thirsty, he crav'd the favour of the gentlemen to bestow a little drink upon him, withal saying there was a cup of very good liquor. They acquiesced to his request, and rid up to the house, where a couple of his companions being planted, ready mounted, they attacked the gentlemen at sword and pistol, with such fury, that after a short resistance, they obliged them to pay their postman about two hundred thirty pounds for safely conducting them into their clutches.

Shortly after this adventure, being thro' his extravagance destitute of a horse, pistols, and accoutrements, fitting for a gentleman-thief, he puts himself into the disguise of a porter, with an old frock on his back, leather breeches, a broad belt about his middle, a hiving hat on his head, a knot on his shoulders, a small cord (an emblem of what would be his fate) at his side, and a sham ticket hanging at his girdle; so going up and down the streets to see how fortune might favour his designs, it was his good luck one evening to go thro' Lombard-Street, when a gentleman was sealing up a couple of hundred pounds bags. He takes the advantage to walk by just as the aforesaid gentleman came to the door, where calling for a porter, he plies him, and the money was delivered to him, to carry along with the gentleman to one Esq. Macklethwait's, living near Red Lyon Square. But Zachary Clare, being tired of his burden, turns up St Martin's le-Grand, and made the best of his way to lighten himself as soon as he could of his load.

The gentleman turning about and missing his suppos'd porter, ran up and down like a distracted lunatick broke out of Bedlam, out of one street into another; in this lane, and that alley; this court and that house; crying out, 'Did you see the man that's run away with my two hundred pounds?' But all his scrutiny was to no purpose, for Zachary having a light pair of heels, made, no doubt, what haste he could to such quarters where he might have a safe retreat from justice.

Clare being thus recruited, he soon metamorphosed his porter's habit into that of a gentleman's; and from a man of carriage, transform'd himself into an absolute highwayman again. One of his consorts buys him a good horse in West Smithfield, whilst another buys pistols, and other materials, requisite for a person that lives by the words 'stand and deliver'. Being thus equipped, he bids London adieu for ever; for it was the last time he ever saw it. His progress now was towards the west of England; where he and his associates robbed the Welsh drovers, and several wagggons, besides coaches; insomuch that they were a dread and terror to all those parts which border upon Wales.

But staying there till the country was too hot for them, they steered their course into Warwickshire; where they committed several robberies with very good success; till one day Zachary Clare, and only one more in company with him, going to give their horses a breathing upon Dunmore-Heath, they attacked Sir Humphrey Jennison and his Lady in their coach, who had then above one thousand one hundred pounds in the seat of it, and the knight being unwilling to lose it, he came out to give them battle. An engagement began betwixt the highwaymen and Sir Humphrey, one of whose two footmen was wounded in the arm, and the other had his horse shot in the buttock. But still Sir Humphrey's courage was not quell'd; he maintained the fight more vigorously with what pistols he had; till the coachman discharging a blunderbuss, shot Zachary's horse dead on the spot, and himself in the foot. His comrade seeing him dismounted, and wounded into the bargain, he fled as fast as he could. Clare was now taken, and Sir Humphrey mounting his footman's horse, that was not wounded, pursued James Lawrence, the highwayman that had left Clare in the lurch, and took him. Then tying them behind one another, with the legs of them under the horse's belly, they were brought into Warwick, and being examined before a magistrate, he committed them to gaol.

Now being in close confinement, they made several attempts to break open the prison; and in order thereto, they had files, chizzels, ropes, and aqua fortis, to facilitate their escape. But being detected by one of their fellow prisoners, they were loaded with the heaviest irons the gaol afforded, and were also stapled down to the floor; under which strict retraint they continued for above four months, when the assizes coming on, they were both brought to a trial, having a great number of indictments exhibited against them, to the great surprize of the whole court, who try'd them upon no less than ten, of every one of which the jury found them guilty.

Being ask'd what they had to say for themselves, before sentence of death was past upon them according to law, James Lawrence said, 'he had always been an unfortunate son of a whore; however, if his Lordship would be pleas'd but to be hanged for him, for one half hour or so, it should be the last favour that ever he should ask of him any more'. Being told he was a hardened impudent rogue, Zachary Clare was ask'd what he had to say for himself, who answered, 'My Lord, I have hanged one man already by swearing to save myself; and to save it once more, if your Lordship pleases, I'll swear right or wrong, against the whole jury, to hang them too; for I vow they have done me the greatest diskindness that ever any men did in my life.'

Being condemned, they were remanded back to gaol again, and secur'd in a dark dungeon under ground; where instead of preparing for their latter end, they did nothing but sing, swear, play at cards, and get drunk from morning till night. So audacious were they, that a grave minister coming to give them good counsel, they had the impudence to throw a pot of drink in his face, crying out at the same time, 'Begone you old formal son of a whore! Have we nothing else to do do you think, than stand to be surfeited with your damned cant?' They were no less impudent when they were conveyed to the place of execution; and when they were there, they would neither pray nor make confession. When the sheriff ask'd them if they had any thing to say before they were turn'd off, Lawrence reply'd, 'I wish I was safe in bed with your wife now!' and Clare cry'd, 'I wish I might have the getting of that young woman's maidenhead there!' The ladder upon this was immediately drawn from under them, and so they miserably ended their lives, in August, 1715, the first of them aged thirty two, and the other twenty six years.

379

Published by the Navarre Society, London.

Langre delin.   Goodnight sculp.

THE MAIL ROBBED near COLNBROOK
by Jn.º Hawkins and Geo. Simpson

THE LIVES OF
JOHN HAWKINS
AND GEORGE
SIMPSON

J ohn Hawkins at the time of his death was about thirty years old. His
father was a farmer at Stains in Middlesex, very honest, but poor; and
therefore could not give his son but a slender education. At fourteen
John waited on a gentleman, but soon left him to be a tapster's boy at the
Red-Lyon at Brentford, where he continued till he got into another gentleman's
service: but being of an unsettled temper, he seldom tarried long in a place. The
last family he was in was Sir Dennis Dutry's where he was butler, and might have
lived happily; for being a handsome creditable servant, he was approved of by his
master and lady. But the opinion he had of his own person made him too assuming, and he thought it a small fault to be out two or three nights a week at the
gaming tables. By his repeated neglect of his master's business, the family was
incens'd against him, and he was turned away, not without a suspicion of having
first been a confederate in robbing the house of a considerable value in plate.
Having been instructed in the nature of trading to France and Flanders, in wines,

brandies, &c. he join'd with his brother, a captain of a vessel or sloop, in fetching those commodities from those places, and commonly paid the King's Custom for them. This way of life was very agreeable to him; but having a strong and violent inclination to arrive at great riches and splendour, on a sudden, he left the uncertain way of dealing at sea, to deal in the South-Sea, and the bubbles; from which he had recourse to bubbling in another way, as some others besides have done, in which vicious courses he had success for a considerable time.

He was now twenty four. His first expedition was to Hounslow-Heath, where he stopp'd a coach, and eas'd the passengers of about eleven pounds. With this booty he returned safe to London, and repairing immediately to the King's-Head at Temple-Bar, he threw it all off. Thus he went on a pretty while by himself, losing at play what he had got upon the road: but finding some difficulties in robbing alone, he chose for his companions Ryley, Commerford, Reeves, and Leonard, an Irish captain. With these he committed several robberies on Hounslow and Bagshot Heaths. But tho' he sometimes acquired considerable prizes by such means, they did him but little service; for he still had such an itching to gaming, that he could never forbear 'till he had lost the last penny; so that he was often put to the pitiful shift of bilking an ordinary for a dinner.

Having followed this course about two years Leonard was made a state prisoner, for being concerned in the Preston rebellion; and Hawkins and one Wooldridge, for attempting to rescue him, were apprehended by the king's messengers, but in a short time they were both discharged. A few days after this, Cummerford, Reeves, and Ryley, were seized at Guilford. Hawkins had been with them, but he could not get a horse. The two former were executed, and Ryley transported, and the government took care of Leonard.

Hawkins now engaged with a new gang, among which was one Pocock, who being apprehended, impeach'd all the rest: this quickly dispers'd them, and one Ralphson, to whom they had entrusted most of their stock, went off with it to Holland. By which means Hawkins was left without money or companions, for they had all forsaken the town, except his brother Will and James Wright. Will was taken on Pocock's information, and Wright was in a salivation. Hawkins himself skulk'd about town, not daring to appear but in such houses as he could confide in, one of which Wilson, who was evidence against him at his trial, frequented. They soon became as familiar as ever, and believing Wilson would not betray him for the sake of the reward, Hawkins told him every thing that we have related concerning him and his companions, and other passages that are omitted: As that he was present when Colonel Floyer shot Wooldridge, and that he himself shot General Evans's footman, which he said happened thus. He stopp'd the general and another gentleman in a coach; the general and the gentleman both fired at him, upon which he shot directly into the coach, but mist them and killed the servant who was behind it.

Hawkins often lamented this misfortune, and when he fell into the company with a clergyman, would always be asking some casuistical questions on cases parallel to his own; but tho' he fancied this was no murder because he had no design against the deceas'd, yet he was always told, that the design against the master made the person as guilty, as if it had been intended against the man who was killed.

Wilson took so much pleasure in hearing Hawkins relate his pranks and robberies, that he grew very fond of his company. Wright being now recover'd, he and Hawkins fell to their old sport, and when they came home at night, Wilson used to drink with them. Their first robbery after this reunion was in Richmond-Lane, upon the Earl of Burlington and the Lord Bruce, from whom they took twenty pounds, two gold watches, and a saphire ring, for which his Lordship offered a hundred pounds to Jonathan Wild. Hawkins pretended he sold it for six pounds, and poor Wright thought that a good price, and gladly accepted of three pounds for his snack, tho' Hawkins then had the ring in his own possession, and afterwards sold it in Holland for forty pounds.

James Wright was born of honest parents, and bred a barber. He was one of the best temper, and greatest fidelity to his companions, that ever was known of a highwayman. How his acquaintance begun with Hawkins is uncertain, but they two for about a month after Wright's salivation, went on very prosperously together, before Wilson engaged with them.

About this time a good-natur'd countryman lent Wilson ten pounds, who had been starving for some weeks, notwithstanding which, he made all the haste he could to the tables and lost it every farthing. From the table he went to Hawkins and Wright, and having drank freely, Hawkins began to talk about robbing, but said a third man was necessary, and ask'd Wilson if he durst take a pistol. Wilson answered, 'Yes, as well as any man, for the want of money has made me ready for any thing.' He, who was always glad of new companions, proffered very kindly to get a horse against next night. They agreed, and so went to bed.

Hawkins was as good as his word, and in the evening they sat to drinking again. At a proper hour Hawkins told us all was ready; and so they mounted about ten o'clock, and soon after robbed Sir David Dalrymple near Winstanley's water-works: they put on upon stopping the coach, to try how capable he was of becoming a man of business. And he perform'd so well, that Hawkins never after cared to part with him.

They took from Sir David about three pounds in money, a snuff-box, and a pocket-book, for which last, Sir David offer'd sixty pounds to Wild; but they return'd it by a porter, gratis; for they had no dealings with Wild, nor did he know either of them.

The next coach they robbed was Mr Hide's of Hackney; they took from him ten pounds and a watch; but miss'd three hundred pounds in bank notes. They seldom fail'd of committing two or three robberies in a week, for a month together. They scarce ever went above five miles out of town, and when they returned to it again, they attack'd the coaches in the streets. One night in August, 1720, when all mankind were turn'd thieves, they robb'd a coach in Chancery-Lane, another in Lincolns-Inn-Fields, and in going off stumbled upon my Lord Westmoreland, who had three footmen behind his coach. They had some diffi-culty in robbing his Lordship, for the watch pour'd in upon them; but at hearing a pistol fir'd over their heads, they retired as fast, and gave them an opportunity of escaping.

Will Hawkins, the brother of John, and Wright, were soon after both priso ners, Hawkins could not impeach any body, because he was impeached himself. Wright indeed might have taken that advantage to have saved his own life; but he told Jack Hawkins's wife that he would hurt no body, and much less her husband, because of his children. How well this generosity was returned will appear hereafter. Hawkins and Wilson, to conceal themselves, went to Oxford, and staid there a month; in which time Hawkins defac'd some pictures in the gallery over the Bodleian Library. The University offered a hundred pounds to any that would discover the person who did it; and a poor taylor, who had distinguished himself for a Whig, was taken up and imprison'd on suspicion, and narrowly escaped a whipping.

The sessions at the Old-Baily being ended, Hawkins was discharged, and Wright reserved for Kingston assizes. The two brothers then went to Holland with all Wright's goods to the value of fifty pounds, and left him starving in jail.

About the end of October they both returned to London, where Wilson joined with them, and they went on together 'till Christmas; when Wilson became of age, and was in possession of a small estate his father left him, which he sold for three hundred and fifty pounds. But he soon lost it all at play, except what he lent to Jack and Will to buy horses.

One night Hawkins and Wilson took a ride to Hampstead, and being elevated with wine, resolved, as they returned, to rob the first coach they met. It happened that about a hundred yards on this side Fig-Lane, they met a chariot with two gentlemen in it. As soon as they pass'd them they muffled up with cape and handkerchief, and overtook 'em at the end of Fig-Lane. The coachman stopt at the first word, and down went the sashes, Wilson on one side, and Hawkins on the other. The gentleman sired both at once. One of them lodg'd three slugs in Hawkins's shoulder, but the other mist Wilson; had they suffered them to have come nearer they might have shatter'd them to pieces. However our highwaymen thought it best to move off, to prevent murther on both sides.

This action was follow'd with such bad weather, that they could do nothing; and when fair weather came, their horses heads were so swell'd that they could not get 'em out of the stable, and so they agreed to rob on foot in Hyde-Park. The first coach they attempted there was Mr Green the brewer's but the coachman whipt his horses and left them. However Wilson shot one of his horses, and endeavouring to fire again shot himself thro' the hand, which made his retreat very difficult having the wall to get over.

Being thus disabled Wilson had leisure to reflect on his deplorable condition, and was convinced that vengance would one day overtake him, and such a course of life be finish'd with scandal at Tyburn! These reflections brought him to a resolution of leaving the town, pursuant to which he borrow'd money of a friend, took a horse out of the stable and set forward for Yorkshire, Feb. 1. 1721.

Thus prepared for an honest life arrived at Whitby, where in a few days he fell into his mother's business, and followed it diligently 'till the succeeding August:

when one day being sent for to a publick-house, to his great surprize, he found his old friend John Hawkins, and a new companion George Simpson. After the usual salutations, Hawkins told Wilson that as he had been like other men, he was now as liable to suffer as any body; for his brother Will had impeached him and all the rest of his companions, and he should be fetch'd away in a few days. This startled Wilson so much, that he agreed to go with them. So they all bought horses, and came to London. Then Wilson found that Hawkins had deceived me, for I was not impeach'd nor was his brother in custody.

George Simpson was about twenty eight when he died. He was born at Putney in Surrey, and brought up at Cowre in Lincolnshire. He had no education, and but poor natural parts: he was never capable of designing; but when any thing was contrived for him, no one was more speedy or bold in the execution; for he was equally brisk and stout. He had been bailiff of a hundred in Lincolnshire; but for some misdemeanor, flying the country, he came to London, and served the Lord Castlemain and other gentlemen in quality of a footman. But discontented with that condition of life, and becoming acquainted with Jack Hawkins he commenced collector on the highway.

However it was not long before Hawkins was in earnest taken by the servants of Sir Edward Lawrence, whom he and Butler Fox had robb'd in the Huntington coach. Will impeached every body that had been concerned with him, tho' none but Fox and Wright were apprehended. Wright was acquitted at Kingston the summer assizes before; and having obtain'd his liberty, fell into an honest employment, which he follow'd till Hawkins impeached him. He was convicted of street-robbery, done about two years before, and hanged. And thus was poor Wright's generosity repaid. He saved Hawkins to be hang'd himself.

Butler Fox was a porter in Milk-Street. He had a wife and three children. His acquaintance with Will Hawkins began at Carter's house by London-Wall, a nest for highwaymen. Hawkins impeach'd him of robbing Colonel Hamilton, and at the trial swore, that himself and Fox committed that robbery, tho' neither of them was concerned in it; for it was done by Jack Hawkins and George Simpson, and no other person; and they, the same night, informed Will of all the particulars. This I had from Jack himself, who own'd he had often exclaim'd against Will for swearing Fox into this robbery.

All this time the rest of the gang play'd least in sight; their most convenient house was by London-Wall. The landlord knew all their circumstances, and found his account in that knowledge; for they seldom committed a robbery, but he had his snack by way of reckoning. As he kept a livery-stable, they had an opportunity of riding out at all hours, so that they harrass'd most of the morning stage-coaches in England. One morning they robb'd the Worcester, the Glocester, the Cirencester, the Bristol, and the Oxford coaches all together. Next morning the Chichester and Ipswich, and the third morning the Portsmouth coach. They were constant customers to the Bury coach; and touch'd it no less than ten times. And for any of these they seldom rode farther than the Stones End. When they met with any portmanteaus, they carried them to Carter, and ransack'd 'em.

Their evening enterprizes were commonly between Richmond, Hackney, Hampstead, or Bow, and London; and often behind Buckingham-Wall. They committed innumerable robberies with great success, and might, perhaps, have continued much longer if they had not meddled with the mails.

One time as they were making up to the Portsmouth coach, a gentleman upon it fired at them, before they spoke to the coachman; for their passing the coach and immediately returning, was a plain indication of what they aimed at. They were treated in the like manner in attempting a mourning coach, but with worse luck; for Wilson's horse received a wound, of which he died. One thing was remarkable enough, and that was their meeting Mr Green and his lady behind Buckingham Wall, and robbing them; because when they once before attacked the same coach, and being on foot the coachman drove away, upon which Wilson told him they should have the luck to meet him again, when they were mounted.

Thus they went on till the beginning of April, 1722, when they began to talk of robbing the mails. This design was first concerted with their landlord Carter. He propos'd to begin with the Harwich mail, but that being as uncertain as the wind, they could not agree to wait for it. At last, they pitched upon the Bristol mail, and prepared every thing for that purpose.

On Sunday, April the 15th, they set out, and next morning they took the mail; and again on Wednesday morning. They robbed it the second time, to get the halves of some bank notes, the other halves of which, they had taken the first time.

387

On Monday, April the 23d, Wilson went after dinner to see his horse in Fenchurch-Street; and from thence to Carter's, where he found two or three men, whose looks made him withdraw abruptly to Moregate coffee-house.—There he fell into a sett of company, among whom was one who appeared to be a Quaker, and told him there was great enquiry made after the robbers of the Bristol mail, and that some were even then searching for them in the neighbourhood. This confirming Wilson's suspicion, he paid for his gill, left the coffee-house, and took a turn in Bedlam; where he determined in his mind to take a passage that night for Newcastle.

With this resolution he went towards Moregate coffee-house again, and in his way, met the persons he had seen at Carter's. As soon as he past 'em, they turned about and followed him, tho' not so closely but he got into the coffee-house unperceived by them; for they went thro' Moregate Arch. He then went out at the fore door, where they stood watching in the street; and as soon as they saw him, they seized him. They carried him to the Post-Office, where he was examined by the Post Master General, who could make nothing of him that night. Next morning he was carried before him again, four or five times to as little purpose, tho' Mr Carteret used the most prevailing arguments to procure a discovery. All the post-officers, in short, were very pressing to no purpose; till one of them called Wilson aside, and shewed him the following letter:

SIR,

I AM one of those Persons who robbed the Mails, which I am sorry for; and to make amends, I will secure my two Companions, as soon as may be. He whose Hand this shall appear to be, will, I hope, be entitled to the Reward and his Pardon.

Wilson knew this to be Simpson's letter, and so presently made a discovery; whereupon, Hawkins and Simpson were apprehended on the Thursday following.

At their trial Hawkins pray'd the court that all the king's witnesses might be examin'd a-part, which the court granted.

Thomas Green, the postboy, depos'd thus. On Monday the 16th of April, about one in the morning, as I was riding by the Pyde-Horse at Slouth, and blowing my horn, I was overtaken by James Ladbrook, who was travelling the same way. We rode in company to Langley-Broom, where a man on a chesnut horse made up to us, and went off again. We rode thro' Colebrook, and then perceived that two men follow'd us at a distance; and on this side Longford they came up to us, with handkerchiefs in their mouths, and their wigs and hats pulled forward over their faces. The foremost of them was on a chesnut horse. He held a pistol to my head, and said, 'You must go along with me'; and then taking hold of my horse's bridle he led me down a narrow lane, and the other man brought Ladbrook after me in the same manner. Then they making us both dismount, he on the chesnut horse said to me, 'Are you the lad that swore against Child?' 'No,' I said, 'I have been post-boy but a very little while.' 'Have you ever been rob'd yet' says he. 'No,' says I. 'Why then,' says he, 'you must pay beverage now, for God damn my blood and 'ouns I'll be revenged upon some-body for poor Child's sake.' Then he cut Ladbrook's horse's bridle, and turned him a drift, and that being done, he went off with the black gelding I rode upon. As soon as he was gone the other man ty'd our hands behind us, bound us back to back, and so fastened us to a tree in a ditch. Then he ask'd Ladbrook what money he had about him. Ladbrook told him he had but 3 s. 6 d. He searched Ladbrook's pocket, and finding no more, he did not take that, nor any thing else from him, but left us bound, and went after his companions. Ladbrook and I, with a great deal of struggling, got from the tree, but could not get from one another: and so, ty'd back to back, we went to an inn in Longford, from whence the ostler came with us, and he went down the lane together, and there we found the gelding loose, and the bags cut open.—It was pretty dark, so that I cannot swear to the persons, or their horses, only I could perceive that one was a chesnut horse.

James Ladbrook confirmed all the post-boy's evidence.

Ralph Wilson. I have known John Hawkins these two years, but was not acquainted with Simpson till August last. We had often consulted together about robbing some mail, but did not agree upon what mail, till five days before the fact was committed, and then we resolved it should be the Bristol mail. Pursuant to this resolution, about eleven o'clock on Sunday morning, the 15th of April, we all three took horse at the Blue-Boar-Inn in Southwark; Hawkins on a tall bay, or brown gelding, Simpson on a chesnut or sorrel mare, and I on a dapple grey. We cross'd the water at Kew ferry, dined at the Three Pidgeons at Brentford, staid there till six in the evening, called at the post-house at Hounslow, and loitered on the road till we came to the post-house at Colebrook, where we supp'd on horseback; we enquir'd of the ostler what time the Bristol mail would come by, and he told us between one and two o'clock in the morning. We went thence, and came to Langley Broom about midnight, where we agreed to dispatch Simpson alone to meet the mail. He went and we loitered about, waiting for his return: and about one o'clock we saw the post-boy and a traveller with him, and Simpson following them. Then we met Simpson, and held a fresh consultation, in which at last it was agreed, that he and I should follow the mail, and that Hawkins should watch at a distance, because he being pretty bulky, would be more remarkable. Then Hawkins and I changed horses, and I and Simpson followed the boy and the traveller thro' Colebrook; and on this side of Longford, we rode up to them, and taking hold of their horses bridles, led them down Harmonsworth Lane, where we made them dismount. I left Simpson to bind them, and took the boy's gelding and mail to the end of the lane, where I found Hawkins waiting, and where in a little time Simpson came to us. We all rifled the bags, and carried several of them to Hounslow-Heath, where we selected those of Bath and Bristol, and left the rest. Thence we rode thro' Kingston and Wandsworth, and going down a bye road we searched the bags, took out what we thought fit, most of which we put in two riding bags, and the rest into our pockets, and what we thought would be of no service to us, we put into the Bristol and Bath bags again, and so threw them over a hedge. Then taking our way through Camberwell, we came along Greenwich Road, to the Hand-Inn in Barnaby-Street, between five and six on Monday morning. There we put up our horses, and drank a pint of burnt wine, and after some time took coach and drove to the Minories; where, to avoid suspicion, we parted, and went by different ways to Frank Green's at the Cock and George in the Minories. We went into a room by ourselves, and to take off all mistrust, we called for a candle, wax, paper, pen and ink, and then locking the door, we examin'd our prize. We reserved only the bank notes, and burnt all the other notes and the letters with the candle which we set in the chimney; we found three 20 *l.* bank notes, one of 25 *l.* half of a 50 *l.* and two halves of 25 *l.* each, which we equally divided. I was apprehended on the Monday following, and made this same confession before Mr Carteret, the Post Master General, and by my directions the prisoners were taken, at Mrs Bowen's (a midwife's) in Green-Arbor-Court in the Little Old-Bailey.

The ostlers at the several inns where they had been, confirmed almost all the circumstances of Wilson's deposition.

Pichard Room Constable. I went with Richard Mills, and others to apprehend the prisoners at a midwife's house, in Green-Arbor-Court, in the Little Old-Bailey, between eight and nine at night. A woman came to the door, and asked what we wanted? We bid her not be frighted, but light a candle, for we were come to search for stolen goods. The prisoners, who were above, over heard us, called out and said, 'We are the men you want, but G—d d—n ye the first that comes up is a dead man.' We told them we were provided for them, let them fire as soon as they would. Then Hawkins's brother came down foremost, and persuaded them to surrender quietly. I told them we were come upon Wilson's information. 'Are you so,' says the prisoner Hawkins, 'why then we are dead men; but we had rather lose our lives, than save them in such a base and infamous a manner as that villain Wilson has saved his.'

Richard Mills depos'd the same in substance. The prisoners then brought several evidences to vindicate their characters; one of which gave the court some trouble, on account of a receipt which he produced; the whole affair is too long to be rehearsed. In fine, at a second going out, the jury brought them in Guilty.

The verdict being recorded, Hawkins exprest himself to this purpose. 'I am altogether innocent of this robbery; though I don't blame my countrymen for their verdict; for their intentions were honourable, but they were over-ruled by a partial judge. I have been ill dealt by: my friend has been brow beat, and hardly suffered to speak. I expect to dye, but yet I would not change conditions, with the villain that has saved his own life, by swearing away mine: for I prefer death to a life sav'd in such an infamous manner. My blood lies upon his head, and upon some others.—I hope your Lordship is not concerned in it.'

When they were convey'd to execution, not being allowed the priviledge of a coach, they appeared in the carts with uncommon tokens of repentance, scarce ever raising their eyes from their books to regard the great crowds about them, not tarrying to drink quantities of liquor, as is usually done.

Being in some confusion he was turned off, and died, not without prodigious difficulty and struggling; contrary to his friend, who was more composed before he died, and more easily lost his breath.

The same day their bodies were carried to Hounslow-Heath, and there hanged in irons on a gibbet erected for that purpose, not far from that on which Benjamin Child was hanged in the same manner—he was convicted at Ailesbury assizes (on the evidence of his man William Wade and the post boy) for robbing the Bristol mail. On Monday the 8th of March, 1722, he was carried on horseback from Ailesbury jail, to the Bear at Slough, where he lay that night, and about ten next day was carried in a coach to the place of execution.

FURTHER READING

Arne Bialuschewski, 'Daniel Defoe, Nathaniel Mist, and the "General History of the Pyrates"', *The Papers of the Bibliographical Society of America*, Vol. 98, No. 1 (March 2004), pp. 21–38.

David J. Cox, *Crime in England 1688–1815* (2014).

Lincoln B. Faller, *Turned to Account: The Forms and Functions of Criminal Biography in Late Seventeenth- and Early Eighteenth-Century England* (1987).

Philip Gosse, *A Bibliography of the Works of Captain Charles Johnson* (1927).

Douglas Hay ... [et al.], *Albion's Fatal Tree: Crime and Society in Eighteenth-Century England* (1976).

Eric Hobsbawm, *Bandits* (1969).

Peter King, *Punishing the Criminal Corpse, 1700–1840: Aggravated Forms of the Death Penalty in England* (2017).

Peter Linebaugh, *The London Hanged: Crime and Civil Society in the Eighteenth Century* (2006).

Andrea McKenzie, 'The Real Macheath: Social Satire, Appropriation, and Eighteenth-Century Criminal Biography', *Huntington Library Quarterly*, Vol. 69, No. 4 (December 2006), pp. 581–605.

Erin Mackie, *Rakes, Highwaymen, and Pirates: The Making of the Modern Gentleman in the Eighteenth Century* (2009).

Frank McLynn, *Crime and Punishment in Eighteenth-Century England* (1989).

John Richetti, *A History of Eighteenth-Century British Literature* (2017).

John J. Richetti, *Popular Fiction Before Richardson: Narrative Patterns, 1700–1739* (1969).

James Sharpe, *Dick Turpin: The Myth of the English Highwayman* (2005).

James Sharpe, *A Fiery & Furious People: A History of Violence in England* (2016).

Gillian Spraggs, *Outlaws & Highwaymen: The Cult of the Robber in England from the Middle Ages to the Nineteenth Century* (2001).

John Sugden, *The Thief of Hearts: Claude Duval and the Gentleman Highwayman in Fact and Fiction* (2015).

Megan Wachspress, 'Pirates, Highwaymen, and the Origins of the Criminal in Seventeenth-Century English Thought', *Yale Journal of Law & the Humanities*, Vol. 26, Issue 2 (Summer 2014), pp. 301–344.

Richard M. Ward, *Print Culture, Crime and Justice in 18th-Century London* (2014).

Tammy Whitlock, 'Wicked Ladies: Provincial Women, Crime and the Eighteenth-Century English Justice System.' *The Historian*, Vol. 78, Issue 1 (Spring 2016), p. 146–147.